MW00834284

Georg Forster

A voyage round the world

In His Britannie Majesty's sloop, Resolution VOL. I

Georg Forster

A voyage round the world
In His Britannie Majesty's sloop, Resolution VOL. I

ISBN/EAN: 9783741194795

Manufactured in Europe, USA, Canada, Australia, Japa

Cover: Foto ©Andreas Hilbeck / pixelio.de

Manufactured and distributed by brebook publishing software
(www.brebook.com)

Georg Forster

A voyage round the world

A

V O Y A G E

ROUND THE

W O R L D,

IN

His BRITANNIC MAJESTY's Sloop, RESOLUTION,

commanded by Capt. JAMES COOK, during the Years 1772, 3, 4, and 5.

By G E O R G E F O R S T E R, F.R.S.

Member of the Royal Academy of MADRID, and of the Society for promoting
Natural Knowledge at BERLIN.

IN TWO VOLUMES.

VOL. I.

On ne repousse point la verité sans bruit,
Et de quelque façon qu'on l'arrête au passage,
On verra tôt-ou-tard que c'était un outrage,
Dont il falloit qu'au moins la *honte* fut le fruit.

DE MISSY.

L O N D O N,

Printed for B. WHITE, Fleet-Street; J. ROBSON, Bond Street; P. ELMSLY, Strand;
and G. ROBINSON, Pater-noster Row.

MDCCLXXVII.

PREFACE.

HISTORY does not offer an example of such disinterested efforts, towards the enlargement of human knowledge, as have been made by the British nation, since the accession of his present Majesty to the Throne. America, with all its riches, might long have remained undiscovered, if the unequalled perseverance and the glorious enthusiasm of Columbus had not providentially surmounted every difficulty, and, in spite of ignorance and envy, forced their way to Ferdinand and Isabella. That immortal navigator was protected at last, only because he opened a new and evident source of gain. But a friendship between Plutus and the Muses was too singular to be sincere; it only lasted whilst they, with no better success than the Danaids, poured heaps of gold into his treasury.

The triumph of science was reserved to later periods of time. Three voyages of discovery, from the most liberal motives, had already been performed, when a fourth was undertaken by order of an enlightened monarch, upon a more enlarged and majestic plan than ever was put in

A 2   execution

P R E F A C E.

execution before. The greateſt navigator of his time, two
able aſtronomers, a man of ſcience to ſtudy nature in all her
receſſes, and a painter to copy ſome of her moſt curious
productions, were ſelected at the expence of the nation.
After completing their voyage, they have prepared to give
an account of their reſpective diſcoveries, which cannot fail
of crowning, their employers at leaſt, with immortal
honour.

The Britiſh legiſlature did not ſend out and liberally ſupport my father as a naturaliſt, who was merely to bring
home a collection of butterflies and dried plants. That
ſuperior wiſdom which guides the counſels of this nation,
induced many perſons of conſiderable diſtinction to act on
this occaſion with unexampled greatneſs. So far from
preſcribing rules for his conduct, they conceived that the
man whom they had choſen, prompted by his natural love
of ſcience, would endeavour to derive the greateſt poſſible
advantages to learning from his voyage. He was only
therefore directed to exerciſe all his talents, and to extend
his obſervations to every remarkable object. From him
they expected a philoſophical hiſtory of the voyage, free
from prejudice and vulgar error, where human nature
ſhould be repreſented without any adherence to fallacious
ſyſtems, and upon the principles of general philanthropy ;
in ſhort, an account written upon a plan which the learned
world had not hitherto ſeen executed.

My

My father performed the voyage, and collected his observations agreeably to the ideas which had thus been entertained of him. Fully refolved to complete the purpofe of
his miffion, and to communicate his difcoveries to the public, and not allowing himfelf any time to reft from the fatigues which he had undergone, he infcribed and prefented
the firft fpecimen of his labours to his majefty within four
months after his return *. The hiftory of the voyage, the
principal performance which was demanded at his hands,
next engroffed his whole attention. It was at firft propofed,
that from his own and captain Cook's journals a fingle
narrative fhould be compofed, in which the important obfervations of each fhould be inferted, and referred to their
proper authors by different marks. My father received a
part of captain Cook's journal, and drew up feveral fheets
as a fpecimen; however, as it was foon after thought more
expedient to feparate the two journals, this plan was not
profecuted. The Right Hon. the Lords Commiffioners of
the Admiralty, being defirous of ornamenting the account
of the late difcoveries with a number of plates, engraved
after the drawing of the artift who went on the voyage,
generoufly granted the whole expence of the engraving †

* Charaſteres Generum Plantarum quas in Infulis maris auftralis colleg. &c.
Joannes Reinoldus Forfter, LL. D. & Georgius Forfter. 4to. Lond. 1776.

† This expence amounts to upwards of 2000 l. all the plates being executed by
the ableſt artiſts.

in

PREFACE.

in equal fhares to captain Cook and my father. An agreement was drawn up on the 13th of April, 1776, between captain Cook and my father, in the prefence, and with the fignature of the earl of Sandwich, fpecifying the particular parts of the account which were to be prepared for the prefs by each of the parties feparately, and confirming to them both jointly the generous gift of the plates from the Board of Admiralty. In confequence of this, my father prefented a fecond fpecimen of his narrative for the perufal of the earl of Sandwich, and was much furprifed at firft that this fecond effay was entirely difapproved; but after fome time he was convinced, that as the word "narrative" was omitted in the agreement, he had no right to compofe a connected account of the voyage. He was told that if he meant to preferve his claim to half the profit arifing from the plates which the Board of Admiralty provided, he muft conform to the letter of the agreement; and though he had always confidered himfelf as fent out chiefly with a view to write the hiftory of the voyage, he acquiefced for the benefit of his family, and ftrictly confined himfelf to the publication of his unconnected philofophical obfervations made in the courfe of the voyage.

I muft confefs, it hurt me much, to fee the chief intent of my father's miffion defeated, and the public difappointed in their expectations of a philofophical recital of facts.

However,

However, as I had been appointed his affiftant in the courfe of this expedition, I thought it incumbent upon me, at leaft to attempt to write fuch a narrative. Every con-fideration prompted me to undertake the tafk, which it was no longer in his power to perform. It was a duty we owed to the public; I had collected fufficient materials during the voyage, and I had as much good will to begin with, as any traveller that ever wrote, or any compiler that was ever bribed to mutilate a narrative. I was bound by no agreement whatfoever, and that to which my father had figned, did not make him anfwerable for my actions, nor in the moft diftant manner preclude his giving me affiftance. Therefore in every important circumftance, I had leave to confult his journals, and have been enabled to draw up my narrative with the moft fcrupulous attention to hiftorical truth.

Two anonymous publications on the fubject of our voyage have already appeared; but the prefent age is too enlightened to credit marvellous hiftories, which would have difgufted even the romantic difpofition of our anceftors. The incidents of our voyage are various, and deeply in-terefting, without the affiftance of fiction. Our courfe has been by turns fertile, and barren of events; but as the induftry of the labourer reaps fome advantage from the moft ungrateful foil, fo the moft dreary folitudes have yielded inftruction to the inquifitive mind.

Another

PREFACE.

Another narrative of this circumnavigation, is faid to have been written by captain JAMES COOK of His Majefty's Royal Navy, under whofe command it was performed. That account will be ornamented with a great variety of plates, reprefenting views of the countries which we vifited, portraits of the natives, figures of their boats, arms, and utenfils, together with a number of particular charts of the new difcoveries; and all thefe plates, engraved at the expence of the Board of Admiralty, are the joint property of captain Cook and my father.

At firft fight it may feem fuperfluous to offer two relations of this voyage to the world; but when we confider them as narratives of interefting facts, it muft be allowed that the latter will be placed in a ftronger light, by being related by different perfons. Our occupations when in harbour were widely different; whilft captain Cook was employed in victualling or refitting the fhip, I went in queft of the manifold objects which Nature had fcattered throughout the land. Nothing is therefore more obvious, than that each of us may have caught many diftinct incidents, and that our obfervations will frequently be foreign to each other. But above all, it is to be obferved, that the fame objects may have been feen in different points of view, and that the fame fact may often have given rife to different ideas. Many circumftances familiar to the navigator, who has been bred on the rough element, ftrike the

the landman with novelty, and furnish entertainment to his readers. The seaman views many objects on shore with a retrospect to maritime affairs, whilst the other attends to their œconomical uses. In short, the different branches of science which we have studied, our turns of mind, our heads and hearts have made a difference in our sensations, reflections, and expressions. This disparity may have been rendered still more evident, as I have slightly passed over all regulations relative to the interior œconomy of the ship and the crew: I have studiously avoided nautical details both at sea and in harbour, nor ventured to determine, how often we reefed, or split a sail in a storm, how many times we tacked to weather a point, and how often our refractory bark disobeyed her Palinurus, and missed stays. The bearings and distances of projecting capes, of peaks, hills, and hummocks, of bays, harbours, ports, and coves, at different hours of the day, have likewise been in general omitted. These instructive particulars thrive in the proper field of the navigator. The history of captain Cook's first Voyage Round the World *, was eagerly read by all European nations, but incurred universal censure, I had almost said contempt. It was the fate of that History, to be compiled by a person who had not been on the voyage; and

* In the Endeavour, from 1768, to 1771, drawn up by Dr. John Hawkesworth.

to the frivolous obfervations, the uninterefting digreffions, and fophiftical principles of this writer, the ill-fuccefs of the work has been attributed; though few are able to determine, with what degree of juftice the blame is thrown upon the compiler. The active life of captain Cook, and his indefatigable purfuits after difcoveries, have made it impoffible for him to fuperintend the printing of his own Journals; and the public, I am much afraid, muft again converfe with him by means of an interpreter. His prefent performance will, in all probability, have another circumftance in common with the former, where many important obfervations, thought obnoxious, have been fuppreffed, as is cuftomary in France. The fame authority which blew off M. de Bougainville from the ifland of Juan Fernandez, could hufh to filence the Britifh guns, whilft the Endeavour cannonaded the Portuguefe fort at Madeira *. Without entering farther into this fubject, I fhall only obferve, that the above remark will give an adequate idea of the authenticity of a performance, which is fubmitted

* The two circumftances here alluded to, are well known facts, though fuppreffed in the publifhed narratives. M. de Bougainville fpent fome time at Juan Fernandez, and completely refrefhed his crew there, though he wifhes to have it underftood, that contrary winds prevented his touching at that ifland. Captain Cook in the Endeavour, battered the Loo-fort at Madeira, in conjunction with an Englifh frigate, thus refenting an affront which had been offered to the Britifh flag.

to cenfure and mutilation, before it is offered to the
public.

The philofophers of the prefent age, to obviate the feeming contradictions in the accounts of different travellers,
have been at the trouble to felect certain authors in whom
they have placed confidence, and rejected as fabulous the
affertions of all the reft. Without being competent judges
of the fubject, they have affumed a few circumftances as
facts; and wrefting even thofe to fuit their own fyftems,
have built a fuperftructure which pleafes at a diftance, but
upon nearer examination partakes of the illufive nature of
a dream. The learned, at laft grown tired of being deceived by the powers of rhetoric, and by fophiftical arguments, raifed a general cry after a fimple collection of facts.
They had their wifh; facts were collected in all parts of the
world, and yet knowledge was not increafed. They received a confufed heap of disjointed limbs, which no art
could reunite into a whole; and the rage of hunting after
facts foon rendered them incapable of forming and refolv-
ing a fingle propofition; like thofe minute enquirers, whofe
life is wholly fpent in the anatomical diffection of flies,
from whence they never draw a fingle conclufion for the
ufe of mankind, or even of brutes. Befides this, two travellers feldom faw the fame object in the fame manner, and
each reported the fact differently, according to his fenfa-

tions,

tions, and his peculiar mode of thinking. It was therefore neceffary to be acquainted with the obferver, before any ufe could be made of his obfervations. The traveller was no longer to truft to chance for a variety of occurrences, but to make ufe of his firft difcovery, as the thread of Ariadne, by the help of which he might guide his fteps through the labyrinth of human knowledge. It was therefore requifite that he fhould have penetration fufficient to combine different facts, and to form general views from thence, which might in fome meafure guide him to new difcoveries, and point out the proper objects of farther inveftigation. This was the idea with which I embarked on the late voyage round the world, and agreeably to which I have collected materials for the prefent publication, as far as the time, my fituation and abilities, would permit. I have always endeavoured in this narrative to connect the ideas arifing from different occurrences, in order, if poffible, to throw more light upon the nature of the human mind, and to lift the foul into that exalted ftation, from whence the extenfive view muft " juftify the ways of God to man." Whether I have fucceeded or failed in the attempt, remains to be decided ; but the rectitude of the intention cannot, I truft, be mifconftrued. I have fometimes obeyed the powerful dictates of my heart, and given voice to my feelings ; for, as I do not pretend to be free from the weakneffes com-

mon

mon to my fellow-creatures, it was neceſſary for every
reader to know the colour of the glaſs through which I
looked. Of this at leaſt I am certain, that a gloomy livid
tinge hath never clouded my fight. Accuſtomed to look
on all the various tribes of men, as entitled to an equal
ſhare of my good will, and conſcious, at the ſame time, of
the rights which I poſſeſs in common with every individual
among them, I have endeavoured to make my remarks
with a retroſpect to our general improvement and welfare;
and neither attachment nor averſion to particular nations
have influenced my praiſe or cenſure.

The degree of pleaſure which may reſult from the peruſal
of a work, depends not only upon the variety of the ſubject,
but likewiſe upon the purity and the graces of ſtyle. We
muſt reſign all pretenſions to taſte and ſentiment, if we did
not prefer a well-told tale to a lame and tedious narration.
Of late, however, the juſt eſteem in which an elegant diction
is held, has been ſo far abuſed, that authors, relying on the
fluency of their language, have paid no attention to the
matter which they propoſed, but deceived the public with a
dry and uninſtructive performance. Such writers may
poſſibly acquire the approbation of ſome individuals,

" Who haunt Parnaſſus but to pleaſe their ear;"

But I am convinced the generality of readers are always juſt
enough to overlook, in ſome meaſure, the defects of ſtyle,.

in.

PREFACE

in favour of the novelty or usefulness of the subject. Without attempting to be curiously elegant, I have aimed at perspicuity; and having paid the strictest attention to this particular, I hope to meet with indulgence, if some errors of less moment have escaped my notice. It was owing to the repeated corrections of some valuable friends, to which I submitted my manuscript, that I sent it late to the press; but from the unexampled activity of the printer, I am enabled to lay my work before the public even sooner than I expected. The Chart, on which our line of circumnavigation is delineated, has been engraved by the ablest artist in that branch*, and I constructed it with the most minute attention from the best authorities, which are mentioned in its margin. After specifying the above particulars, of which I thought it my duty to apprize the reader, it only remains to discharge a promise made in the course of the work, respecting an account of the education and equipment of O-Maï in this country †. (See vol. I. p. 389.) In the narrow limits of a Preface I can only comprehend in a few lines the substance of what might furnish an entertaining volume. O-Maï has been considered either as remarkably

* Mr. W. Whitchurch, Pleasant-row, Islington.

† The native of the Society Islands brought over by captain Furneaux in the Adventure, and vulgarly called Omiah.

stupid,

stupid, or very intelligent, according to the different allowances which were made by those who judged of his abilities. His language, which is destitute of every harsh consonant, and where every word ends in a vowel, had so little exercised his organs of speech, that they were wholly unfit to pronounce the more complicated English sounds; and this physical, or rather habitual defect, has too often been misconstrued. Upon his arrival in England, he was immediately introduced into genteel company, led to the most splendid entertainments of this great and luxurious metropolis, and presented at court amidst a brilliant circle of the first nobility. He naturally imitated that easy and elegant politeness which is so prevalent in all those places, and which is one of the ornaments of civilized society; he adopted the manners, the occupations, and amusements of his companions, and gave many proofs of a quick perception and lively fancy. Among the instances of his intelligence, I need only mention his knowledge of the game of chess, in which he had made an amazing proficiency. The multiplicity of objects which crouded upon him, prevented his paying due attention to those particulars which would have been beneficial to himself and to his countrymen at his return. He was not able to form a general comprehensive view of our whole civilized system, and to abstract from thence what appeared most strikingly useful and applicable to the improvement of his country. His

senses

fenfes were charmed by beauty, fymmetry, harmony, and
magnificence; they called aloud for gratification, and he
was accuflomed to obey their voice. The continued round
of enjoyments left him no time to think of his future life;
and being deflitute of the genius of Tupaïa, whofe fuperior
abilities would have enabled him to form a plan for his
own conduct, his underflanding remained unimproved. It
can hardly be fuppofed that he never formed a wifh to obtain fome knowledge of our agriculture, arts, and manufactures; but no friendly Mentor ever attempted to cherifh
and to gratify this wifh, much lefs to improve his moral
character, to teach him our exalted ideas of virtue, and the
fublime principles of revealed religion. After having fpent
near two years in England, and happily undergone inoccu-
lation for the fmall pox *, he embarked with captain Cook
in the Refolution, which failed from Plymouth in July
1776. The various fcenes of debauchery, which are almoft unavoidable in the civilized world, had not corrupted
the natural good qualities of his heart. At parting from
his friends his tears flowed plentifully, and his filence and
outward behaviour proved him deeply affected. He carried with him an infinite variety of dreffes, ornaments, and
other trifles, which are daily invented in order to fupply our

---

* This difeafe proved fatal to Aotourou, the native of O-Taheitee, whom M. de
Bougainville brought to France, and who received nearly the fame education as
O-Mai.

artificial

artificial wants. His judgment was in its infant flate, and therefore, like a child, he coveted almoft every thing he faw, and particularly that which had amufed him by fome unexpected effect. To gratify his childifh inclinations, as it fhould feem, rather than from any other motive, he was indulged with a portable organ, an electrical machine, a coat of mail, and a fuit of armour. Perhaps my readers expect to be told of his taking on board fome articles of real ufe to his country; I expected it likewife, but was difappointed. However, though his country will not receive a citizen from us much improved, or fraught with valuable acquifitions, which might have made him the benefactor, and perhaps the lawgiver of his people, ftill I am happy to reflect, that the fhips which are once more fent out upon difcovery, are deftined to carry the harmlefs natives of Taheitee a prefent of new domeftic animals. The introduction of black cattle and fheep on that fertile ifland, will doubtlefs increafe the happinefs of its inhabitants; and this gift may hereafter be conducive, by many intermediate caufes, to the improvement of their intellectual faculties. And here I cannot but obferve, that confidering the fmall expence at which voyages of difcovery are carried on *, the nation which favours thefe enterprizes is amply repaid by the benefit derived to our fellow-creatures. I cannot help thinking that our late voy-

* The whole expence of the voyage in which I embarked did not exceed the fum of 25000 l. including all extraordinary difburfements.

P R E F A C E.

age would reflect immortal honour on our employers, if it had no other merit than flocking Taheitee with goats, the Friendly Isles and New Hebrides with dogs, and New Zeeland and New Caledonia with hogs. It is therefore sincerely to be wished, that voyages of discovery, upon a disinterested plan, may still be prosecuted with vigour, as much remains to be done, even in the South Sea; unless it should be in the power of illiberal men to defeat the great and generous views of a monarch, who is justly called the patron of science. A single remark, which may be of extensive use to posterity; a single circumstance, which may make happy our fellow-creatures in those remote parts of the world, repays the toils of the navigation, and bestows that great reward, the consciousness of good and noble actions.

London,
March 1, 1777.

G. FORSTER.

CONTENTS.

BOOK I.

CHAP.

CONTENTS.

A

V O Y A G E

ROUND THE

W O R L D.

B O O K I.

C H A P. I.

Departure—Passage from Plymouth to Madeira—Description of that Island.

Ubi animus ex multis miseriis atque periculis requievit,—finui res gestas—perfcribere ; tamen (hic) imprimis arduum videtur,—quia plerique, quæ delicta reprehenderis, malivolentia et invidia putant ; ubi de magna virtute et gloria bonorum memores, quæ fibi quifque facilia factu putat, æquo animo accipit ; fupra ea, veluti ficta, pro falfis ducit.   SALLUST.

A VOYAGE to explore the high fouthern latitudes of our globe was refolved upon, foon after the return of the Endeavour in 1771. Two ftout veffels, the *Refolution* and the *Adventure*, were fitted as King's floops for that purpofe, and the command of them given to Capt. JAMES COOK and Capt. TOBIAS FURNEAUX. On the 11th of June, 1772, my father and myfelf were appointed to embark in this expedition, in order to collect, defcribe, and draw

VOL. I.   B   the

the objects of natural hiſtory which we might expect to meet with during our courſe. We prepared with the utmoſt alacrity for this arduous undertaking, and in the ſpace of nine days ſent all our baggage on board the Reſolution, then at Sheerneſs, but which failed from thence for Plymouth on the 22d of June.

We left London on the 26th, and in two Days reached Plymouth, where the Reſolution was not yet arrived. The 1ſt of July, we went on board the *Auguſta Yacht*, and waited on the Earl of Sandwich, then Firſt Lord Commiſſioner for executing the office of High Admiral. His Lordſhip expecting the Reſolution to come into Plymouth Sound that day, deſired us to be on board of her, between the hours of five and ſix in the evening. However, to our great diſappointment, ſhe did not appear, and his Lordſhip left Plymouth the next morning.

The 3d of July early, we ſaw the Reſolution lying in the Sound, where ſhe had arrived the night before. Captain Cook purpoſed to ſtay here eight or ten days, and gave orders, that ſome neceſſary ſhelves ſhould be fixed up in our cabins previous to our reception on board. The deſire of letting paſs no opportunity for the improvement of ſcience, and for our own inſtruction, prompted us to paſs theſe leiſure hours in viſiting the tin mines in Cornwall. Having ſatisfied our curioſity, and being both highly en- tertained and much inſtructed by the ſight of the rich extenſive

tenſive works at Poldyce and Kenwyn, we returned to Plymouth on the 8th of July.

On Saturday the 11th, we went on board the Reſolution
ſloop, which was now to ſail with the firſt fair wind. The
next day it blew a freſh gale; and my father, walking on
the quarter-deck, obſerved our veſſel to alter her poſition
conſiderably in regard to the Adventure (which was to accompany us on our voyage) and to a maſt-ſhip, both at
anchor in the Sound; at the ſame time taking notice that
ſhe approached the rocks under the caſtle. He immediately communicated his apprehenſions to Mr. Gilbert, the
maſter, who happened to be upon deck with him. The
maſter found, that the veſſel having been moored to one of
the tranſport buoys in the Sound, the buoy, not intended
to ſupport ſuch a violent ſtrain, had broke from its
ground tackle, and was adrift together with the ſloop. In
an inſtant all hands were on deck, the ſails ſpread, and
the cables cleared. We ſhot paſt the Adventure and maſt-
ſhip, and came to an anchor, after eſcaping the moſt
imminent danger of being daſhed againſt the rocks under
the fort. Our ſeamen looked upon this fortunate event,
as an omen favourable to the ſucceſs of the voyage, while
we could not avoid reflecting on the tutelar gui.'
DIVINE PROVIDENCE, which had thus manifeſte
a critical moment, that might eaſily have put a s

B 2

ſtop to our projects *. We ſhall, in the courſe of this hiſtory, find frequent inſtances of impending deſtruction, where all human help would have been ineffectual, if our better fortune had not prevailed under the ſuperior direction of HIM, without whoſe knowledge not a ſingle hair falls from our heads. We are ever ready to give due applauſe and do full juſtice to the great ſkill and good conduct of our able circumnavigators, but we cannot avoid attributing every thing to its proper ſource, and that eſpecially to a higher power, which human art, though aided by effrontery and irreligion, dares not vindicate to itſelf.

Early on Monday the 13th, we ſet ſail from Plymouth Sound, in company with the Adventure. I turned a parting look on the fertile hills of England, and gave way to the natural emotions of affection which that proſpect awakened; till the beauty of the morning, and the novelty of gliding through the ſmooth water attracted my attention, and diſperſed the gloomineſs of former ideas. We ſoon paſſed by *Eddiſtone* lighthouſe, a lofty and well-contrived tower, which is of the greateſt advantage to navigation and commerce. It was impoſſible to look at it, without ſhuddering with apprehenſions for the lonely

---

* That it is not uncommon for ſhips, under the ſame circumſtances as the Reſolution ſloop, to take conſiderable damage, appears from what happened to the Aldborough, May 19, 1776, which broke from the buoys in the ſame manner, but drove aſhore on Drake's iſland, and was bulged to pieces.

keepers,

Keepers, who are often obliged to pass three months there, deprived of all communication with the main-land. The fate of *Winstanley*, who was really crushed by the downfall of a former structure, which he himself had built on this rock, and the vibrations of the present tower, when winds and waves assail it, must give them strong fears of a dreadful and sudden end.

In proportion as we stood off shore, the wind encreased, the billows rose higher, and the vessel rolled violently from side to side. Those who were not used to the sea, nay some of the oldest mariners, were affected by the sea-sickness, in various degrees of violence. It was of different duration with different persons, and after it had continued three days amongst us, we found the greatest relief from red port wine mulled, with spices and sugar.

On the 20th, we fell in with Cape *Ortegal*, on the coast of *Gallicia* in Spain; the natives call it *Ortiguera*, and it was probably the *Promontorium Trileucum* of the ancients. The country hereabouts is hilly; where the naked rock appears it is white, and the tops of the mountains are covered with wood. I also observed some corn-fields almost ripe, and some spots which seemed to be covered with heath. The eagerness with which every body gazed at this land, powerfully persuaded me, that mankind were not meant to be amphibious animals, and that of course our present situa-

tion

tion was an unnatural one; an idea that feems to have occurred to Horace, when he fays,

Nequicquam Deus abfcidit
Prudens oceano diffociabili
Terras; & tamen impia
Non tangenda rates tranfiliunt vada.   Hor.

•

In vain did Nature's wife command
Divide the waters from the land,
If daring fhips and men profane,
Invade th' inviolable main.   Dryden.

On the 22d, we faw the lighthoufe near *Corunna*, or, as our failors abfurdly call it, the *Groyn*. It was perfectly calm, the water fmooth as a mirror, and the hilly pro-fpect very agreeably varied by corn-fields, inclofures, fmall hamlets, and gentlemen's feats, every thing confpiring to banifh the remains of the fea-ficknefs entirely from amongft us, and to bring back that chearfulnefs which could not well keep company with empty ftomachs and a tempeftuous fea. In the evening we were near a fmall tartan, which we took to be a fifhing veffel from the Spanifh coaft; and in that perfuafion, a boat was hoifted out and fent towards her, in order, if poffible, to purchafe fome frefh fifh. In going thither we obferved the whole furface of the fea every where covered with myriads of little crabs, not above an inch in diameter, which we

found

found were of the species called *cancer depurator* by Linnæus. The little vessel proved to be a French tartan
from Marseilles, of about 100 tons burden, freighted
with flour for *Ferrol* and *Corunna*. The people in her
begged for a small supply of fresh water, having been
driven far from their course by contrary winds during
two months, by which means this necessary article had
been exhausted above a fortnight ago, and they were reduced to live upon bread and a little wine. Whilst they
continued in this distressful situation, they had met with
several ships at sea, and especially with several Spanish
men of war, though none had been humane enough to
alleviate their sufferings. When the officer who commanded our boat heard this account, he sent their empty
barrels on board our vessel to be filled with fresh water,
and their eyes sparkled with the liveliest expression of joy
when they received it. They thanked Heaven and us,
and rejoiced that they should now be able to light their
fire again, and be comforted with some boiled provisions,
after their long abstinence. So true is it, that a man with
a feeling humane heart, may often, at a very cheap rate,
indulge the inclination to assist his fellow-creatures.

The next afternoon, three Spanish men of war passed
us, standing in for *Ferrol*. One of them seemed to be a
74 gun ship, and the two others carried about 60 guns
each. The sternmost first hoisted English colours, but
when

when we shewed ours, she hauled them down, fired a gun to leeward, and hoisted the Spanish ensign. Soon after she fired a shot at the Adventure; but as we kept standing on, the Spaniard put about, and fired another shot just a-head of her. In consequence of this, our vessel brought to, and the Adventure now *seemed only to follow our example.* The Spaniard then hailed the Adventure in English, and asked " what *frigate* that was a-head," (meaning our sloop); and having been satisfied in that particular, he would not answer a question of the same nature, which was put to him, but always replied, " *I wish you a good voyage.*" We continued our course, after a scene so humiliating to the masters of the sea, and passed Cape *Finisterre* during night.

Several porpesses passed us on the 25th, all swimming against the wind, which had been north-easterly ever since we had left Cape Finisterre. At night the sea appeared luminous, particularly the tops of the waves and part of the ship's wake, which were illuminated by a mass of pure light: but, independent of that, there appeared numerous little sparks infinitely brighter than any other part of this phænomenon.

On the 28th, at six of the clock in the morning, we discovered PORTO-SANTO, which is about five or six leagues long, barren and thinly inhabited. It has only one *Villa* or town, of the same name, situated on the eastern side, in a valley which is entirely cultivated, and appeared to

have

have a fine verdure from the numerous vineyards it contains. This little island is under the orders of the governor of Madeira, and the number of its inhabitants amounts to about seven hundred. Soon after we made MADEIRA and the ILHAS DESERTAS, corruptly called the *Deserters* by our seamen. The town of *Santa Cruz* in Madeira was abreast of us at six in the afternoon. The mountains are here interfected by numerous deep glens and vallies. On the sloping ground we observed several country-houses pleasantly situated amidst surrounding vineyards and lofty cypresses, which give the country altogether a romantic appearance. We were towed to the road of *Funchal* in a perfect calm, and came to an anchor in the dark.

Early on the 29th, we were agreeably surprised with the picturesque appearance of the city of FUNCHAL, which is built round the bay, on the gentle ascent of the first hills, in form of an amphitheatre. All its public and private buildings are by this means set off to advantage. They are in general entirely white, many of them two stories high, and covered with low roofs, from whence they derive that elegant eastern stile, and that simplicity, of which our narrow buildings with steep roofs, and numerous stacks of chimnies are utterly destitute. On the sea side are several batteries and platforms with cannon. An old castle, which commands the road, is situated on the top of a fleep black rock, furrounded by the fea at high-water, and called by the Englifh Low-rock. On a neigh-bouring eminence above the town there is another, called San Joao do Pico, or St. John's caftle. The hills beyond the town ferve to complete the beauty of the landfcape, being covered with vineyards, inclofures, plantations, and groves, interfperfed with country-houfes and feveral churches. The whole feemed to raife the idea of a fairy-garden, and enabled us to form fome conception of the hanging gar-dens of queen Semiramis.

About feven o'clock a boat came off to us called the Pratique-boat, having on board a Capitan do Sal, who is one of the two Guarda-Mores of the board of health, appointed to regulate the quarantine of fuch fhips as come from the coaft of Barbary, the Arches, and other parts fufpected of infectious diftempers. This gentleman enquired into the ftate of health of our fhip's company, and the place we came from, and returned on fhore with fatisfactory information on this fubject.

After breakfaft we landed, and went with the captains to the houfe of Mr. Loughnan, a Britifh merchant, who fupplied the king's fhips, as contractor, with all the ne-ceffaries. The conful, Mr. Murray, lately appointed, was not yet arrived, but Mr. Loughnan received us with fuch hofpitality and elegance, as do honour to himfelf and to the nation in general.

The

The city is far from anfwering the expectations which
may be formed from its appearance towards the road. Its
ftreets are narrow, ill-paved, and dirty; the houfes are
built of freeftone, or of brick, but they are dark, and only
a few of the beft, belonging to Englifh merchants or principal inhabitants, are provided with glafs-windows; all
the others have a kind of lattice work in their ftead,
which hangs on hinges and may be lifted up occafionally.
The ground floors are moftly appropriated for the ufe of
fervants, for fhops, and ftore-houfes.

The churches and monafteries are very plain buildings,
without any difplay of the architectonic art: their infide
exhibits a ftriking want of tafte; the little light which is
admitted into them, ferving only to difplay heaps of tinfel
ornaments, arranged in a manner which is truely Gothic.
The convent of Francifcan friars is clean and fpacious, but
their gardens feemed not to be kept in the beft order.
The nuns of *Santa Clara* politely received us at their grate,
but afterwards deputed fome old women, to offer the artificial flowers of their manufacture for fale.

We walked with Mr. Loughman to his country-feat,
which is fituated on the hills, about a mile from the city.
We there met an agreeable company of the principal Britifh
merchants eftablifhed at Madeira. The captains returned on board in the evening, but we accepted of Mr. Loughman's obliging offer of his houfe during our fhort ftay.

C 2

A VOYAGE ROUND THE WORLD.

Our excursions began the next morning, and were continued on the following day. At five o'clock in the morning we went upwards along the course of a stream, to the interior hilly part of the country. About one o'clock in the afternoon we came to a chesnut grove, somewhat below the highest summit of the island, having walked about six miles from Mr. Loughnan's house. The air was here remarkably cooler than below, and a fine breeze contributed to its temperature. We now engaged a negro to become our conductor, and after a walk of at least an hour and a half, we returned to our hospitable mansion.

The next day we prepared for our departure. It was with regret that I left this delightful spot, and such generous friends, who know how to enjoy the unspeakable pleasure of communicating happiness to their fellow-citizens of the world. My heart still preserves those sentiments of gratitude and esteem, which made me loth to part from hence, and to resign myself to the common fate of travellers. I was however, pleased to find British hospitality existing *abroad*, which Smollet could no longer trace in England *.

Before I leave this island, I shall offer such remarks, as I had an opportunity of collecting during my stay; and I am induced to believe they will prove acceptable,

* Vide Humphry Clinker, vol. I. page 102.

as they were communicated by fensible Englishmen, who had been inhabitants of Madeira for many years, and are therefore of the best authority. I am aware indeed, that an account of Madeira may by some be looked upon as a superfluous work; but if, upon a candid perusal, it is found to contain such obfervations as have not yet appeared in the numerous journals of navigators, I hope I shall not need a farther apology. It is very natural to overlook that which is near home, and as it were within our reach, efpecially when the mind looks forward, on difcoveries which it reckons more important, in proportion as they are more remote.

The island of Madeira is about 55 English miles long, and ten miles broad, and was first difcovered on the 2d of July, in the year 1419, by *Jao Gonzales Zarco*, there being no hiftorical foundation for the fabulous report of its difcovery by one *Macham* an Englishman. It is divided into two *capitanias*, named *Funchal* and *Maxico*, from the towns of thofe names. The former contains two judicatures, viz. *Funchal* and *Calbetta*, the latter being a town with the title of a county, belonging to the family of *Caftello Melhor*. The fecond *capitania* likewife comprehends two judicatures, viz. *Maxice* (read Mafhico) and *San Vicente*.

Funchal is the only *cidade* or city in this island, which has alfo feven *villas* or towns; of which there are four, *Calbetta*, *Camara de Lobos*, *Ribiera braba*, and *Ponta de Sol* in the capitania.

capitania of Funchal, which is divided into twenty-fix
parifhes. The other three are in the capitania of Maxico,
which confift of feventeen parifhes; thefe towns are called
Maxico, San Vicente, and Santa Cruz.

The governor is at the head of all the civil and military departments of this ifland, of Porto-Santo, the Salvages,
and the Ilhas Defertas, which laft only contain the temporary huts of fome fifhermen, who refort thither in
purfuit of their bufinefs. At the time when I was at
Madeira, the governor was Don Joam Antonio de Sao Pereira.
He was efteemed a man of good fenfe and temper, but
rather referved and cautious.

The law department is under the corregidor, who is
appointed by the king of Portugal, commonly fent from
Lifbon, and holds his place during the king's pleafure.
All caufes come to him from inferior courts by appeal.
Each judicature has a fenate, and a Juiz or judge, whom
they choofe, prefides over them. At Funchal he is called,
Juiz da Fora, and in the abfence, or after the death of the
corregidor, acts as his deputy. The foreign merchants
elect their own judge, called the Provider, who is at the
fame time, collector of the king's cuftoms and revenues,
which amount in all to about one hundred and twenty
thoufand pounds fterling. Far the greateft part of this
fum is applied towards the falaries of civil and military
officers, the pay of troops, and the maintenance of public
buildings.

buildings. This revenue arises, first from the tenth of all the produce of this island belonging to the king, by virtue of his office as grand master of the order of Christ; secondly, from ten per cent. duties laid on all imports, provisions excepted; and lastly, from the eleven per cent. charged on all exports.

The island has but one company of regular soldiers of a hundred men : the rest of the military force is a militia consisting of three thousand men, divided into companies, each commanded by a captain, who has one lieutenant under him, and one ensign. There is no pay given to either the private men, or the officers of this militia, and yet their places are much sought after, on account of the rank which they communicate. These troops are embodied once a year, and exercised during one month. All the military are commanded by the *Serjeante Mór*. The governor has two *Capitanos de Sal* about him, who do duty as aides-de-camp.

The secular priests on the island are about twelve hundred, many of whom are employed as private tutors. Since the expulsion of the Jesuits, no regular public school is to be found here, unless we except a seminary where a priest, appointed for that purpose, instructs and educates ten students at the king's expence. These wear a red cloak over the usual black gown, worn by ordinary students. All those who intend to go into orders, are obliged to qualify them-

themfelves by ftudying in the univerfity of *Coimbra*, lately re-eftablifhed in Portugal. There is alfo a dean and chapter at Madeira, with a bifhop at their head, whofe income is confiderably greater than the governor's; it confifts of one hundred and ten pipes of wine, and of forty *muys* of wheat, each containing twenty-four bufhels; which amounts in common years to three thoufand pounds fterling. Here are likewife fixty or feventy Francifcan friars, in four monafteries, one of which is at Funchal. About three hundred nuns live on the ifland, In four convents, of the orders of *Merci*, *Sta. Clara*, *Incarnafao*, and *Bom Jefus*. Thofe of the laft-mentioned inftitution may marry whenever they choofe, and leave their monaftery.

In the year 1768, the inhabitants living in the forty-three parifhes of Madeira, amounted to 63,913, of whom there were 31,341 males, and 32,572 females. But in that year 5243 perfons died, and no more than 2198 children were born; fo that the number of the dead exceeded that of the born by 3045. It is highly probable that fome epidemical diftemper carried off fo difproportionate a number in that year, as the ifland would fhortly be entirely depopulated, if the mortality were always equal to this. Another circumftance concurs to ftrengthen this fuppofition, namely, the excellence of the climate. The weather is in general mild and temperate: In fummer the heat is very moderate on the higher parts of the ifland,

whither

whither the better fort of people retire for that feafon; and in winter the fnow remains there for feveral days, whilft it is never known to continue above a day or two in the lower parts. The accuracy of the numbers of dead and born, may however be entirely depended upon, as a complete lift extracted from the parifh books was procured for us, from the governor's fecretary.

The common people of this ifland are of a tawny colour, and well fhaped, though they have large feet, owing perhaps to the efforts they are obliged to make in climbing the craggy paths of this mountainous country. Their faces are oblong, their eyes dark; their black hair naturally falls in ringlets, and begins to crifp in fome individuals, which may perhaps be owing to intermarriages with negroes; in general they are hard featured, but not difagreeable. Their women are too frequently ill-favoured, and want the florid complexion, which, when united to a pleafing affemblage of regular features, gives our Northern fair ones the fuperiority over all their fex. They are fmall, have prominent cheek-bones, large feet, an ungraceful gait, and the colour of the darkeft brunette. The juft proportions of their body, the fine form of their hands, and their large, lively eyes, feem in fome meafure to compenfate for thofe defects. The labouring men in fummer, wear linen trowfers, a coarfe fhirt, a large hat, and boots; fome had a fhort jacket

Vol. I.   D   made

made of cloth, and a long cloak, which they sometimes
carried over their arm. The women wear a petticoat,
and a short corselet or jacket, closely fitting their shape,
which is a simple, and often not inelegant dress. They
have also a short, but wide cloak, and those that are
unmarried, tie their hair on the crown of their head, on
which they wear no covering.

The country people are exceeding sober and frugal;
their diet in general consisting of bread and onions, or
other roots, and little animal food. However, they avoid
eating tripe, or any offals, because it is proverbially said
of a very poor man, " *be is reduced to eat tripe.*" Their common drink is water, or an infusion on the remaining rind
or skin of the grape (after it has passed through the wine-
press) which when fermented, acquires some tartness and
acidity, but cannot be kept very long. The wine for
which the island is so famous, and which their own hands
prepare, seldom if ever regales them.

Their principal occupation is the planting and raising
of vines, but as that branch of agriculture requires little
attendance during the greatest part of the year, they
naturally incline to idleness. The warmth of the climate,
which renders great provision against the inclemencies
of weather unnecessary, and the ease with which the
cravings of appetite are satisfied, must tend to indolence,
wherever the regulations of the legislature do not coun-
                                                    teract

teract it, by endeavouring with the prospect of encreasing happiness, to infuse the spirit of industry. It seems the Portuguese government does not pursue the proper methods against this dangerous lethargy of the state. They have lately ordered the plantation of olive-trees here, on such spots as are too dry and barren to bear vines; but they have not thought of giving temporary assistance to the labourers, and have offered no premium by which these might be induced to conquer their reluctance to innovations, and aversion to labour.

The vineyards are held only on an annual tenure, and the farmer reaps but four tenths of the produce, since four other tenths are paid in kind to the owner of the land, one tenth to the king, and one to the clergy. Such small profits, joined to the thought of toiling merely for the advantage of others, if improvements were attempted, entirely preclude the hopes of a future increase. Oppressed as they are, they have however preserved a high degree of chearfulness, and contentment; their labours are commonly alleviated with songs, and in the evening they assemble from different cottages, to dance to the drowsy music of a guittar.

The inhabitants of the towns are more ill-favoured than the country people, and often pale and lean. The men wear French cloaths, commonly black, which do not seem to fit them, and have been in fashion in the polite

world

world about half a century ago. Their ladies are delicate, and have agreeable features; but the characteriſtic
jealouſy of the men ſtill locks them up, and deprives them
of a happineſs which the country women, amidſt all their
diſtreſſes, enjoy. Many of the better people, are a ſort of
petite nobleſſe, which we would call *gentry*, whoſe genealogical
pride makes them unſociable and ignorant, and cauſes a
ridiculous affectation of gravity. The landed property is
in the hands of a few ancient families, who live at Funchal,
and in the various towns on the iſland.

Madeira conſiſts of one large mountain, whoſe branches
riſe every where from the ſea towards the centre of the
iſle, converging to the ſummit, in the midſt of which, I
was told, is a depreſſion or excavation, called the Val by
the inhabitants, always covered with a freſh and delicate
herbage. The ſtones on the iſle, which we examined,
ſeemed to have been in the fire, were full of holes, and of
a blackiſh colour; in ſhort, the greater part of them were
lava. A few of them were of the kind which the Derby
ſhire miners call dunſtone. The ſoil of the whole iſland
is a tarras mixed with ſome particles of clay, lime,
and ſand, and has much the ſame appearance as ſome
earths we ſince found on the iſle of Afcenſion. From this
circumſtance, and from the excavation of the ſummit of
the mountain, I am induced to ſuppoſe, that in ſome remote period, a volcano has produced the lava, and the
ochreous

ochreous particles, and that the Val was formerly its crater. At first fight of Madeira I was of a different opinion; but the black Loo-rock, the cliff on which St. John's castle stands, the nature of the foil and stones, and the situation of the Val, convinced me, that the whole had formerly undergone a violent change by fire.

Many brooks and small rivulets descend from the summits in deep chasms or glens, which separate the various parts of the isle. We could not however perceive any *plains* mentioned by others *, through which the waters would probably have taken their course, if any such had existed. The beds of the brooks are in some places covered with stones of all sizes, carried down from the higher parts by the violence of winter rains or floods of melted snow. The water is conducted by wears and channels into the vineyards, where each proprietor has the ufe of it for a certain time; some being allowed to keep a constant supply of it, some to ufe it thrice, others twice, and others only once a week. As the heat of the climate renders this supply of water to the vineyards absolutely necessary, it is not without great expence that a new vineyard can be planted; for the maintenance of which, the owners muft purchase water at a high price, from those

* See an Account of the Voyages undertaken by the order of his present Majefty, and successively performed by the Captains Byron, Wallis, Carteret, and Cook.—Compiled by Dr. Hawkesworth. Vol. II. p. 7.

who

who are conflantly fupplied, and are thus enabled to
fpare fome of it.

Wherever a level piece of ground can be contrived in
the higher hills, the natives make plantations of eddoes
(arum esculentum, Linn.) enclofed by a kind of dyke to caufe
a flagnation, as that plant fucceeds beft in fwampy ground.
Its leaves ferve as food for hogs, and the country people
ufe the roots for their own nourifhment.

The fweet potatoe (convolvulus batatas) is planted for
the fame purpofe, and makes a principal article of diet;
together with chefnuts, which grow in extenfive woods,
on the higher parts of the ifland, where the vine will not
thrive. Wheat and barley are likewife fown, efpecially in
fpots where the vines are decaying through age, or where
they are newly planted. But the crops do not produce
above three months provifions, and the inhabitants are
therefore obliged to have recourfe to other food, befides
importing confiderable quantities of corn from North-
America in exchange for wine. The want of manure,
and the inactivity of the people, are in fome meafure the
caufes of this difadvantage; but fuppofing hufbandry to
be carried to its perfection here, I believe they could not
raife corn fufficient for their confumption. They make
their threfhing-floors of a circular form, in a corner of the
field, which is cleared and beaten folid for the purpofe.
The fheaves are laid round about it, and a fquare board

fluck

ftuck full of fharp flints below, is dragged over them by
a pair of oxen, the driver getting on it to encreafe its
weight. This machine cuts the ftraw as if it had been
chopped, and frees the grain from the hufk, from which
it is afterwards feparated.

The great produce of Madeira is the wine, from which
it has acquired fame and fupport. Where the foil, expofure, and fupply of water will admit of it, the vine is
cultivated. One or more walks, about a yard or two
wide, interfect each vineyard, and are included by ftone-
walls two feet high. Along thefe walks, which are arched
over with laths about feven feet high, they erect wooden
pillars at regular diftances, to fupport a lattice-work of
bamboos, which flopes down from both fides of the walk,
till it is only a foot and a half or two feet high, in which
elevation it extends over the whole vineyard. The vines
are in this manner fupported from the ground, and the
people have room to root out the weeds which fpring up
between them. In the feafon of the vintage they creep
under this lattice-work, cut off the grapes, and lay them
into bafkets: fome bunches of thefe grapes I faw, which
weighed fix pounds and upwards. This method of keeping the ground clean and moift, and ripening the grapes
in the fhade, contributes to give the Madeira wines that
excellent flavour and body for which they are remarkable.
The owners of vineyards are however obliged to allot a

certain

certain ſpot of ground for the growth of bamboos; for the lattice-work cannot be made without them; and I was told ſome vineyards lay quite neglected for want of this uſeful reed.

The wines are not all of equal goodneſs, and conſequently of different prices. The beſt, made of a vine imported from Candia, by order of the Infante of Portugal, Don Henry, is called Madeira Malmſey, a pipe of which cannot be bought on the ſpot for leſs than 40 or 42 *l.* ſterling. It is an exceeding rich ſweet wine, and is only made in a ſmall quantity. The next ſort is a dry wine, ſuch as is exported for the London market, at 30 or 31 *l.* ſterling the pipe. Inferior ſorts for the Eaſt India, Weſt India, and North-American markets, ſell at 28, 25, and 20 *l.* ſterling. About thirty thouſand pipes, upon a mean, are made every year, each containing one hundred and ten gallons. About thirteen thouſand pipes of the better ſorts are exported, and all the reſt is made into brandy for the Brazils, converted into vinegar, or conſumed at home.

The encloſures of the vineyards conſiſt of walls, and hedges of prickly pear, pomegranates, myrtles, brambles, and wild roſes. The gardens produce peaches, apricots, quinces, apples, pears, walnuts, cheſnuts, and many other European fruits; together with now and then ſome tropical plants, ſuch as bananas, goavas, and pine apples.

All

All the common domestic animals of Europe are likewise found at Madeira; and their mutton and beef, though small, is very well tasted. Their horses are small, but sure-footed; and with great agility climb the difficult paths, which are the only means of communication in the country. They have no wheel-carriages of any kind; but in the town they use a sort of drays or sledges, formed of two pieces of plank joined by cross pieces, which make an acute angle before; these are drawn by oxen, and are used to transport casks of wine, and other heavy goods, to and from the warehouses.

The animals of the feathered tribe, which live wild here, are more numerous than the wild quadrupeds; there being only the common grey rabbit here, as a representative of the last-mentioned class. We observed the sparrow-hawk, (*falco nisus*); several crows, (*corvus corone*); magpies, (*corvus pica*); sky and wood-larks, (*alauda arvensis, & arborea*); starlings, (*sturnus vulgaris*); yellow hammers, (*emberiza citrinella*); common and mountain sparrows, (*fringilla domestica & montana*); yellow wagtails and robin redbreasts, (*motacilla flava & rubecula*); and wild pigeons, of which we could not determine the species. We likewise saw the house-swallow and swift, (*hirundo rustica & apus*); and some gentlemen of the British factory assured us they had also seen the martin, (*h. urbica*). This last genus of birds lives here all the winter, and only disappears for a few days in very cold weather, retiring to clifts and crevices of the rocks, and returning on the first fair sunny day. The red-legged partridge, *(tetrao rufus)*, is likewise common in the interior parts of the isle, where it is not much disturbed. In Mr. Loughnan's aviary I saw waxbills, *(loxia astrild)*, chaffinches, goldfinches, yellowfinches, and canary-birds, *(fringilla coelebs, carduelis, butyracea, & canaria)*; all which had been caught upon this island. Tame birds, such as turkies, geese, ducks, and hens, are very rare, which is perhaps owing to the scarcity of corn.

There are no snakes whatsoever in Madeira; but all the houses, vineyards, and gardens swarm with lizards. The friars of one of the convents complained, that these vermin destroyed the fruit in their garden; they had therefore placed a brass kettle in the ground to catch them, as they are constantly running about in quest of food. In this manner they daily caught hundreds, which could not get out on account of the smooth sides of the kettle, but were forced to perish.

The shores of Madeira, and of the neighbouring Salvages and Desertas, are not without fish; but as they are not in plenty enough for the rigid observance of Lent, pickled herrings are brought from Gothenburg in English bottoms, and salted cod from New-York and other American ports, to supply the deficiency.

We

We found a few infects here, and might perhaps have collected more, if our stay had been of longer duration; those we met with were of known sorts, and in no great variety. On this occasion I shall mention a general remark, which ought to be applied to all the *islands* we have touched at during the course of our voyage. Quadrupeds, amphibious reptiles, and infects, are not numerous in *islands*, at some distance from a continent, and the first are not to be met with at all, unless they were formerly transported thither by men. Fishes and birds, which are able to pass through water or air, are more frequent, and in greater variety. *Continents*, on the other hand, are rich in the above-mentioned classes of animals, as well as in those of birds and fishes, which are more universal. Africa, which we visited during this voyage, in a few weeks supplied us with a great variety of quadrupeds, reptiles, and infects, whilst all the other lands where we touched, afforded no new discoveries in those classes.

E 2

CHAP.

CHAP. II.

The Passage from Madeira to the Cape Verd Islands, and from thence to the Cape of Good Hope.

1774.
August.

Tuesday 4.

L ATE in the evening on the first of August, we got under sail, in company with the Adventure. A North-east wind forwarded our course so well, that we got sight of Palma on the fourth, early in the morning. This island is one of the group now called the Canaries, known to the ancients by the name of *Insulæ Fortunatæ*, one of them being already at that time distinguished by the name of Canaria [*]. They were entirely forgotten in Europe, till towards the end of the fourteenth century, when the spirit of navigation and discovery was revived. Some adventurers then found them again, and the Biscayans landed on Lanzarota, and carried off one hundred and

---

[*] It is probable that not only the Canaries, but likewise Madeira, and Porto-Santo were known to the ancients; a circumstance from which it is possible to reconcile their various accounts of the number of these islands. See Plin. Hist. Nat. lib. vi. cap. 37. The description given of them by ancient writers, agree with the modern accounts. See Vossius in Pompon. Melam. ad cap. x. v. 30. *Ex iisdem quoque insulis cinnaberit Romam advehdebatur. Sanguineæ frequens est in insulis fortunatis arbor illa quæ cinnaberin gignit. Vulgo* SANGUINEAM DRACONIS *appellant,*—We have Pliny's testimony, lib. vi. cap. 36. that Juba, the Mauritanian king, dyed purple in some of these isles, opposite to the Autololes in Africa.

seventy

seventy of the natives. Luis de la Cerda, a Spanish nobleman of the royal family of Castile, in consequence of a bull from the Pope, in the year 1344, assumed the title of Prince of the Fortunate Islands, but never went to take possession of his estates. Lastly, John, Baron de Bethencourt of Normandy, visited these islands again in the year 1402, took possession of several, and called himself King of the Canaries. His nephew ceded his claims upon them to Don Henry, Infante of Portugal; but they were afterwards left to the Spaniards, who now possess them.

The next day at five o'clock in the morning, we passed the isle of Ferro, remarkable only from this circumstance, that several geographers have reckoned their first meridian from its westermost extremity. The same day, being in about 27 deg. N. latitude, we observed several flying fishes, pursued by bonitos and dolphins, rising out of the water in order to escape from them. They were flying in all directions, and not against the wind only, as Mr. Kalm seems to think. Neither did they confine themselves to a strait-lined course, but frequently were seen to describe a curve. When they met the top of a wave as they skimmed along the surface of the ocean, they passed through, and continued their flight beyond it. From this time, till we left the torrid zone, we were almost daily amused with the view of immense shoals of these fishes, and now and then caught one upon our

decks

decks when it had unfortunately taken its flight too far,
and was ſpent by its too great elevation above the ſurface
of the ſea. In the uniform life which we led between
the tropics, where we found weather, wind, and ſea, almoſt conſtantly favourable and agreeable, the mind catched
at every little circumſtance that could give the hint to a
reflection. When we ſaw the moſt beautiful fiſhes of
the ſea, the dolphin and bonito, in purſuit of the flying
fiſh, and when theſe forſook their native element to ſeek
for ſhelter in air, the application to human nature was
obvious. What empire is not like a tumultuous ocean,
where the great in all the magnificence and pomp of
power, continually perſecute and contrive the deſtruction
of the defenceleſs?—Sometimes we ſaw this picture continued ſtill farther, when the poor fugitives met with
another ſet of enemies in the air, and became the prey
of birds *, by endeavouring to eſcape the jaws of fiſhes.

On the 8th we obſerved the ſea to be of a whitiſh
colour, and tried for ſoundings, but found none with
fifty fathoms of line. In the evening we croſſed the tropic
of cancer. About this time, the captain ordered the ſhip
to be fumigated with gunpowder and vinegar, having
taken notice that all our books, and utenſils became co-

---

* Boobies (*pelecanus piſcator*); men of war birds (*p. aquilus*); and tropic
birds (*phaëthon æthereus.*)

vered

vered with mould, and all our iron and ſteel though
ever ſo little expoſed, began to ruſt. Nothing is more
probable than that the vapours, which now filled the
air, contained ſome ſaline particles, ſince moiſture alone
does not appear to produce ſuch an effect [*]. If it be aſked
how any ſaline particles, generally ſo much heavier than
the aqueous, can be raiſed in vapours, I leave it to the
philoſophers to determine, whether the numerous animal
parts which daily putrefy in the ocean, do not ſupply
enough of the volatile alkali, by the aſſiſtance of which the
above phænomenon might be explained. The great heat
between the tropics ſeems to volatiliſe the marine acid
contained in the brine and common ſalt: for it has been
obſerved, that on rags dipped in a ſolution of any one of
the alkalies, and ſuſpended over one of the pans where
brine is evaporated and ſalt is prepared, cryſtals are ſoon
formed of a neutral ſalt, compounded of the marine acid
and the alkali in which the rags had been immerſed;
hence perhaps we may be allowed to infer, that the marine acid is by the heat of the tropical ſun volatiliſed, and
in that aërial or vaporous form attacks the ſurface of iron
and ſteel; nay, this little quantity of acid may perhaps,
imbibed by the lungs, and pores of the ſkin, become ſalutary; in the firſt caſe to people under pulmonary diſeaſes;

[*] This opinion is very judiciouſly diſcuſſed by Ellis, in his voyage to Hudſon's
Bay.

and

and in the second by gently bracing the habit of bodies relaxed by a tropical heat, and moderating the too violent perfpiration.

The infpiffated effence of beer, of which we had feveral cafks on board, was obferved to be in motion before we left Madeira, and now began to burft the cafks and run out. The captain ordering it to be brought on deck, its fermentation was encreafed by the addition of frefh air, and feveral of the cafks had their heads forced out by the fermenting liquor, with an explofion like that of a fowling-piece. A kind of vapour, like fmoke, always preceded the eruption. A veffel, ftrongly fumigated with fulphur, was, by my father's advice, filled with this effence, by which means the fermentation was ftopped for a few days, but returned afterwards, efpecially in cafks expofed to the free accefs of air. Some cafks, which had been buried in the ballaft-fhingle, were preferved and prevented from burfting. Perhaps the admixture of double-diftilled fpirit, might have hindered the progrefs of fermentation in this effence. The beer made of it, by the fimple addition of warm water, was very good and palatable, though it had a little empyreumatic tafte, caufed by the infpiffation.

Auguft the 11th, we difcovered Bonavifta, one of the Cape-Verd iflands. The next morning, the weather cleared up, after a fhower of rain, and prefented to our fight the

ifle

iſle of Mayo. About noon we approached the iſle of San Jago, and anchored at three o'clock in the afternoon in Porto-Praya.

Early the next morning we went on ſhore, and viſited the commandant of the fort, Don Joſeph de Sylva, a good-natured man, who ſpoke the French imperfectly, and introduced us to the governor-general of the Cape-Verd iſlands. This gentleman, whoſe name was Don Joachim Salama Saldanha de Lobos, commonly reſides at St. Jago, the capital of the iſland; but as he was very ſickly, which his complexion witneſſed for him, he had retired hither about two months ago, where the air is reckoned more ſalubrious. He occupied the apartments of the commandant, who was now obliged to dwell in a wretched cottage, and who gave us ſome information relative to theſe iſlands.

In 1449, Antonio Nolli, probably by others named Antoniotto, a Genoeſe in the ſervice of Don Henry, Infante of Portugal, diſcovered ſome of the Cape-Verd iſlands, and on the firſt of May landed on one of them, which had its name from thence. St. Jago was ſeen at the ſame time. In 1460, another voyage was undertaken in order to ſettle them; and on this occaſion the remaining iſlands were likewiſe diſcovered. San Jago is the greateſt of them, and about ſeventeen leagues in length. The capital, of the ſame name, lies in the interior parts of the country, and is the ſee of the biſhop of all the Cape-

Verd iſlands. This iſle is divided into eleven pariſhes, and the moſt populous of theſe contains about four thouſand houſes, ſo that it is but very thinly inhabited.

Porto-Praya ſtands on a ſteep rock, to which we climbed by a ſerpentine path. Its fortifications are old decayed walls on the ſea ſide, and fences, ſcarce breaſt-high, made of looſe ſtones, towards the land. A ſmall church is incloſed within theſe walls, towards the ſea; but, beſides it, there are only a few cottages. A tolerable building, at a little diſtance from the fort, belongs to a company of merchants at Liſbon, who have the excluſive right to trade to all the Cape-Verd iſlands, and keep an agent here for that purpoſe. When we made application to this indolent Don, by the Governor's direction, to be ſupplied with live cattle, he indeed promiſed to furniſh as many as we wanted, but we never got more than a ſingle lean bullock. The company perfectly tyrannizes over the inhabitants, and ſells them wretched merchandize at exorbitant prices.

The natives of St. Jago are few in number, of a middle ſtature, ugly, and almoſt perfectly black, with frizzled woolly hair, and thick lips, like the moſt ill-looking kind of negroes. The ingenious and very learned Canon Pauw, at Xanten, in his Recherches Philoſophiques ſur les Americains, vol. I. p. 186. ſeems to take it for granted, that they are the deſcendants of the firſt Portugueſe ſettlers, gradually degenerated through nine generations (three
hundred

hundred years) to their prefent hue, which we found darker
than he defcribes it. But whether, according to his and
the Abbé de Manet's * opinion, this change of complexion
was effected merely by the heat of the torrid zone, or
whether they have acquired their fable colour by intermarriages with negroes from the adjacent coaſt of Africa,
is a queſtion which I do not venture to decide, though fo
able and judicious an inveſtigator of nature as Count
Buffon, aſſerts, that " the colours of the human fpecies
depend principally on the climate." See Hiſtoire Naturelle,
in 12mo, vol. VI. p. 260. At prefent there are very few
white people among them, and I believe we did not fee
above five or fix, including the governor, commandant,
and company's agent. In fome of the iſlands, even the
governors and prieſts are taken from among the blacks.
The better fort of them wear ragged European cloaths,
which they have obtained by barter from fhips that touched here, previous to the eſtabliſhment of the monopolizing
company. The reſt content themfelves with a few feparate articles of drefs, either a ſhirt, or a waiſtcoat, or a
pair of breeches, or a hat; and feem to be well pleafed
with their own appearance. The women are ugly, and
wear a long flip of ſtriped cotton over the fhoulders, hanging down to the knees before and behind; but children

* See his Nouvelle Hiſtoire de l'Afrique Françoife, enrichie de Cartes, &c. a
Paris, 1767, 12mo, vol. II. p. 224.

F 2   are

are perfectly naked till the age of puberty. Defpotic
governors, bigotted priests, and indolence on the part of
the court of Lifbon, will always keep thefe people in a
wretched fituation, beneath that of any community of
negroes in Africa, and prevent them from increafing their
numbers, which are the real wealth of a nation. It is
natural for people whofe folids are relaxed in a fervid climate, to incline to floth and lazinefs; but they are confirmed in thefe vices, and muft become indifferent to improvement, when they know the attempt would only
make their fituation more irkfome. With a kind of
gloomy infenfibility they give themfelves up to beggary,
the only ftate which can protect them from the greedy
clutches of tyrannical mafters; and they fhun every labour, which muft encreafe the treafures of others without
benefit to themfelves; and which only breaks in upon
thofe hours of reft, that are now the folace of their precarious condition. Such clouded profpects, that never
admit a gleam of happinefs, cannot be incitements to
marriage, and the difficulty of fupporting a wretched exiftence, is a fufficient reafon to decline the cares annexed
to the relation of parents. Let us add to this, that the
dry foil, whofe fertility depends on the ftated return of
annual rains, is parched up whenever a drought takes
place; all vegetation is then deftroyed, and an inevitable
famine fucceeds. It may be reafonably fuppofed, that the
experience

experience of fuch fatal periods, deters the inhabitants from
indulging in the fweets of conjugal connections, when
they muft apprehend that mifery, and perhaps the horrors
of flavery, await their unhappy offspring *.

The Cape-Verd iflands in general are mountainous,
but their lower hills, which are covered with a fine verdure, have a very gentle declivity, and extenfive vallies
run between them. They are ill fupplied with water,
which in many of them is only found in pits or wells.
St. Jago has, however, a tolerable river running into the
fea at Ribeira Grande, a town which takes its name from
thence. At Porto-Praya there was only a fingle well fet
round with loofe ftones, and containing muddy brackifh
water, in fuch fmall quantities, that we drew it quite dry
twice a day. The valley by the fide of the fort feems to
have fome moifture, and is planted here and there with
cocoa-nut-palms, fugar-canes, bananas, cotton, goava, and
papaw-trees; but the greateft part of it is over-run with
various forts of brufhwood, and another is left for paftures.

* On our return to the Cape of Good Hope, in 1775, we were told of a general famine which had happened in the Cape-Verd iflands in 1773 and 1774, and
which had rifen to fuch a height that hundreds of people had perifhed for want.
The commander of a Dutch fhip, which touched at St. Jago during this diftrefs-
ful feafon, received feveral of the natives, with their wives and children, who
fold themfelves to him, in order to efcape the dreadful confequences of want.
He carried them to the Cape of Good Hope, and fold them; but when the Government there was informed of it, he was ordered to redeem them at his own
expence, to carry them back to their native country, and to bring a certificate
from the Portuguefe governor, importing the execution of thefe orders.

We

We may perhaps conclude from hence, that the Cape Verd iflands in the hands of an active, enterprifing, or commercial nation, would become interefting and ufeful, and might be cultivated to the greateft advantage. The cochineal-plant, indigo, fome fpices, and perhaps coffee, would thrive particularly well in this hot and parched climate; and thefe productions would be fufficient to fupply the natives not only with the neceffaries, but likewife with the conveniencies and luxuries of life, under the benign influence of a free and equal government, like that under which we have the happinefs to live in this country. Inftead of feeding on a fcanty allowance of roots, we fhould fee their board heaped with plenty, and convenient houfes would then fupply the place of wretched hovels.

Some of the lower hills were dry and barren, fcarce any plants growing upon them; but others had ftill fome verdure on them, though we were now at the end of the dry feafon. They are all covered with abundance of ftones, which appear to have been burnt, and are a fpecies of lava. The foil, which is fertile enough in the vallies, is a kind of rubbifh of cinders, and ochreous afhes; and the rocks on the fea-fhore are likewife black and burnt. It is therefore probable, that this ifland has undergone a change from volcanic eruptions; and it will not be deemed unreafonable to form the fame opinion of all the Cape-Verd

Verd iſlands, when we conſider that one of them, the iſland of Fuogo, ſtill conſiſts of a burning mountain. The interior mountains of the country are lofty, and ſome of them appear ſteep and craggy, being perhaps of a more ancient date than the volcanic parts which we could examine.

In the evening we returned on board; but as the ſurf ran conſiderably higher than at our landing, we were obliged to ſtrip in order to wade to our boats, which our beſt ſwimmers had loaded with water-caſks, and ſuch re-freſhments as could be purchaſed on ſhore; not without ſome danger of being hurt by ſharks, which are numerous in the harbour. The captains, aſtronomers, and maſters, had ſpent this day in making aſtronomical obſervations upon the little iſlet in the harbour, named *Ilba dos Codornizes*, or Quail iſland, from the birds which are in great plenty upon it. The commandant of the fort informed us, that the officers of a French frigate had likewiſe made aſtronomical obſervations on this identical ſpot ſome time ago, having ſeveral watches of a new conſtruction on board *.

The next day captain Cook invited the governor-general, and the commandant to dinner, and we ſtaid on board, in order to act as interpreters on this occaſion. The cap-

* This was the 16s frigate, commanded by M. de Fleurieu, on board of which was M. Pingré, with ſeveral time keepers. A journal of the voyage and obſerva-tions made in that ſhip, has ſince been publiſhed in 2 vols. quarto.

tain.

tain fent them his own boat; but when it came on fhore, the governor begged to be excufed, becaufe he was always affected with ficknefs on board any veffel, whether at fea or in harbour. The commandant promifed to come, but having at firſt neglected to afk the governor's leave, the latter retired to take his *fiefta* (or afternoon's repofe) and no one ventured to difturb him.

The extreme fcarcity of refrefhments made our ſtay at Porto-Praya very fhort. We were therefore obliged to content ourfelves with a few cafks of brackifh water, a fingle bullock, a few long-legged goats, with ſtrait horns and pendulous ears, fome lean hogs, turkies, and fowls, and a few hundreds of unripe oranges, and indifferent bananas. The refearches we had made the preceding day, furnifhed us with a few tropical plants, moſtly of known fpecies, with fome new kinds of infects and of fifh. We alfo obferved feveral forts of birds, and among them guinea-hens, which feldom fly, but run very fwiftly, and which, when old, are very tough and dry eating. Quails and red-legged partridges are likewife common, according to the report of the natives, though we did not fee any; but the moſt remarkable bird we found is a fpecies of Kingfifher *, becaufe it feeds on large land-crabs of a blue

* The fame fpecies is found in Arabia Felix; vide Forfkal Fauna Arabica; as alfo in Abyffinia, as appears from the elegant and valuable drawings of James Bruce, Efq.

and

and red colour, whofe numerous habitations are round and deep holes in the dry and parched foil. Our failors, who catch at every thing that may afford them diverfion, purchafed about fifteen or twenty monkies, known by the name of St. Jago, or green monkies (*fimia fabœa*); which were a little bigger than cats, and of a greenifh-brown colour, with black faces and paws. On each fide of their mouth, they had a kind of pouch (like many others of the monkey tribe) which the Englifh in the Weft-Indian colonies, call by their Spanifh name *alforjas*. The antic tricks of thefe little monkies were amufing for fome days, while their novelty lafted; but they foon became infipid companions, were neglected, fometimes cruelly bandied about the veffel, and ftarved to death for want of frefh food, fo that only three of them reached the Cape of Good Hope. A harmlefs race of animals, dragged from the happy recefs of native fhades, to wear out the reft of their lives in continual anguifh and torment, deferve a pitying remembrance, though humanity would fain have drawn the veil over all acts of iron-hearted infenfibility, and wanton barbarifm.

We got under fail in the evening and fteered to the fouthward, having mild weather with frequent fhowers of rain on the following days, and the wind blowing from N. E. by N. to N. N. E. On the 16th, at eight o'clock in the evening, we faw a luminous fiery meteor, of an oblong shape and blueish colour, and having a very quick descending motion: its course was N. W. and it disappeared in the horizon after a momentary duration. Our distance from St. Jago was fifty-five leagues at noon, notwithstanding which, we saw a swallow following our vessel, and making numberless circles round it. The necessary manœuvres of trimming the sails, in the evening disturbed it from its roost on one of the gun-ports, upon which it took shelter in the carved work of the stern. The two following days it continued to attend the ship on her course. During this time we observed many bonitos in the sea around us, which frequently shot past us with great velocity; but notwithstanding our endeavours to catch them with hooks, and strike them with harpoons, we could not take a single one. The crew were more successful in hooking a shark of about five feet in length. Its common attendants, the pilot-fish (*gasterosteus ductor*) and sucking-fish (*echeneis remora*), likewise appeared with it; but with this difference, that the former carefully avoided being caught, and swam about very nimbly; but the latter stuck so fast to the shark's body, that four of them were hauled on deck with it. We dined on part of the shark the next day, and found it a tolerable food when fried, but rather of difficult digestion on account of its fat.

Two

Two days after, Henry Smock, one of the carpenter's crew, being employed on the fides of the fhip, was fuddenly miffed, and probably had fallen over-board and was drowned. His good-natured character, and a kind of ferious turn of mind caufed him to be regretted *even* among his fhipmates, and muft embitter his lofs to thofe, whom the tender ties of parental or conjugal affection had united to him. Humanity ftole a tear from each feeling traveller, the tribute due to a rational fellow creature of a gentle and amiable difpofition.

We had frequent fhowers after leaving St. Jago, and experienced a remarkable heavy fall of rain on the 21ft, during which we caught up feven puncheons of frefh water in our fpread awnings. This fupply, though we were not diftreffed for want of it, was however very feafonable, inafmuch as we were now enabled to give large allowance of this neceffary element to the crew. Captain Cook's remark deduced from long experience, that abundance of frefh water contributes to the prefervation of health in long voyages, is extremely judicious, and feems to be founded on the known principles of phyfiology. If feamen have plenty of water to drink, and fome to wafh themfelves and their linen, this effential precaution will in a great meafure prevent the fea-fcurvy from gaining ground among them. Their blood is diluted, and the wafte of fluids caufed by profufe perfpiration in hot cli-

mates,

mates, is reflored by plentiful drinking, and the infenfible
perfpiration likewife goes on without a check, when the
people frequently fhift their linen, and wafh off any
uncleanlinefs that may obftruct the pores. It is evident that
the greateft danger of putrid diftempers is thus precluded ;
fince the reimbibing of perfpired matter, and the violence
of perfpiration without a frefh fupply to temper and
dilute the faline and cauftic quality of the remaining
fluids, (which are often fuppofed to be the caufes of in-
flammatory fevers) are both in a great meafure prevented.

The heavy rains of this morning, entirely foaked the
plumage of the poor fwallow, which had accompanied
us for feveral days paft ; it was obliged therefore to fettle
on the railing of the quarter-deck, and fuffered itfelf to
be caught. I dried it, and when it was recovered, let
it fly about in the fteerage, where, far from repining at
its confinement, it immediately began to feed upon the
flies, which were numerous there. At dinner we opened
the windows, and the fwallow retook its liberty ; but about
fix in the evening, it returned into the fteerage and cabin,
being fenfible that we intended it no harm. Having
taken another repaft of flies, it went out again, and roofted
that night fomewhere on the outfide of the veffel. Early
the next morning our fwallow returned into the cabin
once more, and took its breakfaft of flies. Emboldened

by

by the ſhelter which we afforded it, and the little diſtur-
bance it ſuffered from us, the poor little bird now ventured to enter the ſhip at every port and ſcuttle which
was open; ſome part of the morning it paſſed very happily in Mr. Wales's cabin; but after having left that it
entirely diſappeared. It is more than probable that it
came into the birth of ſome unfeeling perſon, who caught
it in order to provide a meal for a favourite cat.

From the hiſtory of this bird, which was of the common ſpecies, or a houſe-ſwallow *(hirundo ruſtica* Lin.) we
may deduce the circumſtances that bring ſolitary land-
birds a great way out to ſea. It ſeems to be probable,
that they begin with following a ſhip, from the time ſhe
leaves the land; that they are ſoon loſt in the great ocean,
and are thus obliged to continue cloſe to the ſhip, as the
only ſolid maſs in this immenſe fluid expanſe. If two
or more ſhips are in company, it is alſo eaſy to account
for the expreſſion of *meeting with* land-birds at a great diſtance from land; becauſe they may happen to follow ſome
other ſhip from the ſhore, than that which carries the
obſerver; thus they may eſcape obſervation for a day or
two, or perhaps longer, and when noticed, are ſuppoſed
to be *met with* at ſea. However, great ſtorms are ſometimes
known to have driven ſingle birds, nay vaſt flocks out
to ſea, which are obliged to ſeek for reſt on board of
ſhips,

ſhips, at conſiderable diſtances from any land *, I ſhall
venture another reflection on this incident. In the long
ſolitary hours of an uniform navigation, every little circumſtance becomes intereſting to the paſſenger; it is
therefore not to be wondered at, if a ſubject ſo trifling in
itſelf as putting to death a harmleſs bird, ſhould affect a
heart not yet buffeted into inſenſibility.

Sunday 23. On the 23d, ſeveral cetaceous fiſh, from fifteen to
twenty feet long paſſed the ſhip, directing their courſe
to the N. and N. W. They were ſuppoſed to be grampuſſes,
Tueſday 25. (delphinus orca). Two days after the ſame kind of fiſh,
and a number of leſſer ones of a browniſh colour, called
ſkip-jacks, from leaping frequently out of the water, were
obſerved. The wind for ſeveral days paſt had blown from
the N. W. and obliged us to take a S. E. courſe, ſo that
we were now got to the ſouthward of the coaſt of Guinea.
Several of our navigators, who had frequently croſſed the
Atlantic, looked upon this as a ſingular circumſtance; and
indeed it fairly proves, that though nature in the torrid
zone commonly produces regular and conſtant winds,
nevertheleſs it ſometimes deviates even there from general

* Captain Cook very obligingly communicated to me a fact which confirms
the above aſſertion. Being on board of a ſhip between Norway and England, he
met with a violent ſtorm, during which a flight of ſeveral hundred birds covered
the whole rigging of the ſhip. Among numbers of ſmall birds, he obſerved ſeveral
hawks, which lived very luxuriouſly by preying on thoſe poor defenceleſs
creatures.

rules,

rules, and admits of several exceptions. In this situation we also observed several man-of-war birds, (*pelecanus aquilus*.) It is a common belief among sailors that their appearance denotes a vicinity of land; but we were at present above a hundred leagues from any shore, so that this opinion seems to have no better support than many old prejudices. Each eradication of one of these is a gain to science; and each vulgar opinion, proved to be erroneous, is an approximation to TRUTH, which *alone* is worthy of being recorded for the use of mankind.

On the first of September, several dolphins, (*coryphana hippurus*,) were seen; and we likewise took notice of a large fish close to us, perfectly resembling the figure of a fish given in Willoughby's Histor. Piscium, appendix pag. 5. tab. 9. f. 3. which is taken from John Nieuhoff's account, and which the Dutch call *zee-duyvel*, or sea-devil. In its external shape it was similar to the genus of rays, but seems to be a new species; from whence it is evident, that even in the most frequented seas, such as the Atlantic, many new discoveries in natural history might be made, if those who can distinguish unknown from known objects, had always opportunities of enquiring into them.

On the third of September great numbers of flying-fishes were observed, and a bonito (*scomber pelamys*) was caught, whose meat we found to be dry and less palatable than it is generally represented. We were lucky enough

two

1772.
SEPTEMBER.
Saturday 5. two days after to take a dolphin, (*coryphæna hippurus*,) which is likewise dry meat; but the inimitable brightness of its colours, which continually change from one rich hue to another whilst it is drying, is, in my opinion, one of the most admirable appearances which can occur to the voyager's view during a tropical navigation.

> But here defcription clouds each fhining ray;
> What terms of art can NATURE's pow'rs difplay!
>
> FALCONER.

A boat was this day hoisted out in order to find the direction of the current, and to determine the temperature of the sea-water at a great depth. We sounded with 250 fathoms without finding any bottom. The thermometer in the air stood at 73½ deg. dipped under the surface of the sea it shewed 74 deg. and after being let down to the depth of 85 fathoms and hauled up again, it was fallen to 66 deg. It staid 30' under water, and was 27' in hawling up. Our latitude at noon was 0° 52' north. The boat being out, we had an opportunity of examining that kind of blubber, or sea-nettle, which Linnæus has named *medufa pelagica*; together with another submarine animal called *dris lævis*, and employed ourselves in making drawings of them, and more minute descriptions than have hitherto been published.

Wednesday 9. On the 9th, having passed the line with a light air, our crew ducked such of their shipmates as had never crossed it before,

before, and did not care to redeem themfelves by paying
a certain forfeit of brandy. Thofe who had been obliged
to undergo the briny fubmerfion, changed their linen and
clothes; and as this can never be done too often, efpecially in warm weather, the ducking proved a falutary
operation to them. The quantity of ftrong liquors, arifing
from the forfeits of the reft, ferved to heighten the jovial humour, which is the predominant characteriftic of failors. This
day we likewife obtained a foutherly wind, which gradually,
came round to S. by E. and S. S. E. and fettled into the
ufual trade wind.

This day we caught feveral dolphins, and a flying-fifh
one foot long fell on the quarter-deck. Ever fince the
8th we had daily obferved feveral aquatic birds, fuch
as man of war birds, boobies *(pelecanus aquilus & fula)* petrels,
gulls, and tropic-birds *(phäton æthereus.)* We had alfo at
various intervals, found the fea covered with animals
belonging to the clafs of *mollufca,* one of which, of a blue
colour, in fhape like a fnail, with four arms, divided into
many branches, was named *glaucus atlanticus*; another, tranfparent like a cryftal, and often connected in a long ftring
with individuals of the fame fpecies, was referred to the
genus named *doris*, mentioned in Lieut. Cook's voyage in
the Endeavour *. Two other fpecies of mollufca, which

* See Hawkefworth's compilation, vol. II. p. 2.

seamen call *sallee*, and *Portuguese* men of war, *(medusa velella & holothuria physalis)* likewise appeared about our vessel in great abundance.

On the 27th we tried the direction of the currents, and the temperature of the sea again, with nearly the same result as before. The thermometer, which in open air stood at 72 ½ deg. and under the surface of the sea at 70 deg. after being let down 80 fathom, sunk to 68 deg. It continued 15 min. under water, and was hauled up in 7 min. We likewise took up a new species of the blubber (*medusa*.) For two days past, we had observed a bird, which we were this day enabled to examine, when we knew it to be the common shear-water (*procellaria puffinus*.) Having now reached the latitude of twenty-five degrees south, we found the wind gradually coming round from E. by S. to E. by N. and to N. E. which enabled us to steer to the south-eastward. Our bodies, which the heat of the torrid zone had in a great degree relaxed, now began to feel a considerable alteration in the climate, and though the thermometer was not above ten degrees different from what it used to be near the line, yet I contracted a violent cold, attended with the tooth-ach, swelled gums, and cheeks.

On the fourth of October, we observed great numbers of the common little petrel, of a sooty brown, with white rumps *(procellaria pelagica)*, and found the air cold and sharp.

                                                                The

The next day the albatrofs, *(diomedia exulans)* and the pintadas *(procellaria capenfis)*, made their firſt appearance.

On the 11th it was mild and almoſt calm, after feveral
days of hazy and fqually weather, which had probably
ſharpened the appetite of the ſea birds, and eſpecially the
pintadas; for theſe laſt eagerly fwallowed hooks baited
with pieces of pork or mutton, and no leſs than eight of
them were caught in a ſhort time. In the evening we
obferved an eclipfe of the moon, of which the end at a
medium happened at 6h. 58′ 45″ p. m. our latitude at
noon being 34° 45′ ſouth.

The next day we tried the current and the temperature
of the ſea a third time. We let down the thermometer
100 fathoms, where it continued 20 min. was hauled
up in 7 min. more, and then ſhewed 58 deg. At the
furface it ſtood at 59 deg. and in the air at 60 deg. It
being calm, we employed ourſelves in the boat with
ſhooting ſea-fowl; among which were a ſmall tern, a
ſhear-water, a new ſpecies of albatrofs, and a new petrel:
Several animals of the molluſca tribe likewiſe came within
our reach, together with the *helix janthina*, a violet-coloured
ſhell, remarkable for the extreme thinneſs of its texture,
which breaks with the leaſt preſſure, and ſeems therefore
entirely calculated to keep the open ſea, or at leaſt to ſhun

H 2 rocky

rocky shores *, agreeably to the obfervation in Lieutenant
Cook's voyage in the Endeavour. Albatroffes, pintadas,
and petrels of all kinds, amongſt which was alfo the ful-
mer, (*procellaria glacialis*,) were now daily obferved.

On the 17th, we had an alarm that one of our crew
was overboard, upon which we immediately put about,
but feeing nothing, the names of all perfons on board
the veffel were called over, and none found miffing, to
our great fatisfaction. Our friends on board the Adventure, whom we vifited a few days after, told us they had
indeed fufpected by our manœuvre, the accident which
we had apprehended, but that looking out on the fea,
Capt. Furneaux had plainly obferved a fea-lion, that had
been the caufe of this falfe alarm.

* See Hawkefworth's Compilation, vol. II. p. 14. We find another
remark at the end of that above quoted, which is of very different value, and
feems to indicate that the ancient authors were not confulted. Whoever has
looked into Pliny, can never have the leaſt idea that the thin ſhell afore-men-
tioned could be " the purpura of the ancients." They had feveral kinds of
ſhells, which yielded the purple dye, but thefe were all rock-ſhells. *Eorum
genera plura, pauludé et* SOLO *diſcreta,* lib. ix. cap. 61. *Enquirantur omnes* SCOPULI
getuſi muricibus ac purpuris, lib. v. cap. 1. It is equally clear and uncontrovertible
that the figure and hardnefs of their purple ſhells were very different from thofe
of the little *helix janthina.* PURPURA *vocatur, cuniculatim procurrente roſtro et cuni-
culi latere introrfus tubulato quo profertur lingua,* lib. ix. cap. 61.——*Lingua purpura
longitudine digitalis qua poſſitur, perforando reliqua conchylia,* tanta DUBITIA *a.nbu
eſt,* lib. ix. cap. 60.——*Præterea devotum eſt ad turbinem ufque aculeis in orbem feptenis
fere,* lib. ix. cap. 61. Don Antonio Ulloa, in his voyage to South-America,
book IV. chap. 8. may be confulted on the fubject.

On

On the 19th we had a great southern swell, and saw a large whale, and likewise a fish of the shark genus, of a whitish colour, with two dorsal-fins, and its length about eighteen or twenty feet. As we had been a considerable time at sea, the Captain had for some weeks past ordered sour-krout (or cabbage sliced and fermented) to be regularly served to the crew, at a pint per man on meat-days, which was four times a week. The Lords of the Admiralty, attentive to every circumstance which bids fair to preserve the health of seafaring men, had ordered a very considerable quantity of this salutary and palatable food to be put on board both of the ships, and the event has proved that it is one of the best prophylactics against the sea-scurvy.

On the 24th, the Adventure being a great way astern, the captain ordered a boat to be hoisted out, and several officers and other gentlemen went a shooting, which gave us a fresh opportunity of examining the two sorts of albatrosses, and a large black species of shear-water, (*procellaria aequinoctialis.*) Our navigation, which for nine weeks past had been out of sight of any land, began to appear dull and tedious, and seemed to be distressing to many who were not used to an uniform recluse life on board a ship, without any refreshments or variety of scenes. We should have found this long passage equally disagreeable, if it had not supplied us with employment from time to time,

time, and nursed the hope of making many interesting discoveries relative to the science of nature.

On the 29th, early in the morning, we discovered the land of the extremity of Africa, covered with clouds and fog; and several gannets and small diving-petrels, together with some wild ducks, came out to sea from thence. Soon after the land disappeared entirely, and we could not see it again till three o'clock in the afternoon, when its parts were much plainer, though the clouds still involved them. The wind blowing fresh, and the Adventure being a great way a-stern, we could not venture to get into the Table bay during night, but stood off and on till the next morning, having thick squally weather, and heavy showers of rain.

     The night was scarcely begun, when the water all round us afforded the most grand and astonishing sight than can be imagined. As far as we could see the whole ocean seemed to be in a blaze. Every breaking wave had its summit illuminated by a light similar to that of phosphorus, and the sides of the vessel, coming in contact with the sea, were strongly marked by a luminous line. Great bodies of light moved in the water along our side, sometimes slower, sometimes quicker; now in the same direction with our course, now flying off from it; sometimes we could clearly distinguish their shape to be that of fishes, which when they approached any smaller ones, forced these

these to haften away from them. Defirous of enquiring into the caufe of this aftonifhing phænomenon, we procured a bucket full of the illumined fea-water. The moft accurate attention to it proved, that innumerable minute fparks, of a round fhape, communicated this luminous appearance to the water, and moved about in it with great brifknefs and velocity. After the water had been ftanding for a little while, the number of fparks feemed to decreafe; but on being ftirred again, the whole became as luminous as before. Again, as the water gradually fubfided the fparks were obferved to move in directions contrary to the undulations of the water, which they did not before, whilft the agitation was more violent, and feemed to carry them along with its own motions. We fufpended the bucket, to prevent its being too much affected by the motion of the fhip; the bright objects by this means betrayed more and more a voluntary motion, independent of the agitation of the water caufed by our hands, or by the rolling of the veffel. The luminous appearance always gradually fubfided, but on the leaft agitation of the water, the fparkling was renewed, in proportion as the motion was encreafed. As I ftirred the water with my hand, one of the luminous fparks adhered to my finger. We examined it by the common magnifier of Mr. Ramfden's improved microfcope, and found it to be globular, tranfparent like a gelatinous fubftance, and fomewhat brownifh:

by

1772.
October.

by the greatest magnifier we discovered the orifice of a little tube, which entered the body of this little atom, within which were four or five intestine bags connected with the tube. Having examined several of them, which had much the same appearance, I endeavoured to catch some in water, and bring them under the microscope in a concave glass, where its nature and organs might be better examined: but these minute objects were always hurt with our touch before we could place them in the concave glass, and when dead only appeared as an indistinct mass of floating filaments. In about two hours time the water had lost its luminous appearance. We had another bucket full of it drawn before that time, but all our attempts to catch one of the little atoms in the glass proved ineffectual. Accordingly we hastened to draw the appearance of the first globule, and to write down our observations. The most probable conjecture which we could form concerning these little atomical animalcules was, that they might be the young fry of some species of medusa or blubber, though it may likewise be possible, that they are beings of a distinct genus.

There was a singularity, and a grandeur in the display of this phænomenon, which could not fail of giving occupation to the mind, and filling it with a reverential awe, due to Omnipotence. The ocean covered to a great extent, with myriads of animalcules; these little beings,

or-

organized alive, endowed with locomotive power, a quality of shining whenever they pleafe, of illuminating
every body with which they come in contact, and of laying
afide their luminous appearance at pleafure: all thefe
ideas crouded upon us, and bade us admire the Creator, even
in his minuteft works. It is the natural fault of young
people to think too well of mankind; but I hope I fhall
not have formed too favourable an opinion of my readers,
if I expect that the generality will fympathize with me in
thefe feelings, and that none will be found ignorant or
depraved enough to defpife them.

Turrigeros elephantorum miramur humeros, taurorumque colla et truces in
fublime jactus, tigrium rapinas, leonum jubas; quum rerum natura nufquam
magis, quam in minimis tota fit. Quapropter quæfo, æ noftra legentes,
quoniam ex his fpernent multa, etiam relata faftidio damment, quum in contem-
platione Naturæ nihil poffit videri vacaneum. Plin. Hift. Nat. lib. xi. cap. 2.

The next morning, after a very rainy night, we failed
into Table bay. The mountains at the bottom of it, now
appeared clear of clouds, and furprifed us with their prodigious craggy, fteep, and barren appearance. As we
advanced farther into the bay, we difcovered the town
at the foot of the black Table mountain, and foon came
to an anchor. After faluting the fort, and receiving the
vifit of feveral officers in the fervice of the Dutch Eaft-India
company, we went on fhore with captains Cook and
Furneaux, being prepared to meet with many new acquifitions to fcience, on a continent fo diftant from our
own, and fituated in an oppofite hemifphere.

C H A P.   III.

Stay at the Cape of Good Hope.—Account of that Settlement.

WE were no sooner landed than we all went to wait
upon the governor, baron Joachim van Plettenberg,
a man of a very liberal education, and extensive knowledge, whose politeness and affability immediately gave
us a good opinion of him.   From him we proceeded
to the other members of the council, and at last retired
to take up our lodgings at Mr. Brand's, now commander at False bay, whose house at the Cape town is
commonly frequented by the English captains who happen
to touch there.   Almost every inferior officer of the Dutch
Company's government, the members of the council excepted, let their supernumerary apartments to the officers
and passengers in the various English, French, Danish, and
Swedish ships, which annually put in here, either on their
voyage from or back to Europe.

We were not a little pleased with the contrast between
this colony, and the Portuguese island of St. Jago.   There
we

we had taken notice of a tropical country, with a tolerable appearance, and capable of improvement, but utterly neglected by its lazy and oppressed inhabitants; here, on the contrary, we saw a neat well-built town, all white, rising in the midst of a desart, surrounded by broken masses of black and dreary mountains; or in other words, the picture of successful industry. Its appearance towards the sea-side, is not quite so picturesque as that of Funchal. The store-houses of the Dutch East-India company, are all situated nearest the water, and the private buildings lie beyond them on a gentle ascent. The fort which commands the road, is on the east side of the town, but seems not to be of great strength; besides which, there are several batteries on both sides. The streets in the town are broad, and regular; all the principal ones are planted with oaks, and some have in their middle a canal of running water, which on account of its small quantity, they are obliged to husband by sluices, so that parts of it are sometimes entirely drained, and occasion no very pleasant smell. The national character of the Dutch strongly manifests itself in this particular; their settlements being always supplied with canals, though reason and common sense evidently prove their noxious influence on the health of the inhabitants, especially at Batavia.

Quanto præstantius esset
———viridi si margine clauderet undas
Herba, nec ingenuum violarent marmora tophum !

JUVENAL.

The houses are built of brick, and many of them are
white washed on the outside. The rooms are in general
lofty and spacious, and very airy, which the hot climate
requires. There is but one church in the whole town,
and that is extremely plain, and seems to be rather too
small for the congregation. That spirit of toleration,
which has been so beneficial to the Dutch government at
home, is not to be met with in their colonies. It is but
very lately that they have suffered even the Lutherans, to
build churches at Batavia, and at this place; and at the
present time, a clergyman of that persuasion is not tole-
rated at the Cape, but the inhabitants are obliged to content themselves with the chaplains of Danish and Swedish
East-India-men, who give them a sermon, and administer
the sacrament once or twice a year, and are very hand-
somely rewarded. The government, and the inhabitants
do not give themselves the trouble to attend to a circumstance of so little consequence in their eyes, as the religion of their slaves, who in general seem to have none
at all. A few of them follow the Mahommedan rite, and
weekly meet in a private house belonging to a free Ma-
homedan, in order to read, or rather chaunt several prayers,

and

1772.
OCTOBER.

and chapters of the Koran. As they have no priest among them, they cannot partake of any other acts of worship [*].

The slaves belonging to the company, who amount to several hundreds, are lodged and boarded in a spacious house erected for that purpose, where they are likewise kept at work. Another great building serves as an hospital for the sailors belonging to the Dutch East-India ships, which touch here, and commonly have prodigious numbers of sick on board, on their voyage from Europe towards India. The vast number of men, sometimes six, seven, or eight hundred, which these ships carry out to supply the military in India, the small room to which they are confined, and the short allowance of water and salt provision, they receive on a long voyage through the torrid zone, generally make considerable havock among them: it is therefore no uncommon circumstance at the Cape, that a ship on her passage thither from Europe, loses eighty or a hundred men, and sends between two

---

[*] We would not be understood to throw an odium on the Dutch in particular, when it is well known that the negroes, who wear the chains of the English and French, are equally neglected: it was only intended to awaken a fellow-feeling towards an unhappy race of men, among the colonists of all nations; and to remind them whilst they enjoy, or strive to enjoy the inestimable blessing of liberty, to exert themselves in acts of humanity and kindness, towards those from whom they with-hold it, perhaps, without remorse.

and

and three hundred others dangerously ill to the hospital. A fact no less deplorable than certain, is, that the small expence and facility with which the *ziel-verkoopers* actually carry on their infamous trade of supplying the India company with recruits, makes them less attentive to the preservation of health among these poor people. Nothing is more common, in this and other Dutch colonies, than to meet with soldiers in the company's service who, upon enquiry, acknowledge they have been kidnapped in Holland. There is an apothecary's shop belonging to the hospital, where the most necessary remedies are prepared, but no expensive drug is to be found in it, and the method of administering to all the patients indiscriminately out of two or three huge bottles, full of different preparations, suffice to convince us, that the fresh air of the land, and fresh provisions here, contribute much more to the recovery of the sick, than the skill of their physicians. Patients who are able to walk, are ordered to go up and down the streets every fair morning; and all kinds of greens, pot-herbs, sallads, and antiscorbutics are raised for their use in an adjacent garden belonging to the company. Travellers have sometimes praised and sometimes depreciated this garden, according to the different points of view in which it has been considered. It is true, a few regular walks of indifferent oaks, encompassed with elm and myrtle hedges, are not objects engaging enough

to

to thofe who are ufed to admire the perfection of garden-
ing in England, or who contemplate in Holland and France
cyprefs, box, and yew trees cut out into vafes, ftatues, and
pyramids, or *charmilles* turned into pieces of architecture!
But confidering that the trees were planted in the beginning of this century, more for ufe than ornament; that
they fhelter the kitchen-herbs for the hofpital, againft the
deftructive violence of ftorms; and that they form the only fhady and airy walks, comfortable to voyagers and fick
perfons in this hot climate, I cannot wonder that fome
fhould extoll as " a delightful fpot[*]," what others con-
temptuoufly call " a friar's garden[†]."

The day after our arrival, the aftronomers of both
fhips, Mr. Wales and Mr. Baily, fixed their inftruments
afhore, within a few yards of the identical fpot where
Meffrs. Mafon and Dixon had formerly made their aftro-
nomical obfervations. The fame day we began our botanical excurfions in the country about the town. The
ground gradually rifes on all fides towards the three
mountains which lie round the bottom of the bay, keeping low and level only near the fea-fide, and growing
fomewhat marfhy in the ifthmus between the Falfe and
Table bays, where a falt rivulet falls into the latter. The

---

[*] Commodore (now admiral) Byron. See Hawkefworth's compilation, vol I.
[†] M. de Bougainville. See his Voyage round the World.

marfhy

marfhy part has fome verdure, but is intermixed with a
great deal of fand. The higher grounds, which from the
fea fide have a parched and dreary appearance, are however covered with an immenfe variety of plants, amongst
which are a prodigious number of fhrubs, but fcarce one
or two fpecies that deferve the name of trees. There are
alfo a few fmall plantations wherever a little run of water
moiftens the ground. Abundance of infects of every
fort, feveral fpecies of lizards, land-tortoifes, and ferpents
frequent the dry fhrubbery, together with a great variety
of fmall birds. We daily brought home ample collections
of vegetables and animals, and were much furprifed to
find a great number, efpecially among the latter, entirely
unknown to natural hiftorians, though gathered in fields
adjacent to a town, from whence the cabinets and repofi-
tories of all Europe have been repeatedly fupplied with
numerous and valuable acquifitions to the fcience.

One of our excurfions was directed to the Table mountain. The afcent was very fteep, fatiguing, and difficult,
on account of the number of loofe ftones which rolled
away under our feet. About the middle of the mountain
we entered a bold grand chafm, whofe walls are perpendicular and often impending rocks, piled up in ftrata.
Small rills of water oozed out of crevices, or fell from
precipices in drops, giving life to hundreds of plants and
low fhrubs in the chafm. Another kind of vegetables,
growing

growing on a drier soil, that seemed to concentrate their
juices, spread a fine aromatic scent, which a gentle breeze
wafted towards us from the chasm. At last, after three
hours walk, we reached the summit of the mountain. It
was nearly level, very barren, and bare of soil; several
cavities were however replete with rain-water, or contained a little vegetable earth, from whence a few odoriferous
plants drew their nourishment. Some antelopes, howling
baboons, solitary vultures, and toads are sometimes to be
met with on the mountain. The view from thence is very
extensive and picturesque. The bay seemed a small pond
or bason, and the ships in it dwindled to little boats: the
town under our feet, and the regular compartments of its
gardens, looked like the work of children. The Lion's
Rump now seemed an inconsiderable ridge; we looked
down on the spiry Lion's Head, and only Charles' Mount
rose as it were in competition with the Table. To the
northward, Robben island, the Blue hills, the Tyger hills,
and beyond them a noble chain of mountains, loftier than
that on which we stood, bounded our view. A group of
broken rocky masses inclosed Hout baay (Wood bay) to
the west, and continuing to the southward formed one side
of the Table bay, and terminated in the famous *stormy*
cape which king MANOEL of Portugal named the Cape of
GOOD HOPE. To the south-east our view extended across
the low isthmus between the two bays; beyond it we

discerned the colony of Hottentot Holland, and the mountains about Stellenbosch; and on this side we were delighted with a number of plantations insulated by the vast heath, and finely contrasting their verdure with the rest of the country: Among them we distinguished Constantia, famous in the annals of modern epicures. After a stay of two hours, finding the air very cold and sharp on the mountain, we descended, very well pleased with our excursion, and amply rewarded for the toilsome part of it, by the beauty and extent of the prospect.

The country on the S. E. side of the Table mountain attracted our particular attention, on account of the number of plantations on the sloping grounds, and the variety of plants which that part produced. Its appearance, especially near the hills, is the pleasantest on this side of the isthmus. By the side of every little rivulet a plantation is situated, consisting of vineyards, corn-fields, and gardens, and commonly surrounded with oaks from ten to twenty feet high, which enliven the country, and afford shelter against storms. The late governor Tulbagh, who is looked upon as a father to this colony, rebuilt several houses and gardens here, for the use of the governors, at Rondebosch and Nieuw-land. They are plain, and have nothing particular to recommend them, but that they are kept in the best order, consist of shady walks, and are well supplied with water. The company's granges or sheds are
also

alſo erected hereabouts; and a little farther on there is a brewery, belonging to a private man, who has the excluſive privilege of brewing beer for the Cape. In a fine valley, on the ſide of the mountain, lies the plantation called Paradiſe, remarkable for its delightful grove, and for producing ſeveral fruits, eſpecially ſuch as belong to tropical climates, which come to great perfection there. Alpheu, the ſeat of Mr. Kerſte, (at that time commander in Falſe bay) was the boundary of our excurſions on this ſide. We were here received with real hoſpitality, which our worthy hoſt had brought from Germany, his native country. During a few days it was the centre of our botanical rambles, which always furniſhed us with an abundant harveſt, and gave us the greateſt apprehenſions that with all our efforts, we alone would be unequal to the taſk of collecting, deſcribing, drawing, and preſerving (all at the ſame time) ſuch multitudes of ſpecies, in countries where every one we gathered would in all probability be a nondeſcript. It was therefore of the utmoſt importance, if we meant not to neglect any branch of natural knowledge, to endeavour to find an aſſiſtant well qualified to go hand and hand with us in our undertakings. We were fortunate enough to meet with a man of ſcience, Dr. Sparrman, at this place, who after ſtudying under the father of botany, the great Sir Charles Linné, had made a voyage to China, and another to the Cape in purſuit of knowledge.

K 2 The

The idea of gathering the treasures of nature in countries hitherto unknown to Europe, filled his mind so entirely, that he immediately engaged to accompany us on our circumnavigation; in the course of which, I am proud to say, we have found him an enthusiast in his science, well versed in medical knowledge, and endowed with a heart capable of the warmest feelings, and worthy of a philosopher. But far from meeting with such great discoveries in natural history, as had been made in Lieut. Cook's first voyage on a new continent *, we were obliged to content ourselves with the produce of a few small islands, which we could imperfectly investigate in the short spaces of sometimes a few hours, or a few days, or to the utmost of a few weeks, in unfavourable seasons.

During our stay at the Cape, the people on board our ship set up the rigging, scrubbed and payed the sides, and took in store some brandy and other necessary articles of provision for the crew, together with several sheep for the captains and officers. Several rams and ewes were likewise brought aboard, intended as presents to the natives of the South-Sea; but the length of the voyage, and our run to the frozen zone, reduced them so much, that this useful purpose was entirely defeated. In order to pursue our researches after natural knowledge, with greater cer-

* New Holland.

tainty

tainty of fuccefs, we likewife bought a water-fpaniel here, in hopes that this animal would prove ufeful in fetching any game which fell out of our reach. It was with great difficulty we could meet with one, and we were obliged to pay an exhorbitant price for it; though it afterwards proved of little fervice. It may feem fuperfluous to mention fo trifling an occurrence as this, but I believe it is hardly imagined, how great a number of little objects are to be attended to among many weightier concerns, by a traveller who means to improve his time to the utmoft advantage.

On the 22d we brought all our baggage on board, and the fame day we failed from Table bay. Previous to the mention of farther occurrences, I fhall here endeavour to give a fuccinct account of the ftate of this Dutch colony, which it is hoped will afford fatisfactory inftruction to my readers.

The foutherrmoft extremity of Africa, circumnavigated fo early as the times of the Egyptian king Necho, and again in the reign of Ptolemæus Lathyrus *, was once more

* The proofs of this affertion are enumerated in Schmidt Opufc. diff. Iv. de romerrs. & navigatho. Ægyptior. p. 160. and more fully in Schlözer Handlungs-Gefchichte (or Hiftory of Commerce) p. 300. Herodotus exprefsly fays, that Africa is furrounded by the fea, and that this was found out by fome Phœnician mariners fent out for that purpofe by Pharaoh Necho from the Red Sea, who returned by the Mediterranean. lib. Iv, cap. 42. Strabo, lib. ii. alfo mentions the expedition of one Eudoxus round Africa, in the reign of Ptolemy Lathyrus; and according to Pliny, the Carthaginians likewife have explored

the

difcovered in later times, by Bartolomeo Diaz, a Portuguefe
navigator, in the year 1487. Vafco de Gama was the firft
who made a voyage to India round it in 1497, which was
looked upon as a kind of prodigy. It remained however
ufclefs to Europeans till the year 1650, when Van-Riebeck,
a Dutch furgeon, firft faw the advantage that would ac-
crue to the Eaft-India Company in Holland, from a fettlement at fo convenient a diftance both from home and
from India. The colony which he founded, has ever fince
continued in the hands of the Dutch, and increafed in
value for a confiderable time after his deceafe.

The governor depends immediately upon the Eaft-India
Company, and has the rank of an *Edele Heer*, the title
given to the members of the fupreme council of Batavia.
He prefides here over a council confifting of the fecond,
or deputy governor, the fifcal, the major (who commands
the fort), the fecretary, the treafurer, the comptroller of
provifions, the comptroller of liquors, and the book-keeper;
each of which has a branch of the Company's commerce
affigned to his care. This council has the whole management of the civil and military departments, but the deputy governor prefides over another, named the court of

the coaft of that continent. Hift. Nat. lib. ii. cap. 67. *Et Himno, Carthaginis*
potentia florente, circumvectus a Gadibus ad finem Arabiæ, navigationem eam prodita
fcripto.

juftice,

justice, which tries all offences and crimes, and consists of some of the members of the former; but no two relations can sit and have vote in the same council, to prevent the influence of parties.

The income of the governor is very considerable, for besides a fixed appointment, and the use of houses, gardens, proper furniture, and every thing that belongs to his table, he receives about ten dollars for every leagre of wine which the Company buy of the farmer, in order to be exported to Batavia. The company allows the sum of forty dollars for each leagre, of which the farmer receives but twenty-four; what remains is shared between the governor, and second or deputy, the former taking two thirds, which sometimes are said to amount to 4000 dollars per annum. The second governor has the direction of the company's whole commerce here, and signs all orders to the different departments under him, as well as the governor to others. He and the fiscal have the rank of *upper koopman*. The fiscal is at the head of the police, and sees the penal laws put in execution; his income consists of fines, and of the duties laid on certain articles of commerce, but if he be strict in exacting them, he is universally detested. The sound policy of the Dutch have likewise found it necessary to place the fiscal as a check, to over-awe the other officers of the company, that they may not counteract the interests of their masters, or infringe the

laws

laws of the mother country. He is to that end, commonly well verfed in juridical affairs, and depends folely upon
the mother country. The major (at prefent Mr. Von Prehn,
who received us with great politenefs) has the rank of
koopman or merchant: this circumftance furprifes a ftranger,
who in all other European ftates, is ufed to fee military
honours confer diftinction and precedence, and appears ftill
more fingular to one who knows the contraft in this particular between Holland and Ruffia, where the idea of military rank is annexed to every place, even that of a
profeffor at the univerfity. The number of regular fol-
diers at this colony amounts to about 700, of which 400
form the garrifon of the fort, near the Cape town. The
inhabitants capable of bearing arms form a militia of
4000 men, of whom a confiderable part may be affembled
in a few hours, by means of fignals made from alarm
places in different parts of the country. We may from
hence make fome eftimate of the number of white people
in this colony, which is at prefent fo extenfive, that the
diftant fettlements are above a month's journey from the
Cape ; but thefe remote parts lie fometimes more than a
day's journey from each other, are furrounded by various
nations of Hottentots, and too frequently feel the want of
protection from their own government at that diftance.
The flaves in the colony are at leaft in the proportion of
five or more, to one white perfon. The principal inhabitants

tants at the Cape have fometimes from 20 to 30 flaves,
which are in general treated with great lenity, and fometimes become favourites with their maflers, who give
them very good cloathing, but oblige them to wear neither
fhoes nor flockings, referving thefe articles to themfelves.
The flaves are chiefly brought from Madagafcar, and a
little veffel annually goes from the Cape thither on that
trade; there are however, befides them, a number of Ma-
lays and Bengalefe, and fome negroes. The colonifts
themfelves are for the greateft part Germans, with fome
families of Dutch, and fome of French proteftants. The
character of the inhabitants of the town is mixed. They
are induftrious, but fond of good living, hofpitable, and
fociable; though accuftomed to hire their apartments to
ftrangers *, for the time they touch at this fettlement, and
ufed to be complimented with rich prefents of ftuffs, &c.
by the officers of merchant fhips. They have no great
opportunities of acquiring knowledge, there being no
public fchools of note at the Cape; their young men are
therefore commonly fent to Holland for improvement, and
their female education is too much neglected. A kind of
diflike to reading, and the want of public amufements,
make their converfation uninterefting and too frequently

* The terms are mentioned in Lieut. Cook's Voyage. See Hawkefworth's
compilation, vol. III. p. 393. The members of the council are an exception
in this refpect.

turn it upon scandal, which is commonly carried to a degree of inveteracy peculiar to little towns. The French, English, Portuguese, and Malay languages are very commonly spoken, and many of the ladies have acquired them. This circumstance, together with the accomplishments of singing, dancing, and playing a tune on the lute, frequently united in an agreeable person, make amends for the want of refined manners and delicacy of sentiment. There are however among the principal inhabitants, persons of both sexes, whose whole deportment, extensive reading, and well-cultivated understanding would be admired and distinguished even in Europe *. Their circumstances are in general easy, and often very affluent, on account of the cheap rate at which the necessaries of life are to be procured ; but they seldom amass such prodigious riches here as at Batavia, and I was told the greatest private fortune at the Cape did not exceed one

* Among them we cannot in justice avoid mentioning the governor, Baron Joachim von Plettenberg, a gentleman whose hospitality and affability do great honour to him and his nation; Mr. Hemmy, second governor, and his family ; Mr. Von Prehn, the major ; Mr. Bergh the secretary, a man of science, of a noble, philosophic turn of mind, with a family who distinguish themselves in every mental and bodily accomplishment, above the whole rising generation of the Cape ; Mr. Kersle, Mr. de Wit, and our worthy host Mr. Christophel Brand, commander of the Post at False Bay, with all their families. It is a real satisfaction to perpetuate the memory of valuable members of society, and friends to mankind.

hundred

hundred thoufand dollars, or about twenty-two thoufand
five hundred pounds fterling.

The farmers in the country are very plain hofpitable
people; but thofe who dwell in the remoteft fettlements
feldom come to town, and are faid to be very ignorant;
this may eafily be conceived, becaufe they have no better
company than Hottentots, their dwellings being often
feveral days journey afunder, which muft in a great meafure preclude all intercourfe. The vine is cultivated in
plantations within the compafs of a few days journey
from the town; which were eftablifhed by the firft colonifts, and of which the ground was given in perpetual
property to them and their heirs. The company at prefent never part with the property of the ground, but let
the furface to the farmer for an annual rent, which,
though extremely moderate, being only twenty-five dollars
for fixty acres *, yet does not give fufficient encouragement to plant vineyards. The diftant fettlements therefore
chiefly raife corn and rear cattle; nay many of the fettlers
entirely follow the latter branch of ruftick employment,
and fome have very numerous flocks. We were told
there were two farmers who had each fifteen thoufand
fheep, and oxen in proportion; and feveral who poffeffed

* Each acre of fix hundred and fixty-fix fquare Rhynland roods, the rood of
twelve feet. The proportion of the Rhynland foot to the Englifh is about one
hundred and fixteen to one hundred and twenty.

fix

fix or eight thousand sheep, of which they drive great
droves to town every year; but lions and buffaloes, and
the fatigue of the journey, destroy numbers of their cattle before they can bring them so far. They commonly
take their families with them in large waggons covered
with linen or leather, spread over hoops, and drawn by
eight, ten, and sometimes twelve pair of oxen. They
bring butter, mutton-tallow, the flesh and skins of sea-
cows (hippopotamus), together with lion and rhinoceros'
skins, to sell. They have several slaves, and commonly engage in their service several Hottentots of the poorer sort,
and (as we were told) of the tribe called Boschemans or
Bushmen, who have no cattle of their own, but commonly subsist by hunting or by committing depredations on
their neighbours. The opulent farmers set up a young
beginner by intrusting to his care a flock of four or five
hundred sheep, which he leads to a distant spot, where he
finds plenty of good grass and water; the one half of all
the lambs which are yeaned fall to his share, by which
means he soon becomes as rich as his benefactor.

Though the Dutch company seem evidently to discourage
all new settlers, by granting no lands in private property,
yet the products of the country have of late years sufficed
not only to supply the Isles of France and Bourbon with
corn, but likewise to furnish the mother country with several ship loads. These exports would certainly be made
at

at an eafier rate than at prefent, if the fettlements did not extend fo far into the country, from whence the products muft be brought to the Table bay by land carriage, on roads which are almoft impaffable. The intermediate fpaces of uncultivated land between the different fettlements are very extenfive, and contain many fpots fit for agriculture; but one of the chief reafons why the colonifts are fo much divided and fcattered throughout the country, is to be met with in another regulation of the company, which forbids every new fettler to eftablifh himfelf within a mile of another. It is evident that if this fettlement were in the hands of the commonwealth, it would have attained to a great population, and a degree of opulence and fplendor, of which it has not the leaft hopes at prefent: But a private company of Eaft-India merchants find their account much better in keeping all the landed property to themfelves, and tying down the colonift, left he fhould become too great and powerful.

The wines made at the Cape are of the greateft variety poffible. The beft, which is made at M. Vander Spy's plantation of Conftantia, is fpoken of in Europe, more by report than from real knowledge; thirty leagres * at the utmoft are annually raifed of this kind, and each leagre fells for about fifty pounds on the fpot. The vines from which it is made were originally brought from

* A leagre contains about one hundred and eight gallons, or a pipe.

Shiraz

Shiraz in Perfia. Several other forts grow in the neighbourhood of that plantation, which produce a fweet rich
wine, that generally paffes for genuine Conftantia in
Europe. French plants of burgundy, mufcade, and fron-
tignan have likewife been tried, and have fucceeded extremely well, fometimes producing wines fuperior to thofe
of the original foil. An excellent dry wine, which has a
flight agreeable tartnefs, is commonly drank in the principal families, and is made of Madeira vines tranfplanted
to the Cape. Several low forts, not entirely difagreeable,
are raifed in great plenty, and fold at a very cheap rate,
fo that the failors of the Eaft-India fhips commonly indulge themfelves very plentifully in them whenever they
come afhore.

The products of the country fupply with provifions the
fhips of all nations which touch at the Cape. Corn, flour,
bifcuit, falted beef, brandy, and wine are to be had in
abundance, and at moderate prices; and their frefh greens,
fine fruits *, good mutton and beef, are excellent reflora-
tives to feamen who have made a long voyage. The climate is likewife fo healthy, that the inhabitants are rarely
troubled with complaints, and flrangers foon recover of
the fcurvy and other diftempers. The winters at the Cape
are fo mild that they hardly ever have ice about the
town : but on the mountains, and efpecially thofe far in

* Their grapes and oranges are fome of the beft in the world.

the

the country, they have hard frosts with snow and hail storms; nay a strong south-easterly storm sometimes brings on a frost during night even in the month of November, which is their spring. The only inconvenience which they frequently suffer are colds, brought on by the frequent change of air from strong winds, to which the Cape is subject at all seasons. But notwithstanding the heat, which is sometimes excessive, the inhabitants of Dutch origin seem to have preserved their native habit of body, and both sexes are remarkably corpulent, to which their good living may greatly contribute.

The Hottentots or aboriginal inhabitants of this country, have retired into the interior parts, and their nearest *kraal* or village, is about a hundred miles from the Cape town. From thence they sometimes come down with their own cattle, or attend the Dutch farmers who conduct their flocks to town for sale. We had no opportunity to make new observations upon them, as we only saw a few individuals, in whom we could not discern any peculiarities but such as have already been described by Peter Kolben, in his Present State of the Cape of Good Hope, &c. The circumstantial accounts given by this intelligent man, have been confirmed to us by the principal inhabitants of the Cape town. It is true, that he has been misinformed in regard to some circumstances; and that others, chiefly relative to the colony, have at present another appearance

pearance than in his time: but he still remains the best
author that can be confulted on the fubject, and as fuch
we will venture to refer our readers to him.

We have had an occafion to obferve feveral facts alledged in Kolben, and we likewife find them mentioned
in Lieutenant Cook's voyage. See Hawkefworth's compilation Vol. III. p. 789, &c. The Abbé de la Caille, an
aftronomer, in the account of his voyage, which was publifhed foon after his death, has endeavoured to ruin the
credit of Kolben's book, without giving us any thing better
in its ftead. We fhould not have ventured to mention fo
fuperficial a performance, as that of the Abbé, were it not
neceffary to vindicate from his afperfions, the character of
Kolben, as a faithful and accurate obferver. The Abbé
lived with a family at the Cape, who were of a party directly oppofite to that which had fupported Kolben. He
daily heard invectives againft him, and never failed to
write them down, in order to give himfelf importance
at the expence of the other,

Nul n'aura d'efprit
Hors nous et nos amis.   BOILEAU.

The extremity of Africa towards the fouth is a mafs of
high mountains, of which the outermoft are black, craggy,
and barren, confifting of a coarfe granite, which contains
no heterogeneous parts, fuch as petrified fhells, &c. nor
any

any volcanic productions. The cultivated spots which we saw had a stiff clay mixed with a little sand and small pieces of stone; but the plantations towards False bay are almost entirely on a sandy soil. The colony of Stellenbosch is said to have the most fertile soil of all at the Cape, and the different plantations thrive there incomparably better than any where else, particularly the European oaks, which are said to have attained a considerable height and flourishing appearance, whilst they do not seem to succeed near the town, where the tallest we saw was not above thirty feet high. The interior mountains are certainly metallic, and contain iron and copper; specimens of ores of both kinds were shewn to us by Mr. Hemmy, and some tribes of Hottentots melt both these metals; from whence we may conclude, that the ores they employ must be rich and easy of fusion. Hot springs are likewise found at several places in the interior country; and the inhabitants of the Cape Town resort to one of them at the distance of about three days journey, which is famous for curing cutaneous and other distempers, and is probably of a sulphureous nature.

The variety of plants in this country is surprising. In the little time we staid there, we observed several new species growing in the environs of the town, where we should least have expected them. And though the collections of former botanists from hence are very ample, yet Dr.

Sparrman and the learned Dr. Thunberg * have gathered above a thousand species entirely unknown before. The animal kingdom is proportionably rich in the variety of its productions. The greatest quadrupeds, the elephant, the rhinoceros, and the giraffe or camelopard, inhabit this extremity of Africa; the two first were formerly found within fifty miles of the Cape, but have been so much pursued and hunted, that they are rarely seen at present within many days journey. The rhinoceros particularly is so scarce, that the government have issued an order to prevent its being entirely extirpated. The hippopotamus; there called a sea-cow, which formerly used to come as far as Saldanha bay, is likewise so seldom seen at present, that none must be killed within a considerable distance of the Cape. Its meat is eaten here, and reckoned a great dainty: the taste in my opinion is that of coarse beef, but the fat rather resembles marrow. This animal feeds entirely on vegetables, and we were told can only dive a

* An eminent disciple of Linné, who after arranging and-classing Dr. Burmann's herbals at Leyden, studied botany during three years at the Cape, and having made immense acquisitions to science, was sent to Batavia, at the expence of the Dutch East-India company, in order to proceed to Japan in 1775. The same gentleman was so obliging, at Dr. Sparrman's request, to take with him, on one of his excursions, Francis Masson, employed in the Royal garden at Kew, who had been sent to the Cape on board the Resolution, in order to collect live plants and seeds for the botanical garden. Under Dr. Thunberg's kind guidance, who pointed out to him what was worthy of notice, he has made and brought home an ample collection.

short

short space, not exceeding thirty yards. The wild buffalo
is another huge quadruped, which now inhabits the more
remote settlements of the Cape, and is said to have prodigious strength and ferocity. Its horns resembles those of
the American wild ox *(bison)*, and are represented in the
ixth vol. of M. de Buffon's Natural History. They often
attack the farmers travelling in the country, and kill
many of their cattle, which they trample upon with their
feet. Dr. Thunberg lost his horses in one of these ren-
counters, and his fellow-traveller, the Dutch company's
gardener, narrowly escaped between two trees. A young
one, about three years old, belonging to the second governor, was put before a waggon, with six tame oxen, but
his strength was such that they could not move him out
of his place *. Besides this there is another species of
wild ox, called by the natives *gnu*, which has slender
horns, a mane, and brushes of hair on the nose and wat-
tles, and in the slender make of its limbs seems to resemble an horse or an antelope, more than its cogeneric animals. This species we have drawn and described, and it
has been brought over to the menagerie of the Prince of
Orange. Africa has always been known as the country of

---

* We should have gone into the country to see this animal, but we only
heard of it the day before our departure. This seems to be the animal mentioned by de Manet, Nouvelle Histoire de l'Afrique Françoise, tome ii. p. 129.

M 2

the

the beautiful genus of gazelles or antelopes *, and the
different names which have been improperly given to its
species, have hitherto not a little contributed to obscure
our knowledge of them. A number of the fiercest beasts
of prey likewise infest the Cape, and the colonists can never
be at sufficient pains to extirpate them. Lions, leopards,
tyger-cats, striped and spotted hyænas, (Pennant's Syn. of
Quadr.) jackals, and several others, live on the numerous

* We can only except a few species found in India, and other parts of
Asia, and one in Europe. The different species at the Cape are remarkable,
some for the elegance of their shape, some for their colours, their horns, or their
size. The Coodoo, or Kolben's bock other names (goat without a name), from
whence the name of M. de Buffon's Condoma is probably derived, is the strep-
siceros of Lioné and Pallas, and its height is that of a horse. Its leaps are said
to be of an astonishing height. The Cape elk of Kolben, Pallas's antilope oryx,
is about the size of a stag. The hartebeest bock is the A. scripta of Dr. Pallas. The
antelope which they improperly call a bart or stag at the Cape, is the A. bubalis
of Pallas. The Egyptian antelope, Linné's and Pallas's gazella, and M. de
Buffon's pasan, is here called gems-bock or chamois, which it does not in the
least resemble. The blue antelope, (blaauw bock) is really of a blackish colour,
but when killed soon loses the velvet-like appearance of its fur. The spring-
bock, a beautiful species, named A. pygargus by Pallas, live in vast herds in the
interior parts of Africa, and travel to the southward in the summer season, in
search of food, attended by many lions, panthers, hyænas, and jackals, which
prey upon them. Of this species we had the honour to present one to Her
Majesty alive. Two small species, with several varieties not hitherto noticed,
supply the principal inhabitants with venison of a fine flavour. Their size is
that of a fawn of the fallow deer. The duyker, or diving antelope, so called
from hiding itself among the bushes when pursued, and only emerging from time
to time, is not yet sufficiently known, and the animal named a roebuck here,
likewise deserves the farther attention of travellers.

species

G

species of antelopes, on hares, jerbuas, caviæ, and many lesser quadrupeds with which the country abounds. The number of birds is likewise very great, and among them many are arrayed in the brightest colours. I cannot help mentioning, in confirmation of Kolben's accounts, that we have seen two species of swallows at the Cape, though the Abbé de la Caille censures him for speaking of them, because they did not occur to himself. The Abbé also commits a mistake with regard to the knorhan, which is not a gelinote or grous, as he calls it, but the African bustard. Upon the whole, it would be easy to refute almost every criticism which the Abbé has passed on Kolben, if a work of so little merit deserved so much attention. Reptiles of all kinds, serpents, (among which are many whose bite is mortal,) and a variety of insects swarm about the Cape; and its shores likewise abound in well-tasted fishes, many of which are not yet known to the naturalist. In short, notwithstanding the many spoils of the vegetable and animal kingdom, which have been brought from Africa, its immense interior countries remain almost entirely unknown to the present time, and still contain great treasures of natural knowledge, which wait the future investigation of another THUNBERG or another BRUCE.

CHAP.

CHAP. IV.

Run from the Cape to the Antarctic Circle; first season spent in high Southern Latitudes.—Arrival on the Coast of New Zeeland.

Tuesday 12.

WE failed from Table bay, about four in the afternoon, on the 22d of November, after having faluted the fort. The wind blew in hard fqualls, which continued all night, and gave us once more a rough reception on the boifterous element; while the fame luminous appearance, which we had obferved before our coming into this bay, was perceived again, though in a much flighter degree. Monday 23. The next day towards eight in the morning, we loft fight of the Cape, and directed our courfe to the fouthward. As we were now entering on an unexampled navigation, not knowing when we might meet with a new place of refrefhment, the captain gave the ftricteft orders to prevent the wafte of frefh water; to this end a centry was placed at the fcuttled-cafk *, and a regular allowance of water was daily ferved out to the crew, befides which they were permitted to drink at the cafk, but not to carry any water away. The captain himfelf wafhed with falt-water, and

* An open butt placed on the quarter-deck, and daily filled with frefh water out of the hold, for the ufe of the fhip's cumpany.

all

all our company were obliged to conform to this necessary restriction. The distilling machine improved by Mr.
Irving, was likewise constantly employed, to supply at least
some part of the quantity daily consumed.

On the 24th in the afternoon, the weather being fair Tuesday 14.
and moderate, after a hard gale we caught nine albatrosses
with a line and hook, baited with a bit of sheep's skin.
Several of them measured above ten feet from tip to tip,
between the expanded wings. The younger ones seemed
to have a great mixture of brownish feathers, whereas
the full-grown were almost entirely white except their
wings, which were blackish, and their scapulars which
were barred and sprinkled with dotted lines of black.

A large brown fish resembling the sun fish *(tetrodon
mola)*, was likewise seen close to the ship for a short space
of time.

On the the 29th the wind, which had for three or four Sunday 19.
days past blown a very strong gale, now encreased so much,
that we ran during the last twenty-four hours, almost
under the bare fore-sail. The sea at the same time ran very
high, and frequently broke over the sloop, in which none
of the cabins were prepared for such bad weather, our
course from England to the Cape having been remarkably free of storms. The people, and especially persons
not brought up to sea-affairs, were ignorant how to behave
in this new situation; the prodigious rolling of the vessel
therefore

therefore daily made great havock among cups, faucers, glaffes, bottles, diſhes, plates, and every thing that was moveable; whilſt the humorous circumſtances fometimes attending the general confuſion, made us bear theſe irreparable loſſes with greater compoſure than might have been expected. The decks, and the floors of every cabin were however continually wet; and the howl of the florm in the rigging, the roar of the waves, added to the violent agitation of the veſſel, which precluded almoſt every occupation, were new and awful fcenes, but at the fame feverely felt, and highly difagreeable. The air was likewife unpleafantly ſharp and cold about this time, our latitude being now about 42° fouth; and frequent rains contributed to make the fervice of the feamen hard and comfortlefs. To fecure them in fome meafure againſt the inclemencies of the weather, the captain ordered a general diſtribution of clothes to be made, which had been exprefsly provided at the expence of the Admiralty to ferve this purpofe. Every perfon whofe duty expofed him to the feverity of fouthern climates, from the lieutenant to the failor, was provided with a jacket and a pair of trowfers of the thickeſt woollen ſtuff called *fearnought* [*], or ſtrong flannel, which kept out the wet for a long time, and had this only fault, in common with every thing the navy pro-

---

[*] A diſtribution of the fame nature was made to Captain Cook's crew in his firſt voyage round the world. See Hawkefworth's Compilation, vol. II. p. 40.

vides,

vides, viz. that they were fupplied by contract, and therefore generally too fhort for our people. If we confider
the diftreffes to which M. de Bougainville's crew were
reduced for want of cloathing, we cannot help reflecting
on the better fortune of Englifh feamen, who, under an
equitable government, may expect to be treated with peculiar care; and who, on perilous expeditions, are humanely
and attentively fupplied with neceffaries to face the dangers
of the fea, and fupport their fpirits in adverfity. A trying
moment frequently occurs, where the defpondence caufed
by ill-treatment and heavy fufferings, muft have the moft
fatal confequences, fince its direct oppofite, an undaunted
refolution is then moft neceffary; fuch a moment we experienced in this night. A petty officer in the forepart
of the veffel, awaking fuddenly, heard a noife of water
ftreaming through his birth, and breaking itfelf againft
his own and his mefs-mates chefts; he leaped out of his bed,
and found himfelf to the middle of the leg in water. He
inftantly acquainted the officer of the quarter-deck with
this dreadful circumftance, and in a few moments almoft
every perfon in the fhip was in motion; the pumps were
employed, and the officers encouraged the feamen with an
alarming gentlenefs, to perfevere in their work; notwithftanding which the water feemed to gain upon us; every
foul was filled with terror, encreafed by the darknefs of
the night.

Ponto nox incubat atra,
Præsentemque viris intentant omnia mortem.   VIRGIL.

For what obscured light the heav'ns did grant,
Did but convey unto their fearful minds
A doubtful warrant of immediate death.   SHAKESPEARE.

The chain-pumps were now cleared, and our sailors
laboured at them with great alacrity; at last one of them
luckily discovered that the water came in through a scuttle
(or window) in the boatswain's store-room, which not having
been secured against the tempestuous southern ocean, had
been staved in by the force of the waves. It was immediately repaired, and closely shut up, and we escaped for
this time with the greatest part of the clothes and effects of the sailors and officers thoroughly soaked in salt
water. We should have found it difficult, if not utterly
impossible, to clear the ship of the water, if the midshipman
had not providentially awaked before it had gained too
much upon us: the presence of mind of our officers, and
the spirit of our seamen would have been exerted in vain,
and we must perhaps have gone down to the bottom, in
the midst of a very dark night and turbulent ocean, which
would have effectually prevented our consort from giving
us assistance. A distribution of fishing-hooks and lines
was made about this time to every person on board, as it
was uncertain how soon we might meet with land, and
consequently with an opportunity of making use of them.

The

The stormy weather continued, intermixed with frequent rains and fogs, till the fifth of December *, when we set the top-gallant sails for the first time, after leaving the Cape of Good Hope, and observed the latitude at noon, in 47° 10′ south. In the afternoon, however, the showers returned, and a western swell announced a wind from that quarter, which actually came on during night, blowing at about S. W. and chilled the air so considerably, that the thermometer sunk from 44° to 38° during the night, and some snow began to fall the next morning. The wind soon encreased to a storm again; so that on the 7th in the afternoon, we had only a single sail set. A variety of birds of the petrel and tern genus, had attended us in greater or lesser numbers ever since we had left the Cape, and the high sea and winds seemed to have no other influence on them, than that of bringing more of them about us. The principal forts were the Cape-petrel, or pintada *(procellaria capensis)*, and the blue petrel, so called from its having a blueish-grey colour, and a band of blackish feathers acrofs the whole wing. We likewise saw the two before mentioned species of albatroffes † from time to time, together with a third, less than the others, which we named the *fory*, and our sailors called the

---

* We had lost six large hogs of our live flock, and some sheep, during this uncomfortable weather.

† See p. 51.

N 2   quaker

quaker bird, from its having a greyish-brown colour.
Many birds of all these different species surrounded us on
the 8th of December, the wind still continuing very high,
and the sea very turbulent. We now likewise saw pinguins * for the first time, and some bunches of sea-weed,
of the species called the sea-bamboo *(fucus buccinalis* Lin.)
These appearances greatly favoured the hope of meeting
with land, as it had hitherto been held uncontroverted that
weeds, especially rockweeds, (such as these were) and
pinguins were never to be met with at a great distance from
shores; but experience has shewn that these prognostics
are not to be relied upon, and probably derive all their
credit from single accidental proofs in their favour, supported by the name of some celebrated mariner. Future
observations on the nature of floating rock-weeds, and
drift-wood, might perhaps lead to some more determinate
conclusions; for as these weeds must have been at first
detached from the rocks on which they grew, it is probable
that from the degree of freshness or of putridity which

---

* These birds, which since the time of Sir John Narborough, have
been repeatedly mentioned by almost every navigator that has visited the Southern
extremities of America, are so well known to the English reader, from the account of Anson, Byron, Bougainville, Pernetty, &c. that it is scarce necessary
to describe them. They are in a manner amphibious creatures, and their wings
are unfit for flying, but shaped like strong fleshy membranes, which perform
all the functions of fins. There are upwards of ten different species known to
the naturalists at present.

they

they have when found, the time they have been adrift, *December.*
and in fome rare inflances, the diflances from land, may
be conjectured; but the direction and force of the winds
and waves, and other accidental circumflances, mufl in
that cafe be carefully taken into confideration,

The wind abated during night, fo that we fet our
courfes on the 9th in the morning. The thermometer at *Wednefday 9.*
eight o'clock was however fallen to 35°, and only rofe
one degree at noon, being then in 49° 45′ of fouth latitude. Towards night it grew colder again, and at half an
hour paft ten, we found the thermometer on deck very
near 32°, and the edges of the fcuttled-cafk, filled with
frefh water, were freezing. This great cold preceded the
fight of ice floating in the fea, which we fell in with on
the next morning. The firft we faw, was a lump of con- *Thurfday 10.*
fiderable fize, fo clofe to us, that we were obliged to bear
away from it; another of the fame magnitude a little more
a-head, and a large mafs about two leagues on the weather-
bow, which had the appearance of a white head-land, or a
chalk-cliff.

In the afternoon we paffed another large cubical mafs
about 2000 feet long, 400 feet broad, and at leaft as high
again as our main-top-gallant-maft head, or 200 feet high.
According to the experiments of Boyle and Mairan *, the

* See Mairan's Differtation fur la Glace. Paris, 1749, p. 261.

volume of ice is to that of sea-water, nearly as ten to nine: consequently, by the known rules of hydrostatics, the volume of ice which rises above the surface of the water, is to that which sinks below it, as one to nine. Supposing the piece which we now saw to be entirely of a regular figure, its depth under water must have been one thousand eight hundred feet, and its whole height two thousand feet, allowing its length as abovementioned two thousand feet, and its breadth four hundred feet, the whole mass must have contained one thousand six hundred millions cubic feet of ice.

These prodigious pieces of ice, in all probability, drift but very slowly and imperceptibly, since the greatest part of them being under water, the power of winds and waves can have but little effect; currents perhaps are the principal agents which give them motion, though I much question, whether their velocity is ever considerable enough to carry them two miles in four-and-twenty hours. At the time we met with this first ice, all our conjectures about its formation could not amount to more than bare probabilities, and had not sufficient experience to support them: but after we have made the tour of the globe, without finding the Southern Continent, the existence of which has been so universally believed in Europe; it seems in the highest degree reasonable to suppose this floating ice to

have

have been formed in the sea * ; an idea the more probable, as repeated and decisive experiments have evinced, that salt-water may be frozen.

· This ice likewise served to shew us the great difference between the temperature of the northern and southern hemisphere. We were now in the midst of December, which answers to our June, and the latitude observed at noon gave only 51° 5′ south, notwithstanding which we had already passed several pieces of ice, and the thermometer stood at 36°. The want of land in the southern hemisphere seems to account for this circumstance, since the sea, as a transparent fluid, absorbs the beams of the sun, instead of reflecting them.

On the 11th of December, about three o'clock in the afternoon, we passed to leeward of a large piece, or island of ice, at least half a mile in length. The thermometer on deck, which had been at 36° about two o'clock, was risen to 41°, on account of the fair sunshine, which continued all the afternoon: when we came abreast of the ice, the wind directly blowing from thence, it gradually sunk

* Mr. Adanson, on returning from Senegal, brought several bottles filled with sea-water with him, taken up in different latitudes, which being brought to Paris from Brest in the midst of winter, the water in them froze so as to break them; the ice was perfectly fresh, and the residuum of brine was run out. See his Voyage au Senegal, p. 190. Mr. Edward Nairne, F. R. S. has made experiments on sea-water during the hard frost in 1776, inserted in the LXVI. volume of the Philosophical Transactions, which put it beyond a doubt, that solid and fresh ice may be formed from sea-water.

1772.
December. to 37½; however we had no sooner passed it, than the mer-
cury regained its former station of 41°. We also found
that this difference of four degrees, very perceptibly affected our bodies, and concluded that the large masses of ice
greatly contributed to refrigerate the general temperature of
the air in these inhospitable seas. The waves dashed with
great violence against the island of ice, as against a fixed
body; sometimes they broke entirely over it, notwithstanding its height, which was not much inferior to that of
the beforementioned piece, and we frequently saw the spray
rise very high above it, a phænomenon, which, on account
of the fair weather, had a remarkable fine effect. The sea-
water by this means washed upon the ice, is probably con-
gealed there, and serves to encrease the mass; a circumstance very materially conducive to ascertain the history of
its formation.

Notwithstanding the coldness of this climate, our sloops
were still surrounded by birds of the petrel genus, albatrosses and pinguins. We particularly observed a petrel, about
the size of a pigeon, entirely white, with a black bill and
blueish feet; it constantly appeared about the icy masses,
and may be looked upon as a sure fore-runner of ice. Its
colour induced us to call it the snowy-petrel. A grampus
and several whales likewise made their appearance among
the ice, and in these chilling regions served to vary the

dismal

dismal scene, and gave us some idea of a southern Greenland.

The number of icy masses encreased around us every day, so that we numbered upwards of twenty of a vast size on the 13th in the afternoon. One of them was full of black spots, which were taken for seals by some, and for aquatic birds by others, though we could not find that they even shifted their places. However seals being hitherto looked upon as certain signs of land, we sounded in the evening with a line of one hundred and fifty fathoms, but found no bottom. The latitude we were now in, was that in which Captain Lozier Bouvet had placed his pretended discovery of Cape Circumcision, and our longitude was only a few degrees to the eastward of it: the general expectation of seeing land, was therefore very great, and every little circumstance like the preceding roused all our attention; the clouds a-head were curiously examined at every moment, since every one was eager to be the first to announce the land. We had already had several false alarms from the fallacious conformation of fog-banks, or that of islands of ice half hid in snow storms, and our consort the Adventure had repeatedly made the signals for seeing land, deceived by such appearances: but now, the imagination warmed with the idea of M. Bouvet's discovery, one of our lieutenants, after having repeatedly been up to the mast-head, (about six o'clock in the morning on

VOL. I. O the

the 14th) acquainted the captain that he plainly saw the land. This news soon brought us all upon deck: We saw an immense field of flat ice before us, broken into many small pieces on the edges, a vast number of islands of ice of all shapes and sizes rose beyond it as far as the eye could reach, and some of the most distant considerably raised by the hazy vapours which lay on the horizon, had indeed some appearance of mountains. Several of our officers persisted in the opinion that they had seen land here, till Captain Cook, about two years and two months afterwards (in February 1775) on his course from Cape Horn towards the Cape of Good Hope, sailed over the same spot, where they had supposed it to lie, and found neither land nor even ice there at that time. Numbers of pinguins, pintadas, fulmars, snowy and blue petrels * attended this vast extent of ice, and different species of cetaceous animals spouted up the water around us; two of them, shorter than other whales, were particularly noticed, in respect of their bulk and of a white or rather fleshy colour. A great degree of cold in these icy regions entirely precluded the idea of a summer, which we had expected at this time of the year; our thermometer stood at 31˚ in the morning, and did not rise beyond 33˚ at noon, though the latitude we observed this day was only 54˚ 55ʹ south. We passed through quantities of broken ice in the

* Aptenodytes antarctica; Procellaria capensis, glacialis, nivea, & vittata.

afternoon,

afternoon, and saw another extensive ice-field, beyond which several of our people still persisted in, taking fog-banks for land. It snowed a good deal during night, and in the morning it was almost calm, but very foggy. A boat was hoisted out to try the direction of the current. Mr. Wales the astronomer, and my father, took this opportunity to repeat the experiments on the temperature of the sea at a certain depth. The fog encreased so much while they were thus engaged, that they entirely lost sight of both the ships. Their situation in a small four-oared boat, on an immense ocean, far from any inhabitable shore, surrounded with ice, and utterly destitute of provisions, was truly terrifying and horrible in its consequences. They rowed about for some time, making vain efforts to be heard, but all was silent about them, and they could not see the length of their boat. They were the more unfortunate, as they had neither mast nor sail, and only two oars. In this dreadful suspence they determined to lie still, hoping that, provided they preserved their place, the sloops would not drive out of sight, as it was calm. At last they heard the jingling of a bell at a distance; this sound was heavenly music to their ears; they immediately rowed towards it, and by continual hailing, were at last answered from the Adventure, and hurried on board, overjoyed to have escaped the danger

of

of perishing by flow degrees, through the inclemencies of
weather and through famine. Having been on board
some time, they fired a gun, and being within hail of the
Refolution, returned on board of that floop, to their own
damp beds and mouldering cabins, upon which they now
fet a double value, after fo perilous an expedition. The
rifks to which the voyager is expofed at fea are very numerous, and danger often arifes where it is leaft expected.
Neither can we trace the care of Providence more evidently
in ftorms among hidden rocks and fhoals, and where
water or fire threaten deftruction, than in thefe little circumftances, which the traveller and the reader are both.
too apt to forget or pafs lightly over, if they come to a.
favourable iffue.

The quantity of impenetrable ice to the fouth did not
permit us to advance towards that quarter; therefore, after feveral fruitlefs attempts, we ftood on to the eaftward,.
along it, frequently making way through great fpots covered with broken ice, which anfwered the defcription of
what the northern navigators call packed ice. Heavy hail
fhowers and frequent falls of fnow continually obfcured
the air, and only gave us the reviving fight of the fun.
during fhort intervals. Large iflands of ice were hourly
feen in all directions around the floops, fo that they were
now become as familiar to us as the clouds and the fea;
their

their frequency however still led to new obfervations, which
our long acquaintance with them ferved to confirm. We
were certain of meeting with ice in any quarter where we
perceived a ftrong reflexion of white on the fkirts of the
fky near the horizon. However the ice is not always
entirely white, but often tinged, efpecially near the furface of the fea, with a moft beautiful fapphirine or rather
berylline blue, evidently reflected from the water; this
blue colour fometimes appeared twenty or thirty feet above
the furface, and was there probably owing to fome particles of fea-water which had been dafhed againft the mafs
in tempeftuous weather, and had penetrated into its in-
terftices. We could likewife frequently obferve in great
iflands of ice, different fhades or cafts of white, lying
above each other in ftrata of fix inches or one foot high.
This appearance feems to confirm the opinion concerning
the farther encreafe and accumulation of fuch huge
maffes by heavy falls of fnow at different intervals. For
fnow being of various kinds, fmall grained, large grained,
in light feathery locks, &c. the various degrees of its com-
pactnefs account for the different colours of the ftrata.

We did not lofe fight of our deftination to explore the
fouthern frigid zone, and no fooner perceived the fea more
open than before, than we ftood once more to the fouthward. We made but fmall advances at firft, the wind
being very faint, and almoft falling calm in the morning:

on

on the 23d. We seized this opportunity to hoist out a boat, and continue the experiments on the current, and on the temperature of the sea. The species of petrels which were numerous about us, were likewise examined, described, and drawn this day, having been shot as they hovered with seeming curiosity over our little boat.

We continued standing southerly, and even made a good deal of westing, the wind being S. S. E. The next morning the wind blew pretty fresh, and carried us past several islands of ice; some whales, and a number of birds appearing about us. Our first Christmas day during this voyage, was spent with the usual chearfulness among officers and passengers; but among the sailors, notwithstanding the surrounding rocks of ice, with savage noise and drunkenness, to which they seem to have particularly devoted the day. The next morning we sailed through a great quantity of packed or broken ice, some of which looked dirty or decaying. Islands of ice still surrounded us, and in the evening, the sun setting just behind one of them, tinged its edges with gold, and brought upon the whole mass a beautiful suffusion of purple. A dead calm which succeeded on the 27th, gave us an opportunity of hoisting the boat out, and going to shoot pinguins and petrels. The chace of pinguins proved very unsuccessful, though it afforded great sport; the birds dived so frequently, continued so long under water, and at times skipped

skipped continually into and out of the water, making way with such amazing velocity in a strait line, that we were obliged to give over the pursuit. At last we came near enough to one, to wound it; but though we followed it closely, and fired above ten times with small shot, which we could observe to hit, yet we were at last obliged to kill it with ball. When we took it up, we perceived that its hard, glossy plumage, had continually turned the shot aside. This plumage is extremely thick, and consists of long narrow feathers, which lie above each other as closely as scales, and secure these amphibious birds against the wet, in which they almost constantly live. Their very thick skin and their fat seem wisely appropriated to them by nature, to resist the perpetual winter of these unhospitable climates; their broad belly, the situation of their feet far behind, and their fins, which supply the place of wings, are constructed with equal wisdom to facilitate the progress of their otherwise lumpish bodies through the water. The one that we had now shot weighed eleven pounds and a half. The blue petrels which are seen throughout this immense ocean, and which now settled in flocks of several hundreds on the smooth surface of the water, were not worse fitted out against the cold than the pinguins. Their plumage was amazingly abundant, and increased their bulk in a great proportion; and two feathers instead of one, proceeded

out

out of every root, lying within each other, and formed a very warm covering. As they are almost continually in the air, their wings are very strong, and of a great length to support them. On the ocean, between New Zeeland and America, we have found them above seven hundred leagues from any land; a distance which it would have been impossible for them to have passed, without an amazing strength in their bones and muscles, and the assistance of long wings. Possibly these birds spreading over the whole ocean far from any land, may live a considerable time without fresh supplies of food; that being the case with many animals of prey, both in the class of quadrupeds and that of birds. Our experience should seem in some measure to contradict, and in some degree to confirm, this supposition. For whenever we lamed any of them, they disgorged a quantity of viscid food, to all appearance recently digested, which the rest immediately swallowed up with such avidity as seemed to indicate a long fast. Therefore it may be probable, that several sorts of blubbers (mollusca) inhabit these icy seas, which may come to the surface in fair weather, and supply the weary birds with food. We were glad to meet with subjects from whence these little reflections could be drawn. They afforded us a momentary relief from that gloomy uniformity with which we slowly passed dull hours, days, and months in this desolate part of the world.

world. We were almoſt perpetually wrapt in thick fogs, beaten with ſhowers of rain, ſleet, hail, and ſnow, the temperature of the air being conſtantly about the point of congelation in the height of ſummer; ſurrounded by innumerable iſlands of ice againſt which we daily ran the riſk of being ſhipwrecked, and forced to live upon ſalt proviſions, which concurred with the cold and wet to infect the maſs of our blood. Theſe ſeverities naturally inſpired a general wiſh for a happier change of ſituation and climate, though our ſeamen coming freſh and ſtrong from England, were not yet diſpirited amidſt the number-leſs fatigues and inclemencies to which they were expoſed. The prophylactics, with which we had been ſupplied, and which were regularly ſerved to the crew, namely portable broth, and four krout, had a wonderful effect in keeping them free from the ſea-ſcurvy. Two or three men however, of a bad habit of body, could not reſiſt this dreadful diſeaſe; one of them in particular, George Jackſon, a carpenter, fell ill ten days after leaving the Cape; his gums were ulcerous, and his teeth ſo looſe, as to lie ſideways. A marmalade of carrots, which had been much recommended was tried, but without ſucceſs, it having no other effect than that of keeping him open. Our ſurgeon, Mr. Patton, then began the cure with freſh wort, i. e. the infuſion of malt, by which he gradually recovered, and in the ſpace of a few weeks was perfectly cured, his teeth

faft, and his gums entirely renewed. As the efficient
caufe of his complaint ftill exifted, he was obliged to continue the ufe of wort even after his cure, and by that
means was kept free from all fcorbutic fymptoms. The
encomiums on the efficacy of malt cannot be exaggerated,
and this ufeful remedy ought never to be forgotten on
board of fhips bound on long voyages; nor can we beftow
too much care to prevent its becoming damp and mouldy,
by which means its falutary qualities are impaired, as we
experienced during the latter part of our voyage.

The new year began with fnow-fhowers and frefh cold
gales, which carried us to the weftward, under the meridian, where M. Bouvet placed the difcovery, which he
called Cape Circumcifion. The fight of feals and pinguins once more revived the hopes of fome of our fellow-
voyagers, who bid us look out for land, which by their
account could not be far off. Our courfe however foon
difappointed their expectations, and only ferved to invali-
date their teftimonies of the proximity of land.

The wind fhifted to the north-weftward in the night,
and we ftood back again to the eaft, having firft proceeded
beyond the meridian of M. Bouvet's difcovery. We paffed
the fpot where we had met with much ice on the 31ft of
December, and found it drifted away from thence; after
which we continued our courfe to the S. E.

On

On the 9th, in the morning, we saw a large island of ice, surrounded with many small broken pieces, and the weather being moderate we brought to, hoisted out the boats, and sent them to take up as much of the small ice as they could. We piled up the lumps on the quarter-deck, packed them into casks, and after dinner melted them in the coppers, and obtained about thirty days water, in the course of this day, and in the latitude of 61° 36' south. Two days afterwards we had another opportunity of supplying our sloops with ice, which our people performed with great alacrity, notwithstanding the excoriation of their hands, which the cold and the sharpness of the sea produced. A picturesque view of some large masses of ice, and of our ships and boats employed in watering from small ice, is inserted in Captain Cook's account of this voyage. Some white whales of a huge size, seemingly sixty feet long, were observed here, and many pinguins floated past us, standing upright on small bits of ice. The water we melted out of this ice was perfectly fresh, and had a purer taste than any which we had on board. If any fault could be found with it, it was that the fixed air was expelled from it, by which means almost every one who used it was affected with swellings in the glands of the throat. Water melted from snow or ice is known always to have this effect, and the constant use of it in mountainous countries produces those enormous wens

(goitres)

(goîtres) which are common among Alpine nations, and are become fo habitual that they are looked upon as ornamental. Several perfons on board, unacquainted with natural philofophy, were very ferioufly afraid that the ice, when it began to melt, would burft the cafks in which it was packed, not confidering that its volume muft be greater in its frozen than in its melted flate, fince it floated on the furface. The Captain, to undeceive them, placed a little pot filled with flamped ice in a temperate cabin, where it gradually diffolved, and in that flate took up confiderably lefs fpace than before. Ocular demonftration always goes farther than the clearest arguments; but reafoning never has lefs weight than with failors.

On the 17th, in the forenoon, we croffed the antarctic circle, and advanced into the fouthern frigid zone, which had hitherto remained impenetrable to all navigators. Some days before this period we had feen a new fpecies of petrel, of a brown colour, with a white belly and rump, and a large white fpot on the wings, which we now named the antarctic petrel, as we faw great flights of twenty or thirty of them hereabouts, of which we fhot many that unfortunately never fell into the fhip. About five o'clock in the afternoon, we had fight of more than thirty large iflands of ice a-head, and perceived a ftrong white reflexion from the fky over the horizon. Soon after we paffed through vaft quantities of broken ice, which looked honey-

honey-combed and fpungy, and of a dirty colour. This
continually thickened about us, fo that the fea became
very fmooth, though the wind was frefh as before. An
immenfe field of folid ice extended beyond it to the fouth,
as far as the eye could reach from the maft-head. Seeing
it was impoffible to advance farther that way, Captain
Cook ordered the fhips to put about, and ftood north-eaft
by north, after having reached 67° 15´ fouth latitude,
where many whales, fnowy, grey, and antarctic petrels,
appeared in every quarter.

On the 19th and 20th we faw a bird, which a gentleman, who had been at Falkland's iflands, called a Port-
Egmont hen *, and which proved to be the fkua or great
northern gull *(larus catarractes)*, common in the high latitudes of both hemifpheres. The appearance of this bird,
was likewife conftrued into a prognoftick of land; but our
difappointments had already been fo frequent in this refpect, that we were not eafily led to give credit to bare
affertions. We faw a bird of this fpecies again on the
27th, when we had a great variety of all kinds of petrels
and albatroffes around us. It always foared up to a great
height, perpendicularly over our heads, and looked down
upon us, as it fhould feem with great attention, turning
its head now on one fide, and now on the other. This

* This bird is mentioned in Lieutenant Cook's voyage in the Endeavour, See
Hawkefworth, vol. II. p. 283.

was

was a novelty to us, who were used to see all the other
aquatic birds of this climate keep near the furface of
the fea. The next evening, and on the 29th, we had feveral porpesses passing by us with amazing swiftness in all
directions. They were pied, and had a large blotch of
white on the sides, which came almost up to the back behind the dorsal fin. Their velocity was at least triple that
of our vessels, though we now went at the rate of feven
knots and a half. In the afternoon we faw a small black
and white bird, which fome called an ice-bird, and others
a murr, and which feldom or never go out of fight of
land ; but as we could not come near enough to examine
it more accurately, we rather believed that it might be a
fpecies of petrel. We flood however off and on this night
and the next, finding the fea very moderate, though the
wind blew very fresh. We were the more induced to
take this precaution as we had received intelligence at the
Cape of Good Hope of a discovery of land hereabouts, by
the French captains M. de Kerguelen and M. de St. Allouarn, in January 1772.

As the journal of that voyage has been fuppreffed in
France, I shall here infert such particulars as were communicated to us by feveral French officers at the Cape of
Good Hope. M. de Kerguelen, a lieutenant in the French
navy, commanding the vessel *(flute)* la Fortune, and having
with him a fmaller vessel *(gabarre)* le Gros Ventre, commanded

manded by M. de St. Allouarn, failed from the Iſle of France or Mauritius, the latter end of 1771. On the 13th of January 1772, he ſaw two iſles, which he called the Iſles of Fortune; and the next morning one more, which from its ſhape they called Iſle Ronde. Almoſt about the ſame time, M. de Kerguelen ſaw land, of a conſiderable extent and height, upon which he ſent one of the officers of his ſhip a-head in the cutter to ſound. But the wind blowing freſh, M. de St. Allouarn in the Gros Ventre ſhot ahead of the boat, and finding a bay, which he called the Gros Ventre's bay, ſent his own yawl to take poſſeſſion of the land which was performed with the utmoſt difficulty. Both the boats then returned aboard the Gros Ventre, and the cutter was cut adrift on account of the bad weather. M. de St. Allouarn then ſpent three days in queſt of M. de Kerguelen, who had been driven ſixty leagues to leeward, on account of his weak maſts, and was returned towards the Iſle of France. M. de St. Allouarn continued to take the bearings of this land, and doubled its northern ex-tremity beyond which it tended to the ſouth-eaſtward. In this direction he coaſted it for the ſpace of twenty leagues, and ſeeing it was very high, inacceſſible, and deſtitute of trees, he left it, ſtanding over to the coaſt of New Holland, from thence to Timor and Batavia, and at laſt back to the Iſle of France, where he died ſoon after his arrival. On M. de Kerguelen's return to Europe, he was immediately

ſent

sent out again with a 64 gun ship called the Roland, and the frigate l'Oiseau, captain Rosnevet; but after having just seen the land, which he had discovered in his former voyage, he returned without making farther discoveries. The northern coast of the land which he discovered, is situated in about 48 degrees south latitude, and about 82 degrees east longitude from Ferro, or 6 degrees east of the Isle of France, (i. e. in about 64° 20′ east from Greenwich.)

M. de Marion in his expedition of 1772, in January, fell in with small islands in three different places, about the latitude of 46½° and 47½°, and about the longitudes of 37°, 46½°, and 48½° east from Greenwich. These islands were all of inconsiderable extent, high, rocky, destitute of trees, and almost entirely barren. M. de Marion had two ships under his command, one the Mascarin, captain Crozet, the other the Castrie, captain Du Clesmure. They proceeded to the southern extremity of New Holland, or Diemen's land, first seen by Tasman; and from thence to the bay of islands in New Zeeland, where M. de Marion was killed with 28 of his men by the natives, of which more shall be said in the sequel. After this loss M. de Crozet, on whom the command devolved, passed through the western part of the South Sea to the Philippinas, from whence he returned to the Isle de France. Agreeably to these accounts, the discoveries of the French voyagers have been laid down in an excellent

lent chart of the southern hemisphere, by M. de Vaugondy, under the direction of the duke de Croy, and published in March 1773.

On the 31st in the evening, our latitude being nearly that of 50° south, we passed by a large island of ice, which at that instant crumbled to pieces with a tremendous explosion. The next morning a bundle of sea weeds was seen floating past the sloop; and in the afternoon, captain Furneaux in the Adventure having hailed us, acquainted captain Cook that he had seen a number of divers, resembling those in the English seas, and had past a great bed of floating rock-weeds. In consequence of these observations we stood off and on during night, and continued an easterly course the next morning. We saw many petrels and black shear-waters, some rock-weed, and a single tern (*sterna*) or as the seamen call it an egg-bird, which had a forked tail. At noon we observed in 48° 36' south latitude, which was nearly the same in which the French discoveries are said to be situated. After noon we stood southwestward, but the next day the gale encreased to such a degree, as obliged us to hand our topsails, and stand on under the courses all night; however, at eight o'clock on the 4th, we found a smooth sea again, and set more sail, changing our course to the north-westward at noon. On the 6th our latitude at noon was nearly 48 degrees south, about 60 degrees east from Greenwich, when not seeing

Q any

any land, we gave over the attempt to stand in search of it, and directed our course once more to the south-eastward, to the main object of our voyage. The smoothness of the sea, whilst we had strong easterly gales, however persuaded us, that there was probably some land near us to the eastward, and the situation given to the French discoveries, in M. Vaugondy's late chart, has confirmed our supposition; for, according to it, we must have been at least 2 degrees of longitude to the west of it, on the second of February, when we were farthest to the east in the given latitude. Though we did not fall in with the land itself, yet we have done so much service to geography by our track, as to put it beyond a doubt, that the French discovery is a small island, and not, what it was supposed at first to be, the north cape of a great southern continent.

On the 8th in the morning, we had an exceeding thick fog, during which we lost sight of the Adventure, our consort. We fired guns all that day and the next, at first every half hour, and afterwards every hour, without receiving any answer; and at night we burnt false fires, which likewise proved ineffectual.

On the 10th in the morning, notwithstanding all our endeavours to recover our consort, we were obliged to proceed alone on a dismal course to the southward, and to expose ourselves once more to the dangers of that frozen climate, without the hope of being saved by our fellow-voyagers,

voyagers, in cafe of lofing our own veffel. Our parting
with the Adventure, was almoft univerfally regretted among
our crew, and none of them ever looked around the ocean
without expreffing fome concern on feeing our fhip alone
on this vaſt and unexplored expanfe, where the appearance
of a companion feemed to alleviate our toils, and infpired
cheerfulneſs and comfort. We were likewife not entirely
without apprehenfions, that the Adventure might have
fallen in with land, as the fight of pinguins, of little
diving petrels, and efpecially of a kind of grebe, feemed
to vindicate its vicinity. Indeed, according to the chart
of M. Vaugondy we muft have been but very little to the
fouth of it at that time.

On the 17th we were near 58 degrees fouth, and took
up a great quantity of fmall ice, with which we filled our
water cafks. A variety of petrels and albatroffes, had
attended us continually; and from time to time the fkua,
or great northern gull *(larus catarractes)*, which our people
called a Port Egmont hen, many pinguins, fome feals, and
fome whales had made their appearance near us. A beautiful phænomenon was obferved during the preceding
night, which appeared again this and feveral following
nights. It confifted of long columns of a clear white
light, fhooting up from the horizon to the eaftward, almoft
to the zenith, and gradually fpreading on the whole
fouthern part of the fky. Thefe columns fometimes were

Q 2   bent

1775.
FEBRUARY. bent fideways at their upper extremity, and though in moſt
reſpects fimilar to the northern lights *(aurora borealis)* of our
hemiſphere, yet differed from them, in being always of
a whitiſh colour, whereas ours aſſume various tints, eſpecially thoſe of a fiery, and purple hue. The ſtars were ſometimes hid by, and ſometimes faintly to be ſeen through the
fubſtance of theſe ſouthern lights, *(aurora auſtralis),* which
have hitherto, as far as I can find, eſcaped the notice of
voyagers. The ſky was generally clear when they appeared, and the air ſharp and cold, the thermometer ſtanding at the freezing point.

Wedneſd. 14.   On the 24th, being in about 62 degrees ſouth latitude,
we fell in once more with a ſolid field of ice, which
confined our progreſs to the ſouth, very much to
the ſatisfaction of every body on board. We had now
been long at ſea, without receiving any refreſhment; the
favorable ſeaſon for making diſcoveries towards the frozen
zone, drew to an end; the weather daily became more
ſharp, and uncomfortable, and preſaged a dreadful winter
in theſe ſeas; and, laſtly, the nights lengthened apace, and
made our navigation more dangerous than it had hitherto
been. It was therefore very natural, that our people, ex-
hauſted by fatigues and the want of wholeſome food, ſhould
wiſh for a place of refreſhment, and rejoice to leave a part
of the world, where they could not expect to meet with it.

MARCH.
Wedneſd. 17.   We continued however from this day till the 17th of March

to run to the eaftward, between 61° and 58° of fouth latitude, during which time we had a great fhare of eafterly
winds, which commonly brought fogs, and rains with
them, and repeatedly expofed us to the moft imminent
danger of being wrecked againft huge iflands of ice. The
fhapes of thefe large frozen maffes, were frequently fingu-
larly ruinous, and fo far picturefque enough; among
them we paffed one of a great fize, with a hollow in the
middle, refembling a grotto or cavern, which was pierced
through, and admitted the light from the other fide. Some
had the appearance of a fpire or fteeple; and many others
gave full fcope to our imagination, which compared them
to feveral known objects, by that means attempting to overcome the tedioufnefs of our cruize, which the fight of
birds, porpeffes, feals, and whales, now too familiar to
our eyes, could not prevent from falling heavily upon us.
Notwithftanding our excellent prefervatives, efpecially the
four-krout, feveral of our people had now ftrong fymptoms of fea-fcurvy, fuch as bad gums, difficult breathing,
livid blotches, eruptions, contracted limbs, and greenifh
greafy filaments in the urine. Wort was therefore prefcribed
to them, and thofe who were the moft affected drank five
pints of it per day; the contracted limbs were bathed in
it, and the warm grains applied to them. By this means
we fucceeded to mitigate, and in fome individuals entirely
to remove the fymptoms of this horrid difeafe. The rigours

1775.
March. gours of the climate likewise violently affected the live sheep,
which we had embarked at the Cape of Good Hope.   They
were covered with eruptions, dwindled to mere skeletons,
and would hardly take any nourishment.   Our goats and
sows too, miscarried in the tempestuous weather, or their
off-spring were killed by the cold.   In short, we felt, from
the numerous concurrent circumstances, that it was time
to abandon the high southern latitudes, and retire to some
port, where our crew might obtain refreshments, and
where we might save the few sheep, which were intended
as presents to the natives of the South-sea islands.

On the 16th, being in about 58 degrees of south latitude, we saw the sea luminous at night, though not to
such a degree as we had observed it near the Cape, but only
by means of some scattered sparks.   This phenomenon was
however remarkable, on account of the high latitude we
were in, and the cold weather, our thermometer being at
33½° at noon.   We saw the southern lights again during
the nights of the 16th and 19th; and this last time, the
columns formed an arch across the sky, rather brighter
than any we had hitherto seen.   We now stood to the
north-eastward, in order to reach the south end of New-
Zeeland; and on this course we had strong gales, and frequently saw weeds, especially rock-weeds, together with
numbers of petrels, and other birds.   We were much amused
by a singular chace of several skuas or great grey gulls,

after

after a large white albatrofs. The fkuas feemed to get the better of this bird, notwithflanding its length of wings, and whenever they overtook it, they endeavoured to attack it under the belly, probably knowing that to be the moft defencelefs part; the albatrofs on thefe occafions had no other method of efcaping, than by fettling on the water, where its formidable beak feemed to keep them at bay. The fkuas are in general very flrong and rapacious birds, and in the Ferro Iflands frequently tear lambs to pieces, and carry them away to their nefls. The albatroffes do not feem to be fo rapacious, but live upon fmall marine animals, efpecially of the *mollufca*, or blubber clafs. They appeared in great numbers around us, as we came to the northward of 50 degrees fouth, only few folitary birds having gone fo far to the fouth as we had penetrated; from whence it may be inferred, that they are properly inhabitants of the temperate zone.

As we flood to the northward, we alfo obferved more ftals every day, which came from the coaft of New Zeeland. A large trunk of a tree, and feveral bunches of weeds were feen on the 25th, and greatly exhilarated the fpirits of our failors. Soon after, the land was defcried, bearing N. E. by E. at a vaft diftance. About five o'clock in the afternoon we were within a few miles of it, and faw fome high mountains inland, and a broken rocky coaft before us, where feveral inlets feemed to indicate an extenfive bay or found.

We:

We tried foundings in 30 fathoms, but found none; however, at the mast-head they obferved funken rocks clofe to us, on which we immediately tacked, and ftood off fhore, as the weather was growing dark and mifty. The next morning we found this part of New Zeeland lay to the fouthward of Cape Weft, and had not been explored by captain Cook, in the Endeavour.

Thus ended our firft cruize in the high fouthern latitudes, after a fpace of four months and two days, out of fight of land, during which we had experienced no untoward accident, and had been fafely led through numerous dangers by the guiding hand of Providence, which preferved our crew in good health during the whole time, a few individuals excepted. Our whole courfe, from the Cape of Good Hope to New Zeeland, was a feries of hardfhips, which had never been experienced before; all the difagreeable circumftances of the fails and rigging fhattered to pieces, the veffel rolling gunwale to, and her upper works torn by the violence of the ftrain; the concomitant effects of ftorms, which have been painted with fuch ftrong expreffion, and blacknefs of Colrit, by the able writer of Anfon's Voyage, were perhaps the leaft diftreffing occurrences of ours. We had the perpetual feveritia of a rigorous climate to cope with; our feamen and officers were expofed to rain, fleet, hail, and fnow; our rigging was conftantly encrufted with ice, which cut the hands of thofe who were obliged to touch it; our

provifion

provision of fresh water was to be collected in lumps of ice floating on the sea, where the cold, and the sharp saline element alternately numbed, and scarified the sailors' limbs; we were perpetually exposed to the danger of running against huge masses of ice, which filled the immense Southern ocean: the frequent and sudden appearance of these perils, required an almost continual exertion of the whole crew, to manage the ship with the greatest degree of precision and dispatch. The length of time which we remained out of sight of land, and the long abstinence from any sort of refreshment were equally distressful; for our hooks and lines distributed in November (See pag. 90.) had hitherto been of no service, on account of our navigation in high southern latitudes, and across an unfathomable ocean, where we saw no fish except whales, and where it is well known no others can be expected; the torrid zone being the only one where they may be caught out of soundings.

———Atrum
Defendens pisces hiemat mare. HORAT.

We may add to these the dismal gloominess which always prevailed in the southern latitudes, where we had impenetrable fogs lasting for weeks together, and where we rarely saw the cheering face of the sun; a circumstance which alone is sufficient to deject the most un-

VOL. I.   B   daunted,

daunted, and to four the spirits of the most cheerful. It
is therefore justly to be wondered at, and ought to be
considered as a distinguishing mark of divine protection,
that we had not felt those ill effects which might have
been expected, and justly dreaded as the result of such
accumulated distresses.

C H A P.

C H A P. V.

*Stay at Dusky Bay; description of it, and account of our trans-
actions there.*

AFTER an interval of one hundred and twenty-two
days, and a run of above three thousand five hundred leagues, out of sight of land, we entered Dusky Bay
on the 26th of March about noon. This bay is situated Friday 26.
a little to the northward of Cape West, and captain Cook,
in his voyage in the Endeavour, had discovered and named
it without entering into it *. The soundings gave about
40 fathoms in the entrance, but as we advanced, we had
no ground with 60, and therefore were obliged to push
on farther. The weather was delightfully fair, and ge-
nially warm, when compared to what we had lately experienced; and we glided along by insensible degrees,
wafted by light airs, past numerous rocky islands, each
of which was covered with wood and shrubberies, where
numerous evergreens were sweetly contrasted and mingled
with the various shades of autumnal yellow. Flocks of
aquatic birds enlivened the rocky shores, and the whole
country resounded with the wild notes of the feathered

* See Hawkesworth's compilation, vol. III. p. 424.

tribe.

tribe. We had long and eagerly wished for the land and its vegetable productions, and therefore could not but eye the prospect before us with peculiar delight, and with emotions of joy and satisfaction which were strongly marked in the countenance of each individual.

About three o'clock in the afternoon, we dropped an anchor under a point of an island, where we were in some measure sheltered from the sea, and so near the shore, as to reach it with a hawser. The sloop was no sooner in safety, than every sailor put his hook and line overboard, and in a few moments numbers of fine fish were hauled up on all parts of the vessel, which heightened the raptures we had already felt at our entrance into this bay. The real good taste of the fish, joined to our long abstinence, inclined us to look upon our first meal here, as the most delicious we had ever made in our lives. The view of rude sceneries in the style of *Rosa*, of antediluvian forests which cloathed the rock, and of numerous rills of water, which every where rolled down the steep declivity, altogether conspired to complete our joy; and so apt is mankind, after a long absence from land, to be prejudiced in favour of the wildest shore, that we looked upon the country at that time, as one of the most beautiful which nature unassisted by art could produce. Such are the general ideas of travellers and voyagers long exhausted

by

by diftreffes ; and with fuch warmth of imagination they have viewed the rude cliffs of Juan Fernandez, and the impenetrable forefts of Tinian !

Immediately after dinner two boats were fent out to reconnoitre different parts of the bay, and chiefly to look for a fafe harbour for our veffel, the firft anchoring-place being open, inconvenient, and only ferving the neceffity of the moment. We improved thefe opportunities of purfuing our refearches in natural hiftory, and feparated in order to profit by both excurfions. Each of the parties found convenient and well-fheltered harbours, with plenty of wood and water ; and wherever they went they met with fuch abundance of fish and water-fowl, that they entertained hopes of a conftant fupply of refrefhments during their ftay in thefe parts. This profpect prevailed upon Capt. Cook, who had but curforily examined the fouthern extremities of New-Zeeland in his former voyage, to fpend fome time there, in order to gain a more competent knowledge of its fituation and productions. On our part, we perceived a new ftore of animal and vegetable bodies, and among them hardly any that were perfectly fimilar to the known fpecies, and feveral not analogous even to the known genera. With thefe therefore we hoped to be wholly employed during our ftay, in fpight of the approach of autumn, which feemed to threaten the vegetable creation.

Early

Early the next morning, a small boat having been sent
out towards the shore, returned in three hours time with
as many fishes, caught by the hook, as supplied a plentiful dinner to all on board. The best and most savoury
fish was a species of the cod, which, from its external colour, our sailors called a coal-fish: besides this we caught
several species of excellent flat cavalhas (*sciæna*), some scor-
pens, mullets, horse-mackrel, and many other sorts of a
fine taste, which were entirely unknown in Europe. At
nine o'clock we got under sail and went into Pickersgill
harbour, one of those examined the preceding day, where
the ship was moored head and stern in a small creek, and
so near the shore, that we could reach it by means of a
stage of a few planks. Nature had assisted us for this purpose with a large tree, projecting in an horizontal position
over the water, of which we placed the top on our gunwale, connecting our planks with it. This situation facilitated all our operations, and was particularly adapted to
the conveniency of wooding and watering, for our sloop's
yards were locked in the branches of surrounding trees,
and about half a musket shot a-stern we had a fine stream
of fresh water.

We now began to clear away the woods from a neighbouring hill, in order to fix the astronomer's observatory upon it,
and to establish our forge there, as our iron-works wanted
repairs. Near the watering-place we pitched tents for the
sail-

fail-makers, coopers, waterers, and wood-cutters. Thefe occupations ferved to lower the great idea which our people had conceived of this country; for the prodigious intricacy of various climbers, briars, fhrubs, and ferns which were interwoven throughout the forefts, rendered the tafk of clearing the ground extremely fatiguing and difficult, and almoft precluded the accefs to the interior parts of the country. It is indeed reafonable to fuppofe, that in the fouthern parts of New-Zeeland, the forefts have never been touched by human induftry, but have remained in the rude unimproved ftate of nature fince their firft exiftence. Our excurfions into them gave us fufficient grounds for this fuppofition; for not only the climbing plants and fhrubs obftructed our paffage, but likewife numbers of rotten trees lay in our way, felled by winds and old age. A new generation of young trees, of parafitic plants, ferns, and moffes fprouted out of the rich mould to which this old timber was reduced by length of time, and a deceitful bark fometimes ftill covered the interior rotten fubftance, whereon if we attempted to ftep, we funk in to the waift. The animal creation afforded another proof, that this country had not yet undergone any changes from the hands of mankind, and indeed at firft raifed the idea, that Dufky Bay was wholly uninhabited. Numbers of fmall birds which dwelt in the woods were fo little acquainted with men, that they familiarly hopped upon the

nearest

neareſt branches, nay on the ends of our fowling-pieces, and perhaps looked at us as new objects, with a curioſity ſimilar to our own. This little boldneſs in reality at firſt protected them from harm, ſince it was impoſſible to ſhoot them when they approached ſo near; but in a few days it frequently proved the means of their deſtruction; for a ſly cat on board, had no ſooner perceived ſo excellent an opportunity of obtaining delicious meals, than ſhe regularly took a walk in the woods every morning, and made great havock among the little birds, that were not aware of ſuch an inſidious enemy.

As we had plenty of fiſh, and ſaw a number of water-birds which might afford us a variety of animal food, ſome of our botanical excurſions were in a great meaſure inſtituted in ſearch of uſeful vegetables, to be eaten as greens. From thence the moſt ſalutary effects might be expected, by a ſet of people who had been above ſeventeen weeks at ſea, and whoſe blood muſt have been more or leſs corrupted by living ſo long on ſalt proviſions.

On the firſt day after our arrival we found a beautiful tree in flower, ſomething related to the myrtle genus, of which an infuſion had been drank inſtead of tea in Capt. Cook's former voyage. We immediately repeated the experiment with great eagerneſs, as we had not yet ſeen any plant which was fit to be uſed at our tables. Its leaves were finely aromatic, aſtringent, and had a particular plea-

ſant

fant flavour at the firſt infuſion; but this fine taſte went off at the next filling up of the tea-pot, and a great degree of bitterneſs was then extracted. We therefore never ſuffered it to be twice infuſed. The uſe of this plant, which became general among our crew, probably contributed greatly to reſtore their ſtrength, and to remove all ſcorbutic ſymptoms. A plant, which might be of ſervice to future navigators, deſerved to be drawn, in order that they might know it again. We have therefore very readily permitted Captain Cook to make uſe of our drawing of it, from which a plate has been engraved by order of the Admiralty, intended to accompany his own account of this voyage. In a fine ſoil in thick foreſts it grows to a conſiderable tree, ſometimes thirty or forty feet high, and above a foot in diameter; on a hilly arid expoſure I have, on the contrary, found it as a little ſhrub, ſix inches high, which bore flowers and ſeed; but its uſual ſize is about eight or ten feet, and about three inches in diameter. In that caſe its ſtem is irregular and unequal, dividing very ſoon into branches which riſe at acute angles, and only bear leaves and flowers at top. The flowers are white and very ornamental to the whole plant. Another tree, which grew in great plenty round about us, was likewiſe tried, and afforded a good infuſion; but the reſemblance it bore to the trees of the fir tribe, and a kind of reſinous taſte, ſoon convinced us that it was fitter to ſerve the purpoſes of

1773.
March.
the American fpruce-tree, and that a palatable and wholefome liquor might be brewed from it, as a kind of fubfti-
tute for fpruce-beer *. In effect, with the addition of the
infpiffated juice of wort, and of fome molaffes, we brewed
a very good fort of beer, which we improved very confiderably afterwards, by correcting the too great aftringen-
cy of our new fpruce, with an equal quantity of the new
tea-tree. Its tafte was pleafant, and fomething bitter; and
the only fault we could obferve in it was, that being
taken on an empty ftomach, it frequently caufed a naufea
or ficknefs; but in all other refpects it proved a very falutary drink. The fpruce of New-Zeeland is a very beautiful tree, and confpicuous on account of its pendant
branches, which are loaded with numerous long thread-
like leaves, of a vivid green. It frequently grows to the
height of fifty or fixty, and even one hundred feet, and
has above ten feet in girth. Though the fpruce and the
tea-trees alone afforded articles of refrefhment in Dufky
Bay; yet we found the woods full of trees of various
kinds, very fit for the ufe of fhipwrights, joiners, and
other mechanics; and Capt. Cook was of opinion that,
except in the river Thames on the northern ifland, he had
not obferved a finer growth of timber on all New-Zeeland.

* This ufeful plant deferves a defcription for the benefit of the navigator; but,
notwithftanding all our refearches, we could never find it either in flower or in
fruit, owing to the unfavourable feafons in which we vifited New-Zeeland.

We

We had not been above two days in this bay, before
we found that our opinion of its being uninhabited was premature. On the 28th in the morning several of our officers went a shooting in a small boat, and on entering a cove two or three miles from the ship, perceived several natives upon a beach, who were about to launch their canoe. The New Zeelanders halloo'd at their approach, and seeming by this means more numerous than they really were, the officers thought proper to return and acquaint the captain with their discovery; a step which they found the more necessary, as the weather was very rainy, and might, in case of danger, have prevented their pieces from going off. They were scarcely returned on board, when a canoe * appeared off a point, at about a mile's distance from the sloop; there were seven or eight people in it, who looked at us for some time, but notwithstanding all the signs of friendship which we could make, such as calling to them to come to us, waving a white cloth, and promising beads, they did not care to come nearer, and paddled back again the same way they came. They appeared to be dressed in mats, and had broad paddles with which they managed their canoe, like the inhabitants in the northern parts of New Zeeland.

* We shall always make use of this word to signify an Indian embarkation, unless we mean to describe or specify it more particularly.

Captain

Captain Cook refolved to vifit them in the afternoon, in
order to quiet the apprehenfion which they feemed to have
entertained. We went in two boats, accompanying him
and feveral of the officers into the cove, where the natives
had been firft feen. Here we found a double canoe
hauled upon the fhore, near fome old, low hut, about
which we faw veftiges of fire places, fome fifhing-nets,
and a few fcattered fifh. The canoe which appeared to be
old and in bad order, confifted of two troughs or boats
joined together with fticks, tied acrofs the gunwales with
ftrings of the New Zeeland flax-plant*. Each part confifted of planks fowed together with ropes made of the
flax-plant, and had a carved head coarfely reprefenting a
human face, with eyes made of round pieces of ear-fhell,
which fomewhat refembled mother of pearl. This canoe
contained two paddles, a bafket full of berries of the
cwiaria rufcifolia Lin. and fome fifhes; but the natives were
not to be feen or heard, which gave us reafon to believe
that they had retired into the woods. To conciliate their
good will, we left fome medals, looking-glaffes, beads, &c.
in the canoe, and embarked again after a fhort ftay. We then
rowed to the head of the cove, in order to furvey it, where we
found a fine brook of frefh water coming down on a flat
beach, from whence the water continued fhallow to a con-

* See Hawkefworth's compilation, vol. III. p. 443.

fiderable

siderable extent, so that our boat ran aground several times. Ducks, shags, black oyster-catchers, and some forts of plovers were very numerous here. At our return we visited the canoe again, added a hatchet to the other presents which we had left before, and to shew the use of it, we cut several chips out of a tree, and left it sticking there. No natives appeared this second time, though we imagined they could not be far off, as we thought we could smell the smoke of a fire. However, captain Cook desisted at present from searching in the woods, since they purposely avoided us, and choosing to leave it to time and their own free will to cultivate an intercourse with us, he returned on board late in the evening.

Heavy showers of rain fell all the next morning, but intermitted in the afternoon, giving us an opportunity of going into the woods above our cove, where the rains had so thoroughly soaked the soil, that together with the other impediments in walking in this country, the prodigious slipperiness rendered our excursion laborious and fatiguing. We met however with a few plants, which still shewed some late blossoms, notwithstanding the advanced season; but we were at the same time greatly tantalized by the appearance of numerous trees and shrubs, which had already lost their flowers and fruits, and only served to give us an idea of the great profusion of new vegetables in this country.

The

The two following days we were entirely confined on board, on account of the rain and stormy weather; which not a little damped our spirits, and gave us reason to fear we should spend the remainder of our time very disagreeably.
However, on the 1st of April in the afternoon, we took the advantage of a lucid interval to make another visit to the cove where we had seen the Indians. We found every thing in the same situation as we had left it, and it did not appear that any person had been near the canoe since that time. The weather being now fair, we saw this cove in all its perfection. It is so spacious that a whole fleet of ships may lie at anchor in it, and some of the loftiest hills in all the bay encompass it on the south-west side, and are entirely covered with woods from the summit to the water's side. The different projecting points, and the various islands in the bay, form altogether a picturesque and pleasing scene. The smoothness of the water, illumined by the setting sun, the different degrees of verdure, and the various notes of birds which resounded throughout the whole cove during this calm evening, greatly softened the rude, uncultivated outlines of this landscape.

The pleasure we had enjoyed in the evening, induced us to return to the cove again the next day, which continued to be perfectly fair. We set out at sun-rise, and did not return till late in the evening, with a considerable

able

able acquisition of new birds, and plants. We had a young dog with us at this time, which the officers had taken on board at the Cape of Good Hope, and intended to try, whether we could not train him up to the gun: but we had no sooner discharged the first fowling-piece, than he ran into the woods, and would not return, though we used all possible means to recover him. Captain Cook likewise took the opportunity of the fair weather, to examine different parts of the bay; and touched at a little rock, near our first anchoring place, which had already at that time acquired the name of Seal-rock, from the animals that came to sleep upon it. Here he found a number of seals, and killed three of them, among which one afforded him great sport: for having been repeatedly wounded, it became quite furious, and attacked the boat, where it was at last killed. It weighed 220 pounds, was about six feet long, and very lean. After he had passed several isles, he reached the north-west part of the bay, formed by the land of Point Five-fingers: there, at the bottom of a fine cove, he found a great variety of aquatic birds, of which he killed and brought on board a considerable number.

Another rainy pause of three days followed this excursion, confining us to our ship, where a sort of little crane-flies *(tipula alis incumbentibus)*, which had plagued us ever since our entrance into Dusky Bay, became remarkably troublesome during the bad weather. They were numerous in the

skirts

skirts of the woods, not half so large as gnats or musketoes, and our sailors called them sand-flies. Their sting was extremely painful, and as often as the hand or face grew warm, caused a troublesome itching, the least irritation of which brought on a very violent swelling, attended with great pain. We were, however, not all equally affected; myself in particular, never felt any great inconvenience from them; others, on the contrary, suffered in a very violent degree, especially my father, who could not hold a pen to write down the common occurrences in a journal, and fell into a high fever at night. Various remedies were tried, but all proved ineffectual, except the simple unction with soft pomatum, and the constant use of gloves.

Early on the 6th, several of the officers went into the cove, which the captain had discovered on the 2d; and the latter, accompanied by Mr. Hodges, Dr. Sparrman, my father, and myself proceeded in another boat, to continue the survey of the bay, to copy views from nature, and to search for the natural productions of the country. We directed our course to the north side, where we found a fine spacious cove, from which we had not the least prospect of the sea. Along its steep shores we observed several small but beautiful cascades, which fell from vast heights, and greatly improved the scene; they gushed out through the midst of the woods, and at last fell in a clear column, to which a ship might lie so near, as to fill her casks on board with the greatest

safety,

safety, by means of a leather tube, which the sailors call
a hose. At the bottom there was a shallow muddy part,
with a little beach of shell-sand, and a brook, as in all the
greater coves of the bay. In this fine place, we found a
number of wild fowl,. and particularly wild ducks, of which
we shot fourteen, from whence we gave it the name of
Duck Cove. As we were returning home, we heard a loud
hallooing on the rocky point of an island, which on this
occasion obtained the name of Indian Island; and standing
in to the shore, we perceived one of the natives, from whom
this noise proceeded. He stood with a club or battle-axe
in his hand, on a projecting point, and behind him on the
skirts of the wood we saw two women, each of them having a long spear. When our boat came to the foot of the
rock, we called to him, in the language of Taheitee, *tayo,
harre mai,* " friend, come hither ;" he did not, however,
stir from his post, but held a long speech, at certain intervals pronouncing it with great earnestness and vehemence,
and swinging round his club, on which he leaned at other
times. Captain Cook went to the head of the boat, called
to him in a friendly manner, and threw him his own and
some other handkerchiefs, which he would not pick up.
The captain then taking some sheets of white paper in his
hand, landed on the rock unarmed, and held the paper out
to the native. The man now trembled very visibly, and
having exhibited strong marks of fear in his countenance,

VOL. I.   T   took

took the paper: upon which captain Cook coming up to him, took hold of his hand, and embraced him, touching the man's nose with his own, which is their mode of salutation. His apprehension was by this means dissipated, and he called to the two women, who came and joined him, while several of us landed to keep the captain company. A short conversation ensued, of which very little was understood on both sides, for want of a competent knowledge of the language. Mr. Hodges immediately took sketches of their countenances, and their gestures shewed that they clearly understood what he was doing; on which they called him *tóë-tóë*, that term being probably applicable to the imitative arts. The man's countenance was very pleasing and open; one of the women, which we afterwards believed to be his daughter, was not wholly so disagreeable as one might have expected in New Zeeland, but the other was remarkably ugly, and had a prodigious excrescence on her upper lip. They were all of a dark brown or olive complexion; their hair was black, and curling, and smeared with oil and ruddle; the man wore his tied upon the crown of the head, but the women had it cut short. Their bodies were tolerably well proportioned in the upper part; but they had remarkable slender, ill-made, and bandy legs. Their dress consisted of mats made of the New Zeeland flax-plant *,

* See Hawkesworth's Compilation, vol. III. p. 443.

interwoven

interwoven with feathers; and in their ears they wore
small pieces of white albatrofs skins stained with ruddle
or ochre. We offered them some fishes and wild fowl,
but they threw them back to us, intimating that they did
not want provisions. The approaching night obliged us
to retire, not without promising our new friends a visit
the next morning. The man remained silent, and looked
after us with composure and great attention, which seemed
to speak a profound meditation; but the youngest of the
two women, whose vociferous volubility of tongue exceeded every thing we had met with, began to dance at our
departure, and continued to be as loud as ever. Our feamen passed several coarse jests on this occasion, but nothing
was more obvious to us than the general drift of nature,
which not only provided man with a partner to alleviate
his cares and sweeten his labours, but endowed that partner likewise with a desire of pleasing by a superior degree
of vivacity and affability.

The next morning we returned to the natives, and presented them with several articles which we had brought
with us for that purpose. But so much was the judgment
of the man superior to that of his countrymen, and most
of the South Sea nations *, that he received almost every
thing with indifference, except what he immediately con-

* See Hawkesworth's Compilation.

ceived

ceived the ufe of, fuch as hatchets and large fpike-nails.
At this interview he introduced his whole family to us,
confifting of two women, whom we fuppofed to be his
wives; the young woman, a boy of about fourteen years
of age, and three fmaller children, of which the youngeft
was at the breaft. One of the wives had the excrefcence
or wen on the upper lip, and was evidently neglected by
the man, probably on account of her difagreeable appearance. They conducted us foon after to their habitation,
which lay but a few yards within the wood, on a low hill,
and confifted of two mean huts, made of a few flicks
thatched with unprepared leaves of the flax-plant, and covered with the bark of trees. In return for our prefents
they parted with feveral of their ornaments and weapons,
particularly the battle-axes, but they did not choofe to give
us their fpears. When we were preparing to re-embark,
the man came to the water-fide, and prefented to Captain
Cook a drefs made of the flax plant, a belt of weeds, fome
beads made of a little bird's bones, and fome albatrofs
fkins. We were at firft of opinion that thefe were only
intended as a retribution for what he had received, but he
foon undeceived us by fhewing a ftrong defire of poffeffing one of our boat-cloaks *. We were not charitable
enough to part with our cloaths, when we knew the defi-

* Boat-cloaks are commonly of prodigious dimenfions and great width, fo
that the whole body may be wrapped into them feveral times.

ciency

ciency could not be supplied again; but as soon as we
came on board, Captain Cook ordered a large cloak to be
made of red baize, which we brought to the man at our
next visit.

The rain prevented our going to him the next morning,
but in the afternoon, the weather being a little more promising, we returned to Indian Island. However, at our
approach, instead of being welcomed by the natives on the
shore, we saw none of them, and received no answer when
we shouted to them. We landed therefore, and having
proceeded to their habitation, soon found the reason of
this unusual behaviour. They were preparing to receive
us in all their finery, some being already completely
adorned, and others still busy in dressing. Their hair
was combed, tied on the crown of the head, and anointed
with some oil or grease; white feathers were stuck in at
the top; some had fillets of white feathers all round the
head, and others wore pieces of an albatross skin, with its
fine white down in their ears. Thus fitted out, they shouted at our approach, and received us standing, with marks
of friendship and great courtesy. The captain wore the
new cloak of baize on his own shoulders, and now took
it off and presented the man with it; he, on his part,
seemed so much pleased with it, that he immediately
drew out of his girdle a pattoo-pattoo, or short flat club
made of a great fish's bone, and gave it to the Captain in
return.

return for so valuable an acquisition. We endeavoured to enter into conversation; but, though Captain Cook had taken Gibson, the corporal of marines, with him for that purpose, he being supposed to know more of the language* than any other person on board, yet all our attempts to be understood proved fruitless, because it seemed this family had a peculiar harshness of pronunciation. We therefore took leave of them, and proceeded to survey different parts of the bay, fishing at intervals, shooting birds, and collecting shells, and other marine productions among the rocks. The weather was cloudy all this time, though it did not rain where we were; but when we returned to our ship's cove, we were told it had rained there incessantly in our absence. The same observation we had frequent opportunities of making during our sojourn in Dusky Bay. The probable cause of this difference of weather at such little distances, are the high mountains which run along the south shore of the bay, gradually sloping towards the west cape. These mountains being almost constantly capped with clouds, our cove, which lay immediately under, and was surrounded by them, was of course exposed to the vapours, which perpetually appeared moving with various velocities along the sides of the hills, involving the tops of the trees over which they passed in a

* He was particularly versed in the language of the isle of O-Taheitee; and there is only a difference of dialect between it and the language of New Zeeland.

kind

kind of white femi-opaque mift, and defcending upon us
at laft in rains or in fogs which wetted us to the fkin.
The ifles in the northern part not having fuch high bills
to attract and ftop the clouds coming from the fea, permitted them to pafs freely on to the very bottom of the
bay to the Alps, which we faw covered with perpetual
fnow. The two next days the rains were fo heavy that
no work could be done; the perpetual moifture which
defcended in this place caufed fuch a dampnefs in all
parts of our veffel, as could not fail to become very unwholefome, and to deftroy all the collections of plants
which had been made. Our floop lying fo near the fhore,
which was fteep and fhaggy with over-hanging woods,
was involved in almoft conftant darknefs, even in fair weather, and much more fo during the fogs and rains, fo that
we were obliged to light candles at noon. But the conftant fupply of frefh fifh confiderably alleviated thefe difagreeable circumftances, and, together with the fpruce-
beer and the myrtle-tea, contributed to keep us healthy
and ftrong even in this damp climate. We were now indeed become perfect *ichthyophagi*, for many amongft us entirely lived upon fifh. The fear of being cloyed with this
delicious food, often fet us at work to invent new methods
of preparing it, in order to deceive the palate; and we
accordingly made foups, and pafties, boiled, fried, roafted,
and ftewed our fifhes. But it was pleafant to obferve, that
all

all the arts of cookery only tended to furfeit the fooner, for thofe who wifely confined themfelves to plain boiling in fea water, always did honour to their meals;

> As if increafe of appetite had grown
> By what it fed on.———   SHAKESPEARE.

But what was more fingular than all, was, that in order to prevent any diflike to our food, we confined ourfelves, among a great variety of different forts, chiefly to one fpecies of fifhes, which our failors from its dark colour, called the coal-fifh, and which in tafte nearly refembled our Englifh cod, being of the fame genus. Its meat was firm, juicy, and nutritive; but not fo rich and fat as that of many other fpecies, which we found very delicious, but could not continually feed upon. A very fine fpecies of crayfifh (*cancer homarus* Lin.) larger than the lobfter, fome fhell-fifh, and now and then a cormorant, duck, pigeon, or parrot gave us an agreeable variety at our table, which, compared to its appearance when at fea, was now luxurious and profufe.

Every perfon in our floop experienced the good effects of this change of diet; nay every animal on board feemed to be benefited by it, except our fheep, which were not likely to fare fo well as ourfelves. The nature of the country accounts for this difagreeable circumftance. The whole fouthern extremity of Tavai-poe-namoo, or the fouthern ifland of New Zeeland, and efpecially the land

about

about Dusky Bay consists entirely of steep rocky mountains, with craggy precipices, clad with thick forests, and either barren or covered with snow on their summits. No meadows and lawns are to be met with, and the only flat land we found, was situated at the head of deep coves, where a brook fell into the sea, which probably by depositing the earth and stones it brought from the hills, had formed this low and level ground. But even there the whole was over-run with woods and briars, and we could not find a single spot of ground which might have afforded pasture, the grass which grew on some beaches being very hard and coarse. However, after we had taken pains to furnish our sheep with the freshest sprouts which we could meet with, we were surprised that they would not touch any of them: but upon examination we found that their teeth were loose, and that many of them had every symptom of an inveterate sea scurvy. Of four ewes and two rams which captain Cook brought from the Cape of Good Hope, with an intent to put them on shore in New Zeeland, we had only been able to preserve one of each sex, and these were in so wretched a condition, that their further preservation was very doubtful. If future navigators mean to make such valuable presents, as cattle of any sort to the inhabitants of the South Sea, the only probable method of bringing them safely thither, would be to take the shortest route possible from the Cape to New

Zeeland, in the middle latitudes, and in the best of seasons, when they may expect a quick passage, and no severe cold.

On the 11th, the sky being clear and serene promised a fair day, which was very much wanted, in order to dry our sails and linen, as we had not been able to do either since our arrival in this bay. We likewise obtained the use of a boat, in order to increase the number of our obfervations on the productions of nature. We directed our course to the cove where we had seen the first canoe of the natives, and particularly to a water-fall, which we had observed from afar a few days ago, and which had induced us to call this inlet Cascade Cove. This water-fall, at the distance of a mile and a half, seems to be but inconsiderable, on account of its great elevation; but after climbing about two hundred yards upwards, we obtained a full prospect of it, and found indeed a view of great beauty and grandeur before us. The first object which strikes the beholder, is a clear column of water, apparently eight or ten yards in circumference, which is projected with great impetuosity from the perpendicular rock, at the height of one hundred yards. Nearly at the fourth part of the whole height, this column meeting a part of the same rock, which now acquires a little inclination, spreads on its broad back into a limpid sheet of about twenty-five yards in width. Here its surface is curled, and dashes upon every little eminence

in

in its rapid defcent, till it is all collected in a fine bafon about fixty yards in circuit, included on three fides by the natural walls of the rocky chafm, and in front by huge maffes of ftone irregularly piled above each other. Between them the ftream finds its way, and runs foaming with the greateft rapidity along the flope of the hill to the fea. The whole neighbourhood of the cafcade, to a diftance of an hundred yards around, is filled with the fteam or watery vapour formed by the violence of the fall. This mift however was fo thick, that it penetrated our clothes in a few minutes, as effectually as a fhower of rain would have done. We mounted on the higheft ftone before the bafon, and looking down into it, were ftruck with the fight of a moft beautiful rainbow of a perfectly circular form, which was produced by the meridian rays of the fun refracted in the vapour of the cafcade. Beyond this circle the reft of the fteam was tinged with the prifmatic colours, refracted in an inverted order. The fcenery on the left confifts of fteep, brown rocks, fringed on the fummits with over-hanging fhrubs and trees; on the right there is a vaft heap of large ftones, probably hurried down from the impending mountain's brow, by the force of the torrent. From thence rifes a floping bank, about feventy-five yards high, on which a wall of twenty-five yards perpendicular is placed, crowned with verdure and fhrubberies. Still farther to the right, the broken rocks are clothed with moffes, ferns, graffes,

U 2 and

and various flowers; nay several shrubs, and trees to the
height of forty feet, rife on both sides of the stream, and
hide its course from the sun. The noise of the cascade is so
loud, and so repeatedly reverberated from the echoing rocks,
that it drowns almost every other sound; the birds seemed
to retire from it to a little distance, where the shrill notes
of thrushes, the graver pipe of wattle-birds, and the enchanting melody of various creepers resounded on all sides,
and completed the beauty of this wild and romantic spot.
On turning round we beheld an extensive bay, strewed as
it were with small islands, which are covered with lofty
trees; beyond them on one side, the mountains rise majestic on the main land, capt with clouds and perpetual
snow; and on the other, the immense ocean bounded our
view. The grandeur of this scene was such, that the
powers of description fall short of the force and beauty of
nature, which could only be truly imitated by the pencil
of Mr. Hodges, who went on this voyage with us; and
whose performances do great credit and honour to his
judgment and execution, as well as to the choice of his
employers. Satisfied with the contemplation of this magnificent sight, we directed our attention next to the flowers
which enlivened the ground, and the small birds which
sung very cheerfully all round us. We had as yet found
neither the vegetable nor animal creation so beautiful,
or so numerous, in any part of this bay; perhaps, because

the

the strong refraction of the sun-beams from the perpendi-
lar walls of rock, and the shelter from storms, made the
climate considerably more mild and genial in this spot than
in any other part. The soil was in nothing different
here from that in other parts round the bay, but seemed to
be the same vegetable mould; and the rocks and stones
about the cascade consisted of masses of granite, or moor-
stone (ſarum), and of a kind of brown talcous clay-stone,
in strata, which is common to all New Zeeland.

We returned on board before sun-set, well pleased with
our acquisitions during this excursion. At our return
we were told, that the Indian family, whom we had seen
paddling into the cove, in the morning, in their best attire,
had gradually approached the ship with great caution. Captain Cook meeting them in a boat, quitted it, and went
into their canoe, but could not prevail on them to come
along-side of the ship, and was obliged to leave them to follow their own inclination. At length they went ashore, in
a little creek hard by ours, and afterwards came and sat down
on the shore abreast of the vessel, to which they were near
enough to be heard, and spoken to. The captain gave orders to play the fife and bagpipe, and to beat the drum;
but they entirely disregarded the two first, and were not
very attentive to the last, nor could any thing induce them
to come on board. Several of our officers and seamen then
going on shore to them, were received with great good-
nature,

nature, and attempted to converse with them by signs, which
were for the most part unintelligible, or misunderstood.
However, the young woman shewed a great partiality to a
young seaman, and from her gestures it was supposed she
took him for one of her own sex; but whether he had
taken some improper liberties, or whether she had any other
reason to be disgusted, she would never suffer him to come
near her afterwards. We likewise went on shore to them,
after returning from our excursion, and the man desiring
us to sit down by him, frequently pointed at our boats that
plyed between the ship and the shore, and it appeared that
he was desirous of possessing one of them. They staid all
night about a hundred yards from our watering place,
lighted a fire, and dressed some fish there, thus evidently placing
great confidence in us. In the evening a party of officers
set out in a small boat, to the north side of the bay, where
they intended to pass the night, and continue shooting all
the next day.

Captain Cook, accompanied by my father, went in his
boat the next morning, to survey the rocks and isles in the
mouth of the bay. They entered a fine snug cove, on the
S. E. side of the island, under which we had found our first
anchorage, and which was therefore named Anchor Island.
Here they sat down by the side of a pleasant brook, and
made a slight repast on some boiled craw-fish, which they
had brought with them. From thence they proceeded to
the

the outermost iflands, where they difcovered a number of
feals on the rocks, fhot fourteen of them with ball, which
they carried away with them, and might have killed many
more, had the furf permitted them to land upon all the
rocks in fafety. The feals in Dufky Bay are all of the fpecies called fea-bears *, which profeffor Steller firft defcribed
on Bering's Ifland, near Kamtchatka, and which are confequently common to both hemifpheres. They are very
numerous on the fouthern extremities of the continents of
America and Africa, likewife at New Zeeland, and on
Diemen's Land. The only difference we could perceive between thefe at Dufky Bay, and thofe defcribed at Kamtchatka, confifted in the fize, in refpect of which ours were inferior. They found it difficult to kill them, and many,
though grievoufly wounded, efcaped into the fea, and tinged the rocks and the water with their blood. Their meat,
which is almoft black, and their heart and liver were eatable, the former, by the help of a good appetite, and a
little imagination, might be eaten for beef, and the laft
were perfectly fimilar to a calf's pluck. We were, however, obliged to cut away every bit of fat, before we dreffed
the meat, which otherwife had an infupportable tafte of
train-oil. Captain Cook availed himfelf of this opportunity of laying in a provifion of lamp-oil, which was boiled

* Phoca urfina *Linn.* Urfine Seal, *Pennant. Syn. Quad.* 271.

out

out of the seals fat; he also ordered the skins to be made use of for repairing our rigging.

The success of the preceding day encouraged him to make another trip to the Seal Islands, on which my father accompanied him again; but the sea ran so very high, that it was by no means practicable to come near, and much less to land on them. With a great deal of difficulty they weathered the S. W. point of Anchor Island, where the sea tumbled in with great impetuosity, and was so much agitated, as to affect the mariners with sickness. They then rowed along the north shore of that island, where the captain landed to take the bearings of different points. It happened very fortunately, that they had taken this route; for they now discovered the small boat adrift, which set off from the sloop on the 11th in the evening, and laid hold of it the moment before it was going to be dashed against the rocks. The boat was immediately secured in a small creek, and after refreshing the people with some provisions which they found in it, captain Cook proceeded to the place where he supposed the party of officers to be, from whom it was drifted away. Between seven and eight in the evening they reached the cove, and found them on a small island, to which they could not then approach, because the tide had left it. They landed therefore on an adjacent point, and after many fruitless attempts, at length succeeded in making a fire. Here they broiled some fish, and after

supper

fupper lay down; the ftony beach was their bed, and their covering the canopy of heaven.

At three o'clock in the morning the tide permitted them to take the fportfmen from their barren ifland; after which they immediately failed with a fair wind, accompanied with fhowers of rain, to the cove where they had fecured the other boat. Here they found an immenfe number of petrels of the bluifh fpecies, common over the whole fouthern ocean *, fome being on the wing, and others in the woods, in holes under ground formed between the roots of trees and in the crevices of rocks, in places not eafily acceffible, where they probably had their nefts and young. In day time, not one of them was to be feen there, the old ones then being probably out at fea in queft of food. They now faw them going out for that purpofe, and two days ago they had been obferved at the Seal Iflands, returning in the evening in order to feed their young with the food which they had collected. They now heard a great variety of confufed founds coming from the fides of the hill, fome very acute, others like the croak-ing of frogs, which were made by thefe petrels. At other times we have found innumerable holes on the top of one of the Seal Iflands, and heard the young petrels making a noife in them; but as the holes communicated with each other it was impoffible to come at one of them. We had

* See page 91.

VOL. L.   X   already

already frequently obferved the old petrels flying about us in the evening, when we returned late from our excurfions, but till now they had always been taken for bats. They have a broad bill, and a blackifh ftripe acrofs their bluifh wings and body, and are not fo large as the common fhear-water or Mank's petrel of our feas. The inftinct is very wonderful which actuates thefe birds to burrow holes under ground for their young, to roam all over the ocean in queft of food for their fupport, and to find their way to the fhore when they are feveral hundred leagues diftant from it.

Having replaced the fportfmen in their boat, they all proceeded to the fhip, which they reached at feven in the morning, not a little fatigued from the night's expedition. The natives, probably forefeeing the bad weather, which continued all this day, had left the place they occupied near the fhip on the preceding night, and had retired to their habitations on Indian Ifland.

The weather cleared up a little on the 15th in the morning. Captain Cook therefore fet out to continue his furvey of the N. W. part of the bay, and we accompanied a party of officers to the cove in that part where we intended to take up our quarters for the next night. In our way we rowed along-fide of our fifhing-boat, which conftantly went out in the morning to provide all our crew with their dinner, and took in a fail which we ftood

in

in need of. We were furprifed to fee the young black dog in the boat with them, which ran away from us on the 2d inftant; and were told, that, taking their ftation near the fhore, at day-break they had heard a very piteous howling on the next point, and had found the dog, which came into the boat very readily as foon as they put in fhore. Though this animal had been in the woods during a fortnight, yet it was by no means famifhed, but on the contrary looked well fed and very fleek. A large fpecies of rails, which we called water-hens, and which are very numerous in this part of New Zeeland, with perhaps fome fhell-fifh on the rocks, or fome dead fifh thrown up by the fea, had in all probability afforded it fufficient fupport. We may from hence conclude, that as there is abundance of food for carnivorous animals in New Zeeland, they would probably be very numerous if they exifted there at all, and efpecially if they were endowed with any degree of fagacity, like the fox, or cat tribes. In that cafe they could not have efcaped the notice of our numerous parties, nor of the natives, and the latter would certainly have preferred their furrs, as a valuable article of drefs in their moift and raw climate, for want of which they now wear the fkins of dogs and of birds. The queftion, whether New Zeeland contained any wild quadrupeds, had engaged our attention from our firft arrival there. One of our people, ftrongly per-

fuaded

fuaded that fo great a country could not fail of poffeffing
new and unknown animals, had already twice reported
that he had feen a brown animal, fomething lefs than a
jackal or little fox, about the dawn of morning, fitting on
a ftump of a tree near our tents, and running off at his
approach. But as this circumftance has never been confirmed by any fubfequent teftimony, nothing is more probable than that the want of day-light had deceived him,
and that he had either obferved one of the numerous
wood-hens, which are brown, and creep through the
buſhes very frequently; or that one of our cats, on the
watch for little birds, had been miftaken for a new quadruped.

Having taken the fail on board, we continued our courfe,
and began our refearches in the cove, where we killed
many ducks of four different fpecies. One of them was
remarkably beautiful, and of the fize of the eider duck.
Its plumage was of a blackiſh brown, elegantly fprinkled
with white; all the coverts of the wing were white, the
rump and vent ferruginous, the quill and tail-feathers
black, and the fecondaries green. Another fpecies was
nearly of the fize of our mallard, but all of a light-brown,
every feather being edged with a yellowiſh white, of
which there was a line on the cheek and eye-brows; the
eyes of this fort had irides of a bright yellow, and on the
wings there was a fpot of fine bluiſh green inclofed in

black

black lines. The third fort was a bluish grey whistling duck, about the size of a wigeon; its bill had a remarkable membranaceous substance at the extremity on both sides, probably because the bird is intended to live by sucking the worms, &c. in the mud, when the tide retires from the beaches. Its breast was sprinkled with ferruginous feathers, and on the wings it had a large white spot. The fourth and most common fort is a small brown duck, which is nearly the same as the English gadwall. A little before dark, the captain, having examined all the harbours which lay in his way, shot a number of wild fowl, and caught fish sufficient for all our party, arrived at our rendezvous, where we had erected a tent, by means of the sails and oars. Our keen appetites dispensed with the arts of cookery, and our fish broiled à l'Indienne, over a strong fire, on a bit of a stick, tasted as deliciously as we could desire. With this supper, and a draught of spruce-beer, of which we had carried a small keg with us, we composed ourselves to sleep, and contrived to pass the night, though not quite so comfortably as in our beds. The next morning a boat went up to the head of the cove to start the game, which was done so effectually that almost all the wild-ducks escaped, the rain having wetted all our fire-arms. The captain now landed in the cove, and walked across a narrow isthmus, which separates it from another cove on the north side of the Five-finger Land.

Land. Here he found a prodigious number of the water-hens before mentioned, and brought away ten couple of them, which recompenfed him for the trouble of croffing the ifthmus, through intricate woods, where the water was frequently up to the waift. At nine o'clock we were all affembled again, and fet out on our return to the fhip; but as we continued examining every creek and harbour which we found on our way, and encreafing our collection of wild-fowl, we did not return till feven o'clock in the evening. We brought feven dozen of various forts of birds with us, among which were near thirty ducks, and immediately diftributed them to the feveral meffes of offi-cers, petty-officers, and feamen, as far as they would go. We may take this opportunity to obferve, that there is no part of New Zeeland fo well flocked with birds of all kinds as Dufky Bay. We found feveral forts of wild-ducks, fhags, corvorants, oyfter-catchers or fea-pies, water or wood-hens, albatroffes, gannets, gulls, pinguins, and others of the aquatic kind. The land-birds were hawks, parrots, pigeons, and many leffer ones of new and unknown fpecies. The parrots were of two forts; one fmall and green, and the other very large, greyifh-green, with a reddifh breaft. As the birds of that genus are commonly confined to the warmer climates, we were much furprifed to find them in the latitude of 46°, expofed to the raw rainy weather,

which

which the height of the mountains almost constantly produces in Dusky Bay.

The next day was so rainy, that none of us could venture to stir out of the sloop; but the day after proving a
very fine one, my father went up the hill, along the course
of the brook, from which we filled our casks. About half
a mile upwards, through ferns, rotten trees, and thick
forests, he came to a fine lake of fresh water nearly half
a mile in diameter. Its water was limpid and well tasted,
but had acquired a brownish hue, from the leaves of trees
which dropped into it on all sides; he observed no other
inhabitant in it than a small species of fish *(esox)*, without
scales, resembling a little trout; its colour was brown,
and mottled with yellowish spots in the shape of some
ancient Asiatic characters. The whole lake was surrounded by a thick forest, consisting of the largest trees,
and the mountains rose all round it in a variety of forms.
The environs were deserted and silent, not the least note
of the common birds was heard, for it was rather cold
at this elevation; and not a single plant had blossoms.
The whole scene was perfectly fitted to inspire a kind of
pleasing melancholy, and to encourage hermit-meditation.
The fine weather induced our friends the natives to pay
us another visit; they took up their quarters on the same
spot, where they had been this day sevennight, and when
they were again invited to come on board, they promised

to come the next morning. In the mean while they had a quarrel among themselves, the man beat the two women who were supposed to be his wives; the young girl in return struck him, and then began to weep. What the cause of this disagreement was, we cannot determine; but if the young woman was really the man's daughter, which we could never clearly understand, it should seem that the filial duties are strangely confounded among them; or which is more probable, that this secluded family acted in every respect, not according to the customs and regulations of a civil society, but from the impulses of nature, which speak aloud against every degree of oppression.

In the morning, the man resolved to come on board with the young woman, but sent the rest of his family a-fishing in the canoe. He walked with her round the cove, to the place where we had made a stage or temporary bridge from the vessel to the shore. Before they entered upon this, they were conducted to a place on the hill, where we kept our sheep and goats, which they seemed to be much surprised with, and desired to possess; but as we foresaw that they must die for want of proper food if we left them here, we could not comply with this request. Captain Cook, and my father met them at the stage, and this man after saluting them with his nose against theirs, gave each of them a new cloak or piece of cloth made of the flax-plant, curiously interwoven with

parrot's

parrot's feathers, and prefented the captain with a piece
of green nephritic ftone, or *jadde* *, which was formed into
the blade of a hatchet. Before he ftepped on the bridge, he
turned afide, put a piece of a bird's fkin with white feathers
through the hole in one of his ears, and broke off a fmall
green branch from a neighbouring bufh. With this he
walked on, and ftopping when he could juft reach the
fhip's fides with his hand, ftruck them and the main-
fhrouds feveral times with his branch. He then began to
repeat a kind of fpeech or prayer, which feemed to have
regular cadences, and to be metrically arranged as a
poem; his eyes were fixed upon the place he had
touched, his voice was raifed, and his whole behaviour
grave and folemn. The young woman, though at other
times laughing and dancing, now kept clofe to the
man and was ferious all the while he fpoke, which
lafted about two or three minutes; at the clofe of his
fpeech he ftruck the fhip's fide again, threw the branch
into the main chains, and came aboard. This manner of
delivering folemn orations, and making peace, is practifed
by all the nations which have been feen in the South Sea
before our voyage, as appears from the teftimonies of
various voyagers. Both the man and woman had a fpear
in their hands when they were conducted on the quarter-
deck; there they admired every thing they faw: a few geefe

* See Hawkefworth, vol. II. p. 286.

in our coops particularly attracted their attention; a handsome cat, was likewise much courted, but they always
ftroked it the wrong way, fo as to make the hair ftand upright, though we fhowed them to do it in a contrary direction; probably they admired the richnefs of the furr. The
man looked upon every new object with furprize, but as his
attention could not be fixed to any one object for more than
a fingle moment, many of our works of art muft have appeared to him as incomprehenfible, as thofe of nature.
However, the number and ftrength of our decks and of
other parts of our veffel engroffed his admiration more than
any thing elfe. The girl, feeing Mr. Hodges, whofe pencil fhe had much admired, made him a prefent of a piece
of cloth, of the fame kind as thofe which the man had
given to captain Cook and my father. This cuftom of
making prefents is not fo ufual in other parts of New Zeeland, as in the tropical iflands; but it appears on the whole,
that this family were not always guided by national cuftoms, but took fuch meafures as prudence and integrity
fuggefted in their fituation, which left them at the mercy
of a greater force. We defired them to come into the cabin,
and after a long debate among themfelves, they accepted
the invitation, and defcended by the ladder. Here they
admired every thing, and were particularly pleafed to
learn the ufe of chairs, and that they might be removed
from place to place. They were prefented with hatchets
by

by the captain and my father, and received a great number of trinkets of lefs value. Thefe laft the man laid
down in a heap, and would have gone away without them,
had we not reminded him of them; whereas he never
let a hatchet or fpike-nail go out of his hand, after he had
once taken hold of it. They faw us fit down to our breakfaft, and were feated near us; but all our intreaties could
not prevail on them to touch our victuals. They likewife
exprefsly inquired where we went to fleep, and the captain fhowed them his cot, which was fufpended, at which
they were mightily pleafed. From the cabin they proceeded
to the gun-room, on the deck below; and having received
feveral prefents there, they returned to the captain again.
The man now pulled out a little leather bag, probably of
feals fkin, and having, with a good deal of ceremony, put
in his fingers, which he pulled out covered with oil, offered
to anoint captain Cook's hair; this honour was however
declined, becaufe the unguent, though perhaps held as a
delicious perfume, and as the moft precious thing the man
could beftow, yet feemed to our noftrils not a little offenfive; and the very fqualid appearances of the bag in which
it was contained, contributed to make it ftill more difguft-
ful. Mr. Hodges did not efcape fo well; for the girl, having a tuft of feathers, dipt in oil, on a ftring round her
neck, infifted upon dreffing him out with it, and he was
forced to wear the odoriferous prefent, in pure civility.

We

We left them to amuse themselves in the other parts of the ship, and set out in two boats, with the captain and several officers, to examine a long inlet which ran to the eastward, in sight of our cove. In proportion as we receded from the sea, we found the mountains much higher, more steep, and barren; the trees gradually diminished in height and circumference, and dwindled to shrubs, contrary to what is observed in other parts of the world, where the inland countries have finer forests and better timber than the sea shores. The interior ranges of mountains called the Southern Alps, appeared very distinctly, of a great height, and covered with snow on their summits. We passed by a number of shady islands, which contained little coves and rivulets; and on one of the projecting points, opposite the last island, we saw a fine cascade falling into the water, over a steep rock, clothed with thick bushes and trees. The water was perfectly calm, polished, and transparent; the landscape was distinctly reflected in it, and the various remantic shapes of the steep mountains, contrasted in different masses of light and shade, had an admirable effect. About noon we put into a small cove, where we caught some fish, and shot a few birds. From thence we rowed again till dusk, when we entered a fine cove, at the extremity of this long arm, and were obliged to take up our quarters on the first beach we could land upon, after being prevented by shoals from proceeding to the head of the cove. There
we

we thought we perceived something similar to a smoke, but finding nothing to confirm this opinion, and especially seeing no fire at night, we readily acquiesced in the idea of having been deceived by some misty vapour, or other object, which we might have indistinctly seen. We prepared with great alacrity to pass the night here, and no one was excepted from his task on these occasions. As it may be curious to know the nature of our marooning parties, as our seamen called them, I shall here give some account of our proceedings this night. Having found a beach to land on, with a brook, and a wood close to it, our first care was to bring on shore the oars, sails, cloaks, guns, hatchets, &c. not forgetting a little keg of spruce-beer, and perhaps a bottle of strong liquor. The boats were next secured at a grappling, and with a rope made fast to a tree on shore. Some of us were then busied in collecting dry pieces of wood for fuel, which in such a wet country as New Zeeland, was sometimes very difficult; some erected a tent or wigwam, made of the oars and sails together with strong branches of trees, in a convenient dry spot, sheltered as much as possible, in case of wind and rain. Others lighted the fire in front of the tent, by burning some oakum, in which they had previously rubbed a quantity of gunpowder. The preparations for supper were very short: some of the sailors cleaned our fishes, skinned the waterfowl, split, and lastly broiled them; when they were dressed,

one

-one of the boat's gang-boards, washed clean, answered the several purposes of a table, of dishes, and plates; and our fingers and teeth did yeoman's service, instead of knives and forks. A keen appetite, procured by strong exercise, and excited by the sharp air of the country, soon taught us to overcome the ideas of indelicacy, which civilized nations connect with this way of living; and we never so strongly felt how little is wanting to satisfy the cravings of the stomach, and to support the existence of human beings, as on these occasions. After supper we listened a while to the original comic vein of our boat's crew, who huddled round the fire, made their meal, and recited a number of droll stories, intermixed with hearty curses, oaths, and indecent expressions, but seldom without real humour. Then strewing our tent with heaps of fern leaves, and wrapping ourselves in our boat-cloaks, with our guns and shooting-bags for our pillows, we composed ourselves to sleep.

At day-break Captain Cook and my father, with two men, went in a small boat to take a view of the head of the cove, where they saw some flat land. They went on shore upon it at one corner, and ordered the boat to meet them at the opposite point. They had not walked a great way before they saw some wild-ducks, and, by creeping through the bushes, came near enough to fire and kill one of them. The moment they had fired they heard a hideous shout of several loud and piercing voices round about them

them from different quarters. They fhouted in their turn, and taking up the duck retired towards the boat, which was full half a mile off. The natives continued their clamours, but did not follow them; for indeed a deep branch of a river was between them, and their numbers were too inconfiderable to attempt hoftilities; but thefe circumftances we only learnt in the fequel. We had in the mean while taken a ramble into the woods in fearch of plants; but hearing the fhout of the natives, we embarked immediately in the remaining boat and joined the other, which by this time had taken Captain Cook and my father on board. We therefore proceeded up into a river, which was deep enough for the boats, and amufed ourfelves with fhooting ducks, which were here in great plenty. We now faw a man, woman, and child on the left fhore, and the woman waved to us with a white bird's fkin, probably in fign of peace and friendfhip. On this occafion I could not help admiring, that almoft all nations on our globe have tacitly agreed upon the white colour, or upon green branches, as tokens of a peaceable difpofition, and that with thefe in their hands they confidently rely on a ftranger's placability. Perhaps this general agreement had its origin anterior to the univerfal difperfion of the human fpecies; this will feem the more probable when it is confidered, that neither the white colour, nor the green boughs of a tree, have any intrinfic character, to which the

the idea of amity is naturally and neceſſarily referred.
Our boat being neareſt to theſe natives, Captain Cook deſired the officer in it to land, and accept their proferred
friendſhip, whilſt he meant to take the advantage of the
tide to get as high up in the river as poſſible. Whether
the officer did not underſtand Captain Cook's meaning, or
whether he was too deeply engaged with duck ſhooting,
we did not land; and the poor people, to all appearance
apprehenſive of the worſt conſequences, from a ſet of men
who rejected their propoſals of peace, fled into the woods
with the utmoſt precipitation. The Captain in the mean
while rowed about half a mile higher, where his boat
was ſtopped by the violence of the ſtream, and by ſeveral
huge ſtones which lay acroſs the bed of the river, and redoubled the rapidity of the water. Here, however, he
found a new ſpecies of ducks, the fifth we had obſerved
in Duſky Bay. Its ſize was ſomething leſs than that of a
teal, the colour of a ſhining greeniſh black above, and a
dark ſooty grey below; it had a purple caſt on the head,
a lead-coloured bill and feet, a golden eye, and a white
bar in the leſſer quill feathers. On Captain Cook's return
to us, we perceived two men in the woods along the bank
oppoſite to that where we had ſeen the friendly family.
The captain endeavoured to form an acquaintance with
them, but when the boat came cloſe along ſhore, they always retired into the woods, which were ſo thick, that they

not

1772.
April.

not only covered them from our fight, but alfo made it unadvifeable to follow them. The ebbing tide obliged us to retire out of this river to the place where we had fpent the night; and, after breakfafting there, we embarked in order to fet out on our return to the Refolution. However, when we had fcarce put off, we perceived the two natives, who had walked acrofs the woods to an open fpot, from whence they halloo'd to us. The captain immediately ordered both the boats to row up to them, and coming into fhallow water, he got out unarmed, attended by two men, and waded to the fhore, with a fheet of white paper in his hand. The two natives ftood about one hundred yards from the water's fide, each of them with a long fpear in his hand. When the captain advanced with his two men they retired; he then proceeded alone, but could not prevail on them to lay afide their fpears. At laft one of them ftuck his fpear in the ground, and taking a bunch of grafs in his hand met the captain, and giving him one end of the grafs to hold while he kept the other, he pronounced a folemn fpeech in a loud tone of voice, during a minute or two, in which he made feveral paufes, perhaps waiting for a reply. As foon as this ceremony was over, they faluted each other, and the New Zeelander took a new garment from his own fhoulders and prefented it to the captain, for which he received a hatchet in return. Peace and friendfhip being thus firmly eftablifhed, the

VOL. I.   Z   other

other man likewife came up to falute the captain, and was
prefented with a hatchet; and feveral of us came afhore to
them, at which they were not the leaft alarmed, but received every new comer with great cordiality. We now
perceived feveral other natives, probably women, on the
fkirts of the wood, and the two men earneftly intreated us
to go up to their habitations, intimating by figns, that
they would give us fomething to eat there; but the tide
and other circumftances did not permit us to accept their
invitation. When we had taken leave of them, the two
men followed us to our boats, where they defired us to
remove the mufkets which lay acrofs the ftern, and having
complied with their requeft, they came along-fide, and affifted us to launch the boats, which were aground on account of the ebb. We found however that it was neceffary to have an eye upon them, becaufe they feemed to
covet the poffeffion of every thing they faw or could lay
hands on, except the mufkets, which they would not
touch, being taught to refpect them as inftruments of
death, on account of the havock they had feen us make
among the wild-fowl. We obferved no canoes among
them, and their only means of tranfporting themfelves
acrofs the river, was on a few logs of wood connected together into a kind of raft, which was perfectly fufficient
for that purpofe. Fifh and wild-fowl were in fuch plenty
here, that they can have little occafion to roam to any diftance

1771.
April.

tance in queft of them, as their numbers did not feem to exceed three families; and the whole bay being almoft entirely deftitute of inhabitants, one fingle family more excepted, they need not be apprehenfive of difturbance from bad neighbours. The features of thefe men were rather wild, but not ill-favoured; their complexion refembled that of the family on Indian Ifland, of a mahogany brown; their hair bufhy, and their beards frizled and black. They were of a middling ftature and ftout, but their legs and thighs very flender, and their knees too much fwelled in proportion. Their drefs and general behaviour feemed to be the fame as that of the other family before mentioned. The courage of this people has fomething fingular in it, for it fhould feem, that in fpight of their inferiority of force, they cannot brook the thought of hiding themfelves, at leaft not till they have made an attempt to eftablifh an intercourfe, or prove the principles of the ftrangers who approach them. It would have been impoffible for us, among the numerous iflands and harbours, and in the mazy forefts upon them, to have found out the family which we faw on the Indian Ifland, if they had not difcovered themfelves, and thus made the firft advances. We might alfo have departed from the cove without knowing that it was inhabited, if the natives had not fhouted at the difcharge of our mufkets. In both cafes a certain opennefs and honefty, appear ftrongly to mark

their

their character; for if it had the least admixture of treach-
ery, they would have tried to fall upon us unawares, as
they could not have failed of meeting with frequent opportunities of cutting off our numerous small parties,
when dispersed in different parts of the woods.

It was noon when we left these two men, and proceeded
down on the north side of the long arm, of which captain
Cook took the bearings in his way. The night overtook
us before he had completed this survey; so that we were
forced to leave another arm unexplored, and to hasten to
the vessel, which we reached about eight o'clock at night.
We were told that the native with his companion, the
young woman, had staid on board till noon, after our departure; and having been informed, that we had left some
presents in his double canoe in Cascade Cove, he employed
some of his people to bring them away from thence, after
which the whole family remained in the neighbourhood
of the ship till this morning. They then took their departure, and we never saw them again, which was the
more extraordinary, as they never went away empty handed
from us, but had at different times received nine or ten
hatchets, and four times that number of large spike-
nails, besides other articles. As far as these things may
be counted riches among them, this man was the wealthiest
in all New Zeeland, being possessed of more hatchets, than
there were in the whole country besides, before the second
arrival

arrival of British vessels. The thin population in this part
of the island makes it probable, that the few families in
it lead a nomadic or wandering life, and remove according
as the season, the conveniency of fishing, and other circumstances render it necessary. We were therefore of opinion,
that our friendly family had only removed upon this principle; but we were likewise told that before they went
away, the man had made signs of going to kill men, and
employing the hatchet as an offensive weapon. If this
circumstance was rightly understood, we cannot sufficiently
wonder that a family so secluded from all the rest of the
world, in a spacious bay, where they have a superfluity
of food, and of all the necessaries of life, the fewness of
their wants considered, should still have a thought of
warring with their fellow-creatures, when they might
live peaceably and happily in their retirement. The pleasing hope of facilitating the œconomical operations of these
people, and of encouraging some degree of agriculture
among them, by presenting them with useful tools, was
defeated by this determination. The state of barbarism,
in which the New Zeelanders may justly be said to live,
and which generally hearkens to no other voice than that
of the *strongest*, might make them more liable than
any other nation to resolve upon the destruction of their
fellow-citizens, as soon as an opportunity offered; and
their innate and savage valour may probably assist them

to

1773.
April to put such projects in execution. On this occasion, I
cannot omit mentioning a remarkable instance of courage
which characterised the old man who had now left us;
our officers having fired several musquets in his presence,
he became desirous of discharging one himself, which they
easily granted; the young woman, supposed to be his
daughter, fell prostrate on the ground before him, and
entreated him, with the strongest marks of fear, to desist
from his undertaking; but he was not to be diverted
from his purpose, and fired the musquet with the greatest
resolution, repeating it afterwards three or four times. This
warlike disposition, together with the irascible temper of
the whole nation, that cannot brook the least injury, is
probably the cause which has induced this single family,
and the few in the long inlet we had visited, to separate
from the rest of their fellow-creatures. All the disputes
of savage people commonly terminate in the destruction
of one of their parties, unless they evade it by a well-
timed flight: this may have been the case of the inhabitants of Dusky Bay, and admitting it, their design of going
to fight, is no more than a project of being revenged on
their foes and oppressors.

Friday 23.   On the 23d, early in the morning, several officers, accompanied by Dr. Sparrman, went to Cascade Cove, in order
to ascend one of the highest mountains in the bay, which
was situated on one side of it. About two o'clock they
reached

1775.
APRIL.

reached the summit, which they made known to us by
lighting a great fire there. We should have accompanied
them on this excursion, but a violent flux attended with
gripes confined us on board. It was owing to the care-
lessness of our cook, who had suffered our copper kitchen-
furniture to become full of verdigrise. In the evening
however, we went to meet our travellers in Cascade Cove,
and after searching the woods some time for plants and
birds, we brought them on board with us. At night the
fire had spread in a bright circular garland all round the
summit of the mountain, and made a very elegant illu-
mination in honour of St. George's day. Our party related that they had a prospect of the whole bay, and of
the sea beyond the mountains to the south, S. W. and W.
N. W. for more than twenty leagues all round them, the
weather being remarkably fine and clear. The inland-
mountains were very barren, and consisted of huge broken
and craggy masses, all covered with snow on their summits;
the top of that on which they stood, afforded several low
shrubs and various alpine plants, which we had seen no
where else. A little lower down they saw a taller shrubbery; below this a space covered with dry or dead trees,
and next to those the living woods began, which increased
in size as they descended. The ascent had been fatiguing
enough, on account of the intricacy of briars and climbers,
but the descent also was dangerous, because of many

precipices

Mr.
Arat.

precipices which they met on their way, and along most
of which they contrived to slide down by the help of trees
and bushes. At a considerable height they met with three
or four trees, which they took for palms, and of which
they cut down one, and used its middlemost shoot for their
refreshment. These trees,' however, were not the true
cabbage-palms, nor did they belong at all to the class of
palms, which are generally confined to more temperate
climates. They were properly speaking, a new species
of dragon-trees, with broad leaves, *(dracæna australis)* of
which the central shoot when quite tender, tastes something
like an almond's kernel, with a little of the flavour of
cabbage. We afterwards observed more of them in other
parts of this bay.

The next morning I accompanied captain Cook to the
cove on the N. W. part of the bay, which from the transaction
of this day, received the name of Goose Cove. We had five
tame geese left, of those which we had taken on board
at the Cape of Good Hope, and these we intended to leave
in New Zeeland to breed, and run wild. This cove was
looked upon as the most convenient place for that purpose,
since there were no inhabitants to disturb them, and because it afforded an abundance of proper food. We set
them on shore, and they immediately ran to feed in the
mud, at the head of the cove where we left them, pronouncing over them the *crescite & multiplicamini*, for the
benefit

benefit of future generations of navigators and New Zeelanders. There can be little doubt indeed, but that they
will fucceed in this fecluded fpot, and in time fpread over
the whole country, anfwerable to our original intention. The
reſt of this day was ſpent in ſhooting, and among the different birds killed was a white heron *(ardea alba)*, common
to Europe.

The fair weather, which had laſted eight days fucceſſive-
ly, was entirely at an end on the 15th, when the rain fet
in again towards evening, and continued till the next day
at noon. We had reaſon to believe fuch a continuance of
dry weather very uncommon in Duſky Bay, and particularly at this feaſon, becauſe we never experienced above two
fair days one after another, either before or after this week.
We had, however, improved this opportunity to complete
our wood and water, and put the ſloop in condition to go
out to fea, and having taken on board all our men, we
caſt off our bridge, and removed out of the creek, into the
middle of our cove, ready to fail with the firſt fair wind.
The fuperiority of a ſtate of civilization over that of barbarifm could not be more clearly ſtated, than by the altera-
tions and improvements we had made in this place. In
the courfe of a few days, a fmall part of us had cleared
away the woods from a furface of more than an acre,
which fifty New Zeelanders, with their tools of ſtone, could

VOL. I.   A a   not

not have performed in three months. This spot, where immense numbers of plants left to themselves lived and decayed by turns, in one confused inanimated heap; this spot, we had converted into an active scene, where a hundred and twenty men pursued various branches of employment with unremitted ardour :

> *Quales apes aestate nova per florea rura*
> *Exercet sub sole labor,*   VIRGIL.

> Such was their toil, and such their busy pains,
> As exercise the bees in flowery plains,
> When winter past and summer scarce begun,
> Invites them forth to labour in the sun.   DRYDEN.

We felled tall timber-trees, which, but for ourselves, had crumbled to dust with age; our sawyers cut them into planks, or we split them into billets for fuel. By the side of a murmuring rivulet, whose passage into the sea we facilitated, a long range of casks, which had been prepared by our coopers for that purpose, stood ready to be filled with water. Here ascended the steam of a large cauldron, in which we brewed, from neglected indigenous plants, a salutary and palatable potion, for the use of our labourers. In the offing, some of our crew appeared providing a meal of delicious fish for the refreshment of their fellows. Our caulkers and riggers were stationed on the sides and masts of the vessel, and their occupations gave

life

life to the scene, and struck the ear with various noises, whilst the anvil on the hill resounded with the strokes of the weighty hammer. Already the polite arts began to flourish in this new settlement; the various tribes of animals and vegetables, which dwelt in the unfrequented woods, were imitated by an artist in his noviciate; and the romantic prospects of this shaggy country, lived on the canvas in the glowing tints of nature, who was amazed to see herself so closely copied. Nor had science disdained to visit us in this solitary spot; an observatory arose in the centre of our works, filled with the most accurate instruments, where the attentive eye of the astronomer contemplated the motions of the celestial bodies. The plants which clothed the ground, and the wonders of the animal creation, both in the forests and the seas, likewise attracted the notice of philosophers, whose time was devoted to mark their differences and uses. In a word, all around us we perceived the rise of arts, and the dawn of science, in a country which had hitherto lain plunged in one long night of ignorance and barbarism! But this pleasing picture of improvement was not to last, and like a meteor, vanished as suddenly as it was formed. We re-imbarked all our instruments and utensils, and left no other vestiges of our residence, than a piece of ground, from whence we had cleared the wood. We sowed indeed a quantity of European garden seeds of the best kinds; but it is obvious that the shoots of the surrounding weeds will shortly stifle

A a 2   every

every salutary and useful plant, and that in a few years our abode no longer discernible, must return to its original chaotic state.

A new passage out to sea, to the northward, was discovered on the 27th; and it being more convenient for our purpose, than that by which we entered, we weighed on the 29th in the afternoon, in order to stand up the bay towards it. However, the wind falling calm, we were obliged to come to again in 43 fathom, under the north side of an island which we named Long Island, about two leagues from our cove. At nine the next morning we proceeded with a light breeze at west, which with all our boats towing ahead, was scarce sufficient to stem the current; for after struggling till six in the evening, we had gained no more than five miles, and anchored under the same island, only a hundred yards from the shore.

At daylight the next morning we attempted to work to windward, having a gentle air down the bay, but the breeze dying away, we lost ground, and came with the stern so close to the shore, that our ensign-staff was entangled in the branches of trees, on a perpendicular rock, close to which we could find no bottom. We were towed off without receiving any damage, and dropt an anchor below the place we set out from, in a little cove on the north side of Long Island. Here we found two huts, and two fireplaces, which seemed to prove that the place had lately been

been inhabited. During our stay here, we discovered several new birds and fish; and indeed caught some fish which are common to Europe, viz. the horse-mackarel, the greater dog-fish, and the smooth hound *. The captain was taken ill of a fever and violent pain in the groin, which terminated in a rheumatic swelling of the right foot, contracted probably by wading too frequently in the water, and sitting too long in the boat after it, without changing his cloaths.

We were detained in this cove by calms, attended with continual rains, till the 4th in the afternoon, when, assisted by a light breeze at S. W. we entered the reach or passage leading out to sea. The breeze coming a-head just at that time obliged us to anchor again under the east point of the entrance, before a sandy beach. These little delays gave us opportunities of examining the shores, from whence we never failed to bring on board new acquisitions to the vegetable and animal system. During night we had heavy squalls of wind, attended with rain, hail, and snow, and some loud thunder claps. Day-light exhibited to our view all the tops of the hills round us covered with snow. At two o'clock in the afternoon a light breeze sprung up at S. S. W. which carried us down the passage, though not without the help of our boats, to the last point near the opening into the sea, where we anchor-

Tuesday 4.

Wednesday 5.

* Scomber tracherus, squalus canis, & sq. mustelus, Linn.

ed

ed at eight in the evening. The shores on both sides of the passage were steeper than any we had seen before, and formed various wild landscapes, ornamented with numerous little cascades, and many dragon-trees *(dracæna.)*

The captain being confined to the cabin by his rheumatism, sent an officer, accompanied by my father and myself, to explore the southernmost arm, which ran up eastward from our new passage into the interior country. During our absence he ordered the Resolution to be well cleaned and aired with fires between decks, a precaution which ought never to be neglected in a moist and raw climate.

We rowed up this new inlet, were delighted with many cascades on both sides of it, and found a number of good anchoring places, with plenty of fish and wild-fowl. However, the woods consisted chiefly of shrubberies, and began to look very bare, the leaves being mostly shed, and what remained looking faded of a pale yellow colour. These strong marks of approaching winter seemed to be peculiar to this part of the bay, and it is probable that the adjacent high mountains, all which were now crowned with snow, caused their premature appearance. We put into a little cove about two o'clock to broil a few fishes for our dinner, and then went on till it was dark, taking up our night's quarters on a little beach, almost at the head of the inlet. Here we made a fire, but slept very
little

little on account of the cold of the night and the hardness
of our pillows. The next morning we saw a cove, with
a little flat land, to the north of us, which formed the
end of this spacious inlet or arm, about eight miles from
its entrance. Here we amused ourselves with shooting for
some time, and then set out to return towards the Resolution; but the fair weather which had favoured us hitherto,
was now succeeded by a storm at N. W, which blew in hard
squalls, attended with violent showers of rain. We made
shift to row down the arm into the entrance which led to
the sloop, and there sharing the remains of a bottle of rum
among our boat's crew, by way of encouragement, we
entered the hollow sea in the passage. The violence of
the wind, and the height of the short waves were such, that
in spight of our utmost efforts we were thrown above half
a mile to leeward in a few minutes, and narrowly escaped
being swamped. With the greatest difficulty we regained
the inlet out of which we had passed, and about two
o'clock in the afternoon we put into a small snug cove, at
its north entrance. After securing our boat in the best
manner possible, we climbed on a bleak hill, where we
made a fire on a narrow rock, and attempted to broil some
fishes; but though we were soaked with rain, and severely
cut by the wind, yet it was impossible for us to keep near
our fire, of which the flames were continually whirled
about in a vortex by the storm, so that we were forced to
change

change our places every moment, in order to efcape being fcorched or burnt. The ftorm now encrealed to fuch a violence, that we could hardly ftand on this barren fpot; and therefore it was refolved, for our own and the boat's greater fafety, to crofs the cove, and take up our night's quarters in the woods immediately under the lee of the high mountains. Every one of us feized a firebrand and ftepped into the boat, where we made a formidable appearance, as if we were bound on fome defperate expedition. To our great difappointment the woods were almoft worfe than the rock we had left, being fo wet that it was with the utmoft difficulty our fire would burn; we had no fhelter from the heavy rains which came down upon us in double portions from the leaves; and the wind not allowing the fmoke to afcend, we were almoft ftifled with it. Here we lay down on the moift ground, wrapped in wet cloaks thoroughly foaked and cold, fupperlefs, and tormented with rheumatic pains; and, notwithftanding all thefe inconveniencies, fell afleep for a few moments, being entirely exhaufted with fatigue. But about two o'clock we were roufed by a loud thunder-clap. The ftorm was now at its height, and blew a perfect hurricane. The roar of the waves at a diftance was tremendous, and only overcome at times by the agitation of the forefts, and the crafhing fall of huge timber-trees around us. We went to look after our boat, and at that inftant a dreadful

flafh

flash of lightning illuminated the whole arm of the sea; we saw the billows foaming, and furiously rolled above each other in livid mountains; in a word, it seemed as if all nature was hastening to a general catastrophe.

> Non han piu gli elementi ordine o segno,
> S'odono orrendi tuoni, ognor piu cresce
> De' fieri venti il furibondo sdegno.
> Interspa, s'inlividisce il mar la faccia,
> E s'alza contra il ciel che lo minaccia,   TASSONE.

The lightning was instantaneously followed by the most astonishing explosion we had ever heard, reverberated from the broken rocks around us; and our hearts sunk with apprehension lest the ship might be destroyed by the tempest or its concomitant ætherial fires, and ourselves left to perish in an unfrequented part of the world. In this dismal situation we lingered out the night, which seemed the longest we had ever known. At last about six in the morning the violence of the storm abated, we embarked about day break, and reached the vessel soon after, which had been obliged to strike yards and top-masts. The inlet we had now surveyed, received the name of Wet Jacket Arm, from the dreadful night we passed in it. There now remained only one inlet to the northward of this unexplored; and captain Cook, finding himself recovered, set out, immediately after our return, to examine it. He proceeded up about ten miles, and saw nearly the end of this arm, which like the other, contains good harbours and plenty of fresh water, wood, fish, and wild fowl. On his return his people had the wind and heavy rains to struggle with, and all returned on board thoroughly wet, at nine in the

evening. The next morning the sky being clear, but the wind unfavourable for going out to sea, we accompanied captain Cook once more on a shooting party up the new arm, where we spent the whole day, and met with tolerable good sport; but another party, who had taken a different route, came back almost empty-handed.

The wind continuing westerly and blowing very hard, the captain did not think it adviseable to put to sea; but it falling moderate in the afternoon, he made an excursion to an island in the entrance, on which were abundance of seals. He and his party killed ten of them, of which they took five on board, leaving the rest behind them.

The next morning it was pretty clear, the air very cold and sharp, and all the hills covered with snow almost half way down to the water, so that the winter was now fairly set in. A boat was sent to fetch off the seals killed last night, which had been left behind; and in the mean time we weighed and sailed from Dusky Bay, getting clear of the land at noon.

The

1773.
ALLY.

The ſtay which we had made here of ſix weeks, and
four days, together with the abundance of freſh proviſions
which we enjoyed, and the conſtant exerciſe we uſed, had
contributed to recover all thoſe who had been ill of the
ſcurvy at our arrival, and given new ſtrength to the reſt.
However it is much to be doubted, whether we ſhould have
preſerved our health ſo well as we did, without the uſe of
the fermented liquor or ſpruce-beer which we brewed. The
climate of Duſky Bay, is I muſt own, its greateſt inconvenience, and can never be ſuppoſed a healthy one. During
the whole of our ſtay, we had only one week of continued
fair weather, all the reſt of the time-the rain predominated.
But perhaps the climate was leſs noxious to Engliſhmen
than to any other nation, becauſe it is analagous to their
own. Another inconvenience in Duſky Bay is the want
of celery, ſcurvy-graſs, and other antiſcorbutics, which
may be found in great plenty at Queen Charlotte's ſound,
and many parts in New Zeeland. The intricate foreſts
which clothe the ground, the prodigious ſteepneſs of the
hills, which on that account are almoſt incapable, of cultivation, and the virulent bite of ſand-flies, which cauſes
ulcers like the ſmall-pox, are certainly diſagreeable circumſtances; but of ſmall conſequence to thoſe who only
put in here for refreſhment, when compared to the former.
With all its defects, Duſky Bay is one of the fineſt places

in

in New Zeeland, for a set of people to touch at in our situation, exhausted with labours and hardships of long continuance, and deprived of the sight of land above four months. Nothing is more easy than to sail into it, there being no danger except what is visible above water, and so many harbours and coves existing in every part of it, that it is impossible to miss a convenient anchoring-place, where wood, water, fish, and wild-fowl are to be found in plenty.

CHAP.

CHAP. VI.

Paſſage from Duſky Bay to Queen Charlotte's Sound.—Junction with the Adventure.—Transactions during our ſtay there.

HAVING hoiſted in our boat, which returned loaden with ſeals, we ſtood to the northward, with a heavy S. W. ſwell, and numerous ſooty albatroſſes and blue petrels attending us. As we advanced along ſhore, the mountains ſeemed to decreaſe in height, and in four and twenty hours the thermometer roſe $7\frac{1}{2}$ degrees, having been at 46° on the day after we left Duſky Bay, and ſtanding at $53\frac{1}{2}°$ the next morning at eight o'clock.

Tueſday 11.

On the 14th, being off Cape Foul-wind, our favourable gale left us, as if it meant to authenticate the propriety of the denomination, and we really had a contrary wind. It blew a hard gale all the 16th, attended with heavy rains, and we kept plying the whole day, making one of our boards cloſe in ſhore under Rock's Point.

Thurſday 13.

Sunday 16.

At four o'clock in the morning on the 17th we ſtood to the eaſtward with a fair wind, ſo that we were abreaſt of Cape Farewell at eight o'clock. Here we ſaw the land appearing low and ſandy near the ſea-ſhore, though it roſe into high ſnow-capt mountains in the interior parts. Vaſt flocks of the little diving petrel, (*procellaria tridactyla,*) were ſeen.

1772.
Mar.

seen fluttering on the surface of the sea, or sitting on it,
or diving to confiderable diftances with amazing agility.
They feemed exactly the fame which we had feen on the
29th of January and the 8th of February, in the latitude
of 48° S. when we were in fearch of M. Kerguelen's
Iflands.

In the afternoon, about four o'clock, we were nearly
oppofite Cape Stephens, and had little or no wind. We
obferved thick clouds to the S. W. about that time, and
faw that it rained on all the fouthern parts of that cape.
On a fudden a whitifh fpot appeared on the fea in that
quarter, and a column arofe out of it, looking like a glafs
tube; another feemed to come down from the clouds to
meet this, and they made a coalition, forming what is
commonly called a water-fpout. A little while after we
took notice of three other columns, which were formed
in the fame manner as the firft. The neareft of all thefe
was about three miles diftant, and its apparent diameter, as
far as we could guefs, might be about feventy fathom at
the bafe. We found our thermometer at 56° when this
phænomenon firft took its rife. The nature of water-fpouts
and their caufes being hitherto very little known, we were
extremely attentive to mark every little circumftance attendant on this appearance. Their bafe, where the water
of the fea was violently agitated, and rofe in a fpiral form
in vapours, was a broad fpot, which looked bright and
                                                yellowifh

1773.
MAY.

yellowish when illuminated by the sun. The column was of a cylindrical form, rather encreasing in width towards the upper extremity. These columns moved forward on the surface of the sea, and the clouds not following them with equal rapidity, they assumed a bent or incurvated shape, and frequently appeared crossing each other, evidently proceeding in different directions; from whence we concluded, that it being calm, each of these water-spouts caused a wind of its own. At last they broke one after another, being probably too much distended by the difference between their motion and that of the clouds. In proportion as the clouds came nearer to us, the sea appeared more and more covered with short broken waves, and the wind continually veered all round the compass, without fixing in any point. We soon saw a spot on the sea, within two hundred fathom of us, in a violent agitation. The water, in a space of fifty or sixty fathoms, moved towards the centre, and there rising into vapour, by the force of the whirling motion, ascended in a spiral form towards the clouds. Some hailstones fell on board about this time, and the clouds looked exceedingly black and louring above us. Directly over the whirl-pool, if I may so call the agitated spot on the sea, a cloud gradually tapered into a long slender tube, which seemed to descend to meet the rising spiral, and soon united with it into a strait column of a cylindrical form. We could distinctly observe the

water

water hurled upwards with the greatest violence in a spiral, and it appeared that it left a hollow space in the centre; so that we concluded the water only formed a hollow tube, instead of a solid column. We were strongly confirmed in this belief by the colour, which was exactly like any hollow glass-tube. After some time the last water-spout was incurvated and broke like the others, with this difference, that its disjunction was attended with a flash of lightning, but no explosion was heard. Our situation during all this time was very dangerous and alarming; a phænomenon which carried so much terrific majesty in it, and connected as it were the sea with the clouds, made our oldest mariners uneasy and at a loss how to behave; for most of them, though they had viewed water-spouts at a distance, yet had never been so beset with them as we were; and all without exception had heard dreadful accounts of their pernicious effects, when they happened to break over a ship. We prepared indeed for the worst, by cluing up our topsails; but it was the general opinion that our masts and yards must have gone to wreck if we had been drawn into the vortex. It was hinted that firing a gun had commonly succeeded in breaking water-spouts, by the strong vibration it causes in the air; and accordingly a four-pounder was ordered to be got ready, but our people being, as usual, very dilatory about it, the danger was past before we could try this experiment. How far

electricity

electricity may be confidered as the caufe of this phænomenon, we could not determine with any precifion; fo much
however feems certain, that it has fome connection with it,
from the flaſh of lightning, which was plainly obferved at
the burfting of the laſt column. The whole time, from
their firſt appearance to the diffolution of the laſt, was
about three quarters of an hour. It was five o'clock when
the latter happened, and the thermometer then flood at
54° or 2½ degrees lower, than when they began to make
their appearance. The depth of water we had under us
was thirty-fix fathom. The place we were in was analogous to moſt places where water-fpouts have been obferved, inafmuch as it was in a narrow fea or ſtrait. Dr.
Shaw and Thevenot faw them in the Mediterranean and
Perfian Gulph; and they are common in the Weſt Indies,
the Straits of Malacca, and the Chinefe fea. Upon the
whole, we were not fortunate enough to make any remarkable difcoveries in regard to this phænomenon; all
our obfervations only tend to confirm the facts already noticed by others, and which are fo largely commented upon
by the learned Dr. Benjamin Franklin, F. R. S. His ingenious hypothefis, that whirlwinds and water-fpouts have a
common origin, has not been invalidated by our obfervations. We refer our philofophical readers to his papers,
as containing the moſt complete and fatisfactory account
of water-fpouts *.

* See his Experiments on Electricity, &c. 4to. fifth edition, London, 1774.

About five o'clock the next morning we opened Queen Charlotte's Sound, and about seven we saw three flashes rising from the south end of the *Motu-Aro*, where a *hippab*, or strong hold of the natives, was situated, which is described in Lieutenant Cook's voyage in the Endeavour *. We immediately conceived that they were signals made by Europeans, and probably by our friends in the Adventure; and upon firing some four-pounders, had the pleasure of being answered out of the Ship Cove, opposite the island. Towards noon we could discern our old consort at anchor; and soon after were met by several of her officers, who brought us a present of fresh fish, and gave us an account of what had happened to them after our separation. In the afternoon it fell calm, so that we were obliged to be towed into the cove, where we anchored at seven in the evening. In the mean time Captain Furneaux came on board, and testified his satisfaction at rejoining us, by a salute of thirteen guns, which our people cheerfully returned. Those who have been in situations similar to ours, may form an adequate idea of the reciprocal pleasure which this meeting produced. It was heightened on both sides, by the recent impressions of accumulated dangers to which our separate courses had exposed us, and which under Providence we had happily escaped.

* See Hawkesworth's Compilation, vol. II. p. 395, 400.

The

The Adventure, after lofing our company, had continued her courfe to the northward of us, between the latitudes of 50° and 54° fouth, experiencing very heavy gales from the weftward during the whole time. On the 28th of February, being in about 122° of longitude weft from Greenwich, Captain Furneaux thought it advifeable gradually to defcend into the latitude of Diemen's Land, or the extremity of New Holland, difcovered by Abel Janffen Tafman in November 1642. On the 9th of March he fell in with the S. W. part of this coaft, and running along its fouthern extremity, came to an anchor on the 11th in the afternoon, in a bay on the eaft fide, which he called Adventure Bay, and which is probably the fame where Tafman lay at anchor, diftinguifhed by the name of Frederick Henry Day. The fouthern extremities of this coaft confifted of large broken maffes of barren and blackifh rocks, refembling the extreme points of the African and American continents. The land round the bay rofe in fandy hillocks, of which the innermoft were covered with various forts of trees, rather remote from each other, and without any brufh-wood. They alfo found a lake of frefh water on the weft fide, covered with great flocks of wild-ducks and other aquatic fowls. Several iflands in the offing to the N E. along fhore, were of a moderate height, and likewife covered with wood. Tafman probably took them for one great ifland, which in his charts

C c 2

bears

bears the name of Maria's Ifland. The Adventure lay only
three days in this bay, during which Captain Furneaux
took in a fmall quantity of frefh water, and collected feveral curious animals, among which was a fpecies of Viverra,
and a fine white hawk. Our Europeans perceived no inhabitants during their ftay, but thought they obferved fome
fmoke at a great diftance in the country.

On the 15th in the evening they weighed and failed out
of Adventure Bay, ftanding along fhore to the northward.
They found it confifted of fandy hills of a moderate height,
but faw at the fame time fome much higher in the interior
country. At different parts of this coaft they met with feveral iflands, particularly thofe which Tafman named
Schouten's and Vander Lyn's Iflands. About the latitude
of 41° 15' fouth, they opened a little bay, which, on account of feveral fires, probably lighted by the natives, they
named the Bay of Fires. They continued examining the
coaft, not without running fome danger from numerous
fhoals, till the 19th of March at noon, when being in the
latitude of 39° 20' fouth, and ftill feeing the land about
eight leagues to the north-weftward, they concluded that
Diemen's Land was connected with the continent of New
Holland, and directed their courfe towards the rendezvous at
New Zeeland. However, as they had been obliged, by the
frequency of fhoals, to keep out of fight of the coaft feveral
times, and there remained a fpace of twenty leagues from
the

the northernmost land they had seen, to Point Hicks, the
southern boundary of captain Cook's discoveries in the Endeavour; it is still undetermined, whether a strait or passage
does not exist between the main of New Holland and Diemen's Land, though the appearance of quadrupeds upon
the latter, rather seems to favour the idea of their being
connected together. Be this as it may, there is perhaps
no part of the world which so well deserves future investigation as the great continent of New Holland, of which
we do not yet know the whole outline, and of whose productions we are in a manner entirely ignorant. Its inhabitants, from the accounts of all the voyagers who have
visited them, are but few in number, probably dwell on the
sea-coasts only, go perfectly naked, and seem by all description to lead a more savage life than any nation in
warm climates. There is consequently a vast interior space
of ground, equal to the continent of Europe, and in great
measure situated between the tropics, entirely unknown,
and perhaps uninhabited: nothing is more certain, from
the vast variety of animal and vegetable productions, collected on its sea-coasts in captain Cook's voyage in the Endeavour, than that the inner countries contain immense
treasures of natural knowledge, which must of course become of infinite use to the civilized nation, which shall first
attempt to go in search of them. The south-west corner
of

of this continent, which hitherto remains wholly unexplored, may perhaps open a way to the heart of the country; for it is not likely, that so great an extent of land, situated under the tropic, should be destitute of a great river, and no part of the coast seems better situated than that for its passage into the sea.

After leaving this coast, the Adventure continued fifteen days at sea, on account of contrary winds, and at length made the coast of New Zeeland, near Rock's Point, on the southern island, on the third of April, at six in the morning, and came to an anchor at Ship Cove, Queen Charlotte's Sound, on the 7th.

During their stay here, they had made the same establishments on shore as we had done at Dusky Bay, except the brewery, which they were not yet acquainted with. They had found the *hippah*, or strong-hold of the natives, at the southern end of Motu-Aro forsaken, and their astronomer had fixed his observatory upon it. The inhabitants of this sound, who amount to some hundred persons, in several distinct and independent parties, often at variance with each other, had begun an intercourse with them, and paid them several visits, coming from the interior parts. They had been extremely well received, and did not hesitate to come on board, where they eat freely of the sailor's provisions, showing a particular liking to our biscuit, and

pease-

pease-soup. They had brought with them great quantities of their clothing, tools, and weapons, which they eagerly exchanged for nails, hatchets, and cloth.

On the 11th of May, being the same day we sailed out of Dusky Bay, several of the Adventure's people, who were at work on shore, or dispersed on shooting parties, distinctly felt a shock of an earthquake; but those who remained on board, did not perceive any thing of it. This circumstance may serve to evince the probability of volcanoes on New Zeeland, as these two great phænomena on our globe seem to be closely connected together.

We arrived in Queen Charlotte's Sound, at the time when the Adventure's crew began to despair of ever meeting with us again, and had made preparations to spend the whole winter in this harbour, in order to proceed to the eastward, with the ensuing spring, to explore the South Sea in high latitudes. Captain Cook, however, was by no means inclined to lie inactive during so many months, especially as he knew, that considerable refreshments were to be had at the Society Isles, which he had visited in his former voyage. He therefore gave directions to put both sloops in condition to go to sea, as soon as possible; and the Resolution being entirely prepared for that purpose, her crew assisted that of the Adventure for the sake of greater dispatch.

We

1773.
MAY.
Wednesd. 19.

We began our excursions the day after our arrival, and found the productions of the forests very similar to those of Dusky Bay, but the season and climate infinitely more favourable to our botanical researches. We were fortunate enough to meet with several species of plants still in flower, and also found some birds, which we had not seen before. But the antiscorbutic plants, which grew on every beach, gave this port the most distinguished advantage over our first place of refreshment. We immediately gathered vast quantities of wild celery, and of a well-tasted scurvy-grass (*lepidium*) which were daily boiled with some oat-meal or wheat for breakfast, and with pease-soup for dinner; and the people on board the Adventure, who had hitherto not known the use of these greens, now followed our example. We also found a species of sow-thistle (*sonchus oleraceus,*) and a kind of plant which our people called lamb's quarters, (*tetragonia cornuta*[*],) which we frequently used as sallads; and if we had not such plenty of wild-fowl and fishes as at Dusky Bay, we were amply recompensed by these excellent vegetables. The spruce and the tea-tree of New Zeeland likewise grew in great plenty hereabouts, and we taught our friends to make use of both for their refreshment.

* See Hawkesworth, vol. III. p. 44t.

The

The next day we went to the Hippah, or fortification of the natives, where Mr. Bailey, the astronomer of the Adventure had fixed his observatory. It is situated on a steep insulated rock, which is accessible only in one place, by a narrow difficult path, where two persons cannot go abreast. At the top it had been surrounded by some palisadoes, but these were in most parts removed, and had been used for fuel by our people. The huts of the natives stood promiscuously within the enclosure, and had no walls, but consisted only of a roof, which rose into a steep ridge. The inner skeletons of these huts were branches of trees plaited so as to resemble hurdles; on these they had laid the bark of trees, and covered the whole with the rough fibres of the flag, or New Zeeland flax-plant. We were told, that the people from the Adventure had found them exceeding full of vermin, and particularly fleas, from which it should seem that they had been but lately inhabited; and indeed it is not unlikely, that all these strong places are only the occasional abode of the natives, in case of danger from their enemies; and that they forsake them, whenever their personal safety does not require their residence. Our fellow-voyagers likewise found immense numbers of rats upon the Hippah rock, so that they were obliged to put some large jars in the ground, level with the surface, into which these vermin fell during night, by running backwards and forwards; and great number of them were caught in this

VOL. I.   D d   manner.

manner. It is therefore very probable, that rats are indigenous in New Zeeland, or at least that their arrival there,
is prior to its discovery by European navigators. Captain
Furneaux shewed us several spots of ground on the top
of this rock, which he had ordered to be dug, and on
which he had sown a great variety of garden-seeds; these
succeeded so well that we frequently had sallads, and many
dishes of European greens at our table, notwithstanding
the season of winter was now far advanced. But the
climate in this part of New Zeeland is extremely mild,
when compared to that of Dusky Bay; and notwithstanding
the vicinity of the snowy mountains, I am inclined to believe it seldom freezes hard in Queen Charlotte's Sound;
at least we experienced no frost during our continuance
there to the 6th of June.

On the 22d we went over to an island in the sound,
to which captain Cook had given the name of Long Island
in his former voyage. It consists of one long ridge, of
which the sides are steep, and the back or top nearly level,
though in most places very narrow. On its N. W. side
we saw a fine beach, surrounding a little piece of flat land,
of which the greatest part was marshy, and covered with
various grasses; the rest was full of antiscorbutics, and the
New Zeeland flax-plant *(phormium)*, growing round some
old abandoned huts of the natives. We cleared some spots
of ground here, and sowed European garden seeds on them,
                                                      which

which we thought were likely to thrive in this place. We also climbed to the top of the ridge, which we found covered with dry grasses, intermixed with some low, shrubby plants; and among them a number of quails exactly like those of Europe, had their residence. Several deep and narrow glens which ran down the sides of the ridge to the sea, were filled with trees, shrubs, and climbers, the haunt of numerous small birds, and of several falcons; but where the cliffs were perpendicular, or hanging over the water, great flocks of a beautiful sort of shags, built their nests on every little broken rock, or if possible in small cavities about a foot square, which seemed in a few instances to be enlarged by the birds themselves. The argillaceous stone, of which most of the hills about Queen Charlotte's Sound consisted, is sometimes sufficiently soft for that purpose. It runs in oblique strata, commonly dipping a little towards the south, is of a greenish-grey, or bluish, or yellowish-brown colour, and sometimes contains veins of white quartz. A green talcous or nephritic stone, is also found in this kind of rock, and when very hard, capable of polish, and semi-transparent; it is used by the natives for chissels, hatchets, and sometimes for panoo-pattoos: it is of the same species which jewellers call the jadde. Several softer sorts of this stone, perfectly opaque, and of a pale green colour, are more numerous than the flinty semi-transparent kind; and several species of horn-

stone

1773.
MAY.

stone and argillaceous slate likewise are seen running in great strata through some of the mountains. The latter is commonly found in great quantity, and broken pieces, on the sea beeches, and is what our seamen call shingle, by which name it is distinguished in the account of captain Cook's former voyage. On these beaches we also met with several sorts of flinty stones and pebbles, and some loose pieces of black, compact, and ponderous basaltes, of which the natives form some of their short clubs, called pattoo-pattoos. In many places we likewise saw strata of a blackish *saxum* Lin. consisting of a black and compact mica or glimmer, intermixed with minute particles of quartz. The argillaceous slate is sometimes found of a rusty colour, which seems evidently to rise from irony particles; and from this circumstance, and the variety of minerals just enumerated, there is great reason to suppose that this part of New Zeeland contains iron ore, and perhaps several other metallic bodies. Before we left this place, we found some small pieces of a whitish pumice-stone on the sea-shore, which, together with the basaltine lava, strongly confirm the existence of volcanoes in New Zeeland.

Sunday 23.

On the 23d in the morning, two small canoes came towards us, in which were five men of the natives, the first we had seen since the arrival of our sloop in this harbour. Their appearance was nearly the same as that

of

of the Dusky Bay people, with this difference, that they seemed much more familiar and unconcerned. We bought some fish of them, and likewise made them some presents, conducting them into the cabin, as they did not hesitate to come on board. Seeing us sit down to dinner, they freely partook of our provisions, but drank pure water, refusing to touch either wine or brandy. They were so restless, that they removed from our table to that of the officers in the steerage, where they likewise eat with great appetite, and drank great quantities of water sweetened with sugar, of which they were remarkably fond. Every thing they saw, or could lay hands upon they coveted, but upon the least hint, that we either could not, or would not part with what they had taken up, they laid it down without reluctance. Glass bottles, which they called taw-haw, were however particularly valuable to them; and whenever they saw any of them, they always pointed to them, and then moved the hand to their breast, pronouncing the word *mòkh*, by which they used to express their desire of possessing any thing. Among the variety of little presents we made them they did not notice beads, ribbons, white paper, &c. but were very eager after iron, nails, and hatchets; a proof that the intrinsic value of these tools cannot fail to make an impression on the minds of these people in the long run, though they were at first indifferent to them, as not knowing their use and durability.

bility. Some of our people having made use of their canoes in the afternoon to transport themselves to the shore, they came into the cabin complaining to the captain, whose authority over the rest they very well conceived; and their embarkations being restored to them, they all went away highly pleased.

The next morning at day-break they returned, but brought four other persons with them, one of them a woman, with some children, and traded as usual about the ships. The captains embarked with us after breakfast, in order to visit an extensive inlet on the northern shore of the sound, which was called West Bay in the Endeavour's voyage. On our way we met a double canoe, manned with thirteen persons, who, coming along side, made acquaintance with Captain Cook, and seemed to recollect him, by enquiring for Tupaya, the native of O-Taheitee, whom he had taken on board during his former voyage, and who had lived to visit this country with him. When they were told that he was dead, they seemed much concerned, and pronounced some words in a plaintive tone. We made signs for them to go on board the vessels lying in Ship Cove; but when they saw us going on to the south, they returned to the cove from whence they came.

We found the country not quite so steep as at the southern extremity of New Zeeland, and the hills near the sea-side were in general of an inferior height. In most parts,
however,

however, they were covered with forests, equally intricate
and impenetrable as those of Dusky Bay, but containing a
greater number of pigeons, parrots, and small birds,
which perhaps abandon that rude climate during the cold
season, and pass their winter in these milder regions.
Oyster-catchers or sea-pies, and various sorts of shags,
likewise enlivened the sea shores here, but ducks were extremely scarce.   West Bay contains a number of fine coves,
each of which affords excellent anchorage; the hills rise
gently all round it, covered with shrubs and trees, and
many of their summits are clear of woods, but overgrown with a common species of fern, *(acrosticum furcatum.)*
This is likewise the case with many islands in the sound,
and great part of the south-east shore of the sound from
Cape Koamaroo to East Bay.   After collecting a number of
new plants, among which was a species of pepper, very
much resembling ginger in the taste, and shooting many
birds of all sorts, we returned on board late in the evening.

The launch, which had been sent out in the morning to
an adjacent cove, in order to cut greens for the ship's
company and some grass for our goats and sheep, did not
return that day; but staying out all the next likewise, we
began to be very uneasy about the twelve people in her,
among whom were our third lieutenant, the lieutenant of
marines, Mr. Hodges, the carpenter, and the gunner. Our
apprehensions were the more just, as the wind and wea-

ther

ther had been favourable for their return from almost any part of the bay, till the morning of the 25th; soon after which it began to be, very rainy and stormy. On the day we had gone to West Bay, a large canoe with twelve of the natives came from the north to our ship, and after selling a variety of their dresses, some stone hatchets, clubs, spears, and even paddles, they returned the way they came.

On the 26th, after noon, the weather being somewhat cleared up, our launch arrived on board, but all the people in her were exhausted with fatigue and hunger. All the provision they had taken out with them consisted of three biscuits and a bottle of brandy; and they had not been able to succeed in catching a single fish during the tempestuous weather. After being tossed about by the waves, attempting in vain to return to the vessels, they had put into a cove, on which they found a few deserted huts of the natives, where they took shelter, and just kept themselves from starving by eating a few muscles that adhered to the rocks.

The next morning we made our researches round the bottom of the cove, in quest of plants and birds; and in the afternoon we went out along the rocky shores towards Point Jackson, to kill some shags, which we had now learnt to relish instead of ducks. Between these two excursions we received another visit of the Indian family, whom we had seen before, on the 23d. They seemed to be come for

no

1771.
Nov.

no other purpofe than that of eating with us, having brought nothing with them to exchange for our iron-work. We now enquired for their names, but they were a long time before they could underſtand us; however, comprehending our meaning at laſt, they gave us a collection of words, which had a ſingular mixture of gutturals and vowels. The oldeſt among them was called Towahàngha; the others Kotughà-a, Koghoàà, Khoàà, Kollàkh, and Taywaherùa. This laſt was a boy about twelve or fourteen years of age, who had a very promiſing countenance, and ſeemed to be the livelieſt and moſt intelligent among them. He came into the cabin and dined with us, eating very voraciouſly of a ſhag-pye, of which, contrary to our expectation, he preferred the cruſt. The captain offered him ſome Madeira wine, of which he drank ſomething more than one glaſs, making a great many wry faces at firſt. A bottle of a very ſweet Cape wine being brought upon the table, a glaſs was filled out to him, which he reliſhed ſo well that he was continually licking his lips, and deſired to have another, which he likewiſe drank off. This draught began to elevate his ſpirits, and his tongue ran on with great volubility. He capered about the cabin, inſiſted on having the captain's boatcloak, which lay on a chair, and was much vexed at the refuſal; he next deſired one of the empty bottles, and this requeſt likewiſe proving fruitleſs, he went out of the cabin highly offended. On deck he faw fome of our fervants folding up linen which had been hung out to dry, and immediately feized on a table-cloth; but this being taken from him, his paffion was at the higheft pitch, he ftamped, threatened, then grumbled, or rather grunted awhile, and at laft became fo fullen that he would not fpeak a word. The impatient temper of this nation never appeared more diftinctly than in this boy's conduct; but at the fame time we had room to confider, feeing the effect of ftrong liquors upon him, how fortunate it was that they were ufed to no kind of intoxicating draught, which would perhaps ferve to make their temper ftill more fierce and ungovernable than it is at prefent.

About thirty natives furrounded us in feveral canoes the next morning, and brought a few of their tools and weapons to fell, for which they received great quantities of our goods in exchange, owing to the eagernefs with which our crews outbid each other. There were a number of women among them, whofe lips were of a blackifh blue colour, by punctuation; and their cheeks were painted of a lively red, with a mixture of ruddle and oil. Like thofe at Dufky Bay, they commonly had flender and bandy legs, with large knees; defects which evidently are deducible from the little exercife they ufe, and their mode of fitting crofs-legged and cramped up almoft perpetually in canoes. Their colour was of a clear brown, between the olive and

mahogany

mahogany hues, their hair jetty black, the faces round, the nose and lips rather thick but not flat, their black eyes sometimes lively and not without expression; the whole upper part of their figure was not disproportionate, and their assemblage of features not absolutely forbidding. Our crews, who had not conversed with women since our departure from the Cape, found these ladies very agreeable; and from the manner in which their advances were received, it appeared very plainly that chastity was not rigorously observed here, and that the sex were far from being impregnable. However their favours did not depend upon their own inclination, but the men, as absolute masters, were always to be consulted upon the occasion; if a spike-nail, or a shirt, or a similar present had been given for their connivance, the lady was at liberty to make her lover happy, and to exact, if possible, the tribute of another present for herself. Some among them, however, submitted with reluctance to this vile prostitution; and, but for the authority and menaces of the men, would not have complied with the desires of a set of people who could, with unconcern, behold their tears and hear their complaints. Whether the members of a civilized society, who could act such a brutal part, or the barbarians who could force their own women to submit to such indignity, deserve the greatest abhorrence, is a question not easily to be decided. Encouraged by the lucrative nature of this

E e 2   infamous

infamous commerce, the New Zeelanders went through the
whole veſſel, offering their daughters and ſiſters promiſcu-
ouſly to every perſon's embraces, in exchange for our iron
tools, which they knew could not be purchaſed at an
eaſier rate.   It does not appear that their married women
were ever ſuffered to have this kind of intercourſe with
our people.   Their ideas of female chaſtity are, in this reſpect, ſo different from ours, that a girl may favour a
number of lovers without any detriment to her character;
but if ſhe marries, conjugal fidelity is exacted from her
with the greateſt rigour.   It may therefore be alledged,
that as the New Zeelanders place no value on the conti-
nence of their unmarried women, the arrival of Europeans
among them, did not injure their moral characters in this
reſpect; but we doubt whether they ever debaſed themſelves ſo much as to make a trade of their women, before
we created new wants by ſhewing them iron-tools; for the
poſſeſſion of which they do not heſitate to commit an
action that, in our eyes, deprives them of the very ſhadow
of ſenſibility.

It is unhappy enough that the unavoidable conſequence of all our voyages of diſcovery, has always
been the loſs of a number of innocent lives; but this
heavy injury done to the little uncivilized communities
which Europeans have viſited, is trifling when compared
to the irretrievable harm entailed upon them by corrupting

their

their morals. If thefe evils were in fome meafure compenfated by the introduction of fome real benefit in thefe countries, or by the abolition of fome other immoral cuftoms among their inhabitants, we might at leaft comfort ourfelves, that what they loft on one hand, they gained on the other; but I fear that hitherto our intercourfe has been wholly difadvantageous to the nations of the South Seas; and that thofe communities have been the leaft injured, who have always kept aloof from us, and whofe jealous difpofition did not fuffer our failors to become too familiar among them, as if they had perceived in their countenances that levity of difpofition, and that fpirit of debauchery, with which they are generally reproached.

Several of thefe people were invited into the cabin, where Mr. Hodges applied himfelf to fketch the moft characteriftic faces, while we prevailed on them to fit ftill for a few moments, keeping their attention engaged, by a variety of trifles which we fhewed, and fome of which we prefented to them. We found feveral very expreffive countenances among them, particularly fome old men, with grey or white heads and beards; and fome young men, with amazing bufhy hair, which hung wildly over their faces, and increafed their natural favage looks. The ftature of thefe people was middle-fized in general, and their form and colour almoft entirely the fame as that of the Dufky Bay people; their drefs was likewife made in the fame man-

ner

ner of the flax-plant, but never interwoven with feathers, in lieu of which they had bits of dog-skin at the four corners of their cloaks, which the others were not fortunate enough to possess. The *bogbee-bogbee*, or shaggy-cloak, which hangs round their neck like a thatch of straw*, was almost constantly worn by them, on account of the season, during which the air began to be sharp, and rains were very frequent. But their other kinds of cloth ‡ were here commonly old, dirty, and not so neatly wrought as they are described in captain Cook's first voyage. The men wore their hair hanging in a very slovenly manner about them, but the women had theirs cut short, which seems to be the general practice among them. They also wore the head-dress, or cap of brown feathers, mentioned in the account of captain Cook's former voyage. After these people had been on board a few hours, they began to steal, and secrete every thing they could lay their hands on. Several of them were discovered in conveying away a large four-hour glass, a lamp, some handkerchiefs, and some knives; upon which they were ignominiously turned out of the sloop, and never permitted to come on board again. They felt the whole weight of shame, which this proceeding brought upon them; and their fiery temper, which cannot brook any humiliation, was up in arms at this

* See Hawkesworth's Compilation, vol. III. p. 453, &c.
‡ Ibid. p. 455.

punish-

1771.
MAY.

punishment; so that one of them uttered threats, and made violent gestures in his canoe. In the evening they all went on shore, abreast of the sloops, and made some temporary huts of the branches of trees, near which they hawled their canoes on the dry land, and made fires, over which they prepared their suppers. Their meals consisted of some fresh fishes, which they had caught in their canoes not far from shore, with a kind of scoop-net, described in captain Cook's former voyage, which they managed with a dexterity peculiar to themselves.

The next morning we had fine mild weather, and Sunday 19. made a trip over to Long Island, in order to look after some hay, which our people had cut there, and to collect greens for the ship's company, near the huts which the natives had abandoned. We were fortunate enough at the same time to find some new plants, and shoot several little birds, different from those which had hitherto fallen into our hands. In the afternoon, many of our sailors were allowed to go on shore, among the natives, where they traded for curiosities, and purchased the embraces of the ladies, notwithstanding the disgust which their uncleanliness inspired. Their custom of painting their cheeks with ochre and oil, was alone sufficient to deter the more sensible from such intimate connections with them; and if we add to this a certain stench which announced them even at a distance, and the abundance of vermin which not only infested

fested their hair, but also crawled on their clothes, and which they occasionally cracked between their teeth, it is astonishing that persons should be found, who could gratify an animal appetite with such loathsome objects, whom a civilized education and national customs should have taught them to hold in abhorrence.

———————— Unde

Hæc tetigit, Gradive, tuos urtica nepotes?   Juvenal.

Before they returned on board again, a woman stole a jacket belonging to one of our sailors, and gave it to a young fellow of her own nation. The owner finding it in the young man's hands, took it from him, upon which he received several blows with the fist. These he believed were meant in joke, but as he was advancing to the water-side, in order to step into the boat, the native threw several large stones at him. The sailor was rouzed, and returning to the fellow, began to box him after the English manner, and in a few moments had given the New Zeelander a black eye, and bloody nose; upon which the latter, to all appearance much terrified, declined the combat, and ran off.

Captain Cook, who was determined to omit nothing which might tend to the preservation of European garden-plants in this country, prepared the soil, sowed seeds, and transplanted the young plants in four or five different parts

of

of this found. He had cultivated a fpot of ground on the
beach of Long Ifland, another on the Hippah rock, two
more on the Motu-Aro, and one of confiderable extent
at the bottom of Ship Cove, where our veffels lay at anchor.
He chiefly endeavoured to raife fuch vegetables as have
ufeful and nutritive roots, and among them particularly
potatoes, of which we had been able to preferve but few in
a ftate of vegetation. He had likewife fown corn of feveral forts, beans, kidney-beans, and peafe, and devoted the
latter part of his ftay in great meafure to thefe occupations.

Early on the firft of June feveral canoes full of natives
came on board, whom we had not feen before. Their canoes were of different fizes, and three of them had fails,
which are but feldom feen among them. The fail confifted
of a large triangular mat, and was fixed to a maft, and a
boom joining below in an acute angle, which could both be
ftruck with the greateft facility. The upper edge, or broadeft
part of the fail, had five tufts of brown feathers on its extremity. The bottom of thefe canoes confifted of a long
hollow trunk of a tree, and the fides were made of feveral
boards or planks above each other, which were united by
means of a number of ftrings of the New Zeeland flax-
plant, paffed through fmall holes, and tied very faft. The
feams between them are caulked with the downy or woolly
fubftance of the reed-mace *(typha latifolia.)* Some of the ca-

noes were double, that is, two fastened along side of each other, by means of transverse sticks, lashed on with ropes; but where that was not the case, they had an outrigger, or narrow piece of plank fixed parallel to one side of the canoe, by means of transverse poles, to prevent their oversetting. All those we now saw had not that profusion of carving and fine workmanship, mentioned in captain Cook's first voyage, which he observed in the canoes of the northern islands; but seemed rather old, and worn out; they were not, however, different in the general conformation from those described there, and always had the distorted human face at the head, the high stern, and the neat sharp-pointed paddles. The people in them brought for sale several ornaments, which were new to us, especially pieces of green nephritic stone, cut into various forms. Some were of a flat shape, with a sharp edge, and served as the blades of hatchets, or adzes; some were formed into long pieces, which are hung into the ear; others were little chissels, inserted in a wooden handle, and again others were cut out with great labour into a contorted and squatted figure, something resembling the carricature of a man, in which a pair of monstrous eyes were inserted, made of the mother of pearl of an ear-shell. This last, which they called *heegbre*, was worn by persons of both sexes, hanging on the breast, from a string passed about the neck, and may perhaps relate to some religious matters. They sold us an apron,

made

made of their close-wrought cloth, covered with red feathers, faced with white dog-skin, and ornamented with
pieces of the ear-shell, which is said to be worn by the women in their dances. They brought a number of their
fish-hooks, which are of a remarkable clumsy form, made
of wood, and barbed with a piece of bone, which was jag-
ged, and which they assured us was human bone. Several
rows of human teeth, drawn on a thread, hung on their
breasts, in the place of, or along with the *teegbee*, but they
readily sold them to us, in exchange for iron tools, or
trinkets. A good many dogs were observed in their canoes, which they seemed very fond of, and kept tied
with a string, round their middle; they were of a rough
long-haired sort, with pricked ears, and much resembled
the common shepherd's cur, or count Buffon's *chien de berger*
(see his Hist. Nat.) They were of different colours, some
spotted, some quite black, and others perfectly white.
The food which these dogs receive is fish, or the same as
their masters live on, who afterwards eat their flesh, and
employ the fur in various ornaments and dresses. They
sold us several of these animals, among which the old ones
coming into our possession, became extremely sulky, and refused to take any sustenance, but some young ones soon
accustomed themselves to our provisions. Several of the
New Zeelanders came into the vessel, and some were conducted into the cabin, where they received some presents;

but

but none of them shewed that astonishment, and that degree of reflection and attention, which our old friend at Dusky Bay had manifested on coming aboard. Some of them were strangely marked in the face with deeply excavated spiral lines; and one of them in particular, a tall and strong man, and nearly middle-aged, had these marks very regular on his chin, cheeks, forehead, and nose, so that his beard, which would otherwise have been very thick, now consisted only of a few straggling hairs. This man's name was Tringho-Waya, and he seemed to have some authority with his people, which was more than we had hitherto observed among the small number who had visited us. The chief object of their commerce were shirts and bottles, of which last they were remarkably fond; perhaps because they have nothing in which to keep liquids, except a minute kind of calabash or gourd, which grows only in the northern island, and was extremely scarce among the people in Queen Charlotte's Sound. They were not inclined however to make disadvantageous bargains, and demanded the best price for every little trifle which they offered for sale, though they were never offended with a refusal. Some of them being in remarkable good spirits, gave us a *hriva*, or dance, on the quarter-deck. They placed themselves in a row, and parted with their shaggy upper garments: one of them sung some words in a rude manner, and all the rest accompanied the gestures

he

1773.
JUNE.

be made, alternately extending their arms, and stamping with their feet in a violent and almost frantic manner. The last words which we might suppose the burden of the fong, or a chorus, they all repeated together; and we could eafily diftinguifh fome fort of metre in them, but were not fure they had rhimes. The mufic was extremely rough, and of no great extent in thefe kinds of fongs. In the evening they all went off again, and returned to the upper part of the found from whence they came.

The next morning we accompanied the captains Cook Wednefday 1. and Furneaux to Eaft Bay, and Grafs Cove, where they intended to collect a load of antifcorbutic greens. We had not only endeavoured to leave ufeful European roots in this country, but we were likewife attentive to flock its wilds with animals, which in time might become beneficial to the natives, and to future generations of navigators. To this purpofe captain Furneaux had already fent a boar and two fows to Canibal Cove, where they had been turned into the woods to range at their own pleafure; and we now deprived ourfelves, with the fame view, of a pair of goats, male and female, which we left in an unfrequented part of Eaft Bay. Thefe places had been fixed upon, in hopes that our new colonifts would there remain unmolefted by the natives, who indeed were the only enemies they had to fear, as their inconfiderate and barbarous temper would not fuffer them to make any reflection on the

the advantages which future ages might reap from the propagation of such a valuable race of animals. On this excursion we saw a large animal in the water about Grass Cove, which seemed to be a sea-lion by its magnitude, but which we could not get a shot at. We had already discovered a small species of bats in the woods, so that the list of the indigenous quadrupeds in New Zeeland was increased to five, including the domestic dog of the natives; and it is much to be doubted whether it is possible to add a sixth to that number. After we had ranged the woods in different parts, collected several plants, shot a few birds, and taken in a great load of wild celery and scurvy-grass, we returned late on board.

On the third of June, we sent some boats to Long Island to fetch our hay on board; and having laid in a sufficient quantity of wood and water, put the ship in a condition to go to sea, and refreshed our crews with vast quantities of greens, we were ready to sail with the first opportunity. One of our boats in returning saw a large double canoe, and another in which they counted about fifty men, who immediately chaced them: but our people not being armed, hoisted sail, and soon got away from them, so that the New Zeelanders gave over the pursuit, and returned towards East Bay from whence they came. We can by no means pretend to assert that their intentions were hostile in any degree, but prudence naturally suggested to our

people

people, not to place themselves in the power of a set of uncivilized men, who follow their own caprice instead of laws.

The next morning we hoisted St. George's colours, the jack and pennant in honour of His Majesty's birth-day, which we prepared to celebrate with the usual festivities. The family of natives, whose name I have mentioned page 209, and who by living constantly in a neighbouring cove, were now intimate with us, came on board very early, and breakfasted with us. Whilst we were sitting in the steerage, an officer acquainted the captain with the approach of a large double canoe, well manned with New Zeelanders, coming from the northward. We immediately went on deck, and saw the canoe about a musket shot from us, containing twenty-eight men, making towards our sloop, which from her size they probably took to be the commanding one. Our friends on board very earnestly told us they would be our enemies, and persisted to fire at them; nay Towahanga, the head of the family jumped on the arm chest, which was placed on our quarter deck, and taking hold of a stick, made a number of warlike motions with it, and soon after spoke to them very violently, but with some degree of solemnity, at the same time brandishing, as it seemed in defiance, a large hatchet, of green nephritic stone, which he had never shewn us before. In the mean time the canoe approached, without

taking.

taking much notice of our friend, whom we perfuaded at laft to be filent. Two people of a fine ftature, one at the ftern, and another about the middle of the canoe ftood upright, while all the reft continued feated. The former had a perfect black cloak of the clofe-wrought kind, patched in compartments with dog-fkin; he held a green plant of the New Zeeland flag in his hand, and now and then fpoke a few words. But the other pronounced a long fpeech well articulated, loud, and very folemn, and gave his voice great variety of falls and elevations. From the various tones in which he fpoke, and a few geftures with which he accompanied his words, he appeared by turns to queftion, to boaft, to threaten, to challenge, and to perfuade us; he was fometimes running on in a moderate tone, then all at once breaking out into violent exclamations; after which he made fhort paufes in order to recover his breath. Having finifhed his oration, he was invited to come on board by the captain, who came to the fhip's fide; he feemed at firft dubious and miftruftful, but his natural fpirit foon overcoming that diffidence, he ventured on board, and was prefently followed by all his people, who traded with the greateft eagernefs for our iron wares. They immediately faluted the family of natives on board, with the ufual application of nofes, or as our failors expreffed it, they nofed each other, and paid every one of us upon the quarter-deck the fame compliment. The

two

1771.
JULY.

two fpeakers were taken into the cabin, where we learnt the fecond orator's name was Teiratu, and that he came from the oppofite fhore of the northern ifland, called Teera Whittee. They immediately enquired for Tupia (*Tupaya*), and, like thofe mentioned p. 206, feemed much concerned, and pronounced fome words in a mournful or plaintive voice on hearing of his death. So much had this man's fuperior knowledge, and his ability to converfe in their language rendered him valuable, and beloved even among a nation in a ftate of barbarifm. Perhaps with the capacity which Providence had allotted to him, and which had been cultivated no farther than the fimplicity of his education would permit, he was more adapted to raife the New Zeelanders to a ftate of civilization fimilar to that of his own iflands, than ourfelves, to whom the want of the intermediate links, which connect their narrow views to our extended fphere of knowledge, muft prove an obftacle in fuch an undertaking.

Teiratu and all his companions were a taller race of people than we had hitherto feen in New Zeeland, none of them being below the middle fize, and many above it. Their drefs, ornaments, and arms were richer than any we had obferved among the inhabitants of Queen Charlotte's Sound, and feemed to fpeak a kind of affluence, which was entirely new to us. Among their dreffes were feveral cloaks entirely lined with dog-fkin, upon which

VOL. I.   G g   they

they set a high value, and which indeed gave them a very comfortable appearance in the cold weather that now began to be felt. Many of their cloaks, made of the fibres of the New Zeeland flag (*phormium*), were new, and had elegant borders, very symmetrically wrought in red, black, and white; so that they might have passed for the work of a much more polished nation[*]. The black is so strongly fixed upon their stuffs, that it deserves the attention of our manufacturers, who greatly want a lasting dye of that colour on vegetable productions; but the little progress we could make in their language, rendered it impossible to gain intelligence from them on this point. Their cloaks are square pieces, of which two corners were fastened on the breast by strings, and stuck together by a bodkin of bone, whalebone, or green jadde. A belt of a sort of close matting of grass, confined the lower extremities of their cloak to their loins, beyond which it extended at least to the middle of the thigh, and sometimes to the mid-leg. Notwithstanding this superiority over the natives of Queen Charlotte's Sound, they resembled them perfectly in their uncleanliness, and swarms of vermin marched about in their cloaths. Their hair was dressed in the fashion of the country tied on the crown, greased, and stuck with white feathers; and several of them had large combs, of some cetaceous animal's bone, stuck upright just

[*] See Hawkesworth, vol. III.

behind

behind the bunch of hair on the head. Many of them were strongly carved with spirals in the face; several had painted it with red ochre and oil, and were always much pleased when we laid some vermilion on their cheeks. We likewise saw some little calabashes among them, neatly carved, in which they kept some stinking oil; but whether it was animal or vegetable I could never learn. All their tools were very elegantly carved, and made with great attention. They sold us a hatchet, of which the blade was of the finest green jadde, and the handle curiously ornamented with fretwork. They also brought some musical instruments, among which was a trumpet, or tube of wood, about four feet long, and pretty strait; its small mouth was not above two inches, and the other not above five in diameter; it made a very uncouth kind of braying, for they always founded the same note, though a performer on the French horn might perhaps be able to bring some better music out of it. Another trumpet was made of a large whelk, *(murex tritonis,)* mounted with wood, curiously carved, and pierced at the point where the mouth was applied; a hideous bellowing was all the sound that could be procured out of this instrument. The third went by the name of a flute among our people, and was a hollow tube, widest about the middle, where it had a large opening, as well as another at each end. This and the first trumpet were both made of

two

two hollow femicylinders of wood, exactly fitted and moulded together, fo as to form a perfect tube. Their double canoe was about fifty feet long, and feemed to be new; both the high ftern and the head were very curioufly carved with fretwork and fpiral lines, as defcribed in Capt. Cook's former voyage. A mifhapen thing, which with fome difficulty we perceived was meant to reprefent a human head, with a pair of eyes of mother of pearl, and a long tongue lolling out of its mouth, conftituted the foremoft extremity or *prora* of the canoe. This figure is the moft common in all their ornaments, and principally in every thing that relates to warlike affairs. The cuftom of lolling out the tongue in contempt and defiance of the enemy, feems to have given rife to the frequent reprefentations of it; the figure of the tongue forms the heads of their war-canoes, it is placed on the narrow extremity of their battle-axes, and they wear it on their breaft, tied to a ftring round the neck; nay they carve it on their very fcoops with which they bale the water, and on the paddles with which they manage their canoes.

Thefe people made but a very fhort ftay with us, for feeing it began to blow frefh, they all embarked and paddled over to the Motu-Aro. The captain, accompanied by feveral gentlemen, followed them about noon, and found feven canoes there hauled on fhore, which had carried about ninety perfons to that ifland, who were all bufied
making

making huts for their temporary shelter. Our people were received with every mark of friendship, and the captain distributed many presents to them. Among these was a number of brass medals, gilt, about one inch and three quarters in diameter, which had been struck on purpose to be left as a memorial of this voyage among the nations we should meet with: on one side was the head of his present majesty, with the inscription, GEORGE III. KING OF GREAT BRITAIN, FRANCE, AND IRELAND, &c. On the reverse, the representation of two men of war, with the names RESOLUTION and ADVENTURE over them; and the exergue SAILED FROM ENGLAND MARCH MDCCLXXII *. Some of these medals had already been given to the natives of Dusky Bay, and those of Queen Charlotte's Sound. In exchange for iron, cloth, and beads, our people collected a great number of arms, tools, dresses, and ornaments, as curiosities among them, they having greater quantities of these things than any New Zeelanders we had seen. The captain and his company perceived that Teiratu seemed to be the principal or chief among them, by a certain degree of regard which the rest paid to him: they could not, however, determine any thing with precision on this subject. Respect is always paid to the old men among them, who may be supposed to owe their consequence to the long experience they have gained. But their.

* It was originally intended that the sloops should sail so early as March..

chiefs,

chiefs, such as we believed this Teiratu to be, are strong, active, young men, in the prime and flower of their age. These are perhaps elected, as among the North American savages; being men of avowed courage, strength, and military sagacity; from a consciousness that a body of men, in case of war, necessarily requires a leader to animate them as a soul, and upon whose superior talents they may confidently place all their hopes. The more we consider the warlike disposition of the New Zeelanders, and the numerous small parties into which they are divided, this form of government will appear indispensible; for it must be evident to them that the qualifications of a chief are not to be inherited, or propagated from father to son; and it is likewise probable, that this free people may have had opportunities of making the obvious reflection, that hereditary government has a natural tendency towards despotism.

Captain Cook, apprehensive lest the natives should find our garden and destroy it, not knowing for what purpose it was intended, conducted Teiratu thither, and shewed him every plant in it, especially the potatoes. He expressed a great liking to the last, and seemed to know them very well, evidently because a similar root, the Virginian or sweet potatoe, (convolvulus batatas,) is planted in some parts of the Northern Island, from whence he came. The captain parted from him, after obtaining the promise

that

that he would not deſtroy his plantations, but leave every
thing to grow up and propagate, and returned aboard the
Reſolution, where the marines fired three vollies, and our
crews gave three hearty cheers in token of affection to
their king.

The wind freſhened conſiderably after noon, and continued to blow very hard for two days following, ſo that
we were obliged to lie at anchor till the 7th in the morning, when we weighed and ſailed out of Ship Cove, in
company with the Adventure.   Our ſtay here had proved ſo
beneficial to our crews, that they might now be ſaid to be
to the full as healthy as when they left England; and we
had only a ſingle ſick man, a marine, on board our ſloop,
who had laboured under a conſumption and dropſy ever
ſince we had left England.

CHAP.

C H A P. VII.

*   *Run from New Zeeland to O-Taheitee.*

W E entered Cook's Strait after noon, and standing
down to the southward, beheld the immense ocean
before us, which goes by the name of the South Sea.
This vast expanse of sea, through which many former
navigators had passed, in the happy climate of the torrid
zone, but whose middle latitudes no European vessel, except the Endeavour bark, had hitherto attempted to explore, has always been believed to contain a large tract of
land, distinguished by geographers with the name of a
Southern Continent. Previous to the Endeavour's voyage,
New Zeeland was thought the western coast of this unknown land, and certain pretended discoveries near America were asserted as its eastern shores. Captain Cook in
that voyage having cut off both these by his course, and
even penetrated to 40 degrees of south latitude without
finding land, the southern continent was restrained within
narrower limits, though these were still considerable enough
to engage the attention of future navigators. We were
now to enter on this unexplored part, and running to the
eastward between the 50th and 40th degrees of south latitude, to search for undiscovered countries in the depth of
winter.

winter. Many among our fellow-voyagers proceeded on
this dangerous expedition in the firm belief that we should
speedily find the coasts we went in quest of, whose novelty
and valuable productions would amply reward our perseverance and fatigues. But captain Cook, and several
others, judging from what had been done in the former
voyage, and what they had already experienced on this,
were far from expecting to discover new lands, and greatly
doubted the existence of a southern continent.

We were still in the mouth of the strait at eight the
next morning, and saw the high mountains of the southern isle loaded with snow, from whence they had their
name, whilst the weather below was clear and mild, our
thermometer being about $51°$ in the shade. Great shoals
of cetaceous fish, of a perfectly black colour, with a white
spot before the back-fin, passed by us. They were fired
at from our vessel, and one of them being shot through
the head, could no longer plunge under water, but began
to beat about furiously on the surface, and tinged the sea
with its blood. It seemed to be about three yards long,
and was slender and blunt-headed, from whence our sailors
called it the bottle-nose, a name which Dale applies to a
very different fish, the beaked whale, of which the beak
or nose resembles the neck of a bottle *. We went at the

* See Pennant's British Zoology.

1773.
June. rate of three knots and a half at this time, so that it was not thought proper to bring to, for the sake of taking up the dead fish.

Wednesday 9. An infinite number of albatrosses, of all the three species, hovered about us, after we were out of sight of the land. The common or large sort were of diverse colours, which we believed to differ according to age, and that the oldest were almost wholly white, those next them somewhat more sprinkled with brown, and the youngest quite brown. Some of our sailors, who had formerly sailed on board of East-India ships, after comparing the facility of those voyages to the hardships of the present, propagated the ludicrous idea among their messmates, that these birds contained the departed souls of old India captains; who now, exiled to a part of the ocean which they shunned before, were forced to gather a precarious subsistence instead of enjoying their former affluence, and were made the sport of storms which they had never felt in their cabbins. This stroke, which may pass for witty enough, confirms what I have before observed of the original humour of sea-faring men.

The officers, who could not yet relish their salt provisions, after the refreshments of New Zeeland, had ordered their black dog, mentioned p. 135, to be killed, and sent the captain one half of it; this day therefore we dined for the first time on a leg of it roasted, which tasted so exactly like mutton, that it was absolutely undistinguishable. In
our

our cold countries where animal food is so much used, and where to be carnivorous perhaps lies in the nature of men, or is indispensibly necessary to the preservation of their health and strength, it is strange that there should exist a Jewish aversion to dogs-flesh, when hogs, the most uncleanly of all animals are eaten without scruple. Nature seems expressly to have intended them for this use, by making their offspring so very numerous, and their encrease so quick and frequent. It may be objected, that the exalted degree of instinct, which we observe in our dogs, inspires us with great unwillingness to kill and eat them. But it is owing to the time we spend on the education of dogs, that they acquire those eminent qualities which attach them so much to us. The natural qualities of our dogs may receive a wonderful improvement, but education must give its assistance, without which the human mind itself, though capable of an immense expansion, remains in a very contracted state. In New Zeeland, and (according to former accounts of voyages) in the tropical isles of the South Sea, the dogs are the most stupid, dull animals imaginable, and do not seem to have the least advantage in point of sagacity over our sheep, which are commonly made the emblems of silliness. In the former country they are fed upon fish, in the latter on vegetables, and both these diets may have served to alter their disposition. Education may perhaps likewise graft new

In-

instincts; the New Zeeland dogs are fed on the remains of their masters' meals; they eat the bones of other dogs, and the puppies become true cannibals from their birth. We had a young New Zeeland puppy on board, which had certainly had no opportunity of tasting any thing but the mother's milk before we purchased it; however it eagerly devoured a portion of the flesh and bones of the dog, on which we dined to-day; while several others of the European breed taken on board at the Cape, turned from it without touching it.

We kept standing to the south-eastward till the 16th at noon, attended by numerous birds of the petrel and albatross kind, together with now and then a skua, or Port-Egmont hen. Beds of sea-weeds frequently were seen floating on the sea, but we were now too much accustomed to their appearance, to attempt to draw any conclusions from it. The thermometer, which at our departure from New Zeeland, stood at 51° at eight o'clock in the morning, sunk in proportion as we came to the southward to 48°, and sometimes to 47° at the same time of day; but the temperature of the air upon the whole was extremely variable, and the weather equally unsettled. From thence it arose, that we daily observed rainbows, or parts of them about the horizon, especially in the morning. The wind during this time was likewise very changeable, and veered round the compass in a direction contrary to the course

of

of the fun, that is, from weft round by the north towards eaft, and fo further on; but it chiefly prevailed from
the eafterly quarter, where we leaft expected it, fo that our
fituation became tedious, and was made more irkfome by
frequent fogs, rains, and heavy fwells. Having reached
the latitude of 46' 17' fouth, we directed our courfe to
the north-eaftward, as much as the wind would permit.

On the 23d, the weather being mild and the wind
very moderate, captain Furneaux came on board, and dined
with us. He acquainted captain Cook, that all his people
continued in good health, except one or two, who were
infected with a naufeous difeafe, which is propagated by
connections with the other fex. This information gave us
great uneafinefs, it being evident that the diftemper had
already reached New Zeeland, fince our men muft have
received it there. Struck with the horrid confequences
which this evil would entail on the New Zeelanders, we
recapitulated the opportunities which thofe people had of
catching the infection from Europeans. The firft dif-
coverer of this country, in 1642, Abel Janffen Tafman,
had not the leaft amicable intercourfe with the inhabitants,
and none of his people appear to have been afhore upon
it. Captain Cook, the next navigator, who vifited it in the
Endeavour Bark, 1769 and 1770, came from O-Taheitee
and the Society Ifles, where feveral of his people had contracted venereal complaints. However, as his paffage lafted
neal:

nearly two months, the furgeon reported, when they made
the coaft, that no man had any fymptoms of the diftemper
about him. Notwithflanding this affurance captain Cook
had the precaution, not to fuffer any perfon to go on fhore,
who had been under cure, and might be fufpected to
have fome latent remains of this infectious evil; and to
preclude the poffibility of communicating it to a guiltlefs
people, he never fuffered the women to come on board.
M. de Surville, a French navigator, failed from Pondichery
in the St. Jean Baptifle, paffed through the Straits of Malacca, touched at the Bafhee Ifles, went round Manila, faw
land to the S. E. of New Britain, about the latitude of 10½°,
and longitude 158° eaft, which he called Port Surville;
touched at New Zeeland, and proceeded to Callao, in South
America, in order to trade there: but being drowned in the
landing, and all his letters of recommendation being loft
with him, the fhip was detained near two years, and then
fent to France, with all her merchandize. M. de Surville
lay in Doublefs Bay, on the 9th of December, 1769, and
faw the Endeavour ftanding paft him, though captain Cook
could not fee his veffel, which lay under the land. What
ftay M. de Surville made there, and upon what terms he
was with the natives, I know not; but the diftance between
this place and Queen Charlotte's Sound, and the want of
intercourfe between the inhabitants of both ports, make it
improbable, even fuppofing the complaint to have exifted
                                    among

among his crew, that it could have reached so far south.

The same thing may be said with regard to M. de Marion and captain Crozet, two French officers, whose expedition, in 1772, I have mentioned page 112, for the communications which their crews had with the natives, was confined to the environs of the Bay of Islands, in the northernmost part of the northern isle. Our two sloops were the next in order, which touched at New Zeeland; but we had not the least reason to suppose, that they carried any venereal complaint to that country. They had left the Cape of Good Hope, the last place where it is possible the sailors might contract this disorder, six months before they came to Queen Charlotte's Sound, five of which they had been at sea; an interval in which a radical cure may be expected, unless the disease be of too inveterate a nature. However, they were far from having any patients of this sort on board, and it is not likely that the poison could lay dormant during that long interval of time, in a set of men who had no other than salt provisions to live upon, and spirituous liquors to drink, and who were exposed to wet and cold, and all the rigours of southern climates. We therefore concluded, that from all the concurring circumstances, the venereal disease was indigenous in New Zeeland, and not imported by Europeans; and we have hitherto had no reason to alter our opinion on this subject. But if, in spite of appearances, our conclusions should prove erroneous, it is

another

another crime added to the fcore of civilized nations, which muft make their memory execrated by the unhappy people, whom they have poifoned. Nothing can in the leaft atone for the injury they have done to fociety, fince the price at which their libidinous enjoyments were pur- chafed, inftils another poifon into the mind, and deftroys the moral principles, while the difeafe corrupts and ener- vates the body. (fee pag. 212.) A race of men, who amidft all their favage roughnefs, their fiery temper, and cruel cuftoms, are brave, generous, hofpitable, and incapable of deceiving, are juftly to be pitied, that love, the fource of their fweeteft and happieft feelings, is converted into the origin of the moft dreadful fcourge of life.

The wind ftill continued as changeable as before, till the beginning of July, having veered all round the compafs againft the fun, more than four times. During this fpace albatroffes, petrels, and fea-weeds, were frequently feen; rainbows alfo appeared almoft every morning, nay one night we obferved this phænomenon pretty ftrong, caufed by the refracted light of the moon.

On the 9th of July we were nearly in the fame longi- tude, where captain Cook, in the Endeavour, had reached 40° 22' fouth *, but our latitude was about two degrees and a quarter more foutherly. Here we loft a young he-

---

* See Hawkefworth's Compilation, vol. II. p. 282.

goat,

goat, which fell over board, and notwithſtanding all poſſible means were tried for his recovery, ſuch as chafing,
injecting clyſters of the fumes of tobacco, &c. our endeavours proved entirely ineffectual.

July 17th, having paſt the longitude of 227° eaſt, and
being in about 40° ſouth latitude, we began to run due
north, after a very tedious courſe in ſearch of the ſouthern
continent, the exiſtence of which, in the latitudes we had
now paſſed through, had been poſitively aſſerted. The uncomfortable ſeaſon of the year, the many contrary winds,
and the total want of intereſting incidents united to make
this run extremely tedious to us all, and the only point
we had gained by it, was the certainty that no great land
was ſituated in the South Sea about the middle latitudes.
In five days time our latitude being 31° ſouth, we began
to loſe ſight of albatroſſes and petrels, and the thermometer was riſen to 61½, ſo that we began to
change our winter clothes for others, conſiderably thinner, for the firſt time after leaving the Cape of Good Hope.
The ſpirits of all our people were much exhilarated in
proportion as we approached to the tropics, and our ſailors
diverted themſelves with a variety of plays every evening.
The genial mildneſs of the air was ſo welcome to us,
after a long abſence from it, that we could not help preferring the warm climates as the beſt adapted for the abode
of mankind. We ſaw a tropic bird on the 25th in the
afternoon, a ſure ſign that we were arrived into the tem-

perate climates below 30° of latitude. The setting sun illumined the clouds with the most brilliant tints of gold, which confirmed us in the opinion that the colours of the sky are no where so rich and beautiful as between or near the tropics.

On the 28th we spoke with the Adventure, and heard that they had buried their cook three days ago, and that about twenty of her people were very ill of the scurvy. This was the more surprising to us, as we had but very few people affected with any symptoms of that disorder, and only one who was dangerously sick. The next day captain Cook sent one of his seamen with a warrant to act as cook on board the Adventure; and several of our gentlemen took the opportunity of going to dine with their friends. They found captain Furneaux and some others very ill of a rheumatic complaint, and many of the people had fluxes. Their carpenter was remarkable ill of the scurvy, and had great livid blotches on his legs. This difference between the salubrity of the two vessels probably arose from the want of fresh air in the Adventure, our sloop being higher out of the water, so that we could open more scuttles in bad weather than our consort. Our people likewise made a greater consumption of sour-krout and wort, and particularly applied the grains of the latter to all blotches and swelled parts, a regimen which had been omitted by those in the Adventure. On this occasion it is not improper to remark, that the scurvy is more dangerous and

and virulent in warm climates than in cold. As long as we had kept in high latitudes it did not make its appearance, or was at least confined to a few individuals, who were naturally of a bad habit of body; but we had scarcely had ten days of warm weather when one man died, and a number of others were affected with the worst symptoms of this dreadful distemper, on board the Adventure. It should therefore seem that the heat contributes to inflammation and putrefaction; and its general effect, even among those who had no dangerous scorbutic complaints, was a great degree of languor and debility.

On the 4th of August a young bitch, of the terrier breed, taken on board at the Cape of Good Hope, and covered by a spaniel, brought ten young ones, one of which was dead. The New Zeeland dog, mentioned above, which devoured the bones of the roasted dog, now fell upon the dead puppy, and ate of it with a ravenous appetite. This is a proof how far education may go in producing and propagating new instincts in animals. European dogs are never fed on the meat of their own species, but rather seem to abhor it. The New Zeeland dogs, in all likelihood, are trained up from their earliest age to eat the remains of their master's meals; they are therefore used to feed upon fish, their own species, and perhaps human flesh; and what was only owing to habit at first, may have become instinct by length of time. This was

I i 2 remarkable

remarkable in our canibal-dog, for he came on board so young, that he could not have been weaned long enough to acquire a habit of devouring his own species, and much less of eating human flesh; however, one of our seamen having cut his finger, held it out to the dog, who fell to greedily, licked it, and then began to bite into it.

On the 6th, in the afternoon, being in about 19½ deg. of south latitude, we got the easterly trade-wind, which set in fresh after several calms, attended with heavy showers of rain. The sun being at this time still in the opposite hemisphere, was probably the cause of our meeting with this wind so much later than usual, the tropics being generally reckoned its limits. Agreeable to the observation which we now made, we had found the trade-wind, in August 1772, at Madeira, though that island is situated in 33° of north latitude. But the most remarkable occurrence in our run was the nature of the winds previous to our obtaining the trade-wind. We had expected that, by going in a middle latitude between 50 and 40 deg. south, we should meet with regular westerly winds, which are common in our seas during the winter months; instead of this we found them veering round the compass in two or three days time, never settling in any other than the eastern quarter, and sometimes blowing with great violence. Thus the name of Pacific Ocean, which has formerly been given to the whole South Sea, is, in my opinion, applicable

ble only to a part of it between the tropics, where the winds are steady and uniform, the weather in general fair and mild, and the sea not so much agitated as in higher latitudes.

Albecores, bonitos, and dolphins gave chace to many shoals of flying-fish, in the same manner as we had observed them in the Atlantic; while several large blackbirds, with long wings and forked tails, which are commonly called men of war *(pelecanus aquilus,* Linn.) soared at a vast height in the air, and sometimes descending into a lower region, viewed a fish swimming under them, and darted down with amazing velocity, never failing to strike the fish with their bill. It is a well known fact, that gannets, which are birds of the same genus in the English seas, catch fish in a similar manner. The fishermen on the coast frequently fix a pilchard or herring on the point of a knife fastened to a floating board, and the bird darting down upon it transfixes itself on the knife.

On the 11th, in the morning, we discovered a low island to the southward of us, which seemed about four miles long, and about six miles distant. It appeared to be almost level with the sea, only some groups of trees rose above the horizon, and among them a few cocoa-nut palms out-topped the rest. To people in our situation, exhausted with a tedious passage, the bare sight of land was sufficient to give some consolation, though we could not

expect

expect to reap any benefit from its productions; and therefore this island, though divested of every thing strikingly beautiful, yet pleased the eye by the simplicity of its form. Our thermometer was now constantly between 70 and 80 degrees in the morning; but the heat was far from being troublesome, as the fair weather was accompanied by a strong pleasant trade-wind, and our awnings were spread over the quarter-deck. This island, which was called RESOLUTION Island, seems to have been seen by M. de Bougainville. Its latitude is 17° 24′ south, and its longitude 141° 39′ west from Greenwich. Our observation at noon was 17° 17′ south, our course being nearly east. In the evening, at half past six o'clock, we saw another island of the same nature as the preceding, about four leagues distant, which was named DOUBTFUL Island. It being after sun-set, we stood to the northward till we

had passed by it. The next morning, before day-break, we were alarmed by the sudden appearance of breakers within half a mile a-head of us. We changed our course instantly, apprized our consort of the danger by proper signals, and then stood along the reef. As soon as it was light we distinguished an island of a circular form, including a large bason or lagoon of sea-water; the northern shores were covered with trees and palms in various clusters, which had a very elegant appearance; but all the rest was a narrow ledge of rocks, over which the surf beat

with

with great violence; within it the lagoon was shallow near us, but deeper under the wooded part; a difference which could easily be diftinguished by the whiter or the bluer colour of the water. Captain Cook gave this ifle the name of FURNEAUX Ifland; it is fituated in 17° 5′ fouth latitude, and 143° 16′ weft longitude. Standing along this reef we faw a canoe failing near the northern part of the ifle, and by the help of glaffes we obferved fix or feven men in it, one of which was placed at the ftern fteering with a paddle. They did not feem to have embarked in order to reconnoitre us, as they did not approach the fouthern reef, but kept clofe in with the wooded part of the ifland. We proceeded all day with a favourable breeze and fair weather till fun-fet; but the navigation between thefe low iflands and reefs being extremely dangerous, becaufe they can only be feen at fhort diftances, we were obliged to bring to at night in order to avoid meeting with them unawares. Early the next morning we left another ifland of this kind on our ftarboard quarter, which was called ADVENTURE Ifland; it lies in 17° 4′ fouth latitude, and 144° 30′ weft longitude. We fpoke with the Adventure about the fame time, and were told fhe had above thirty men on the fick lift, moft of them ill of the fcurvy. Our floop ftill kept rather free of this diftemper, and every precaution was taken to preferve our crew in health by a plentiful ufe of four-krout, by airing the

hammocks

1773.
August. hammocks every day, and frequently smoaking the ship with gunpowder and vinegar.

In the afternoon we saw an island right a-head, consisting of several clumps of trees, united by one reef, and from its situation we judged it was the same which Captain Cook named Chain Island in his former voyage *. To prevent losing our time by bringing the sloops to at night, we hoisted a boat out, and sent it to sail ahead of our vessels, with a light, and to make signals in case of danger. The South Sea between the tropics contains many low islands, singularly constructed, which are level with the sea in most places, and at the utmost a yard or two above it. They have frequently a circular form, including a lagoon or bason of sea-water in their centre, and the depth of the sea all round them is unfathomable, the rocks rising perpendicularly from the bottom. Their productions must be few, and cocoa nut-trees are probably the most useful which they contain; but notwithstanding this circumstance and their small size, many of them are inhabited. The question how such little spots came to be peopled is not easily to be answered; but it is not easier to determine how the higher islands in the South Sea have acquired their inhabitants. Commodore (now Admiral) Byron, and Captain Wallis, who sent some of their people on shore upon these low islands, found their inhabitants shy and jealous of

* See Hawkesworth, vol. II. p. 77.

strangers;

strangers; a disposition which is perhaps owing to the difficulty of preserving their existence from the scanty provisions on their narrow circle, and which may be heightened by the consciousness that their small numbers render them liable to oppression. The language of these people, and their customs, are therefore still unknown, and these are the only circumstances from which the origin of nations, who have no records among them, can be traced.

Early on the 15th of August we saw a high peak with a flattish summit, first discovered by Captain Wallis, who called it Osnabruck Island, and afterwards by M. de Bougainville, in whose chart it has the names of Pic de la Boudeuse, or le Boudoir. The mountain appeared of a considerable height, and its top was broken or excavated perfectly like the crater of a volcano, which seemed evidently to have existed here. The island was nearly of a circular form, and the mountain rose steep to a conical shape from all parts of the sea-shore, there being but little level land round its foot. The whole mountain was green, and the bottom or low land was covered with trees. While we eagerly feasted our eyes with this pleasing prospect, one of our officers, who had formerly been sent close in shore there by Captain Wallis, told us that the trees were of the kind which bear the bread-fruit, so much extolled in the voyages of Anson, Byron, Wallis, and Cook. He acquainted us at the same time, that the natives were of the race as those who dwell on O-Taheitee and the Society Isles, of which the first is within half a day's sail; and that they give the name of *Maitea** to their own island. We never came nearer than four leagues to it, which was probably the reason that no canoes came off to visit us. Having very little wind we hoisted a boat out, which went on board the Adventure, and brought Captain Furneaux to dine with us. We had the pleasure to learn from him, that the flux among his crew was ceased, and that none of his people were in any imminent danger from the scurvy; we hoped therefore, from our vicinity to O-Taheitee, to have a speedy opportunity of restoring their health by a wholesome vegetable diet.

In the evening, about sun-set, we plainly saw the mountains of that desirable island, lying before us, half emerging from the gilded clouds on the horizon. Every man on board, except one or two who were not able to walk, hastened eagerly to the forecastle to feast their eyes on an object, of which they were taught to form the highest expectations, both in respect of the abundance of refreshments, and of the kind and generous temper of the natives, whose character has pleased all the navigators who have visited them. The first discoverer was probably a Spaniard, PEDRO FERNANDEZ DE QUIROS, who sailed from Lima in Peru, on the 21st of December 1605. He made

* See Hawkesworth, vol. II. p. 78. Maitea.

an

an island on the 10th of February 1606, calling it *la Sagit-
taria* [*], which, from all the concurring circumstances, seems
to have been O-Taheitee. He found no harbours on the
south part, where he fell in with it; but the people he sent
ashore were treated with the greatest marks of friendship
and kindness. Captain Wallis next found this island on
the 18th of June 1767, and called it George the Third's
Island. Some unhappy misunderstanding arising between
him and the natives at first, he fired upon them, killed
about fifteen, and wounded a great number; but these
good tempered people, forgetting the great loss they had
sustained, and the wounds their brethren had received,
made peace with him soon after, and furnished him with
a profusion of refreshments, consisting of several roots,
many sorts of rich fruit, fowls, and hogs. M. de Bougainville arrived in the eastern part on the 2d of April
1768, or about nine months and a half after the departure
of Captain Wallis, and discovered the true indigenous name
of this island; sensible of the amiable character of the inhabitants, he staid ten days among them, giving and receiving
frequent marks of friendship and regard. Captain Cook,
in the Endeavour, arriving here in April 1769, to observe the transit of Venus, circumnavigated the whole
island in a boat; and, during a stay of three months, had

[*] See an Historical Collection of the several Voyages and Discoveries in the
South Pacific Ocean, by Alexander Dalrymple, Esq. vol. I. p. 109 to 117.

daily

daily opportunities of confirming the obfervations already made upon this fubject.

We ftood on towards this ifland all night, and the favourable ideas which were raifed by the accounts of former navigators, made us pafs fome happy hours in expectation of the morning. We refolved to forget our fatigues and the inclemencies of fouthern climates; the clouds which had hitherto hung lowering upon our brows were difperfed; the loathed images of difeafe and the terrors of death were fled, and all our cares at reft.

> —————— Somno pofiti fub nocte filenti
> Lenibant curas, et corda oblita laborum. VIRGIL.

CHAP.

CHAP. VIII.

Anchorage in O-Aitepeha harbour, on the lesser peninsula of O-Taheitee. —Account of our stay there.—Removal to Matavai Bay.

Devenere locos lætos et amœna vireta
Fortunatorum nemorum, sedesque beatas.
Largior hic campos æther, et lumine vestit
Purpureo.   VIRGIL.

I T was one of those beautiful mornings which the poets   Monday 16.
of all nations have attempted to describe, when we
saw the isle of O-Taheite, within two miles before us. The
east-wind which had carried us so far, was entirely vanished,
and a faint breeze only wafted a delicious perfume from
the land, and curled the surface of the sea. The mountains,
clothed with forests, rose majestic in various spiry forms,
on which we already perceived the light of the rising sun :
nearer to the eye a lower range of hills, easier of ascent,
appeared, wooded like the former, and coloured with several
pleasing hues of green, soberly mixed with autumnal
browns. At their foot lay the plain, crowned with its
fertile bread-fruit trees, over which rose innumerable
palms, the princes of the grove. Here every thing seemed
as yet asleep, the morning scarce dawned, and a peaceful
shade still rested on the landscape. We discerned however,
a number of houses among the trees, and many canoes
                                                        hauled

hauled up along the fandy beaches. About half a mile from the fhore a ledge of rocks level with the water, extended parallel to the land, on which the furf broke, leaving a fmooth and fecure harbour within. The fun beginning to illuminate the plain, its inhabitants arofe, and enlivened the fcene. Having perceived the large veffels on their coaft, feveral of them haftened to the beach, launched their canoes, and paddled towards us, who were highly delighted in watching all their occupations.

The canoes foon paffed through the openings in the reef, and one of them approached within hale. In it were two men almoft naked, with a kind of turban on the head, and a fafh round their waift. They waved a large green leaf, and accofted us with the repeated exclamation of *tayo* */ which even without the help of vocabularies, we could eafily tranflate into the expreffion of proffered friendfhip. The canoe now came under our ftern, and we let down a prefent of beads, nails, and medals to the men. In return, they handed up to us a green ftem of a plantane, which was their fymbol of peace, with a defire that it might be fixed in a confpicuous part of the veffel. It was accordingly ftuck up in the main fhrouds, upon which our new friends immediately returned towards the land. In a fhort time we faw great crouds of people on the feafhore gazing at us, while numbers in confequence of this

* See Bougainville's Voyage, Englifh Edition, p. 217.

treaty

treaty of peace, which was now firmly established, launched
their canoes, and loaded them with various productions of
their country. In less than an hour we were surrounded
by an hundred canoes, each of which carried one, two,
three, and sometimes four persons, who placed a perfect
confidence in us, and had no arms whatsoever. The welcome sound of *tayo* resounded on all sides, and we returned it with a degree of heart-felt pleasure, on this favourable change of our situation. Coco-nuts, and plantanes in great quantity, bread-fruit and several other vegetables, besides some fresh fish were offered to us, and
eagerly exchanged for transparent beads, and small nails.
Pieces of cloth, fish hooks, hatchets of stone, and a number
of tools, were likewise brought for sale and readily disposed
of; and many canoes kept plying between us and the
shore, exhibiting a picture of a new kind of fair. I immediately began to trade for natural productions through
the cabin-windows, and in half an hour had got together
two or three species of unknown birds, and a great number
of new fishes, whose colours while alive were exquisitely
beautiful. I therefore employed the morning in sketching
their outlines, and laying on the vivid hues, before they
disappeared in the dying objects.

The people around us had mild features, and a pleasing
countenance; they were about our size, of a pale mahogany
brown, had fine black hair and eyes, and wore a piece of cloth
round-

round their middle of their own manufacture, and another wrapped about the head in various picturefque fhapes like a turban. Among them were feveral females, pretty enough to attract the attention of Europeans, who had not feen their own country-women for twelve long months paft. Thefe wore a piece of cloth with a hole in the middle, through which they had paffed the head, fo that one part of the garment hung down behind, and the other before, to the knees; a fine white cloth like a muflin, was paffed over this in various elegant turns round the body, a little below the breaft, forming a kind of tunic, of which one turn fometimes fell gracefully acrofs the fhoulder. If this drefs had not entirely that perfect form, fo juftly admired in the draperies of the ancient Greek ftatues, it was however infinitely fuperior to our expectations, and much more advantageous to the human figure, than any modern fafhion we had hitherto feen. Both fexes were adorned, or rather disfigured, by thofe fingular black ftains, occafioned by puncturing the fkin, and rubbing a black colour into the wounds, which are mentioned by former voyagers. They were particularly vifible on the loins of the common men, who went almoft naked, and exhibited a proof how little the ideas of ornament of different nations agree, and yet how generally they all have adopted fuch aids to their perfonal perfection. It was not long before fome of thefe good people came aboard. That peculiar gentlenefs of

disposition

difpofition, which is their general characteriftic, immediately manifefted itfelf in all their looks and actions, and
gave full employment to thofe, who made the human
heart their ftudy. They expreffed feveral marks of affection in their countenance, took hold of our hands, leaned
on our fhoulder, or embraced us. They admired the white-
nefs of our bodies, and frequently pufhed afide our clothes
from the breaft, as if to convince themfelves that we were
made like them.

Many of them feeing us defirous of learning their language, by afking the names of various familiar objects, or
repeating fuch as we found in the vocabularies of former
voyagers, took great pains to teach us, and were much
delighted when we could catch the juft pronunciation of a
word. For my own part, no language feemed eafier to
acquire than this; every harfh and fibilant confonant being
banifhed from it, and almoft every word ending in a vowel.
The only requifite, was a nice ear to diftinguifh the numerous modification of their vowels, which muft naturally occur in a language confined to few confonants, and which,
once rightly underftood, give a great degree of delicacy to
converfation. Amongft feveral other obfervations, we immediately found that the O or E with which the greateft
part of the names and words in lieutenant Cook's firft
voyage, begin, is nothing elfe than the article, which
many eaftern languages affix to the greater part of their

fubftantives. In confequence of this remark, I fhall always in the fequel either omit this prefix, or feparate it from the word itfelf by a hyphen: and I cannot help taking notice that M. de Bougainville has been fortunate enough to catch the name of the ifland without the additional O, and expreffed it as well as the nature of the French language will permit, by Taïti, which, with the addition of a flight afpirate, we pronounce Taheitee, or Tahitee.

Seeing an opening in the reef before us, which was the entrance to the harbour of Whaï-Urua, in the leffer peninfula of O-Taheitee, we fent a boat to found in it, which found convenient anchorage. The boat afterwards proceeded to the fhore, where a croud of the natives gathered round it, and we heard the fqueaking of pigs, which was at this time a more welcome found to us, than the mufic of the moft brilliant performer. Our people, however, were not fo fortunate as to purchafe any of them, all their offers being conftantly refufed, under the pretext that thefe animals belonged to the *aree*, or king.

A canoe now came alongfide, of a fomewhat larger fize than the reft, and brought a handfome man, above fix feet high, and three women, who all came on board. The man who immediately informed us, that his name was O-Taï, feemed to be a perfon of fome confequence in this part of the ifland, and we fuppofed he belonged to that

clafs

clafs of vaffals, or freeholders, who are called Manahounas in the firft voyage of captain Cook. He came on the quarter-deck, to all appearance thinking, that a place where our chiefs were ftationed, beft became him. He was remarkable fairer than any of the natives we had yet feen, and refembled in colour the Weft Indian Meftizos. His features were really handfome and regular; he had a high forehead, arched eyebrows, large black eyes, fparkling with expreffion, and a well-proportioned nofe; there was fomething remarkably fweet and engaging about his mouth; the lips were prominent, but not difagreeably large; and his beard was black, and finely frizzled; his hair was of a jetty colour, and fell in ftrong curls down his neck; but feeing that we all had ours queued, he made ufe of a black filk neckcloth, which Mr. Clerke made him a prefent of, to imitate our fafhion. The body was in general well proportioned, though fomewhat too lufty, and his feet were rather too large to harmonize perfectly with the reft. By the help of vocabularies we afked this man feveral queftions. One of the firft was, whether Tootaldh was well? to this we were anfwered, that he was dead, being killed by the men of Tiarraboo, or the fmaller peninfula, and that O-Aheatua was *eree*, or the king of the latter; which was confirmed by all the other natives. Of his three female companions, one was his wife, and the other two his fifters: the latter took great pleafure in teaching us to

call

1773.
August.

call them by their names, which were both sufficiently
harmonious, one was called Maroya, and the other Marorai.
They were still fairer than O-Taï, but their stature was
small in comparison to his, being at least nine or ten inches
less.   The last mentioned was a graceful figure, with the
most delicate and beautiful contours, in the hands and all
above the zone.   Their face was round, and their features
far from being so regular as those of the brother; but an
ineffable smile sat on their countenances.   They seemed
never to have been aboard of a ship before, so much were
they struck with admiration on beholding its variety of
objects.   They did not content themselves with looking
around the deck, but descended into the officers cabins,
whither a gentleman conducted them, and curiously examined every part.   Marorai took a particular fancy to a
pair of sheets which she saw spread on one of the beds,
and made a number of fruitless attempts to obtain them
from her conductor.   He proposed a special favour as the
condition; she hesitated some time, and at last with seeming reluctance consented; but when the victim was just
led to the altar of Hymen, the ship struck violently on the
reef, and interrupted the solemnity.   The affrighted lover,
more sensible of the danger than his fair mistress, flew in
haste upon deck, whither all the rest of our people crowded
from their several occupations.   The tide, during a perfect
calm, had driven us by insensible degrees towards the reef

of

of rocks; and actually fet us upon it, before we could
come into the entrance of the harbour, which was as it
were within our reach. Repeated shocks made our situation every moment more terrifying; however, providentially there was no fwell which broke with any violence
on the rocks, and the fea breeze, which muft have brought
on abfolute deftruction to us, did not come in all day. The
officers, and all the paffengers, exerted themfelves indifcriminately on this occafion, hoifted out the launch, and afterwards by heaving upon an anchor, which had been carried out to a little diftance, fucceeded in bringing the veffel
afloat. The natives on board, feeing us work fo hard,
affifted us in manning the capftan, hauling in ropes, and
performing all forts of labour. If they had had the leaft
fpark of a treacherous difpofition, they could not have
found a better opportunity of diftreffing us; but they approved themfelves good-natured, and friendly in this, as
on all other occafions. The heat during this violent exertion of our ftrength was immenfe; the thermometer being
upwards of ninety degrees in the fhade, and the fun blaz-
ing in a perfectly clear fky. The Adventure was clofe to
us, and efcaped fharing the fame diftreffes, by dropping an
anchor in time. It was another fortunate circumftance,
that the reef fhelved in this place fo as to admit of anchorage, which is indeed rarely the cafe, the coral rock being
perpendicular in moft parts. It was about three o'clock
                                                    when

when we were afloat again, after working for about an hour and a half. We now took fome refreſhments in a hurry, and as our fituation was ſtill extremely precarious, in cafe an eafterly wind had come on, we manned the boats of both ſloops, and were towed off to ſea, where we felt a land-breeze gently fwelling our fails, about five o'clock. As foon as we were fure of it, we difpatched the boats to the affiftance of the Adventure; but fhe had already flipped her cables, in order to take advantage of the favourable wind, and followed us. We ſtood off and on all night, and faw the dangerous reefs illuminated by a number of fires, by the light of which the natives were fifhing. One of the officers retiring to reft, found his bed deprived of the fheets, which in all probability the fair Maroraï had taken care of, when forfaken by her lover; though fhe muſt have managed this little concern with confiderable ingenuity, as fhe had appeared on deck before any fufpicion had fallen upon her.

The next morning we refumed our courfe towards the fhore, and ſtood in along the north part of the leſſer peninfula. We were in a fhort time furrounded, as the day before, by the natives, who in a great number of canoes brought us abundance of vegetable, but no animal food, and whofe clamours were fometimes loud enough to ſtun our ears. Thefe canoes very frequently overfet, but the natives were not much difcompofed by fuch accidents, as

both

both sexes were expert swimmers, and re-established themselves in a moment. Seeing that I enquired for plants, and other natural curiosities, they brought off several, though sometimes only the leaves without the flowers, and vice versa; however, among them we saw the common species of black night-shade, and a beautiful *erythrina*, or coral flower; I also collected by these means many shells, coralines, birds, &c.

About eleven o'clock we anchored in a little harbour called O Aitepeha, on the north-east end of the southern or lesser peninsula of Taheitee, named Tiarraboo. Here the concourse of natives still increased, and we saw their canoes coming towards us from all parts. They were eager to obtain our beads, nails, and knives, for which an immense quantity of their cloth, mats, baskets, and various tools, as well as abundance of coco-nuts, bread-fruit, yams, and bananas were exchanged. Many of them came on deck, and took the opportunity of conveying away a number of trifles; nay, some went so far as privately to throw over board the coco-nuts, which we had already purchased, to their comrades, who immediately picked them up, and sold them to our people again. To prevent our being imposed upon for the future in this manner, the thieves were turned out of the vessel, and punished with a whip, which they bore very patiently.

The

The heat was as great as it had been the day before, the thermometer standing at 90° in the shade, when the sky was covered with clouds; the wind likewise dying away again at noon to a perfect calm. Notwithstanding the waste of fluids which the weather occasioned, we could not say that we found the climate affected us too much, or was very disagreeable. On the contrary, allowing for the violent exercise we had undergone at the striking of the ship, we found ourselves more refreshed by the bare proximity of the shore, than we could have expected. The bread-fruit and yams proved a luxurious and most welcome sub-stitute for worm-eaten biscuit; while plantanes, and a fruit of the shape of an apple, called *e-vee* by the natives, furnished out a delicious desert. Our only remaining wish, with regard to eatables, was to be able to purchase some hogs and fowls, which might supply the place of salt beef.

In the afternoon the captains, accompanied by several gentlemen, went ashore the first time, in order to visit O-Aheatua, whom all the natives thereabouts acknow-ledged as *aree*, or king. Numbers of canoes in the mean while surrounded us, carrying on a brisk trade with veget-ables, but chiefly with great quantities of the cloth made in the island. The decks were likewise crouded with na-tives, among whom were several women who yielded without difficulty to the ardent follicitations of our sailors.

Some

Some of the females who came on board for this purpose, seemed not to be above nine or ten years old, and had not the least marks of puberty. So early an acquaintance with the world seems to argue an uncommon degree of voluptuousness, and cannot fail of affecting the nation in general. The effect, which was immediately obvious to me, was the low stature of the common class of people, to which all these prostitutes belonged. Among this whole order we saw few persons above the middle size, and many below it; an observation which confirms what M. de Buffon has very judiciously said on the subject of early connections of the sexes, (see his Histoire Naturelle.) Their features were very irregular, and in general very ordinary, except the eyes, which were always large and full of vivacity; but a natural smile, and a constant endeavour to please, had so well replaced the want of beauty, that our sailors were perfectly captivated, and carelessly disposed of their shirts and cloaths to gratify their mistresses. The simplicity of a dress which exposed to view a well proportioned bosom and delicate hands, might also contribute to fan their amorous fire; and the view of several of these nymphs swimming nimbly all round the sloop, such as nature had formed them, was perhaps more than sufficient entirely to subvert the little reason which a mariner might have left to govern his passions. A trifling circumstance had given cause to their taking the water. One of the officers on the quarter-deck intended to drop a bead into a canoe for a little boy about fix years old; by accident it miffed the boat and fell into the fea; but the child immediately leaped overboard, and diving after it brought it up again. To reward his performance we dropped fome more beads to him, which fo tempted a number of men and women, that they amufed us with amazing feats of agility in the water, and not only fetched up feveral beads fcattered at once, but likewife large nails, which, on account of their weight, defcended quickly to a confiderable depth. Some of them continued a long while under water, and the velocity with which we faw them go down, the water being perfectly clear, was very furprifing. The frequent ablutions of thefe people, already mentioned in Captain Cook's former voyage, feem to make fwimming familiar to them from their earlieft childhood; and indeed their eafy pofition in the water, and the pliancy of their limbs, gave us reafon to look on them almoft as amphibious creatures. They continued this fport, and their other occupations about us, till fun-fet, when they all withdrew by degrees to the fhore.

In the evening the captains with their company return-ed on board, without having feen the king, who, perhaps miftrufting their intentions, had fent word, that he intend-ed to vifit us the next day. They had taken a walk along the fhore to the eaftward, attended by a great croud of

the

the natives, who infifted on carrying them on their fhoulders over a fine brook. After they had paffed it, the natives left them, and they proceeded accompanied by one man, who guided them to an uncultivated projecting point, where different kinds of plants grew in wild luxuriance among feveral forts of fhrubs. On coming out of the fhrubbery they faw a building of ftones, in form of the fruftum of a pyramid; the bafe might meafure about twenty yards in front, and the whole confifted of feveral terraces or fteps above each other, which were ruinous and overgrown with graffes and fhrubs, efpecially on the back or inland part. This the native faid was a burying-place and place of worfhip, *marai*, and diftinguifhed it by the name of *marai no-Aheatua*, the burying-place of Aheatua, the prefent king of Tiarroboo. Around it were placed perpendicularly, or nearly fo, fifteen flender pieces of wood, fome about eighteen feet long, in which fix or eight diminutive human figures of a rude unnatural fhape were carved, ftanding above each other, male or female promifcuoufly, yet fo that the uppermoft was always a male. All thefe figures faced the fea, and perfectly refembled fome which are carved on the fterns of their canoes, and which they call *e-tee*. Beyond the morai they faw a kind of thatch erected on four pofts, before which a lattice of fticks was placed in the ground, hung with bananas and cocoa-nuts *no t' Eatua*, " for the Divinity." They fat down to reft them-

felves

felves under the fhade of this roof, and their guide feeing
them a good deal exhaufted, took feveral of the bananas
and offered them, with the affurance that they were *mda
maitai*, " good eating." They accepted them after this recommendation, and finding them really as delicious as they
had been defcribed, made no fcruple to feaft with the
gods. As the evening was now advancing, they returned
to the fea-fhore, well pleafed with their reception among
thefe good-natured people, and brought on board a few
plants, which we foon recognized as the productions
common to tropical countries.

We contemplated the fcenery before us early the next
morning, when its beauties were moft engaging. The
harbour in which we lay was very fmall, and would not
have admitted many more veffels befides our own. The
water in it was as fmooth as the fineft mirrour, and the fea
broke with a fnowy foam around us upon the outer reef.
The plain at the foot of the hills was very narrow in this
place, but always conveyed the pleafing ideas of fertility,
plenty, and happinefs. Juft over againft us it ran up between the hills into a long narrow valley, rich in plantations, interfperfed with the houfes of the natives. The
flopes of the hills, covered with woods, croffed each other
on both fides, varioufly tinted according to their diftances;
and beyond them, over the cleft of the valley, we faw the
interior mountains fhattered into various peaks and fpires,
among

among which was one remarkable pinnacle, whoſe ſummit was frightfully bent to one ſide, and ſeemed to threaten its downfall every moment. The ſerenity of the ſky, the genial warmth of the air, and the beauty of the landſcape, united to exhilarate our ſpirits.

The launches of both ſhips were ſent to *o Wbai-urua*, to fetch the anchors which we had left there when we ſtruck on the reef. A party of marines and ſeamen were ordered on ſhore at the ſame time, to carry on a trade for proviſions, and to fill our empty caſks with freſh water. For this purpoſe they occupied the remains of an abandoned ſhed or cottage on the beach, which at once gave them ſhelter from the ſun, and ſecured them againſt the thieviſh diſpoſition of the people. Before captain Cook went aſhore he received a viſit from a man of ſome note, called o-Poôe, who brought his two ſons on board. They preſented the captain with ſome of their cloth and ſome little trifles, and in return they received knives, nails, beads, and a ſhirt, in which having dreſſed themſelves, they accompanied us to the ſhore.

Our firſt care was to leave the dry ſandy beach, which could afford us no diſcoveries in our ſcience, and to examine the plantations, which from the ſhips had an enchanting appearance, notwithſtanding the browniſh caſt which the time of the year had given. We found them indeed to anſwer the expectations we had formed of a
country

1773.
August.
country defcribed as an elyfium by M. de Bougainville, (fee
the Englifh edition, p. 228.)   We entered a grove of bread-
trees, on moft of which we faw no fruit at this feafon of
winter, and followed a neat but narrow path, which led to
different habitations, half hid under various bufhes. Tall
coco-palms nodded to each other, and rofe over the reft
of the trees; the bananas difplayed their beautiful large
leaves, and now and then one of them ftill appeared loaded with his cluftering fruit.   A fort of fhady trees, covered
with a dark-green foliage, bore golden apples, which refembled the anana in juicinefs and flavour.   Betwixt thefe
the intermediate fpace was filled with young mulberry-
trees *(morus papyrifera,)* of which the bark is employed by
the natives in the manufacture of their cloth; with feveral
fpecies of arum or eddies, with yams, fugar-canes, and
other ufeful plants.

We found the cottages of the natives fcattered at fhort
diftances, in the fhade of fruit-trees, and furrounded by
various odoriferous fhrubs, fuch as the gardenia, guettarda,
and calophyllum.   The neat fimplicity of their ftructure
gave us no lefs pleafure than the artlefs beauty of the
grove which encompaffed them.   The pandang * or palm-
nut tree had given its long prickly leaves to thatch the

* *Athrodactylis.* Char. Gen. Nover. Forfter. London 1776. *Brouffia fyl-*
veftris. Linn. Flor. Zeyl. *Kaers.* Forfkal. Flora Arab. *Pandanus.* Rumph.
Ambain.

roofs

roofs of the buildings, and these were supported by a few
pillars made of the bread-tree, which is thus useful in
more respects than one. As a roof is sufficient to shelter
the natives from rains and nightly dews, and as the climate of this island is perhaps one of the happiest in the
world, the houses seldom have any walls, but are open on
all sides. We saw, however, a few dwellings constructed
for greater privacy, which were entirely enclosed in walls
of reeds, connected together by transverse pieces of wood,
so as to give us the idea of large bird-cages. In these
there was commonly a hole left for the entrance, which
could be closed up with a board. Before every hut, on
the green turf or on dry grass, we observed groups of inhabitants lying down or sitting in the eastern stile, and
passing their happy hours away in conversation or repose.
Some of them got up at our approach, and joined the
croud that followed us; but great numbers, especially
those of a mature age, remained in their attitude, and only
pronounced a kind *tayo* as we passed by them. Our attendant croud seeing us gather plants, were very ready to
pluck and offer the same sorts to us, which they found
attracted our notice. Indeed a variety of wild species
sprung up amidst the plantations, in that beautiful disorder
of nature, which is so truly admirable when checked by
the hand of industry, and infinitely surpasses the trimness
of regular gardens. Among them we found several species

of

of graffes, which though thinner than in our northern
countries, yet by growing always in the fhade, looked
frefh and formed a foft bed of verdure.   The foil was by
their means kept fufficiently moift to give nourifhment to
the trees, and both were in a thriving ftate, owing to the
reciprocal affiftance which they gave each other.   Various
little birds dwelt in the fhade of the bread-fruit and other
trees, and had a very agreeable note, though common report among Europeans has denied the powers of harmony
(I know not on what grounds) to the birds of warm climates.   The heads of the talleft coco-trees were the ufual
refidence of a kind of very fmall perroquets of a beautiful
fapphirine blue, while another fort of a greenifh colour,
with a few red fpots, were more common among the bananas, and appeared frequently tame in the houfes of the
natives, who feemed to value them for their red feathers.
A king's fifher, of a dark-green, with a collar of the fame
hue round his white throat, a large cuckoo, and feveral
forts of pigeons or doves, were frequently feen hopping
from branch to branch, and a bluifh heron gravely ftalk-
ed along the fea fide, picking up fhell-fifh and worms.   A
fine brook, rolling over a bed of pebbles, came down a
narrow valley, and fupplied our waterers at its difcharge
into the fea.   We followed its ftream for a little while till
we were met by a great croud of natives at the heels of
three men, dreffed in various pieces of their red and yellow
                                                      cloth,

cloth, and provided with elegant turbans of the fame. Each of them had a long stick or wand in his hand, and one of them was accompanied by a woman, whom upon enquiry we found to be his wife. We demanded what their appearance meant, and were answered they were the Te-apoonee; but when they observed we did not understand enough of their language to comprehend this term, they added that they were Tata-no-t'Eatooa, men belonging to the divinity, and to the Marai, or burying-place; I suppose we might call them priests. We stopped with them some time, but as we did not see that any religious, or other ceremony was performed, we returned to the beach. About noon captain Cook re-imbarked with us, and with the two sons of O-Poe mentioned page 269, without having seen Aheatua, who for reasons unknown to us, still refused to admit us to his presence.

The two young fellows sat down to dinner with us, and partook of the vegetables, but did not touch our salt provisions. After dinner, one of them took an opportunity of stealing a knife and a pewter spoon, not contented with a number of presents which he had received from the captain, without having made any return on his part, and which ought to have prevented him from infringing the laws of hospitality. The theft being discovered, he was kicked from the deck, jumped overboard, and swam to the next canoe, where he seated himself, perhaps in defiance

of our power. Captain Cook fired a musket over his head,
upon which he took to the water again, and overset the
canoe. A second musket was levelled at him, but he
dived when he saw the flash, and did the same when the
third was discharged. Captain Cook now manned his boat,
and went to take the canoe, under which the man took
shelter; but he soon abandoned it, and swam to a double
canoe near the first, which was accordingly pursued. This
canoe however got ashore through the surf, and the natives
on the beach took up stones, which they levelled at our
boat's crew, who thought it advisable to retreat. However,
a four pounder directed towards the shore, frightened the
inhabitants sufficiently, so that our people could seize two
large double canoes, and bring them along-side of the ship.

We left the ship after this disturbance, in order to take
an afternoon's walk ashore near the watering-place, and
to restore the confidence of the people, who had entirely
forsaken us on account of our open hostilities. We pursued a different path from that which we had taken in
the morning, and found great quantities of bananas,
yams, eddies, &c. planted round every cottage, inhabited by friendly good-natured people, who seemed however a little more shy or reserved than usual, on account of what had happened. At last we arrived at a
large house, neatly constructed of reeds, which we were
told belonged to Aheatua, who was in another district.

at prefent. Here we faw a hog, and a couple of
fowls, the firft which the natives expofed to our fight,
having hitherto been very careful to conceal them, and
always refufing to part with them, under the pretext that
they were the property of the aree or king. They made
ufe of the fame excufe at prefent, though we offered a
hatchet, which in their eyes was the moft valuable mer-
chandife we had. After a fhort ftay, we returned the fame
way we came, and brought a fmall collection of new plants
on board. About fun-fet a boat was fent off, out of the
harbour, to bury in the fea one Ifaac Taylor, a marine,
who died this morning of a complication of diforders.
Ever fince we had left England, this man had been feverifh,
confumptive, and afthmatic; his complaints always kept
increafing, and at laft turned to a dropfy, which carried
him off. All our people on board were now well, except
one, whofe remarkable fcorbutic habit of body always laid
him up as foon as we came out to fea, where prophylactics
and wort could but juft keep him alive. However this
man, as well as the Adventure's crew, who were much
affected with the fcurvy when they came in here, recovered
amazingly by walking on fhore, and eating quantities
of frefh fruit.

Early the next morning fome of the natives came off
to us in a fmall canoe, and begged for the reftitution of
thofe larger ones which had been taken from them on the

　　　　　　　　day

day before. Captain Cook, who perceived the trade to have
flackened in confequence of that feizure, none of the inhabitants coming to the fhip, and few to the watering-
place, returned the canoes, as the beft means to reconcile
us to the confidence of the natives ; and though the effects
of his indulgence were not inflantaneous, yet in a day or
two our trade was perfectly re-eftablifhed.

After this peaceful prelude we went on fhore, in purfuit
of botanical difcoveries. A fmart fhower of rain which
had fallen over night, had cooled the air confiderably, and
made our walk extremely pleafant, before the fun could
become troublefome. The whole country had profited by
this rain, for every plant and tree feemed revived by it, and
the groves exhaled a fweet refrefhing fmell. Whether it
was owing to the early hour of our excurfion, or to the
beauty of the morning, our ear was faluted by the fong
of many fmall birds, which enlivened this delightful country. We had not walked far, when we heard a loud noife
in the wood, which refembled the ftrokes of a carpenter's
hammer. We followed the found, and at laft came to a
fmall fhed, where five or fix women were fitting on both
fides of a long fquare piece of timber, and beat the fibrous
bark of the mulberry-tree here, in order to manufacture it
into cloth. The inftrument they ufed for this purpofe was
a fquare wooden club, with longitudinal and parallel
furrows, which run fmaller and clofer together on the
                                          different

different fides *. They ceafed a little while to give us time to examine the bark, the mallet, and the timber on which they performed their operations. They alfo fhewed us a kind of glutinous water in a coco-nut fhell, which was made ufe of from time to time, to make the pieces of bark cohere together. This glue, which, as we underftood, was made of the *hibifcus efculentus*, is indifpenfibly neceffary in the manufacture of thofe immenfe pieces of cloth, fome-times two or three yards wide, and fifty yards long, which are compofed of little bits of bark, taken from trees never fo thick as the wrift. We carefully examined their plan-tations of mulberry-trees, but never found a fingle old one among them; as foon as they are of two years growth they are cut down, and new ones fpring up from the root, for fortunately this tree is one of the moft prolific in na-ture, and if fuffered to grow till it flowered and could bear fruits, might perhaps totally over-run the country. The bark muft always be taken from young trees; and thefe are carefully drawn into long ftems, without any branches, except juft at the top, fo that the bark is as entire as pof-fible. The method of preparing it before it comes under the mallet, we were not yet acquainted with at this time. The women employed in this manner, were dreffed in old and dirty rags of their cloth, and had very hard and callous

* See Dr. Hawkefworth's compilation, vol. II, p. 213, and plate No. 9.

hands.

hands. We proceeded a little farther up in a narrow valley, where a well-looking man invited us to sit down in the shade before his house. There was a little area paved with broadish stones, on which he spread banana leaves for us, and brought out a little stool made of the bread-tree-wood, cut out of one piece, on which he desired one of us to sit down, whom he took to be the principal person. Seeing us all seated he ran into his house, and brought out a quantity of bread-fruit baked, which he laid before us on fresh banana leaves. To this he added a matted basket full of the vee, or Taheitee apples, a fruit of the *spondias* genus, which resembles the anana, or pine-apple in the taste, and entreated us to partake of these refreshments. We breakfasted with a hearty appetite, sharpened by the exercise we had taken, the fine air of the morning, and the excellence of the provisions. We found the Taheitee method of dressing bread-fruit and other victuals, with heated stones under ground, infinitely superior to our usual way of boiling them; in the former all the juices remained, and were concentrated by the heat; but in the latter, the fruit imbibed many watery particles, and lost a great deal of its fine flavour and mealiness. To conclude this treat our host brought us five fresh coco-nuts, which he opened by pulling the fibres off with his teeth. The cool limpid liquor contained in them he poured into a clean cup, made of a ripe coco-nut-shell, and offered that to each of us in our

turns,

turns. The people in this country had on all occasions
been good-natured and friendly, and for beads sometimes
sold us coco-nuts and fruit, if we called for them; but
we had not yet seen an instance of hospitality exercised in
so complete a manner during our short stay. We therefore
thought it our duty to recompense our friend as much as
lay in our power, and presented him with a number of
transparent beads and iron nails, with which he was
highly satisfied and contented.

We continued our walk into the country from this seat
of patriarchal hospitality, notwithstanding the uneasiness
which many of the natives expressed, among the croud that
followed us. When they saw us persist in our expedition,
the greatest part of them dispersed to their different habitations, and only a few of them attended us, who made it
their business to act as our guides. We came to the foot
of the first hills, where we left the huts and plantations
of the natives behind us, and ascended on a beaten path,
passing through an uncultivated shrubbery mixed with
several tall timber-trees. Here we searched the most intricate parts, and found several plants and birds hitherto
unknown to natural historians. With these little acquisitions we returned towards the sea, at which our friends
the natives expressed their satisfaction. We found a vast
concourse of inhabitants on the beach at our trading-place,
and saw that our people had brought a great quantity of

large

large eddies and other roots, but few bread-fruits, which
were now very scarce, only a few trees bearing them
so late in the season, while most of the others were already
shooting forth the embryo of a new crop. The excessive
heat of the sun, now tempted us to bath in a branch of
the adjacent river, which formed a deep pond of some
extent; and being refreshed with this bath we returned
on board to dinner. In the afternoon we had heavy rains,
attended with wind, during which the Adventure drove
from her moorings, but was brought up again by a timely
manœuvre. This bad weather confined us on board,
where we arranged the plants and animals which we had
hitherto collected, and made drawings of such as were
not known before. Our three days excursions had supplied
us only with a small number of species, which in an island
so flourishing as Taheitee, gave a convincing proof of its
high cultivation; for a few individual plants occupied that
space, which in a country entirely left to itself, would
have teemed with several hundred different kinds in wild
disorder. The small size of the island, together with its
vast distance from either the eastern or western continent,
did not admit of a great variety of animals. We saw no
other species of quadrupeds than hogs, and dogs which
were domestic, and incredible numbers of rats, which the
natives suffered to run about at pleasure, without ever trying
to destroy them. We found however a tolerable number

of

of birds, and when the natives gave themselves the trouble to fish, we commonly purchased a confiderable variety of fpecies, as this clafs of creatures can eafily roam from one part of the ocean to the other, and particularly in the torrid zone, where certain forts are general all round the world.

If the fcarcity of fpontaneous plants was unfavourable to the botanift, ftill it had the moft falutary effects with regard to the whole company on board of both our veffels, fince their place was occupied by great quantities of whole- fome vegetables. We daily bought abundance of yams, eddies, and Taheitee apples; together with fome bananas and bread-fruit, which, on account of the feafon, were grown very fcarce. The wholefome regimen which we had by this means been able to keep, had vifibly, and I might almoft fay miraculoufly, operated to reftore to their health, all thofe who were ill of the fcurvy at our arrival; and the only inconvenience we felt from it was a kind of flux, owing to the fudden change of diet, with which a few of the people were afflicted. Not content with this fortunate fupply, we could not help cafting longing eyes towards the hogs which we faw in great numbers on all our excurfions into the country, though the natives were always careful to hide them in low ftyes, covered over with boards, forming a kind of platform, on which they fat or lay down. We tried all poffible means to engage the people to fell fome of them to us, and offered hatchets,

shirts, and other goods of value to the Taheitians, but still
without success, their constant answer being, that these animals were the king's (*aree's*) property. Instead of acquief-
cing in this refusal, and acknowledging the kind difposition of the natives, who furnished us at least with the
means of recovering our strength, and restoring our sick,
a proposal was made to the captains, by some persons in
the ships, to sweep away by force a sufficient number of
hogs for our use, and afterwards to return such a quantity
of our goods in exchange to the natives, as we should think
adequate to the spoil we had taken. This proposal, which
nothing but the most tyrannical principles, and the meanest
felfishness could have dictated, was received with the contempt and indignation which it justly deserved.

Our acquisitions in natural history being hitherto so inconfiderable, we had leisure every day to ramble in the
country in search of others, as well as to pick up various
circumstances which might serve to throw a light on the
character, manners, and present state of the inhabitants.

On the 20th towards noon, I directed my walk, in
company with several officers, to the eastern point of the
harbour. We soon came to a rivulet, which was wide and
deep enough to admit a canoe upon it, by means of which
we ferried over to the opposite shore, where we perceived a
house of some extent, among the bushes. Before it we saw
a quantity of the finer sorts of Taheitee cloth spread out on
the

the grafs, which the natives told us, had been wafhed in the river; and clofe to the houfe, fufpended on a pole, we obferved a target of a femicircular form, made of wicker-work, and plaited ftrings (of the coco-nut fibres,) covered with the glolfy bluifh-green feathers of a kind of pigeon, and ornamented with many fhark's teeth, difplayed in three co-centric femicircles; I enquired whether it was to be pur-chafed, but was anfwered in the negative, and concluded that it was only expofed to the air, in the fame manner as we are ufed to do from time to time, with things which we preferve in clofe boxes. A middle-aged man, who lay ftretched at his eafe in the hut, invited us to fit down by him, and curioully examined my drefs; he had long nails on his fingers, upon which he valued him-felf not a little, and which I found were a mark of diftinc-tion, fince only fuch perfons, as had no occafion to work, could fuffer them to grow to that length. The Chinefe have the fame cuftom, and pride themfelves as much in it; but whether the Taheitians derive it from them, or whether chance has led them both to the fame idea, without any communication with each other, is poffibly beyond the art of Needham and Des Guignes to determine. In different corners of the hut we faw fome women and fome men, feparately eating their dinner of bread-fruit and bananas, and both parties, as we approached them, defired us to par-take of their provifions. The fingular cuftom, which forces

O o 2

the

the fexes to fhun each others company at their meals, is already mentioned by former voyagers, who have been equally unfuccefsful with ourfelves in difcovering its caufe.

We left this hut, and ftrolled through an odoriferous fhrubbery to another, where we found O-Taï, his wife, and children, and his fifters Maroya and Maroraï.   The officer who had loft his bed-fheets was with us, but thought it to no purpofe to enquire for them, and rather tried to ingratiate himfelf with the fair one.   Beads, nails, and various trifles were prefented to her, which fhe readily accepted, but remained inexorable to the paffionate folliciations of her lover.   As fhe had in all probability obtained the poffeffion of the fheets, which fhe coveted, and for which alone fhe could have fubmitted to proftitution, it feems nothing could afterwards tempt her to admit the tranfient embraces of a ftranger.   This is the moft likely conftruction we could put upon her conduct, and it became more probable to us, when we confidered, that fhe belonged to a family of fome note, and that, during captain Cook's long ftay on the ifland in the Endeavour, there had been few, if any inftances, that women among the better fort of people had demeaned themfelves fo far.   After a fhort ftay with them, I returned to our trading place, but finding all our boats gone off, ventured to embark in a fingle canoe, without an outrigger, and was fafely brought on board the Re-
                                                                          folution

solution for a single bead, which was all I had left after this excursion.

At day-break the next morning we went ashore again, on another walk to the eastward. We observed the plain to widen, as we advanced beyond the east point of Aitepeha harbour, and of course growing richer in bread-fruit and coco-nut trees, bananas, and other vegetable productions, on most of which we saw the buds of a future crop. The houses of the natives were likewise found to be more numerous, and many seemed to us neater and newer than those near our anchoring-place. In one of them, which was of the closer sort, walled in with reeds, we saw a great many bundles of cloth, and cases for targets suspended from the roof, all which, as well as the house itself, we were informed belonged to Aheatua. We walked about two miles in the most delightful groves or plantations of fruit-trees, where the natives were just returning to their various employments. Among them we easily noticed the manufacturers of cloth, by the hollow sound of the mallet. However, it must not be supposed, that the necessities of these people urgently required their constant application to work; for our appearance soon gathered a croud of them about us, who followed us all day as far as we went, and sometimes even neglected their meals on our account. It was not without some interested motives, that they attended upon us. Their general behaviour towards

wards

wards us was good-natured, friendly, and I may fay offi-
cious; but they watched every opportunity of conveying
away fome trifles with amazing dexterity, and many among
them, whenever we returned the kind looks they gave us,
or fmiled upon them, thought that a proper time to take
advantage of our good difpofition, and immediately with
a begging tone faid, *tayo, poë*, "friend, a bead!" which,
whether we complied with or refufed, did not alter their
good temper. When thefe petitions became too frequent,
we ufed to mock them, by repeating their words in the
fame tone, which always produced a general peal of good-
humoured laughter amongft them. Their converfation was
commonly loud, and it feemed that our appearance was
their principal topick; every new-comer was immediately
made acquainted by the others with our names, which they
reduced to a few vowels and fofter confonants, and was
entertained with a repetition of what we had faid or done
that morning. His firft requeft was generally to hear a
mufket fired off, which we complied with on condition
that he fhould fhew us a bird as a mark. However, we
were frequently at a lofs how to behave, when he pointed
out a bird at four or five hundreds yards diftance, as they
had no idea that the effects of our fire-arms were limited
to a certain fpace. As it was not prudent to let them into
this myftery, we always pretended that we could not fee
the bird, till we came near enough to fhoot it. The firft
explofion

explosion frightened them considerably, and on some produced such violent consternation that they dropped down
on the ground, or ran back about twenty yards from us,
where they remained till we quieted their fears by profef-
sions of friendship, or till their more courageous brethren
had picked up the bird which we had killed. But they soon
became more familiar, and though they always expressed
some sudden emotion, yet they conquered by degrees the
appearance of fear.

Notwithstanding the friendly reception which we met
with on all sides, the natives were very anxious to keep
their hogs out of sight, and whenever we enquired for
them seemed uneasy, and either told us they had none, or
assured us they belonged to Aheatua their king. As we
perceived their reluctance to part with these animals, we
thought it best to take no farther notice of them, and
though we saw great numbers of them confined in pigstyes
almost in every hut, we pretended not to know that there
were any, or not to care for them; this proceeding we always found had the good effect of encreasing the confidence
of the people towards us.

Having advanced a mile or two, we sat down on a few
large stones, which formed a kind of paved area before
one of the cottages, and desired the inhabitants to bring us
some bread-fruit and coco-nuts, in exchange for beads.
They very readily supplied us with a quantity of each, on
which

which we breakfasted. The croud who followed us, sat
down at a distance from us, at our desire, in order that
they might have no opportunity of snatching up any of our
arms, or other apparatus, which we were obliged to lay
out of our hands, while we made our meal. To add to
our good cheer, we were presented with a coco-nut shell
full of a kind of diminutive fresh fish, which the natives are
used to eat raw, without any other sauce than salt water.
We tasted them, and found them far from disagreeable;
however, as we were not used to eat them without being
dressed, we distributed them, with the remains of the fruit,
to our favourites among the croud.

Thus refreshed, we continued our walk, but turned towards the hills, notwithstanding the importunities of the
natives, who urged us to continue on the plain, which we
easily perceived arose merely from their dislike to fatigue.
We were not to be diverted from our purpose; but leaving
behind us almost the whole croud, we entered, with a few
guides, a chasm between two hills. There we found several
wild plants which were new to us, and saw a number of
little swallows flying over a fine brook, which rolled impe-
tuously along. We walked up along its banks to a perpendicular rock, fringed with various tufted shrubberies, from
whence it fell in a crystalline column, and was collected at
the bottom into a smooth limpid pond, surrounded with
many species of odoriferous flowers. This spot, where we
had

had a profpect of the plain below us, and of the fea beyond
it, was one of the moft beautiful I had ever feen, and could not fail of bringing to remembrance the moft fanciful defcriptions of poets, which it eclipfed in beauty. In the fhade of trees, whofe branches hung over the water, we enjoyed a pleafant gale, which foftened the heat of the day, and amidft the folemn uniform noife of the waterfall, which was but feldom interrupted by the whiftling of birds, we fat down to defcribe our new acquifitions before they withered. Our Taheitian companions feeing us employed, likewife refted among the bufhes, viewing us attentively and in profound filence. We could have been well pleafed to have paffed the whole day in this retirement; however, after finifhing our notes, and feafting our eyes once more with the romantick fcenery, we returned to the plain. Here we obferved a great croud of the natives coming towards us, and at their near approach perceived two of our fhipmates, Mr. Hodges and Mr. Grindall, whom they furrounded and attended on their walk. We foon joined them, and refolved to continue our excurfion together. A youth, of a very promifing countenance, who had diftinguifhed himfelf by fhewing a particular attachment for thefe gentlemen, was entrufted with Mr. Hodges's port-folio, where he preferved the fketches and defigns, which he had frequent opportunities of making on his walk. No favour, or mark of affection could I believe have given this youth

VOL. I.   P p   fo

so much real pleasure, as the confidence they had placed in him, upon which he seemed to value himself among his countrymen. Perhaps this circumstance, joined to the peaceable appearance of our gentlemen, who walked without arms of any kind, had a general effect upon all the people that surrounded us, as their familiarity and affection seemed much encreased. We entered a spacious hut together, where we saw a large family assembled. An old man, with a placid countenance, lay on a clean mat, and rested his head on a little stool, which served as a pillow. His head, which was truly venerable, was well furnished with fine locks of a silvery grey, and a thick beard as white as snow descended to his breast. His eyes were lively, and health sat on his full cheeks. His wrinkles, which characterize age with us, were few and not deep; for cares, trouble, and disappointment, which untimely furrow our brows, cannot be supposed to exist in this happy nation. Several little ones, whom we took to be his grand-children, and who, according to the custom of the country, were perfectly naked, played with their aged ancestor, while his actions and looks convinced us, that the simple way of living to which he had been used, had not yet blunted his senses. Several well-made men and artless nymphs, in whom youth supplied the want of beauty, surrounded the old man, and as we came in seemed to be in conversation after a frugal meal. They desired us to sit

down

down on the mats among them, and we did not give them
time to repeat their invitation. Their curiofity, which had
perhaps never before been gratified with the fight of ftrangers, now prompted them to examine our drefs and our arms,
without beftowing their attention longer than a moment on
any fingle objeft. They admired our colour, preffed our
hands, feemed to wonder that we had no punctures on them,
nor long nails on our fingers, and eagerly enquired for our
names, which when known, they were happy to repeat.
Thefe names, as they pronounced them, were not fo like the
originals that an etymologift could eafily have deduced
them, but in return they were more harmonious, and eafily pronounced. Forfter was changed into *Matara*, Hodges
into *Oree*, Grindall into *Terino*, Sparrman into *Pamanee*, and
George into *Teoree*. The hofpitality which we had found
under every roof, was not wanting here, and we were offered fome coco-nuts and *eevees* to quench our thirft after
the laft walk. One of the young men had a flute made of
a bamboo, which had but three holes; he blew it with
his noftrils[*], whilft another accompanied him with the
voice. The whole mufic, both vocal and inftrumental,
confifted of three or four notes, which were between half
and quarter notes, being neither whole tones nor femi-tones.
The effect of thefe notes, without variety or order, was only a kind of drowfy hum, which could not indeed hurt

[*] See Hawkefworth.

the

the ear by its difcordant founds, but made no pleafing im-
preffion on our minds.   It is furprifing that the tafte for
mufic fhould be fo general all over the world, when the
ideas of harmony among different nations are fo diftinct!
Charmed with the picture of real happinefs, which was
thus exhibited before us, Mr. Hodges filled his port-folio
with feveral fketches, which will convey to future times
the beauties of a fcene, of which words give but a faint
idea.   While he was drawing, all the natives looked on
with great attention, and were highly pleafed to find out
the refemblance between his performances and different
perfons among them.   Our acquaintance with their language, which we were at great pains to improve, was as
yet very imperfect, and deprived us of the pleafure which
we might have received from a converfation with thefe
good people.   A few feparate words, and an interlude of
dumb mimickry, was all that we had to fupply the place
of a coherent fpeech.   However, even this was fufficient to
amufe the natives, and our docility and endeavours to pleafe
feemed to be at leaft as agreeable to them, as their focial
temper and willingnefs to give inftruction appeared to us.
The old man, without changing his attitude, and continuing to recline his head on the ftool, afked us feveral little
queftions, fuch as the captain's name, the name of the
country we came from, how long we fhould ftay, whether
we had our wives on board, &c.   It feemed that he was
                                                    already

already apprifed of all thefe things by common report, but wifhed to have them confirmed from our own mouths. We fatisfied his curiofity as well as we could on thefe points, and after diftributing little prefents of beads, medals, and other trifles to his family, we fet forwards once more on our excurfion. The many paufes which we made at the hofpitable huts of the natives, always refrefhed us fo much, that we felt no manner of inconvenience, and could with eafe have walked round the whole ifland in the fame manner. The plain at the foot of the mountains offered no impediment to our progrefs; on the contrary, its paths were well beaten, and its whole furface perfectly level, and covered in many places with a fine growth of graffes. Not a fingle noxious animal appeared to deter us, and not even a gnat or mufketoe hummed unpleafantly about us, or made us apprehenfive of its bite. The bread-fruit groves, with their abundant foliage, intercepted the rays of the meridian fun, whofe action was greatly mitigated by a frefh fea-breeze: The inhabitants however, who were ufed to pafs the middle of the day in repofe, dropt off one by one in the bufhes, fo that only a few remained with us. After we had walked about two miles farther to the fouth eaftward, we came to the fea-fhore at a place where it formed a little inlet. Here, furrounded on all fides with plantations, we met with a glade, or lawn, in the midft of which we faw a marai (burying-place) built up of three

ranges

1773.
AUGUST.

ranges of ftones, like fteps, each about three feet and a
half in height, and covered with graffes, ferns, and fmall
fhrubs.   Towards the country, at fome diftance from the
building, there was an oblong enclofure round it made of
ftone, about three feet high, within which two or three
folitary coco-palms and fome young cafuarinas, with their
weeping branches, gave an air of folemnity and pleafing
melancholy to the fcene.   At a little diftance from the
maraï, furrounded by a thick fhrubbery, we faw an inconfiderable hut or fhed, (tupapou,) where, on a kind of
ftage about breaft high, a corpfe was placed, covered with
a white piece of cloth, which hung down in various folds.
Young coco-trees and bananas were fpringing up, and
dragon-trees bloffoming around it.   Near this we faw
another hut, where a quantity of eatables lay for the divinity, (eatua,) and a pole was ftuck in the ground, on which
we faw a dead bird wrapped in a piece of a mat.   In this
laft hut, which ftood on a fmall eminence, we obferved a
woman fitting in a penfive attitude, who got up at our
approach, and would not fuffer us to come near her.   We
offered her a fmall prefent, but fhe refufed to touch it.
We underftood from the natives who were with us, that
fhe belonged to the maraï, and that the dead corfe was alfo
a woman's, whofe obfequies the firft perhaps was performing.

After

After Mr. Hodges had made several drawings we returned from this place, which had really something grand in its appearance, and seemed calculated to favour religious meditation. In our return we kept along the sea-shore, till we came to a spacious house, very pleasantly situated amidst a grove of low coco-palms, loaded with fruit. Two or three fried little fishes, which one of the natives sold us for a few beads, were here shared among us, to stay our appetite, grown very keen again since our breakfast. Several of our company likewise bathed in the sea, as a farther refreshment in this warm climate, and having afterwards bought some pieces of cloth, (ahow's) of the country fabrick, dressed in them, after the Tahcitee fashion, to the infinite pleasure of the natives. Our walk continued along the shore beyond another marai, much like the first, to a neat house, where a very fat man, who seemed to be a chief of the district, was lolling on his wooden pillow. Before him two servants were preparing his desert, by beating up with water some bread-fruit and bananas, in a large wooden bowl, and mixing with it a quantity of the fermented four paste of bread-fruit, (called mahei.) The consistence of this mixture was such, that it could properly be called a drink, and the instrument with which they made it, was a pestle of a black polished stone, which appeared to be a kind of basaltes [*]. While this was doing, a woman who sat down

[*] See Hawkesworth, vol. II. p. 202.

near him, crammed down his throat by handfuls the remains of a large baked fiſh, and ſeveral bread-fruits, which
he ſwallowed with a voracious appetite. His countenance
was the picture of phlegmatic inſenſibility, and ſeemed to
witneſs that all his thoughts centred in the care of his
paunch. He ſcarce deigned to look at us, and a few mo-
noſyllables which he uttered, were only directed to remind
his feeders of their duty, when we attracted their attention.
The great degree of ſatisfaction which we had enjoyed on
our different walks in this iſland, and particularly the pleaſure of this day's excurſion, was diminiſhed by the appearance and behaviour of the chief, and the reflections which
naturally aroſe from thence. We had flattered ourſelves
with the pleaſing fancy of having found at leaſt one little
ſpot of the world, where a whole nation, without being
lawleſs barbarians, aimed at a certain frugal equality in
their way of living, and whoſe hours of enjoyment were
juſtly proportioned to thoſe of labour and reſt. Our diſappointment was therefore very great, when we ſaw a
luxurious individual ſpending his life in the moſt ſluggiſh
inactivity, and without one benefit to ſociety, like the pri-
vileged paraſites of more civilized climates, fattening on
the ſuperfluous produce of the ſoil, of which he robbed the
labouring multitude. His indolence, in ſome degree, re-
ſembled that which is frequent in India and the adjacent
kingdoms of the Eaſt, and deſerved every mark of indignation

1773.
AUGUST.

tion which Sir John Mandeville expreſſed in his Aſiatic travels.   That worthy knight, who, top-full of chivalry, and the valourous ſpirit of his time, devoted his life to conſtant activity, was highly incenſed at the ſight of a monſter of lazineſs, who paſſed his days " withouten " doynge of ony dedes of armes," and lived " everemore " thus in eſe, as a ſwyn that is fedde in ſty, for to ben " made fatte *."

On

* For the ſatisfaction of my readers I ſhall here inſert the account which the knight gives of the voluptuary who attracted his cenſure, eſpecially as ſeveral little circumſtances ſerve to make the ſimilarity between him and the Tabeitian chief more perfect.—" From that lond, in returnynge he ten journeys thorge out " the lond of the grete Chane, is another gode yle and a great kyngdom, where " the kyng is fulle riche and myghty.   And amonges the riche men of his " contree is a paſſynge riche man, that is no prynce, ne duke, ne erl; but he " hath mo that holden of him londes and other lordſchipes: for he is more " riche.   For he hathe every zeer of annuelle rents 300000 bors charged with " corn of dyverſe greynes and rys; and ſo he ledethe a fulle noble lif and a " delycate, after the cuſtom of the contree.   For he hathe every day 50 fair " damyſeles, alle maydenes, that ſerven him evere more at his mete, and for to " lye by him o night, and for to do with hem that is to his pliſaunce.   And " when he is at the table, thei bryngen him hys mete, at every tyme 5 and " 5 togedre.   And in bryngynge hire ſervyce, thei ſyngen a ſong.   And after " that, thei kutten his mete, and putten it in his mouthe, for he toucethe " no thing, ne handlethe nought, but holdethe everemore his hondes before " him upon the table.   For he hathe ſo longe nayles, that he may take no- " thing, ne handle no thing, for the nobleſſe of that contree is to have longe " nayles, and to make hem growen alle ways to ben as longe as men may.—— " And alle weys theiſe damyſeles, that I ſpak of beforn, ſyngen all the tyme " that this riche man etethe; and when that he etethe no more of his firſt " cours, thanne other 5 and 5 of faire damyſeles bryngen him his ſeconde " cours alle weys ſyngynge as thei dide before.   And ſo thei don contynuelly

1773.
August.

On leaving this Taheitian drone we feparated, and I
accompanied Meff. Hodges and Grindall, whofe good-natured friend, the carrier of the port-folio, had earneflly
invited us to his habitation. We arrived there towards five
in the evening, and found it a fmall but cleanly cottage,
before which a great abundance of frefh leaves were fpread
on a flony place, and a prodigious quantity of the beft
coco-nuts and well-roafted bread-fruit were laid out in
fine order. He immediately ran to two elderly perfons,
who were bufy in frightening the rats from this plentiful
ftore of provifions, and introduced them to us as his parents. They expreffed great joy on feeing the friends of
their fon, and entreated us to fit down to the meal which
lay before us. We were at firft ftruck with aftonifhment
on finding it entirely prepared at our arrival, but we foon
recollected that our friend had fent off one of his comrades feveral hours beforehand, very probably with directions to provide for our entertainment. As this was the
firft regular meal to which we fat down this day, it will
eafily be conceived that we fell to with a good appetite,
and gave infinite fatisfaction to the good-natured old people and the generous-minded youth, who all feemed to

" every day to the ende of his mete. And in this manere he ledethe his lif, and
" fo did thei beforn him that weren his aunceftres, and fo fchulle thei that
" comen after him." See the Voyages and Travaylls of Sir John Maundevile, knight,
pag. 376.

                                                    think

think themselves happy in the honour which we did to their excellent cheer. With such a venerable pair ministring to us, if I may be allowed to indulge in a poetical idea, we ran some risk of forgetting that we were men, and might have believed ourselves feasted by the hospitable Baucis and Philemon, if our inability to reward them had not reminded us of mortality. However, all the beads and nails which we could muster amongst us were offered to them, rather as a mark that we preserved a grateful sense of their good heart, than as any retribution. The youth went on with us to the beach opposite to our vessels, and brought on board a great quantity of provisions, which we had left unconsumed at our dinner. He was there presented with a hatchet, a shirt, and various articles of less value by his friends, and returned that very evening on those to his parents, being probably enriched beyond his warmest expectation.

The usual trade had been carried on about the ships, and on the beach opposite to them, during our absence, without any material incident, except Captain Cook's meeting with Tuahow, the same native who had accompanied him a considerable way when he made the circuit of Taheitee in a boat, in the course of his first voyage *. We found him and two of his countrymen on board at our return, they having resolved to make up their night's lodging

* See Hawkesworth, vol. II. p. 160, 162, &c.

Q q 2

with

1773.
August.
with us, which, though ufual at Matavaï Bay during the
Endeavour's voyage, none had hitherto ventured upon in
this place. Tuahow being already familiarized with our
way of living, and acquainted with the various objects
which commonly ftruck his countrymen with wonder,
eagerly entered into difcourfe with us, as he found us attentive to his queftions. He enquired after *Tabane*, Mr.
Banks; *Tolano*, Dr. Solander; *Tupaya*, (Tupia) and feveral
perfons in the Endeavour whofe names he recollected. He
rejoiced to hear that Mr. Banks and Dr. Solander were
well, and having often renewed his queftion, always received the fame anfwer to it; upon which he afked whether
they would not come back to Taheitee, accompanying it
with a look which ftrongly expreffed the wifh of feeing
them again. When he heard of Tupaya's death, he was
defirous of being informed whether it had been violent or
natural, and was well pleafed to hear from fuch circumftances as we could by broken words and figns communicate to him, that ficknefs had put a period to his life. In
return, we queftioned him concerning the death of *Tootahah*, who had appeared as the acting chief of the ifland in
Captain Cook's former voyage. We plainly underftood that
a great naval fight had happened between that chief and
old *Ahoatua*[*], the father of the prefent king of Tiarraboo;
in which neither party had gained a decifive advantage;

[*] Called *Wahroas* in Hawkefworth, vol. II. p. 157, 158.

but

but that Toorahàh afterwards marching his army acrofs
the ifthmus, which feparates the two peninfulas, had been
defeated in an obftinate engagement, in which himfelf,
Tuboraï-Tamaide, and many other perfons of diftinction
on his fide were flain. A peace was foon after concluded
with *O-Tu* the king of O-Taheitee*, who, after Toorahàh's deceafe, had affumed the power of the fovereignty, of
which before he had only enjoyed the title.   Old Aheatua,
according to Tuahow's account, died but a few months
after this peace, and his fon, of the fame name, who, according to the cuftom of this country, had already, during
his father's life-time, borne the title of *te-aree* † (the king,)
and received the honours annexed to that dignity, now
likewife fucceeded to its more effential part, the management of affairs.

This fubject being exhaufted, we took out the map of
O-Taheitee, (engraved for captain Cooke's former voyage)
and laid it before Tuahow, without telling him what it
was. He was however too good a pilot, not to find it out
prefently ; and overjoyed to fee a reprefentation of his own
country, immediately with his finger pointed out the fituation of all the wheunuas or diftricts upon it, naming them
at the fame time in their order, as we faw them written

* Called *Outra* in Hawkefworth, vol. II. p. 154.
† See Hawkefworth, vol. II. p. 158, 159, 160, 175, where this *title* is
conftantly expreffed as his *name*.

on

on the chart. When he came to O Whai-urua the next diſtrict with a harbour, to the ſouth of our preſent anchoring-place, he pulled us by the arm to look on attentively, and related that there had been a ſhip (paheï) which he called paheï no Peppe, and which had lain there five days; that the people in her had received ten hogs from the natives, and that one of the crew ran away from the ſhip, and now lived upon the iſland. From this account we concluded that the Spaniards had ſent another veſſel to examine O-Taheitee, probably firſt diſcovered by their navigators, and which of late years had been ſo frequently viſited by the Engliſh, as might juſtly rouſe their attention, on account of the proximity of their own extenſive poſſeſſions in South America. Strange as it may ſeem, the name of Peppe confirmed us in our conjectures, notwithſtanding its vaſt difference from Eſpaña, from whence we ſuppoſed it originated; becauſe we were by this time well acquainted with the cuſtom of mutilating all foreign names, which the Taheitians poſſeſs, even in a higher degree than the French and Engliſh. We put ſeveral queſtions relative to this ſhip to Tuahow, but could never obtain any farther intelligence from him, except that the man who had left it, always accompanied Aheatua, and had given him the advice not to furniſh us with any hogs. Whatever ſelfintereſted or bigoted motives that man may have had to give Aheatua ſuch an advice, yet it ſeems to have been in

reality

reality the moſt friendly and valuable which he could have
offered to his protector. The way to keep the riches of
his ſubjects, among which are their hogs in the country,
and to prevent new wants from prevailing among a happy
people, was to get rid of us as ſoon as he could, by denying
us the refreſhments of which we ſtood moſt in need. It
were indeed ſincerely to be wiſhed, that the intercourſe
which has lately ſubſiſted between Europeans and the
natives of the South Sea iſlands may be broken off in time,
before the corruption of manners which unhappily cha-
racteriſes civilized regions, may reach that innocent race
of men, who live here fortunate in their ignorance and
ſimplicity. But it is a melancholy truth, that the dictates
of philanthropy do not harmonize with the political ſyſtems of Europe!

Several of our people having taken a walk on ſhore,
the next day returned on board with the news, that they
had met with Aheatua, who was at laſt come to this diſtrict
in order to give us an audience. They had been admitted
into his preſence without any ceremony, and his majeſty,
in the midſt of all his court, had given up one half of his
ſtool (pappa), to Mr. Smith, one of our mates, who was
of the party. He had at the ſame time graciouſly aſſured
him, that he wiſhed to ſpeak to captain Cook, and had
as many hogs to give him, as he had hatchets to pay for
them, which was by far the moſt agreeable news we had
heard

heard for some time. They also reported that they had seen a man resembling an European in colour and feature, but that upon speaking to him, he had retired into the croud. Whether this was really an European, or whether the story which Tuahow had told us the evening before, had wrought upon the fancy of our men we cannot determine; so much however is certain, that none of us ever saw him afterwards.

In consequence of Aheatua's declaration, the captains, with several officers, Dr. Sparrman, my father, and myself, went on shore early on the 23d. We proceeded about a mile along the river from which we filled our casks, being conducted by Opao, one of the natives, who had lodged on board. A great croud coming down towards us, those who surrounded us pulled off their upper garments, so as to uncover their shoulders, which is a mark of respect due to the king. We presently joined the croud, in the midst of whom Aheatua sat down on a large stool, cut out of solid wood, which one of his people had hitherto carried. He immediately recollected captain Cook, and made room for him on his stool, while captain Furneaux, and the rest of us, chose large stones for our seats. An immense number of natives thronged about us on all sides, and included us in a very narrow circle, increasing the heat to such a degree, that the king's attendants were frequently obliged to keep them back, by beating them.

O-AHEATUA,

1774.
August.

O-AHEATUA, the king of O-Taheitee-eetee, (Little Ta-heitee) which is otherwise called Tiarraboo, was a youth of seventeen or eighteen years of age, well-made, about five feet six inches high, and likely to grow taller. His countenance was mild, but unmeaning; and rather expressed some signs of fear and distrust at our first meeting, which suited ill with the ideas of majesty, and yet are often the characteristics of lawless power. His colour was of the fairest of his people, and his lank hair of a light-brown, turning into reddish at the tips, or being what is commonly called sandy. He wore at present no other dress than a white sash, (marro) round the waist to the knees, made of the best kind of cloth, and his head as well as all the rest of his body was uncovered. On both sides of him sat several chiefs and nobles, distinguishable by their superior stature, which is the natural effect of the immense quantity of food which they consume. One of them was punctured in a surprising manner, which we had never seen before, large black blotches of various shapes, almost covering his arms, legs, and sides. This man, whose name was E-Tee, was also remarkable for his enormous corpulence, and for the deference which the aree (king) paid to him, consulting him almost upon every occasion. The king, during the time he sat on the stool, which was his throne, preserved a grave or rather stiff deportment, scarce to be expected at his years, though it seemed to be

R r studied

1773.
August.

studied and assumed, only to make our meeting more solemn. This may be looked upon as a kind of recommendation by some men, but it is unhappily a mask of hypocrify, which we should hardly have expected at Taheitee. After the first salutation, captain Cook presented Aheatua with a piece of red baize, a bed-sheet, a broad axe, a knife, nails, looking-glasses, and beads; and my father gave him similar presents, among which was an aigrette or tuft of feathers fixed on a wire, and dyed of a bright crimson; upon this his majesty set a particular value, and at the sight of it the whole croud gave a general shout of admiration, expressed by the word *wáu!* The king now enquired for Mr. Banks, which only Tuahow had done before him, and then asked how long we intended to stay, expressing at the same time, that he wished we might remain five months. Captain Cook's answer was, that as he did not receive sufficient supplies of provisions, he must sail immediately. The king confined his first request to one month, and at last to five days, but captain Cook persisted in his resolution; Aheatua then promised to send us hogs the next day, but as this had been repeatedly said without any consequence, we took no notice of it now; for even in a state so little refined as Tiarraboo, we found that the real benevolence of the middle class, which manifested itself towards us in hospitality and a number of good

and

and noble actions, gave us no right to trust the specious politeness of the court and courtiers, who fed our hopes with empty promises.

During this conference the croud, amounting at least to five hundred persons, was so excessively noisy, that it was impossible at times to distinguish a word; and on those occasions some of the king's attendants with a Stentor's voice called out *mamů!* (be silent,) and enforced his command by dealing out hearty blows with a long stick. The aree seeing that captain Cook was not to be persuaded to prolong his stay in this harbour, got up, and walked down along the river with us, while his attendants carried his wooden stool, and the kingly presents which he had received. On this walk he laid aside the gravity, which was not natural to him, and talked with great affability to our common people. He desired me to tell him the names of all the persons from on board both sloops, who were present, to which he added the question, whether they had their wives on board? Being answered in the negative, his majesty in a fit of good humour desired them to look for partners among the daughters of the land, which they understood it was meant at present, in the light of a mere compliment. He sat down soon after close to a house of reeds, into which we all retired, when the sun appeared through the clouds. Here he called for some coco-nuts, and began to tell the story of the *Pahi no Peppe*, or Spanish

ship,

ship, of which Tuahow had given us the first intimation.
According to the king's account it seemed clear, that the
ship had been at Whaï Urua five months before us, and had
lain there ten days. He added, that the captain had hanged
four of his people, and that the fifth had escaped the same
punishment by running away. This European, whom
they named O-Pahoòtu, we enquired after to no purpose,
for a long while; till his majesty's attendants seeing us
very eager to become acquainted with him, assured us he
was dead. We have since heard that about the time mentioned by the natives, Don Juan de Langara y Huarte, sent
out from the port of Callao in Peru, had visited O-Taheitee,
but what the particulars of that voyage are, has never trans-
pired. While we remained in the house E-Tee, the fat
chief, who seemed to be the principal counsellor of the king,
very seriously asked us, whether we had a God *(Eatuâ)* in
our country, and whether we prayed to him *(epore?)*
When we told him, that we acknowledged a Divinity, who
had made every thing, and was invisible, and that we also
were accustomed to address our petitions to him, he seemed
to be highly pleased, and repeated our words with
notes of his own to several persons who sat round him.
To us he seemed to signify, that the ideas of his countrymen corresponded with ours in this respect. Every thing
concurs indeed to convince us, that this simple and only
just conception of the Deity, has been familiar to mankind
in

1773
August.

In all ages and in all countries, and that only by the ex-
ceffive cunning of a few individuals, thofe complex fyftems
of abfurd idolatry have been invented, which difgrace the
hiftory of almoft every people. The love of empire, or the
purfuit after voluptuoufnefs and indolence, feem to have
infpired the numerous branches of heathen priefts with the
idea of keeping the minds of the people in awe, by
awakening their fuperftition. The natural love of the miraculous has made it eafy for them not only to put their
projects in execution, but likewife to weave their prejudices
fo firmly into the web of human knowledge, that to this
moment the greater part of mankind pay them homage,
and blindly fuffer themfelves to be cheated in the groffeft
manner.

While E-Tee was converfing on religious matters, king
Ahcatua was playing with Captain Cook's watch. After
curioufly examining the motion of fo many wheels, that
feemed to move as it were fpontaneoufly, and fhewing
his aftonifhment at the noife it made, which he could not
exprefs otherwife than by faying it "fpoke," *(parou.)* he returned it, and afked what it was good for. With a great
deal of difficulty we made him conceive that it meafured
the day, fimilar to the fun, by whofe altitude in the heav-
ens he and his people are ufed to divide their time. After
this explanation, he called it a little fun, to fhew us that
he perfectly underftood our meaning. We were juft getting.

ting up to return towards the beach, when a man arrived
who brought a hog along with him, which the king prefented to the captain, at the fame time promifing to give
him another. With this fmall beginning we refted fatisfied, and taking our leave, without any troublefome ceremony, only pronouncing a hearty *tayo*, (friend,) which had
more meaning in it than many a ftudied fpeech, we returned on board.

In the afternoon the captains went on fhore with us
again to the king, whom we found where we had left him
in the morning. He took that opportunity of requefting
the captains again to prolong their ftay at leaft a few days;
but he received the fame anfwer as before, and was plainly told, that his refufing to provide us with live flock was
the reafon of their intended departure. Upon this he immediately fent for two hogs, and prefented one to each of the
captains, for which he received fome iron-wares in return.
A highlander, who was one of our marines, was ordered
to play the bagpipe, and its uncouth mufic, though almoft
infufferable to our ears, delighted the king and his fubjects
to a degree which we could hardly have imagined poffible.
The diftruft which we perceived in his looks at our firft interview was now worn off; and if we had ftaid long
enough, an unreferved confidence might have taken its
place, to which his youth and good-nature feemed to make
him inclinable. The ftudied gravity which he had then affected,

fected, was likewiſe laid aſide at preſent, and ſome of his actions rather partook of puerility, among which I cannot help mentioning his amuſement of chopping little ſticks and cutting down plantations of bananas with one of our hatchets. But, inſtead of cultivating any farther acquaintance with him, we took our laſt leave towards the cloſe of the evening, and returned to the ſloops, which unmoored before night.

The inhabitants ſeeing us prepare for ſailing the next morning, came off in a vaſt number of ſmall canoes, loaded with coco-nuts and other vegetable proviſions, which they ſold exceſſively cheap, rather than miſs the laſt opportunity of obtaining European goods. The taſte for baubles, which unaccountably prevails all over the world in different degrees, was ſo extravagant here, that a ſingle bead was eagerly purchaſed with a dozen of the fineſt coco-nuts, and ſometimes preferred even to a nail, though the laſt might be of ſome uſe, and the bead could ſerve merely as an inſignificant ornament. We obſerved that the trade was carried on much fairer this time than at our arrival, the natives being perhaps apprehenſive that any little fraud might break off a commerce, in which they now appeared deeply intereſted. They accompanied us for this purpoſe till we were a mile or two without the reefs, and then returned to the beach, where we had left lieutenant Pickerſ-

gill

1773.
August.

gill with a boat, in order to take advantage of their present disposition.

We were now able to breathe a little, after the continual
hurry which had been the necessary consequence of the
multiplicity of new objects around us, and of the short
space of time which we had to observe them. This interval of repose was the more acceptable, as it gave us leisure
to indulge the reflections which had crouded upon us during our stay. The result of these was a conviction, that
this island is indeed one of the happiest spots on the globe.
The rocks of New Zeeland appeared at first in a favourable
light to our eyes, long tired with the constant view of sea,
and ice, and sky; but time served to undeceive us, and gave
us daily cause of dislike, till we formed a just conception
of that rude chaotic country. But O-Taheitee, which had
presented a pleasing prospect at a distance, and displayed
its beauty as we approached, became more enchanting to
us at every excursion which we made on its plains. Our
long run out of sight of land might have been supposed
at first to have had the same effect as at New Zeeland; but
our stay confirmed instead of destroying the emotions
which we had felt at the first sight; even though we had
no room to be so well pleased with the refreshments we
had obtained, which were not by far so plentiful as the fish
and wild-fowl of New Zeeland, and still obliged us to have
recourse

recourfe to falt provifions. The feafon of the year, which
anfwered to our month of February, had naturally brought
on a fcarcity of fruits; for though it does not manifeft itfelf here by refrigerating the air, as in countries remote
from the tropics, yet it is the feafon when all vegetation
recovers the juices which have formed the late crop, and
prepares them for a new one. At this time feveral trees entirely fhed their leaves, feveral plants died away to the
very root, and the remaining ones looked parched on account of the want of rain, which commonly takes place
then, becaufe the fun is in the oppofite hemifphere. The
whole plain therefore was arrayed in a fober brownifh and
fometimes fallow colour. Only the lofty mountains preferved richer tints in their forefts, which are fupplied with
more moifture from the clouds that hang on their fummits
almoft every day. From thence, among other things, the
natives brought great quantities of wild plantanes *(vehee)*,
and that perfumed wood *(t-abii)*, with which they give
their coco-nut oil *(mmöe)*, a very fragrant fmell. The
fhattered ftate in which we faw the tops of thefe mountains, feemed to have been the work of an earthquake;
and the lavas, of which many of the mountains confift,
and of which the natives make feveral tools, convinced us
of the exiftence of former volcanoes on this ifland. The
rich foil of the plains, which is a vegetable mould, mixed
with volcanic decays, and a black irony fand, which is

Vol. I.   S s   often

often found at the foot of the hills, are farther proofs of
this affertion. The exterior ranges of hills are fometimes
entirely barren, and contain a great quantity of yellowifh
clay, mixed with iron-ochre; but others are covered with
mould, and wooded like the higher mountains. Pieces of
quartz are fometimes met with here, but we never faw indications of precious minerals or metals of any kind, iron
excepted, and of that there were but fmall remains in the
lavas which we picked up; but the mountains may perhaps contain fome iron-ore rich enough for fufion. As to
to the piece of falt-petre, as big as an egg, which Captain
Wallis mentions as a product of Taheitee *, with all refpect
for his nautical abilities, I beg leave to doubt of its exiftence, fince native falt-petre has never yet been found in
folid lumps, as appears from Cronftedt's Mineralogy.

The view of O-Taheitee, along which we now failed
to the northward, fuggefted thefe curfory obfervations on
its foffil productions, while our eyes remained eagerly fixed
on the fpot which had afforded us fuch a fund of real
amufement and inftruction. Our reflections were only
interrupted by the fummons to dine on frefh pork, which
was inftantly obeyed with an alacrity, that fufficiently
proved our long abftinence. We were agreeably furprifed to find this pork entirely free from the lufcious
richnefs which makes it refift the ftomach fo foon in Eu-

* See Hawkefworth, vol. I. p. 437.

rope;

rope; the fat was to be compared to marrow, and the lean had almost the tender taste of veal. The vegetable diet which the hogs are used to at O-Tahcitee, seems to be the principal cause of this difference, and may have had some influence even on the natural instincts of these animals. They were of that small breed which is commonly called the Chinese, and had not those pendulous ears, which according to the ingenious count de Buffon, are the characters of slavery in animals. They were likewise much cleanlier than our European hogs, and did not seem to have that singular custom of wallowing in the mire. It is certain that these animals are a part of the real riches of the Taheitians, and we saw great numbers of them at Aitepèha, though the natives took great pains to conceal them. But they are so far from being their principal dependence, that I believe their total extirpation would be no great loss, especially as they are now entirely the property of the chiefs. They kill their hogs very seldom, perhaps only on certain solemn occasions; but at those times the chiefs eat pork with the same unbounded greediness, with which certain sets of men are reproached at the turtle-feasts in England; while the common sort rarely, if ever taste a little bit, which is always held as a great dainty among them. Notwithstanding this, all the trouble of breeding, bringing up, and fattening the hogs is allotted to the lowest class of people.

We

1773.
August.
Wedneld. 25.

We were becalmed in the evening, and during a great part of the night, but had a S. E. wind the next morning, so that we stood in shore again, in sight of the northernmost part of O-Taheitee, and of the adjacent isle of Eimeo. The mountains here formed larger masses, which had a more grand effect than at Aitepeha. The slopes of the lower hills were likewise more considerable, though almost entirely destitute of trees or verdure; and the ambient border of level land, was much more extensive hereabouts, and seemed in some places to be above a mile broad. Towards ten o'clock we had the pleasure to see several canoes coming off from the shore towards us. Their long narrow sails, consisting of several mats sowed together, their streamers of feathers, and the heap of coco-nuts and bananas on board, had all together a picturesque appearance. For a few beads and nails they disposed of their cargoes, and returned on shore to take in another. About noon our boat arrived with lieutenant Pickersgill, who had been very successful in trading at Aitepeha, having purchased nine hogs and a quantity of fruit. His majesty, Aheatua, had been present at the trading-place the whole time, and after seating himself near the heap of iron wares, which our people had brought on shore, desired to market for them, and was extremely equitable in giving hatchets of different kinds for hogs of proportionate sizes. In the intervals however, he amused himself as he had done the evening.

1773.
AUGUST.

evening before, with chopping fmall flicks, with which our failors were much entertained, and after their manner made many fhrewd obfervations on triflers. Mr. Pickerfgill having expended his flock in trade, put off from Aitepeha in the afternoon, and came the fame evening to Hiddea, the diftrict of O-Rettee (Ereti) where M. de Bougainville lay at an anchor in 1768. Here he was hofpitably entertained by the worthy old chief, who is fo juftly celebrated by that gallant French navigator; and the next morning his brother Tarooree embarked with our officer, in order to vifit the fhips which they faw in the offing. When he came on board we found he had a kind of impediment in his organs of fpeech, by which means he fubflituted a K wherever the language required a T; a fault which we afterwards obferved in feveral other individuals. He favoured us with his company at dinner, as well as another native named O-Wahow, who was the firft that had come aboard from this part of the ifland, and to whom my father had immediately prefented a few beads and a fmall nail, merely to try his difpofition. In return he produced a fifh-hook neatly made of mother of pearl, which he gave to his new friend. A larger nail was the reward of this good-natured action; and on the receipt of this he fent his boy to the fhore in his canoe. Towards four o'clock the canoe returned, and brought on board this man's brother, and a prefent of a number of coco-nuts, feveral

bunches.

bunches of bananas, and a clothing-mat. There was something fo generous in O-Wahow's way of acting, above all the little ideas of bartering, that we could not fail to exprefs the highest regard for him. A much more confiderable prefent was returned to him, rather to confirm him in his noble fentiments, than as a compenfation for his gift. With that he retired in the evening, promifing to return to us again, and expreffing fuch extravagant emotions of joy as are commonly the effects of unexpected good fortune.

In the mean while we gradually approached the fhore, a faint breeze helping us on, and the evening-fun illuminating the landfcape with the richeft golden tints. We now difcerned that long projecting point, which from the obfervation made upon it, had been named Point Venus, and eafily agreed, that this was by far the moft beautiful part of the ifland. The diftrict of Matavaï, which now opened to our view, exhibited a plain of fuch an extent as we had not expected, and the valley which we traced running up between the mountains, was itfelf a very fpacious grove, compared to the little narrow glens in Tiarraboo. We hauled round the point about three o'clock, and faw it crouded with a prodigious number of people, who gazed at us with fixed attention; but as foon as we came to an anchor, in the fine bay which it fhelters, the greater part of them ran very precipitately round the whole beach, and acrofs

One-

One-tree-hill to O-Parre, the next diſtrict to the weſtward. Among the whole croud, we ſaw only a ſingle man whoſe ſhoulders were covered with a garment, and he, according to our friend O-Wahow's teſtimony, was O-Too, the king of O-Taheitee-Nuc (the Greater Taheitee.) His perſon was tall, and very advantageouſly proportioned, but he ran very nimbly along with his ſubjects, which the natives on board attributed to his apprehenſions on our account.

Though it was near ſun-ſet when we came to an anchor, yet our decks were in a ſhort time crouded with natives of all ranks, who recognized their old friends in many of our officers and ſailors, with a degree of reciprocal joy, which cannot eaſily be deſcribed. Among them was the old, venerable O-Whaw, whoſe peaceable character and good offices to our people, are taken notice of in the account of Lieutenant Cook's firſt voyage, particularly upon the occaſion when one of the natives was murdered *. He immediately recollected Mr. Pickerſgill, and calling him by his Taheitean name, Petrodero, enumerated on his fingers, that this was the third viſit he made to the iſland, that gentleman having been here both in the Dolphin and the Endeavour. A chief, named Maratata ‡, paid captain Cook a viſit with his lady, (Tedua)-Erararee, who was a very well-looking young woman, and both received a number

* See Hawkeſworth, vol. II. p. 83, 90, 91.
‡ Ibid. p. 157. Maraitata.

of

of prefents, though it appeared that thefe were their fole
motives for coming on board. A very tall, fat man, the
father-in-law of Maratata, accompanied them, and was
equally fortunate in collecting prefents amongft us, which
he took no other method to obtain, than down-right
begging. They all exchanged names with us in fign of
friendfhip, every one choofing a particular friend, to whom
he was attached; cuftoms which we had never obferved in
our former anchoring place, where the natives were infinitely more referved, and in fome degree diffident of our
intentions. Towards feven o'clock they left the fhip, not
without promifing to return the next morning, which,
from the good reception they had met with, did not feem
to admit of a doubt.

All night the moon fhone clear in a cloudlefs fky, and
filvered over the polifhed furface of the fea, while the
landfcape lay before us like the gay production of a fertile
and elegant fancy. A perfect filence reigned in the air,
which was agreeably interrupted by the voices of feveral
natives that had remained on board, and enjoyed the beauty
of the night with their friends, whom they had known in
a former voyage. They were feated at the fides of the
veffel, and difcourfed on feveral topics, making their words
more intelligible by different figns. We liftened to them,
and found that they chiefly put queftions concerning what
had happened to our people fince their laft feparation, and
gave

gave accounts in their turn of the tragical fate of Tootahah, and his friends. Gibson, the marine, who was so much delighted with this island, in captain Cook's former voyage, that he made an attempt to stay behind[*], was now chiefly engaged in this conversation, as he understood more of the language than the rest of the crew, and was on that account greatly valued by the natives. The confidence which these people placed in us, and their familiar, unreserved behaviour, gave us infinite satisfaction, as it contrasted so well with the conduct of the people of Aitepèha. We now saw the character of the natives in a more favourable light than ever, and were convinced that the remembrance of injuries, and the spirit of revenge, did not enter into the composition of the good and simple Taheitians. It must surely be a comfortable reflection to every sensible mind, that philanthropy seems to be natural to mankind, and that the savage ideas of distrust, malevolence, and revenge, are only the consequences of a gradual depravation of manners. There are few instances where people, who are not absolutely sunk to a state of barbarism, have acted contrary to this general peaceable principle. The discoveries of Columbus, Cortez, and Pizarro in America, and those of Mendanna, Quiros, Schouten, Tasman‡, and Wallis in the South Sea, agree in this particular. It is highly probable,

* See Hawkesworth, vol. II. p. 176, 179.
‡ We except the savages of New Zealand.

that

that the attack which the Taheitians made upon the Dolphin, took its origin from some outrage unknowingly committed by the Europeans; and supposing it did not, if self-preservation be one of the first laws of nature, surely from all appearances these people had a right to look on our men as a set of invaders, and what is more than all, to be apprehensive that even their liberty was at stake. When, after a fatal display of superior European force, they were convinced that nothing farther than a short stay for refreshment was intended, that the strangers who came among them were not entirely destitute of humane and equitable sentiments; in short, when they found that Britons were not more savage than themselves, they were ready to open their arms to them, they forgot that they had had a difference, and bid them partake of each kindly production of their isle. They all exerted themselves in acts of hospitality and testimonies of friendship from the lowest subject to the queen, that every one of their guests might have reason to say, he regretted his departure from this friendly shore:

Invitus, regina, tuo de littore cessi!   VIRGIL.

CHAP.

C H A P. IX.

Account of our Transactions at Matavai Bay.

CAPTAIN Cook, in his voyage in the Endeavour, had
observed that, in order to obtain a sufficient supply
of refreshments at Matavai Bay, it was absolutely necessary
to conciliate the favour of the sovereign, unless peaceable
measures were entirely to be rejected, and the tragedies of
former times be repeated. With this view he resolved to
begin his operations here in the morning, by going to the
province of O-Parre, where king O-Too resided. He did
not, however, leave the ship till Maratata and his wife had
been on board agreeable to their promise. In return for
the presents which they had received the evening before,
they gave some pieces of their best cloth to the captain, and
were very proud to be admitted into the great cabin, while
the rest of their countrymen were obliged to stay without.
As soon as Captain Furneaux was come on board from the
Adventure, Captain Cook embarked in the pinnace with
him, accompanied by Doctor Sparrman, my father, and
myself. Maratata, without any ceremony, likewise came
in with his wife, and immediately occupied the best place
in the stern. A croud of attendants followed them, till the
boat was so full, that our people found it impossible to ply

T t 2   their

their oars. The greater part of thefe unbidden guefts were
therefore obliged to leave it, to their vifible difappointment; for they feemed to have fet a great value upon the
liberty of fitting in our boat, which was frefh painted, and
had a pleafant green awning to fkreen us from the fun.
We rowed acrofs the bay, and approached the fhore near a
point where a thick fhrubbery furrounded a marai of ftone,
fuch as we had already obferved in Aitepeha. This cemetery and place of worfhip was known to Captain Cook by
the name of Tootahah's marai, but when he called it by
this name, Marataua interrupted him, intimating that it
was no longer Tootahah's after his death, but was known
at prefent as O-Too's marai. A fine moral for princes,
daily reminding them of mortality whilft they live, and
teaching them that after death they cannot even call the
ground their own which their dead corfe occupies!—The
chief and his wife on paffing by it, took their upper garment from their fhoulders, which is a mark of refpect
indifcriminately paid at the marai by all ranks of people,
and feems to annex a particular idea of fanctity to thefe
places. Perhaps they are fuppofed to be favoured with the
more immediate prefence of the Deity, agreeably to the
opinion that has been entertained of public places of worfhip at all times and among all nations.

After paffing the marai, we rowed for fome time clofe
along one of the fineft diftricts of O-Taheitee, where the
plains

plains feemed to be very fpacious, and the mountains ran
with a very eafy flope into a long point. A prodigious
number of inhabitants lined the fhores, which were covered
with graffes, and fhaded with numerous palms clofe to the
water's edge. Here we landed, amidft the joyful acclamations of the multitude, and were conducted to a group of
houfes, hid under fpreading fruit-trees. Before one of the
largeft we faw an area twenty or thirty yards fquare, furrounded by an enclofure of reeds, not above eighteen inches
high, in the middle of which the king was feated crofs-legged on the ground, in a great circle of perfons of both fexes,
who feemed to be of the higheft rank in the ifland from
their ftature, colour and deportment. Some of our failors
laid down a number of prefents before him, which ferved
as Captain Cook's credentials. We all followed, and were
intreated to fit down around the king. The refpect which
was paid to the fovereign by all ranks of people, and which
confifted in uncovering the fhoulders in his prefence, did
not prevent them from thronging around us on all fides
with the greateft eagernefs of curiofity. The croud was
beyond comparifon more numerous than at our interview
with Aheatua, and the king's attendants in different corners
of the area were obliged to exert themfelves in order to
keep them within bounds. One in particular difplayed
his activity in a furious manner to clear the way for us,

by

by beating them unmercifully, breaking feveral flicks on their heads, and no doubt breaking their heads too.

> E come quel ch' ancor de la pazzia
> Non era ben guarito interamente ;
> Per allargare innanzi al Re la via,
> Menava quella mazza fra la gente,
> Ch' un imbriaco fvizzero paria
> Di quei, che con villan modo infolente,
> Sogliono innanzi 'l Papa il dì di fefta,
> Rompere a chi le braccia, a chi la tefta.   TASSONI.

Notwithftanding this fevere treatment, they returned as obftinately to the charge as an Englifh mob, but bore the infolence of the king's officers with more patience. The king of O-Taheitee had never feen our people during captain Cook's firft voyage, probably in confequence of the political views of his uncle Tootahah, who at that time had the whole management of affairs in his hands, and who might be apprehenfive of lofing his confequence among the Europeans, if they fhould once know that he was not the greateft man on the ifland. Whether Tootahah's power was to be confidered as an ufurpation, or not, is not eafily to be determined; fo much however may be alledged againft him, that the king himfelf feemed to us to be a man of twenty-four or twenty-five years of age. O-Too was the talleft man whom we faw on the whole ifland which he governs, meafuring fix feet and three inches in height. His whole body was proportionately ftrong and well-made,

without

without any tendency to corpulence. His head, notwithstanding a certain gloominefs which feemed to exprefs a
fearful difpofition, had a majeftic and intelligent air, and
there was great expreffion in his full black eyes. He wore
ftrong whifkers, which with his beard, and a prodigious
growth of curled hair, were all of a jetty black. His
portrait is engraved from Mr. Hodges's drawing, for captain Cook's account of this voyage. The fame habit of
body, and the fame fingular quantity of hair, which ftood
puffed up all about the head intricately entwined and curled, characterifed his brothers, one a youth of about fixteen,
another ten years of age, and likewife his fifters, of which
the eldeft now prefent feemed about twenty-fix. The women of O-Taheitee in general, cut their hair rather fhort;
it was therefore a very uncommon appearance on the heads
of thefe ladies, and may, for ought we know, be a privilege
referved only to thofe of the royal family. Their rank
however did not exclude them from the general etiquette of
uncovering the fhoulders in the king's prefence, a ceremony
which afforded the whole fex numberlefs opportunities of
difplaying an elegant figure to the greateft advantage.
The fimple drapery of a long white piece of cloth, like a
muflin, was to be turned an hundred different ways, according to the convenience, or the talents and fine tafte of
the wearer; no general fafhions force them to disfigure, inftead of adorning themfelves, but an innate gracefulnefs

was

was the companion of fimplicity. The only perfon exempted from the general cuftom of uncovering the fhoulder
was the king's *bòs* *, one of his fervants, whom we could
not better compare than to the lord in waiting, and of
whom we underftood there were twelve who officiated by
turns. Some of them were the fame gentlemen who had
difplayed their dexterity before, by dealing out hearty blows
to the crowd. The number of uncles, aunts, coufins, and
other relations of his majefty, amongft whom we were
feated, vied with each other in beftowing kind looks upon
us, making profeffions of friendfhip, and—begging for
beads and nails. The methods to obtain thefe trifles from
us were very different, and confequently not always equally
fuccefsful. When we diftributed a few beads to one fet of
people, fome young fellows would impudently thruft
their hands in between them, and demand their fhare, as
though it had been their due; thefe attempts we always
made it our bufinefs to difcourage by a flat refufal. It was
already become difficult to deny a venerable old man, who
with a hand not yet palfied by age, vigoroufly preffed
ours, and with a perfect reliance upon our good nature,
whifpered the petition in our ears. The elderly ladies in
general made fure of a prize, by a little artful flattery.
They commonly enquired for our names, and then adopted

* See Hawkefworth, vol. II. p. 243. *eua te Feartt*, by which is meant *e-boa
oe te erm*, (a friend to the king.)

U s

us as their fons, at the fame time introducing to us the feveral relations, whom we acquired by this means. After a feries of little careffes, the old lady began, *Aima poe-tetee no te tayo mettua?* "Have you not a little bead for your kind mother?" Such a trial of our filial attachment always had its defired effect, as we could not fail to draw the moft favourable conclufions from thence in regard to the general kind difpofition of the whole people: for to expect a good quality in others, of which we ourfelves are not poffeffed, is a refinement in manners peculiar to polifhed nations. Our other female relations in the bloom of youth, with fome fhare of beauty, and conftant endeavours to pleafe, laid a claim to our affections by giving themfelves the tender name of fifters; and all the world will agree that this attack was perfectly irrefiftible.

In a little time we met with an ample return for our prefents, efpecially from the ladies, who immediately fent their attendants (Towtows) for large pieces of their beft cloth, dyed of a fcarlet, rofe, or ftraw colour, and perfumed with their choiceft fragrant oils. Thefe they put over our cloathes, and loaded us fo well that we found it difficult to move in them. A variety of queftions concerning Tabane (Mr. Banks), Tolano (Dr. Solander), and many of their former acquaintances, immediately followed the more material bufinefs of receiving prefents; but Tupaya (Tupia) or as he was more commonly called Parua, notwithftanding

the extenfive knowledge of which he feems to have been
poffeffed, and which we expected fhould have endeared him
to his countrymen, was only mentioned by one or two
perfons, who received the news of his death with perfect
indifference.   Whilft we were engaged in this converfation,
our Highlander performed on the bag-pipe to the infinite
fatisfaction of all the Taheitians, who liftened to him with
a mixture of admiration and delight.   King O-Too in particular was fo well pleafed with his mufical abilities, which
I have already obferved were mean enough, that he ordered
him a large piece of the coarfer cloth as a 'reward for his
trouble.

As this vifit was merely a vifit of ceremony, we foon
got up to return to our boat, but were detained a little
longer by the arrival of E-Happaï* the father of the
fovereign.   He was a tall, thin man, with a grey beard
and hair, feemed to be of a great age, but was not yet
entirely worn out.   He received the prefents which our
captains made him, in a cold carelefs manner, which is
natural to old people whofe fenfes are confiderably impaired.   The accounts of former voyagers had already
apprifed us of that ftrange conftitution, by virtue of which
the fon affumes the fovereignty in his father's life time†,
but we could not without furprize, behold the aged Happaï,

* See Hawkefworth, vol. II. p. 154. Whappai.   † Ibid, p. 154.

242   naked

naked to the waist in his son's presence, conform to the general custom. Thus the ideas universally annexed to consanguinity, are suppressed in order to give greater weight to the regal dignity, and I cannot help thinking that such a sacrifice to political authority, argues a greater degree of civilization than has been allowed to the Tahitians by our former navigators. However, though Happaï was not invested with the supreme command, his birth and rank entitled him to deference from the common people, and to a proper support from the king. The province or district of O-Parre, was therefore under his immediate orders, and supplied not only his wants, but those also of his attendants. After a very short stay with this old chief, we parted from him, and from the king his son, and returned on board in the pinnace, which Maratata had occupied during the whole time of our interview, priding himself very much on his supposed interest with us. During our absence several tents had been erected on Point Venus, for the convenience of our wood-cutters and waterers, and the sick of the Adventure. The astronomers of both vessels had likewise fixed their observatory nearly on the same spot, where Mr. Green and captain Cook had observed the transit of Venus. We found a great number of inhabitants about the vessels, and among the rest several of the better sort of people, who having access to all parts of the ship, followed every body with their petitions for

U u 2

beads

1773.
August. beads and other prefents. The captains to evade their
endlefs importunities went on fhore to the tents, and thither
we accompanied them in order to fee what natural productions the country afforded. Another excurfion of the
fame kind was made in the afternoon, but as both were
confined to an inconfiderable diftance, our difcoveries only
confifted of a few plants and birds which we had not feen
at Aitepèha.

Friday 27. The next morning very early, a number of canoes
came to the fhip from Parre, and in one of the fmalleft,
the king in perfon brought many prefents to captain Cook.
A live hog, a very large fifh called a cavalha *(fcomber hippos)*,
and an albecore ready dreffed, about four feet long, with
many bafkets of palm-leaves containing bread-fruit and
bananas, were handed up to the deck fucceffively. Captain
Cook ftood on the fhip's fide, entreating his majefty to
come on board, but he did not ftir from his feat, till an
immenfe quantity of the beft cloth of the country had
been wrapped round the captain, encreafing his bulk to
a prodigious dimenfion. After this ceremony, Too, with
a countenance which betrayed a good deal of diffidence,
ventured to come upon the quarter-deck, and embraced
the captain, who in conjunction with his officers and
ourfelves, devifed all poffible means to quiet thefe apprehenfions. Our quarter-deck was now fo crouded with the
king's relations, that he was requefted to come into the
cabin ;

cabin; but the defcent between decks was fo hazardous an enterprize according to his ideas, that he could by no means be prevailed on to attempt it, till he had fent down his brother, a fine active youth about fixteen years of age, who placed a perfect confidence in us. Having reconnoitred the cabin, and finding it to his liking, he made his report accordingly to the king, who immediately ventured down. He received a great number of valuable prefents from captain Cook, who began to find himfelf very warm under his load of cloth. The principal people accompanied his majefty into the cabin, but they crouded in fo faft, that it was almoft impoffible to ftir for them. Every one of thefe, as I have already mentioned, chofe his particular friend amongft us, and reciprocal gifts fealed every new connection. Captain Furneaux being arrived on board, we took an opportunity of fitting down to our breakfaft, when they feemed perfectly eafy, having prevailed on them to feat themfelves on chairs, which ftruck them with their novelty and convenience. The king paid great attention to our breakfaft, which was a mixture of English and Taheitian provifions, and was much furprifed to fee us drink hot-water *, and eat bread-fruit with oil †. Though he could not be perfuaded to tafte our food, feveral of his attendants were not fo cautious, but eat and drank very heartily of whatever we fet

* Tea.   † Butter.

before

before them. After breakfaſt O-Too ſaw my father's ſpaniel, a fine dog, but in very bad order at that time, and very dirty from the pitch, tar, and other uncleanlineſs on board the ſhip. Notwithſtanding theſe defects, the king expreſſed a great deſire of becoming his maſter, and made a requeſt to that purpoſe, which was readily complied with. He immediately commanded one of the lords in waiting, or *boa*, to take the dog into his cuſtody; and in conformity to his orders, this man ever after carried the dog behind his majeſty. The king ſoon after told captain Cook that he wiſhed to return on ſhore, and went on deck with all his attendants, carrying with him the preſents which he had received. Captain Furneaux took that opportunity of preſenting to him a fine pair of goats, male and female, which he had brought from on board his own veſſel the ſame morning. We ſucceeded very well in our attempt to make him comprehend the value of theſe animals, and the manner of treating them; for he promiſed that he would never kill nor ſeparate them, and take great care of their offspring. The pinnace was now ready, and the king embarked in it, with the captains and ſeveral other gentlemen, and proceeded to the royal reſidence at O-Parre. During this paſſage he appeared highly contented, aſked a number of queſtions, and ſeemed to have entirely conquered his former fears. His enquiries chiefly concerned the goats, which had attracted all his attention, and we

could

could never tell him too often what they should feed upon, and how they were to be managed. As soon as we came on shore, we pointed out to him a fine spot of ground, covered with a good bed of grasses, in the shade of breadfruit trees, and desired that the goats might always be kept in such places. At our landing the shore was crouded with people, who expressed their joy on seeing their sovereign by loud acclamations. Among them we discerned the late Tootahah's mother, a venerable grey-headed matron, who, on seeing captain Cook, ran to embrace him, as the friend of her deceased son, and wept aloud at the remembrance of her loss. We paid the tribute of admiration due to such sensibility, which endears our fellow-creatures to us wherever it is met with, and affords an undeniable proof of the original excellence of the human heart.

From hence we hastened away to our tents at Point Venus, where the natives carried on a regular trade with vegetables of all sorts, which sold at very low rates, a single bead being given for a basket of bread-fruit or a bunch of coco-nuts. My father there met his friend O Wáhow, who presented him with a great quantity of fruit, some fish, some good cloth, and some mother of pearl hooks. This present deserved a compensation, but the generous Taheitian absolutely refused to take any thing, saying that he gave these things as a friend, and without any lucrative view. It seemed as if every thing
had

had confpired this day to give us a favourable idea of the amiable nation among whom we refided.

We returned on board to dinner, and paffed the afternoon there in the occupations of defcribing and drawing objects of natural hiftory. The decks in the mean while were conftantly crouded with natives of both fexes, prying into every corner, and ftealing whenever they found an opportunity. In the evening we beheld a fcene new and ftriking to ourfelves, though familiar to thofe who had been at Taheitee before. A great number of women of the loweft clafs, having been previoufly engaged by our failors, remained on board at fun-fet, after the departure of all their countrypeople to the fhore. We had obferved inftances of the venality of the Taheitian females at Aitepeha; but whatever might have been their condefcenfion towards our people in day-time, they had never ventured to pafs a night on board. The women of Matavai had ftudied the difpofitions of Britifh feamen much better, and knew that they ran no rifk by entrufting themfelves to their care; but on the contrary might make fure of every bead, nail, hatchet, or fhirt which their lovers could mufter. This evening was therefore as completely dedicated to mirth and pleafure, as if we had lain at Spithead inftead of O-Taheitee. Before it was perfectly dark the women affembled on the forecaftle, and one of them blowing a flute with the noftrils, all the reft danced a variety of

dances

dances ufual in their country, amongft which there were fome that did not exactly correfpond with our ideas of decency. However, if we confider that the fimplicity of their education and of their drefs, makes many actions perfectly innocent here, which, according to our cuftoms, would be blameable, we cannot impute that degree of unbounded licentioufnefs to them, with which the proftitutes of civilized Europe are unhappily reproached. As foon as it was dark they retired below decks, and if their lovers were of fuch a quality as to afford them frefh pork, they fupped without referve, though they had before refufed to eat in the prefence of their own countrymen, agreeably to that incomprehenfible cuftom which feparates the fexes at their meals. The quantities of pork which they could confume were aftonifhing, and their greedinefs plainly indicated that they were rarely if ever indulged with that delicious food in their own families. The inftances of fenfibility in Too-tahah's mother and in O-Wahow, and the favourable ideas which we had from thence formed of the Taheitians were fo recent in our memories, that we were much hurt at the fight of thefe creatures, who had entirely forgot the duties of life, and abandoned themfelves to the brutal fway of the paffions. That there fhould exift fo great a degree of immorality in a nation, otherwife fo happy in its fimplicity, and in the fewnefs of its wants, is a reflection very difgraceful to human nature in general, which, viewed to its greateft advantage here, is neverthelefs imperfect. Is it not to be lamented, that the beft gifts of a benevolent Creator feem to be the moft liable to frequent abufe, and that nothing is fo eafy to mankind as error!

Early the next morning O-Too, with his fifter Tedua-Towraï, and feveral relations, came along-fide, and fent up a hog and a large albecore into our veffel, but would not come on board. He had a fimilar prefent for captain Furneaux, but refufed to go to the Adventure till my father went with him. The ceremony of fwaddling the captain in O-Taheitee cloth was performed again before his majefty ventured on board; but that being over, he feemed to think himfelf fafe amongft us, and came on the deck, where captain Furneaux gave him a variety of prefents. His fifter Tedua-Towraï was on board the Refolution in the mean while, and all the women paid her the fame refpect by uncovering the fhoulders, which the whole nation owes to the king. The active youth T'-Aree WATOW, who was with the king his brother, had the fame honours paid to him; and it appeared to us that the title Aree, though common to all the chiefs of diftricts, and the nobility in general, was yet applied by way of excellence to the perfons of the royal family. O-Too foon left the Adventure, rejoined his fifter on board the Refolution, and was accompanied by both the captains to Parre.

On

On the 29th at day-break we landed at our tents, and proceeded into the country with an intention to examine its productions. A copious dew, which had fallen during night, had refreshed the whole vegetable creation, and contributed, together with the early hour of the morning, to make our walk extremely pleasant. We found but few natives at the tents, some of whom attended us to the ford in the river, and for a bead a-piece carried us across, where it was twenty yards wide, without our wetting a foot. As we entered the grove, we perceived the inhabitants in their houses just getting up, and saw many of them performing their customary ablution in the adjacent river of Matavaï. There can be no doubt, that frequent bathing in this warm climate is extremely salutary, and particularly in the morning, when the water, being fresh and cool, cannot but be highly instrumental in bracing the fibres, which might otherwise become too much relaxed. The cleanliness which results from this custom, is certainly one of the best preservatives against putrid disorders, and has the farther advantage of making these people enjoy the comforts of society in a higher degree than those savages who seem to shun the water, and become indifferent to each other, and loathsome to strangers by their squalid appearance, and fetid exhalations. We walked on till we came to a little hut, the lowly dwelling of a poor widow with a numerous family. Her eldest son, Noona, a lively boy

X x 2

about

about twelve years old, had always been particularly attached to the Europeans, and being extremely quick of apprehension, underſtood us much better at half a word,
than many of his countrymen with all the geſtures we
could invent, and after we had ranſacked our vocabularies.
This boy, who, with a dark almoſt cheſnut-brown colour, com-
bined a ſet of pleaſing, good-natured features, had agreed
the evening before, to become our guide on this day's excurſion. At our approach we found his mother, who had
provided a number of coco-nuts and ſome other proviſions
for us, ſitting on the ſtones before her cottage, and her
children aſſembled about her, the youngeſt of which was
not above four years old. She ſeemed to be active enough,
but however of ſuch an age, that we had ſome difficulty
to believe her the mother of ſuch young children, in a
country where we knew that the commerce of the ſexes
begins at an early age. The arrival of a well-looking woman, about three or four and twenty years old, who was
Noona's eldeſt ſiſter, ſoon accounted for the wrinkles on
her mother's brow. Inſtead of verifying the general obſervation, that women in hot countries loſe their ſightlineſs
much ſooner than with us, we had now reaſon to be ſurpriſed, that they ſhould be ſo prolific here, as to bear
children during a period of almoſt twenty years. It was
natural that our thoughts ſhould return to the happy ſimplicity in which the life of the Taheitians ſmoothly rolls
along,

along, and which, undisturbed by cares and wants, is the cause of the great population of their island.

A stout fellow, whom we hired for a few beads, carried the provisions which the hospitable old woman had offered us, suspending them in equal portions on the two extremities of a strong pole, about four feet long, which he placed on his shoulder. Young Noona, and his little brother Toparree, about four years old, cheerfully accompanied us, after we had enriched the whole family with beads, nails, looking-glasses, and knives.

The first part of our march was a little difficult, on account of a hill on which we mounted, in hopes of meeting with something to reward our trouble. But, contrary to our expectations, we found it entirely destitute of plants, two dwarfish shrubs, and a species of dry fern excepted. Here, however, we were much surprised to see a large flock of wild ducks rising before us, from a spot which was perfectly dry and barren, without our being able to imagine what had brought them thither from the reeds and marshy banks of the river, where they commonly resided. We soon crossed another hill, where all the ferns and bushes having lately been burnt, blackened our clothes as we passed through them. From thence we descended into a fertile valley, where a fine rivulet, which we were obliged to cross several times, ran towards the sea. The natives had placed several stone weirs across this rivulet, in order

to

to raife the water, which might by that means be introduced into their plantations of the tarro, or eddy-root
(arum efculentum,) that requires a very marfhy, and fometimes an inundated foil. We found two fpecies of it, one
of which has large gloffy leaves, and roots about four feet
long, but is very coarfe; the other with velvet leaves and
fmall, but more palatable roots. Both are excceffively pun-
gent and cauftic, till boiled in feveral waters; however, hogs
eat them raw without any reluctance. The valley became
narrower as we advanced up along the rivulet, and the
hills which included it were much fteeper, and covered with
forefts. Every part of the level ground was, however,
planted with coco-nut, apple, and bread-fruit trees, with
bananas, cloth-trees, and various roots, and a number of
houfes were conveniently fituated at fhort diftances from
each other. In different parts we met with immenfe beds
of loofe pebble-ftones in the rivulet and on its banks,
which feemed to have been wafhed out of the mountains,
and worn into round or oblong fhapes, by the continual
motion and agitation of the water. On the fides of the
hills we gathered feveral new plants, fometimes at the rifk
of breaking our necks, on account of the pieces of rock
which rolled away under our feet. A great number of inhabitants affembled about us, and among them feveral who
brought us abundance of coco-nuts, bread-fruit, and
apples for fale. We bought as much as we thought neceffary

ceſſary for our proviſion, and hired ſome of the natives to carry it. After proceeding up about five miles from the ſea-ſide we ſat down in the ſhade of a number of trees, on a pleaſant green turf, and made our meal, which conſiſted of the fruit we had purchaſed, and of ſome pork and fiſh which we had taken from on board. The natives formed a circle round us; but thoſe who had been our guides and aſſiſtants were permitted to ſit by us, and partook of our cheer with a very good appetite. They were moſt ſurpriſed at the ſalt, which we had taken care to provide, and which they ſaw us eat with all ſorts of victuals, bread-fruit not excepted. Some of them were deſirous of taſting it, and among theſe there were a few who reliſhed it very well, becauſe they are uſed to employ ſea-water as a ſauce both to fiſh and to pork [*].

It was about four o'clock in the afternoon, when we thought of returning to the ſea-ſide with our acquiſitions. About this time a number of inhabitants came acroſs the hills with loads of horſe-plantanes, a coarſe ſort, which grows almoſt without cultivation, and which they brought for ſale to our ſhips. We followed them along the ſide of the rivulet to a place where ſome children offered us a few little prawns picked out between the ſtones in the bed of the river. We had no ſooner taken them as a curioſity, and rewarded the children with beads, than

[*] See Hawkſworth, vol. II. p. 100, 201.

upwards

upwards of fifty perfons of different ages and fexes fet about the fame employment, and brought us fo many of thefe little creatures, that we were foon obliged to refufe them. In the fpace of two hours we reached our tents on Point Venus, where we found O-Wahow, the generous native who had brought my father another prefent of provifions. In the courfe of this walk, we had obferved more idle perfons than at Aitepeha; the houfes and plantations appeared more ruinous and neglected, and from feveral people inftead of invitations, or marks of hofpitality, we only received importunate petitions for beads and nails. Still upon the whole we had great reafon to be contented with our reception among them, and the liberty of roaming at pleafure through all parts of their delightful country. We had now and then experienced their difpofition to theft, but had never loft any thing of value; for our handkerchiefs, which were the eafieft to come at, were made of their own thinner cloth, fo that they found themfelves difappointed as often as they had dextroufly picked our pockets, and with great good humour returned them to us. In my opinion this vice is not of fo heinous a nature among the Taheitians, as amongft ourfelves. People whofe wants are fo eafily fatisfied, and in whofe manner of living there is fo much equality, can have very few motives to fteal from each other, and their open houfes without doors and bars, are fo many proofs of mutual

fafety

safety. The blame then lies in a great meafure upon us, for bringing temptations in their way too powerful to be withftood. They feem indeed not to think their tranfgreffions of great fignification, perhaps from a reflection that they do not materially injure us by any little larceny.

During our abfence the captains had paid a vifit to the king at Parre, where they were highly entertained by the fight of a dramatic dance, which her royal highnefs Towraï performed, in a drefs exactly defcribed in captain Cook's former voyage, and with the fame geftures which are there mentioned *. Two men danced at different intervals, when the princefs refted, and, with many ftrange diftortions, fpoke or fung fome words, probably relative to the fubject of their dance, which was unintelligible to our people. The whole entertainment lafted about an hour and a half, during which Tedua Towraï difplayed a wonderful activity, which furpaffed every thing that had been feen at the ifle of Ulietea in the former voyage.

Early the next morning captain Cook fent lieutenant Pickerfgill to the fouth-weft part of the ifland, in order to purchafe fome frefh provifion, and particularly fome hogs, of which we had hitherto received only two from the king. We continued on board the whole day, defcribing the plants which we had found on our laft excurfion. In the even-

---

* See Hawkefworth, vol. II. p. 264, 265. See alfo the plate No. 7, though that conveys no idea of Taheitians.

VOL. I.   Y y   ing,

ing, about ten o'clock, we heard a great noise on shore abreast of our vessels, apparently occasioned by some of our men. The captains immediately sent their boats ashore, with proper officers, who brought on board several marines and a sailor. They had obtained leave to take a walk from the commanding officer at the tents, but had exceeded their time, and beaten one of the natives. They were immediately secured in irons, as it was of the utmost consequence towards continuing upon an amicable footing with this nation, to punish them in an exemplary manner. O-Too had promised to come on board with his father the next morning, but this noise, of which he had received advice within half an hour after it had happened, made him so justly diffident of our intentions, that he sent his messenger or ambassador *(Whanno no t'aree*,)* who was one of the principal lords of his court, named E-Tee, to make an apology for his non-appearance. Before he came on board, however, Dr. Sparrman went on shore with me near the place where the disturbance had happened, with a view to make another excursion into the interior parts of the country. O-Whaw†, the old man, who had on former occasions shewed his pacific disposition, met us on the beach, and spoke of the offence of the last night not without expressing some displeasure; but when we assured him that the of-

---

* See Hawkesworth, vol. II. p. 243.

† See before, p. 413; and Hawkesworth, vol. II. p. 83, 90, 91.

fenders

fenders were in irons, and would be feverely punifhed, he feemed perfectly fatisfied. As we had nobody from the veffel to affift us, we defired O-Whaw to point out a native whom we might entruft with the botanizing apparatus. Several people having offered their fervices, he chofe a ftrong well-made man, who was immediately furnifhed with an empty bag, for the reception of plants, and with fome bafkets full of Taheitee apples, which we had purchafed on the fpot. We croffed One-tree-hill, and defcended into one of the firft vallies of O-Parre, where we were gratified with the fight of one of the moft beautiful trees in the world, which we called the Barringtonia. It had a great abundance of flowers, larger than lilies and perfectly white, excepting the tips of their numerous chives, which were of a bright crimfon. Such a quantity of thefe flowers were already dropped off, that the ground underneath the tree was intirely ftrewed with them. The natives called the tree *huddo*, and affured us that the fruit, which is a large nut, when bruifed, mixed up with fome fhell-fifh, and ftrewed into the fea, intoxicates or poifons the fifh for fome time, fo that they come to the furface of the water and fuffer themfelves to be taken with the hands. It is fingular that various maritime plants in tropical climates have fuch a quality; the *cocculi indici*, in particular, are well known and ufed for that purpofe in the Eaft-Indies. We were unwilling to defer the examination of fo remark-

Y y 2

able

ble a plant till after our return on board, and therefore retired to a neat house, built up of reeds, round which several odoriferous shrubs and some very fine coco-trees were
planted. The owner, with that hospitality which I have
already often celebrated, sent a boy up one of the tallest
palms to procure us some of the nuts, which he performed with surprizing agility. He tied a piece of the tough
rind of a banana stalk to both his feet, in such a manner
that they could just encompass the tree on both sides, the
piece of rind serving as a sort of step or rest, whilst he
lifted himself higher with his hands. The natural growth
of the coco-palm, which annually forms a kind of elevated
ring on the stem, certainly facilitated the boy's ascent, but
the quickness and ease with which he walked up and
down were really admirable. We should have ill deserved
this mark of kindness and attention if we had not made
our host a little present at parting, and rewarded the boy
for the pleasure which we had felt in observing his dexterity.

From hence we proceeded up the valley, which having
no rivulet in its middle, began to rise in proportion as we
advanced. We resolved therefore to go upon the steep hill
on our left, and with much difficulty accomplished our
plan. Our Taheitian friend langhed at us, when he saw
us faint with fatigue, and sitting down every moment to
recover our breath. We heard him blow or breathe slowly

but

but very hard, with open mouth, as he walked behind us; we therefore tried the same experiment, which nature had probably taught him, and found it answered much better than our short panting, which always deprived us of breath. At last we reached the ridge of the hill, where a fine breeze greatly refreshed us, after our fatiguing ascent. When we had walked upwards along that ridge for some time, exposed to the burning rage of the sun, reverberated from all parts of the barren soil, we sat down under the scanty shade of a solitary *pandang*, or palm-nut tree *, which was at this time acceptable even to our friendly native. The prospect from hence was delightful; the reef which surrounded O-Taheitee, the bay with the ships, and numerous canoes, and the whole plain of Matavai with its beautiful objects, lay as it were under our feet, while the meridian sun threw a steady and calm light on the whole landscape. At the distance of about six leagues, the low island called Tedhuroa, appeared before us, forming a little circular ledge of rocks, covered with a few palms; and far beyond it the immense ocean bounded the view. The Taheitian who was with us, pointed out the direction of all the neighbouring islands which were not in sight at present, and informed us of their produce, whether they were high or low, inhabited or only occasionally visited. Tedhuroa,

* *Pandang*. Rumph. Herbar. Amboin.—*Athrodactylis*. Forst. Nov. Gen. Plantar.—*Kiera*. Forskol.

which

which we faw was of the laſt ſort, and two canoes with their
ſails ſet, were at that time returning from thence, where
our guide informed us they often went to catch fiſh in the
lagoon. Having reſted a little while, we advanced up towards the interior mountains, which now appeared diſtinct-
ly before us. The rich groves which crowned their ſummits,
and filled the vallies between them, invited us to advance, and
promiſed to reward our preſeverance with a load of new
productions. But we ſoon perceived a number of barren
hills and vallies which lay between us and thoſe deſireable
foreſts, and found it was in vain to attempt to reach them
this day. We conſulted amongſt ourſelves, whether we
ſhould venture to paſs a night on theſe hills, but this was
unadviſeable, on account of the uncertainty of the time
when our ſhips were to ſail, and likewiſe impracticable
for want of proviſions.—Our Taheitian told us, we ſhould
meet with no inhabitants, dwelling, or proviſions on the
mountains, and pointed out a narrow path which led down
the ſteep ſide of the hill into the valley of Matavaï. We began to deſcend therefore, but found it more dangerous than
when we came up: we ſtumbled every moment, and in
many places were obliged to ſlide down on our backs. Our
ſhoes were rather a diſadvantage to us, being made extremely ſlippery by the dry graſſes over which we had walked,
while the native with his bare feet was ſurpriſingly ſure-
footed. In a ſhort time we gave him our fowling-pieces,

10

to enable us to make use of our hands, and at last we re-
sumed them again, and letting him go before, leaned on
his arm in the most difficult places. When we were about
half-way down, he hallooed very loud to some people
whom he saw in the valley; but we did not believe at that
time that they had heard him, especially because he received
no answer. However, presently after we observed several
people coming up towards us, who ascended very fast, so
as to meet us in about half an hour. They brought us three
fresh coco-nuts, which, whether they were really excellent
in their kind, or whether our great fatigue recommended
them to our taste, we looked upon as the best we had ever
emptied. The natives bid us rest a while, and told us that
a little farther down they had left a number of coco-
nuts, which they would not bring up lest we should drink
too hastily at first. Their precaution was very laudable,
but our thirst made us very impatient till they would permit us to move forward. At last we set out, and coming
on a more level ground, entered a delicious little shrubbery,
where we sat down in the fresh grass, and indulged with
the cool nectar which our friends had provided. This
draught enabled us to come down into the valley, where
we were presently surrounded by a croud of the natives,
and prepared to return with them over the plain to the
sea-side; when a well-looking man, accompanied by his
daughter, a young girl about sixteen, invited us to his
house,

house which lay farther up, where he wished to entertain
us with a dinner.   Though we were much exhausted with
fatigue, we agreed not to disappoint him, and returned
about two miles along the delightful banks of the river
Matavai, through groves of coco, bread-fruit, apple, and
cloth-trees, and numerous plantations of bananas and eddoes.
The river formed various windings in the valley from
side to side, so that we were obliged to cross it several
times, and our new host with one of his servants always
insisted upon carrying us over on their backs.   At last we
arrived at his house, which was situated on a little eminence, where the river gently murmured over a bed of pebbles.   An elegant mat was spread for us on the dry grass
in a corner of the house, which was of the closer sort,
being walled in with reeds.   We were immediately surrounded by a great number of our friend's relations, who
seated themselves near us ; and his daughter, who in elegance
of form, clearness of complexion, and agreeable features,
equalled, if not surpassed the Taheitian beauties we had
hitherto seen, together with some of her young companions,
were very assiduous in their endeavours to be agreeable.
The most efficacious remedy they employed besides their
smiles, to recover us from the great weariness which we
felt, was to chafe our arms and legs with their hands,
squeezing the muscles gently between the fingers and the
palm.   Whether this operation facilitated the circulation

of

of the blood through the minuter veffels, or reftored the over-ftrained mufcles to their natural elafticity, I cannot determine; but its effect was certainly fo falutary, that our ftrength was perfectly reftored, and we did not feel the leaft remaining inconvenience from the fatiguing journey of the day. Captain Wallis mentions a fimilar inftance of the excellence of this remedy, and of the bene-ficence of the inhabitants of Taheitee *; and Ofbeck, in his voyage to China, defcribes this operation as a common practice among Chinefe barbers, who are faid to be very expert at it †. Mr. Grofe too, in his voyage to the Eaft Indies, gives a very circumftantial account of the art of *champing*, which feems to be a luxurious refinement upon this wholefome reftorative. It deferves to be mentioned here, that this ingenious author has given quotations from Martial and Seneca, which make it evident that the Romans were acquainted with this practice ‡.

> Percurrit agili corpus arte tractatrix,
> Manumque doctam fpargit omnibus membris. MARTIAL.

We had no longer reafon to complain of the want of appetite which had been the confequence of our fatigue; but as foon as our dinner was placed before us, confifting

* See Hawkefworth, vol. I. p. 463.
† See Ofbeck's and Torcen's Voyages to China, vol. I. p. 231. and II. p. 246.
‡ See Grofe's Voyage, vol. I. p. 113.

of vegetable food, fuitable to the frugal fimplicity of the natives, we partook of it very heartily, and foon found ourfelves in as good fpirits as we had fet out with in the morning. We paffed about two hours with this hofpitable family, and during that time diftributed the greateft part of the beads, nails, and knives which we had brought from the fhip to our generous hoft, to his fair daughter, and her companions, whofe care had reftored our ftrength much fooner than we had a right to expect after fo laborious an expedition. About three o'clock we fet out on our return, and walked paft numerous dwellings, whofe inhabitants enjoyed the beauty of the afternoon in various parties, under the fhade of their fruit-trees. In one of thefe houfes we obferved a man at work, in preparing a red dye, for fome cloth made of the bark of the paper-mulberry, which we commonly called the cloth-tree. Upon enquiring for the materials which he made ufe of, we found to our great furprize that the yellow juice of a fmall fpecies of fig, which they call mattee, and the greenifh juice of a fort of fern, or bind-weed, or of feveral other plants, by being fimply mixed together, formed a bright crimfon, which the women rubbed with their hands if the whole piece was to be uniformly of the fame colour, or in which they dipped a bamboo reed, if it was to be marked or fprinkled in different patterns. This colour fades very foon and becomes of a dirty red, befides being

liable

liable to be fpoiled by rain and other accidents; the cloth, however, which is dyed or rather ftained with it, is highly valued by the Taheitians, and only worn by their principal people. We bought feveral pieces of cloth of different kinds for beads and fmall nails, and then walked on till we arrived at the tents, which ftood at leaft five miles from the place where we had dined. Here we difcharged our trufty friend whom O-Whaw had recommended, and who had behaved with a degree of attachment and fidelity to us, which from the thievifh character of the nation we had no room to expect. This behaviour was the more meritorious as our fituation frequently had afforded him excellent opportunities of running off with all our nails and knives, and with one of our fowling-pieces; temptations which required an uncommon degree of honefty to withftand. We next embarked in one of the canoes which plied between the fhips and the fhore, and for a couple of beads were fafely brought on board. Here we found the captain and my father juft returned from a long excurfion to the weftward. E-Tee, the king's ambaffador, who arrived on board immediately after our departure, had brought a prefent of a hog and fome fruit, but acquainted the captain that O-Too was *matow*, a term which at once expreffed that he was afraid and difpleafed. To convince him that the outrages of laft night were not approved of, the offenders were brought to the gangway,

and

1773.
August.
and received a dozen of lashes in his presence, to the great terror of all the Taheitians on board.   Captain Cook then ordering three wether-sheep from the Cape, which were all we had left, to be put in his boat, embarked with captain Furneaux and my father, in order to regain the confidence of O-Too, without which he knew that no provisions were to be bought in the country.   When they arrived at Parre, they were told that he was gone to the westward; accordingly they went after him, about four or five miles farther, and landing in a district called Tittahàh, waited several hours for him there; his fears having been so strong, as actually to make him remove about nine miles farther from us than usual.   There was something in this conduct seemingly too much allied to cowardise; but we should likewise consider, that the power of Europeans had formerly been displayed here in the terrific shape of destruction.   It was three o'clock in the afternoon before he arrived with his mother; he expressing the most manifest signs of fear and distrust, and she with her eyes swimming in tears.   The report of E-Tee, the present of a new kind of animals, and all possible assurances of friendship on the part of our people, succeeded to quiet their apprehensions.   At the king's desire, the bagpiper was ordered to play before him, and his performance produced an effect similar to that of David's harp, whose harmonious sounds soothed the atrabilarious temper of Saul.   He
sent

sent for a hog, which was presented to captain Cook; and soon after for another, which he gave to captain Furneaux. The captains believing this to be the last opportunity of obtaining presents from him, desired that a third might be brought for *Matarra* (my father's Taheitian name.) A little pig was given him, at which our people expressed some dislike; upon this, one of the king's relations, in the ascending line, who are all styled *Medooa* (Father,) stepped forward from the throng, and spoke very loud, with many violent gestures, to O-Too, pointing at our people, at the sheep they had presented, and at the little pig which they had received. As soon as his speech was finished, the pig was taken back again, and after a short interval a large hog brought in its stead. Our people then produced their iron wares and a variety of trinkets, which they distributed very freely; and in return were wrapped up in several *ahbus*, or pieces of Indian cloth. They then took their leave of the whole court, and returned to their vessels about five o'clock.

Preparations were made for sailing from this island the next morning, whilst the natives crouded about us with fish, shells, fruit, and cloth, of which we purchased all that was to be had. Lieutenant Pickersgill returned from his excursion to the westward about three in the afternoon. He had advanced beyond the fertile plains of Paparra, where

O-Amno,

1771.
SEPTEMBER.
O-Ammo*, who had once been the king of all Taheitee, refided with his fon the young T-Aree Deare †. He took up his firft night's lodging on the borders of a fmall diftrict, which was now the property of the famous queen O-Poorea (Oberea.) As foon as fhe heard of his arrival fhe haftened to him, and met her old acquaintance with repeated marks of friendfhip. She had feparated from her hufband ‡ fome time after the departure of captain Wallis, and was now entirely deprived of that greatnefs which had once rendered her confpicuous in ftory, and auguft in the eyes of Europeans §. The civil wars between the two peninfulas of the ifland had ftripped her, as well as the whole diftrict of Paparra, of the greateft part of her wealth, fo that fhe complained to the lieutenant that fhe was poor, (teiter,) and had not a hog to give her friends. The next morning therefore they left her, and in their return touched at Paparra, where they faw Ammo, who, after parting with O-Poorea, had taken one of the handfomeft young women of the country to his bed, and appeared to be aged and indolent. His fair one gave a hog to our people, and, with fome of her female attendants, ftepped into the boat at their departure, and went the whole day with them, her own canoe attending to take her back again.

---

* See Hawkefworth, vol. II. p. 153, 154. O-ms.
† Ibid. vol. II. p. 154. Terri-Erai.
‡ Ibid. vol. II. p. 154.   § Ibid. vol. II. p. 156.

On

On this excurfion fhe expreffed a great degree of curiofity, which feemed never to have been gratified before by the fight of Europeans, infomuch that fhe was doubtful whether they were formed at all points like her own countrymen, till her eyes removed every doubt. With her they landed at Attahooroo, where a chief named POTATOW [*] received them very cordially, and entertained them at his own houfe during the fecond night. He too had parted with his wife *Polatebèra*, and taken a younger to his bed, while the lady had provided herfelf with a lover or a hufband, and they all continued to live very peaceably in the fame family. The next morning at parting Potatow promifed to accompany Mr. Pickerfgill to Matavaï, in order to vifit captain Cook, provided he might be fure of good treatment. Mr. Pickerfgill affured him of the beft reception; but the chief, for greater fafety, produced a few fmall yellow feathers, tied together into a little tuft, which he defired Mr. Pickerfgill to hold, whilft he repeated his promife, " that *Toòte* (captain Cook) would be the friend " of Potatow." This done, he carefully wrapped the feathers into a bit of Indian cloth, and put it in his turban. We knew, from former accounts, that red and yellow feathers were employed by the inhabitants of this ifland to fix their attention while they prayed to the Deity; but this ceremony conveyed an idea of a folemn affirmation or oath,

[*] See Hawkefworth, vol. II. p. 170.

which

The Friendly... which was quite new to us. Potatow was so well satisfied of the integrity of his friends, after this ceremony, that he and his wives, and several of their attendants, carrying with them two hogs and abundance of cloth, marched towards the boat, amidst an immense croud of people. He was, however, no sooner arrived at the water's side, than the whole multitude eagerly pressed him not to venture amongst our people, and clinging to his feet endeavoured to hold him back; several women, with a flood of tears, repeatedly cried aloud that Toote would kill him as soon as he came on board; and an old man, who, by living at the chief's own house, seemed to be a faithful servant to the family, drew him back by the skirts of his garment. Potatow was moved; for a moment he expressed some marks of diffidence; but instantly arming himself with all the resolution he was master of, he thrust the old man aside, exclaiming "*Toote aipa matte te toyo*," (Cook will not kill his friends!) and stepped into the boat with an air of undaunted majesty, that struck our Britons with astonishment. As soon as he was on board the ship, he descended into the cabin, accompanied by his wife *Whainee-òw*, his former wife, and her friend, and brought his presents to captain Cook. Potatow was one of the tallest men we had seen upon the island, and his features were so mild, comely, and at the same time majestic, that Mr. Hodges immediately applied himself to copy from them, as

from

from the noblest models of nature. His portrait is inserted in captain Cook's own account of this voyage. His
whole body was remarkably strong and heavily built, so
that one of his thighs nearly equalled in girth our stoutest
sailor's waist. His ample garments, and his elegant white
turban, set off his figure to the greatest advantage, and his
noble deportment endeared him to us, as we naturally
compared it with the diffidence of O-Too. Polatchera, his
former wife, was so like him in stature and bulk, that we
unanimously looked upon her as the most extraordinary
woman we had ever seen. Her appearance and her conduct were masculine in the highest degree, and strongly
conveyed the idea of superiority and command. When
the Endeavour bark lay here, she had distinguished herself
by the name of captain Cook's sister, *(tuahine no* TOOTE;)
and one day, being denied admittance into the fort on
Point Venus, had knocked down the sentry who opposed
her, and complained to her adopted brother of the indignity which had been offered to her. After a short stay,
being told that we intended to get under way immediately,
they asked, with every demonstration of friendship and
with tears in their eyes, whether we intended to return.
Captain Cook promised to be here again in the space of
seven months, with which they rested perfectly satisfied,
and departed immediately to the westward, their own canoes having followed our boat all the way.

VOL. I.   A a a   In

In the mean while a young Taheitian, of the common class, who was very well made, and about seventeen years old, having talked to the captain of going *no u whenua tei Britane*, (to the land of Britain,) for several days past, had arrived on board with his father. His whole equipment consisted of a small piece of the Indian cloth wrapped about his loins; so entirely did he depend upon our care and protection. Captain Cook gave his father, who seemed to be a middle aged man, a hatchet and some presents of lesser value, with which he descended into his canoe with great composure and firmness, without manifesting any signs of grief. We had scarce cleared the reefs, when a canoe arrived with two or three natives, who demanded the youth back in the name of O-Too, and shewed some pieces of cloth which they intended as presents to the captain: but as they could not produce the iron-work which he had bestowed on the poor fellow's account, they were obliged to return without him. The youth, whose name was *Porèa*, spoke to them, but would not leave us, though, to terrify him, we understood that they presaged his death amongst us. However, when they were at some distance, he looked wishfully after them, leaned over the railing on the quarter-deck, and shed a flood of tears in an agony of grief. To divert him from this gloomy mood, we took him into the cabin, where he complained that he must surely die, and that his father would weep for his loss.

Captain

Captain Cook and my father comforted him, faying they *1773.* would be his fathers, upon which he hugged and killed them, and pafled from the extreme of defpondence by a quick tranfition to a great degree of chearfulnefs. About fun-fet he ate his fupper, and lay down on the floor of the cabin; but feeing that we did not follow his example, he got up again, and remained with us till we had fupped.

It was with great regret that we daparted from this delightful ifland, at a time when we were juft become acquainted with its happy inhabitants. We had only paffed fourteen days on its coaft, two of which had been fpent in removing from one port to the other. During this fhort fpace of time, we had lived in a continual round of tumultuous occupations, which had left us little leifure to ftudy the nature of the people. An immenfe variety of objects relative to their œconomy, their cuftoms and ceremonies, all which appeared new and interefting to us, had engaged our attention; but we afterwards found moft of them had been obferved by former navigators. Thefe therefore, for fear of prefuming too far on the indulgence of my readers, I have omitted in this narrative, and refer for the particular defcriptions of the dwellings, drefs, food, domeftic amufements, boats and navigation, difeafes, religion, and funeral rites, wars, weapons, and government, to the hiftory of captain Cook's voyage in the Endeavour

bark

bark, compiled by Dr. Hawkefworth (vol. II. from page 184 to page 248). All the merit of the preceding pages concerning the ifle of Taheitee, muft therefore confift in a few gleanings and elucidations on feveral fubjects. However, I am in hopes that the particular point of view in which I have beheld, and confequently reprefented circum-stances already familiar to the reader from former accounts, will not prove uninterefting, and may in feveral inftances fuggeft new and valuable reflections.

The breeze with which we failed was fo moderate, that we continued near the fhore the whole evening, and were able to diftinguifh the exuberant fcenery of the plain, beautiful enough, even at this dead feafon of winter, to vie with the richeft landfcapes, which nature has lavifhed on different parts of the globe. Its fertile foil, and genial climate, which produces all forts of nutritive vegetables almoft fpontaneoufly, infures the felicity of its inhabitants. Allowing for the imperfect ftate of fublunary happinefs, which is comparative at beft, there are not, I believe, many nations exifting whofe fituation is fo defirable. Where the means of fubfiftence are fo eafy, and the wants of the people fo few, it is natural that the great purpofe of human life, that of multiplying the number of rational beings, is not loaded with that multitude of miferies which are attendant upon the married ftate in civilized countries. The impulfes of nature are therefore followed

without

1771.
September.

without reſtraint, and the conſequence is a great population, in proportion to the ſmall part of the iſland which is
cultivated. The plains and narrow vallies are now the
only inhabited parts, though many of the hills are very fit
for culture, and capable of ſupporting an infinite number
of people. Perhaps, in courſe of time, if the population
ſhould encreaſe conſiderably, the natives may have re-
courſe to theſe parts, which are now in a manner uſeleſs
and ſuperfluous. The evident diſtinction of ranks which
ſubſiſts at Taheitee, does not ſo materially affect the felicity
of the nation, as we might have ſuppoſed. Under one
general ſovereign, the people are diſtinguiſhed into the
claſſes of aree, manahouna, and towtow, which bear ſome
diſtant relation to thoſe of the feudal ſyſtems of Europe.
The ſimplicity of their whole life contributes to ſoften
theſe diſtinctions, and to reduce them to a level. Where
the climate and the cuſtom of the country do not abſolute-
ly require a perfect garment; where it is eaſy at every ſtep
to gather as many plants as form not only a decent, but
likewiſe a cuſtomary covering; and where all the neceſſa-
ries of life are within the reach of every individual, at the
expence of a trifling labour, ambition and envy muſt in a
great meaſure be unknown. It is true, the higher claſſes
of people poſſeſs ſome dainty articles, ſuch as pork, fiſh,
fowl, and cloth almoſt excluſively; but the deſire of indulging the appetite in a few trifling luxuries, can at moſt
render

render individuals, and not whole nations, unhappy. Absolute want occasions the miseries of the lower class in some civilized states, and is the result of the unbounded voluptuousness of their superiors. At O-Taheitee there is not, in general, that disparity between the highest and the meanest man, which subsists in England between a reputable tradesman and a labourer. The affection of the Taheitians for their chiefs, which they never failed to express upon all occasions, gave us great room to suppose that they consider themselves as one family, and respect their eldest-born in the persons of their chiefs. Perhaps the origin of their government was patriarchal, and the king might only be dignified by virtue of being considered as the father of his people, till by degrees the constitution settled into its present form. Still there remains much ancient simplicity in that familiarity between the sovereign and the subject. The lowest man in the nation speaks as freely with his king as with his equal, and has the pleasure of seeing him as often as he likes. This intercourse would become more difficult as soon as despotism should begin to gain ground. The king at times amuses himself with the occupations of his subjects, and not yet depraved by the false notions of an empty state, often paddles his own canoe, without thinking such an employment derogatory to his dignity. How long such an happy equality may last, is uncertain; since the indolence of the chiefs is already, notwithstanding the

exuberant

exuberant fertility of the foil, a ftep towards its deftruction.   Though cultivation is a labour fcarce felt at prefent
by the townows, to whom it is allotted ; yet by infenfible
degrees it will fall heavier upon them, as the number of
chiefs muft naturally increafe in a much greater proportion, than their own clafs, for this obvious reafon, becaufe
the chiefs are perfectly unemployed.   This addition of labour will have a bad effect on their bodies, they will grow
ill-fhaped, and their bones become marrowlefs : their
greater expofure to the action of a vertical fun, will blacken
their fkins, and they will dwindle away to dwarfs, by the
more frequent proftitution of their infant daughters, to the
voluptuous pleafures of the great.   That pampered race,
on the contrary, will preferve all the advantages of an extraordinary fize, of a fuperior elegance of form and features, and of a purer colour, by indulging a voracious appetite, and living in abfolute idlenefs.   At laft the common people will perceive thefe grievances, and the caufes
which produced them ; and a proper fenfe of the general
rights of mankind awaking in them, will bring on a re-
volution.   This is the natural circle of human affairs ; at
prefent there is fortunately no room to fuppofe, that fuch a
change will take place for a long feries of years to come ; but
how much the introduction of foreign luxuries may haften
that fatal period, cannot be too frequently repeated to Eu-
                                                    ropeans.

ropeans. If the knowledge of a few individuals can only be acquired at fuch a price as the happinefs of nations, it were better for the difcoverers, and the difcovered, that the South Sea had ftill remained unknown to Europe and its reftlefs inhabitants.

CHAP.

C H A P. X.

Account of our Transactions at the Society Islands.

THE wind with which we failed from O-Taheitee,
freshened after fun-fet, and favoured our departure
from that happy island, which we still discerned by moon-
light.

The next day, at eleven o'clock, we saw the isle of Thursday 2
Huahine, which is about twenty-five leagues from Taheitee,
and was first discovered by captain Cook, on the 11th of
July, 1769. A number of our people now felt the effects
of their intercourse with the women at Matavaï Bay, and
had symptoms of a disagreeable complaint. All the patients,
however, without exception, had this disease only in a very
slight and benign degree. The question which has been agitated between the French and English navigators, concerning
the first introduction of this evil to Taheitee, might be decided very favourably for them both, by supposing the dif-
ease to have existed at Taheitee previous to their arrival.
The argument, that none of captain Wallis's people received the infection, does not seem to controvert this supposition, but only proves, that the women, who prostituted
themselves to his crew, were free from it: which was per-
VOL. I.   B b b   haps

1773.
SEPTEMBER. haps owing to a precaution of the natives, who might be
apprehensive of exposing themselves to the anger of the
strangers, by conferring such a desperate gift upon them *.
We heard, however, of another disease of a different nature,
whilst we staid upon the island; and which they called
o-pay-no-Peppe, (the sore of Peppe,) adding, that it was
brought by the ship which they designed by that name,
and which, according to different accounts, had either been
two, three, or five months before us at Taheitee. By the
account of the symptoms, it seemed to be a kind of le-
prosy. Nothing is more easy than to imagine, how the
strangers (Spaniards,) who visited Taheitee in that ship,
might be innocently charged with introducing that disease.
In order to give rise to a general error of this sort, it is
sufficient that it broke out nearly about the time of their
arrival, and that some distant connections between them
and the persons affected, could be traced. This is the
more probable, as it is certain, that there are several sorts
of leperous complaints existing among the inhabitants,
such as the elephantiasis, which resembles the yaws; also
an eruption over the whole skin, and lastly a monstrous
rotting ulcer, of a most loathsome appearance. However,

* See M. de Bougainville's Voyage, English Edition, pag. 273. 274. 285.
286. and Hawkesworth, vol. I. p. 489. 490. and vol. II. p. 231. M. de Bougainville, with the politeness of a well-bred man, doubts, whether the disease existed
at Taheitee previous to his arrival or not; the English seaman asserts his opinion as fact in positive terms.

all

all thefe very feldom occur, and efpecially the laft; for the excellence of their climate, and the fimplicity of their vegetable food, which cannot be too much extolled, prevent not only thefe, but almoft all dangerous and deadly diforders.

Towards fun-fet we brought to within two leagues of Huahine; and the next day, at four o'clock, doubled the north end of that ifland, and then bore up for the harbour of O-Wharre. Huahine is divided by a deep inlet into two peninfulas, connected by an ifthmus entirely overflowed at high-water. Its hills are much inferior to thofe of Taheitee in height, but their appearance ftrongly indicated them as the former feats of a volcano. The fummit of one of them had much the appearance of a crater, and a blackifh fpungy rock was feen on one of its fides, which feemed to be lava. At fun-rife we beheld fome of the other Society Ifles, called O-Raietea (Ulietea,) O-Taha, and Barabora (Bolabola.) The laft forms a peak like Mahtea, but infinitely higher and more confiderable, on the top of which there appeared alfo the crater of a volcano. There are two entrances to O-Wharre harbour; of thefe we chofe the fouthermoft, and having a very fteady breeze off fhore, our navigators tried their fkill in working in. The entrance might be about three or four hundred yards long, and barely a hundred yards wide between two reefs. However in this fpace we made fix or feven trips with

B b b 2   amazing

amazing dexterity, each trip lasting about two or three minutes. We had not yet worked in, when the Adventure came in after us, but unfortunately approached too near one of the reefs, just as she was putting about, and leaned on the side of the coral rock. We were for the present intent only in saving our own ship for fear of the worst that might happen, and soon after came to an anchor. As soon as that was done, our boats were dispatched to the assistance of our consort, and she was towed into the harbour. Her bottom being examined, it was found that she had suffered no damage, which was likewise the case with the Resolution, when she struck on the coast of Tiarraboo.

The appearance of the country was exactly the same here as at Taheitee, but upon a much smaller scale; the circumference of the whole isle being only about seven or eight leagues. The plains are therefore very inconsiderable, and there are hardly any intermediate hills between them and the higher mountains, which take their rise immediately from the skirts of the plain. The country, however, contained a variety of pleasant little spots. Not a single canoe came off to us here beyond the reefs, but we had not been long at anchor before a few of them arrived loaded with coco-nuts, bread-fruit, and large fowls. We were very glad to meet with these birds, having obtained only a single pair at Taheitee, where they had been entirely

tirely fwept away by former navigators. Amongft the natives who came on board, there was one who had a mon-
ftrous rupture or hernia, which did not feem to incumber
him much, as he came up the fides of the fhip with great
agility. The natives fpoke the fame language, had the
fame features, and wore the fame cloth, made of bark, as
thofe of Taheitee; but none of their women appeared.
They bartered very fairly for our beads and nails, and in a
little time had fold us a dozen of very large cocks, of a
beautiful plumage; but it may be remarked, that they
feldom brought the hens for fale. Towards eleven o'clock
the captains went on fhore to a large fhed, of which the
fides reached to the ground, and which gave fhelter to a
double canoe. Here they appointed a perfon to trade with
the natives, which they did fo regularly that we collected
upwards of twenty hogs this day for large fpike nails or
fmall hatchets, and about a dozen of dogs, which feemed
to be the moft ftupid animals of their kind, but were
reckoned excellent provifion by the natives. During our
firft walk we found two plants which we had not feen before; and we took notice that all the bread-trees in that
part had already young fruit, of the fize of fmall apples,
which, as the natives faid, would not be ripe in lefs than
four months. The diftrict where we landed feemed to be
entirely deftitute of bananas; the natives, however, brought
us fome bunches of this fruit from other parts, which
proves

proves that they have the art of managing some of their plantations so as to produce at different seasons; but these late crops are, as may be easily conceived, very trifling in quantity, and reserved for the luxury of their chiefs.

We returned on board to dinner, and afterwards made another excursion on shore, where we were told, that the chiefs of the island would make their appearance the next day. We were not much incommoded by the inhabitants on our rambles, our train seldom exceeding fifteen or twenty, except near a place of general resort, such as the shed where our trade was carried on. The smallness of the island might be the principal cause of the difference from what we had experienced at Taheitee; but it must be added, that the natives here were not well enough acquainted with our disposition to expect to reap any advantage from following us; and did not, upon the whole, express that degree of curiosity, nor of fear, which was inherent in the Taheitians, who had had sufficient cause to dread the superior power of our fire-arms.

Our Taheitian friend Porea went ashore with us in a linen frock and a pair of trowsers, and carried captain Cook's powder-horn and shot-pouch. He told us that he was desirous to be looked upon as one of our people, and therefore never spoke the Taheitian language, but continued to mutter some unintelligible sounds, which actually imposed upon the multitude. To favour the illusion, he
would

would no longer hearken to his Taheitian name Porea,
but defired to have an English one; the failors immediately called him Tom, with which he was extremely well pleafed, and foon learnt the ufual anfwer of Sir, which he expreffed Yorro. What aim he propofed to himfelf in affuming this difguife, we could not conceive, unlefs it was, that he expected to have greater confequence in the character of an English failor, than that of a Taheitian towtow.

The next day my father accompanied the captains to the trading-place, and from thence to the north part of the harbour, where they found the acting chief, Oree, who was the uncle of the prefent king Territarea (perhaps T'-Aree-Tarea.) They put afhore near a houfe on the water-fide, where Oree was feated amidft a number of his attendants. Two of the natives who were in the boat, feeing our gentlemen preparing to land, defired them to fit ftill a while, till they had brought fome plantane-ftems, in fign of peace and friendfhip. They prefented two of thefe to our people, and defired them to ornament them with large nails, looking-glaffes, medals, &c. This requeft being complied with, the ftems thus loaded were brought on fhore and prefented, whilft they bid our people pronounce to the firft *no t'Eatua,* " for the Divinity," and to the fecond, *na te taye O-Toote no Oree,* " from the friend, Cook, to Oree." This

This done, our people received in their turn five plantane-stalks succeſſively under the following denominations.

1. The firſt, accompanied with a pig, *no t'Aree* " from the king," (meaning T'-aree-tarea who was a boy about ſeven or eight years old).

2. The ſecond, with another pig, *no t'Eatua,* " for the divinity."

3. The third, *no te Taimee.* This term was entirely un-intelligible to our people at that time, but it appeared from ſubſequent explanations, to ſignify " a welcome."

4. The fourth with a dog, *no te Toura,* " from the rope." Here, though the words were underſtood, the meaning was, if poſſible, more obſcure than in the preceding article, and what is worſe, we could never obtain any light upon the ſubject.

5. The laſt with a pig, *no te tayo O-Oree no Toote,* " from the friend Oree to Cook."

To conclude this ceremony, the ſame man who brought all theſe things, likewiſe preſented a red bag, containing a piece of pewter with this inſcription, " His Britannic Ma-jeſty's ſhip, Endeavour. Lieutenant Cook commander, 16th of July, 1769. Huahine," together with a counter *. This teſtimony of captain Cook's firſt viſit to the iſland of Huahine, which he had left to Oree with an injunction never to part

* See Hawkeſworth, vol. II. p. 253.

with

with it, was probably laid before him at prefent, to fhew that his directions had been ftrictly adhered to. As foon as he had received it, he ftepped afhore with all his company, and embraced Oree, who was an old man between fifty and fixty, thin, and very blear-eyed. He received our people very cordially as known friends, and prefented feveral large bales of cloth to the captain; after which the inhabitants flocked in great numbers to his houfe, with abundance of fowls, hogs, and dogs, which they eagerly fold for the trifling confideration of nails, knives, and fmall hatchets.

In the mean while Dr. Sparrman and myfelf, after landing at the trading-place, proceeded to Oree's houfe by land. On this walk we faw great numbers of hogs, dogs, and fowls. The laft roamed about at pleafure through the woods, and roofted on fruit-trees; the hogs were likewife allowed to run about, but received regular portions of food, which were commonly diftributed by old women. We obferved one of them in particular, feeding a little pig with the four fermented bread-fruit pafte, called mahei; fhe held the pig with one hand, and offered it a tough pork's fkin, but as foon as it opened the mouth to fnap at it, fhe contrived to throw a handful of the four pafte in, which the little animal would not take without this ftratagem. The dogs in fpite of their ftupidity, were in high favour with all the women, who could not have

VOL. I.   C c c   nurfed

nurfed them with a more ridiculous affection, if they had
really been ladies of fafhion in Europe. We were witneffes
of a remarkable inftance of kindnefs, when we faw a middle aged woman, whofe breafts were full of milk, offering
them to a little puppy which had been trained up to fuck
them. We were fo much furprifed at this fight, that we
could not help expreffing our diflike of it ; but fhe fmiled
at our obfervation, and added, that fhe fuffered little pigs
to do the fame fervice. Upon enquiry however, we found
that fhe had loft her child, and did her the juftice amongft
ourfelves to acknowledge that this expedient was very innocent and formerly practifed in Europe *. The dogs of
all thefe iflands were fhort, and their fizes vary from that
of a lap-dog to the largeft fpaniel. Their head is broad,
the fnout pointed, the eyes very fmall, the ears upright,
and their hair rather long, lank, hard, and of different
colours, but moft commonly white and brown. They
feldom if ever barked, but howled fometimes, and were
fhy of ftrangers to a degree of averfion.

We met with fome of the birds here, which we had
already feen at Taheitee, and alfo a blue white-bellied
king's-fifher, and a greyifh heron. We fhot fome of each
fort, but found a number of people among the croud,

* The Indian women in America, whofe milk is remarkably abundant,
have frequent recourfe to this expedient to drain their breafts. See the Canon
Pauw's Recherches Philofophiques fur les Americains, vol. I. p. 55.

who

who annexed an idea of holiness to these birds, and called them eatooas, which is the same name by which they design God. There were however at all times, at least an equal, if not greater number of people who desired us to shoot them, and were very ready to point them out. Neither did any of them express a mark of disapprobation after we had killed the birds. It is certain that they do not look upon them as divinities, because these according to their ideas are invisible; but the name of eatooa which they bestow on them, seems to convey an idea of a much greater veneration, than that which protects swallows and other birds in England, against the mischievous pursuit of unlucky boys. Here and in many other circumstances relative to civil, political, and religious institutions, we are entirely at a loss; and on account of our short continuance among these islanders, as well as for want of knowing their language, could never obtain any satisfactory information.

With the acquisitions which we had made, we continued our excursion to the northern arm of the harbour, where Mr. Smith, one of our mates, superintended the waterers. We found a number of natives assembled about him, who brought so many hogs for sale, that we were plentifully supplied with fresh meat, and could serve it every day to both ships companies. Vegetables on the

other

1773.
September.

other hand were so scarce here, that we rarely got plantanes, bread-fruit, and coco-nuts, but contented ourselves
with some good yams, which when boiled supplied the
place of bread.   Towards noon we reached Oree's house,
after walking along a beach of small white shell sand,
amidst a low kind of coco-palms, affording a good deal of
shade, which is always acceptable in these climates.   Captain Cook had been more successful in trading than all
the other parties, so that when we returned into the boat,
we had scarce room enough to sit in it.   In the afternoon
we returned to Oree's house, where we found him surrounded by a great number of the principal people of the
island.   They appeared to be so exactly like the Taheitians, that we could perceive no difference, nor could
we by any means verify that assertion of former navigators,
that the women of this island were in general fairer and
more handsome *; but this may vary according to circumstances.   They were however not so troublesome in
begging for beads and other presents, nor so forward to
bestow their favours on the new comers, though at our
landing and putting off, some of the common sort frequently performed an indecent ceremony, which is described in the accounts of former voyagers, but without
any of the preparatory circumstances which Ooratooa had

* See Hawkesworth, vol. II. p. 254.

prac-

1773.
SEPTEMBER.

practised †. We had likewise much less reason to extol
the hospitality of the inhabitants, their general behaviour
being rather more indifferent, and the Taheitian custom of
reciprocal presents almost entirely unknown. On our
walks we were unmolested, but their conduct was bolder
and more unconcerned than that of the Taheitians, and the
explosion, as well as the effects of our fowling-pieces did
not strike them with fear and astonishment. These differences were certainly owing to the various treatment which
the people of both islands had met with on the part of
Europeans. There were, however, not wanting instances
of hospitality and good-will even here. A chief, named
Townia, entreated my father to come to his house, which
lay in the interior part of the plain. He accepted the invitation, and was very well entertained; besides having an
opportunity of purchasing one of those targets or breast-
plates which I have already mentioned.

Oree came on board early the next morning with his
sons, the eldest of them a handsome little boy, about eleven
years old, who received our presents with great indifference; but he, as well as all the people of the island, were
highly delighted with the bagpipe, and required it to be
constantly played. With Oree, who now went by the name
of Cookee, as he had done whilst the Endeavour lay here [*],

Sunday 5.

---

† See Hawkesworth, vol. II. p. 125. See also vol. I. p. 438, 440. They
lifted up their garments from the knee to the waist.

[*] See Hawkesworth, vol. II. p. 251.

WE

we returned on fhore, where we difperfed in fearch of
plants and other curiofities. In the evening we all met
together again, when Dr. Sparrman, who had been entirely by himfelf towards the north point of the ifle, acquainted us that he had met with a large lagoon of falt-water,
which extended feveral miles parallel to the coaft, and had
an intolerable ftench on account of the putrid mud which
lay on its fhores. Here he had met with feveral plants,
which are common enough in the ifles and coafts of the
Eaft Indies, but not fo frequent in other parts of the South
Sea iflands. A fingle native, whom he had entrufted with
his plant-bag, had proved extremely faithful to him. Whenever the doctor fat down to defcribe, the native feated himfelf behind him, and took both the fkirts of his coat, containing his pockets, in his hand, in order, as he faid, to
prevent the thieves from coming at them. By this means
the doctor had not loft any thing when he came on board;
feveral of the natives, however, feeming to think him in
their power, had beftowed upon him fome ill-natured looks
and opprobrious names.

The next day he ventured out again entirely by himfelf,
while we remained at the trading-place with captain Cook.
One of the natives, named Tubaï, a tall man, dreffed in feveral large pieces of the cloth of bark, ftained with red,
and who had feveral bundles of birds feathers hanging at
his girdle, prohibited the fale of hogs and bread-fruit, and

actually

actually feized a bag of nails which the captain's clerk
held in his hand. However, when the latter called for
affiftance, he let it go again, and perceiving one of our
young gentlemen trying to ftrike a bargain for a large
fowl, he took a nail from him by force, and threatened to
beat him with his club. A complaint being made to captain Cook, juft as he was going aboard in a boat, he returned afhore, and bid Tubaï to leave the place. Upon
his refufal, the captain went up to him and feized two
large clubs which the naüve had in his hand; but the
latter ftruggled with him, till captain Cook drew his hanger,
on which he made off. The clubs, which were made of
the cafuarina wood, were broken and the pieces thrown
into the fea, by the captain's order, while he recalled the
reft of the natives, who began to be alarmed, and were
preparing to leave the trading-place. They all agreed that
this Tubaï was a bad man, *(tata-eeno.)* and feemed to think
that we had done him juftice. However, as captain Cook
was going to fend his boat on board for a party of
marines to protect our traders, the whole croud difperfed
at once and left us alone. We had not been above two
minutes at a lofs to account for their behaviour, when Dr.
Sparrman arrived almoft ftripped naked, and with the
marks of feveral violent blows. He had been accofted on
his walk by two of the natives, who had invited him to
proceed farther into the country, with many proteftations
of

of friendſhip, and repetitions of the word *taye*. At once,
taking the advantage of an unguarded moment, they tore
from his ſide a hanger, the only weapon he had, and gave
him a blow over his head as he was ſtooping to arm himſelf with a ſtone. He ſtumbled, and they tore a black ſat-
tin waiſtcoat and ſeveral looſe parts of dreſs from him.
However, diſengaging himſelf, he ran towards the beach
and outſtripped them, when ſome bind-weeds caught his
feet, and detained him till the villains came up. They
gave him repeated blows over his temples and ſhoulders,
which ſtunned him; ſtripped his ſhirt over his head, and
were juſt preparing to cut his hands, becauſe the ſleeve-
buttons held the ſhirt, when he fortunately opened them
with his teeth, and they made off with their booty. Not
above fifty yards farther on, ſome natives were at dinner,
who, ſeeing him paſſing by, came out and invited him to
ſtop, but he hurried on towards the ſea. In his way,
however, he met two natives, who immediately took off
their own cloth, *(ahow,)* dreſſed him in it, and attended
him to the trading-place. Theſe honeſt people were rewarded to the beſt of our power with various preſents, and
we all hurried on board to reinforce our party. Dr. Sparrman being dreſſed again, accompanied us to Oree's houſe
to whom we made our complaint. The old chief immediately reſolved to aſſiſt captain Cook in the ſearch after
the thieves, but his noble reſolution filled all his relations
with

with terror. Upwards of fifty people of both sexes began to weep when he stepped into the boat; some with the most pathetic and moving gestures tried to dissuade him, and others held him back and embraced him; but he was not to be prevailed upon, and went off with us, saying, that he had nothing to apprehend, because he was not the guilty person. My father offered to remain on shore as an hostage, but he would not admit of it, and took only one of his relations in the boat with him. We rowed up a deep creek opposite the ships, where this villainy had been committed, and afterwards took a long walk into the country to no purpose; for all Oree's messengers, who were sent to apprehend the robbers, did not perform their duty. At last we returned to the boat, where Oree re-embarked with us, notwithstanding the tears of an old lady and of her handsome daughter. The young woman, in a fit of frantic grief, took up some shells and cut herself on the head with them, but her mother tore them out of her hands, and actually accompanied Oree to the ship. Here he dined with us very heartily, but the woman, according to the custom of the country, would not touch our provisions. After dinner we brought him back to his house, which was crouded with different groups of the principal families on the island, who sat on the ground, and many of whom shed tears plentifully. We sat down amongst these disconsolate people, and with all the Tahei-

Vol. I.   D d d   tian

tian oratory we were mafters of, endeavoured to footh them into content and good humour. The women, in particular, fhewed a great fenfibility, and could not recover for a long while. At laft we fucceeded to appeafe their violence of grief; and, as fome of us could not behold their diftrefs, without admiring the excellence of their hearts, we naturally fympathized with them, with a degree of fincerity which entirely regained their confidence. It is indeed one of the happieft reflections which this voyage has enabled us to make, that inftead of finding the inhabitants of thefe ifles wholly plunged in fenfuality, as former voyagers have falfely reprefented them, we have met with the moft generous and exalted fentiments among them, that do honour to the human race in general. Vicious characters are to be met with in all focieties of men; but for one villain in thefe ifles, we can fhew at leaft fifty in England, or any civilized country.

In a little time the trade went on as brifkly as ever, and we were particularly fortunate in obtaining a fupply of vegetables. Towards evening two of Oree's meffengers arrived with the hanger and a part of Dr. Sparrman's waiftcoat, which were reftored to him, and with thefe foon after we returned on board.

In the morning, at day-break, the captains went to Oree's houfe, and returned the piece of pewter on which the commemoration of the firft difcovery was engraved.

At

At the fame time they gave him a piece of copper, with this
infcription: HIS BRITANNICK MAJESTY'S SHIPS RESOLUTION AND ADVENTURE, SEPTEMBER 1773. to which they added a number of medals, and defired him to fhew it to any ftrangers that happened to touch here. As foon as they were on board again, the feamen hove the anchor, and we got under fail, in company with the Adventure. The quantity of live flock which we had purchafed during our three days ftay was amazing, and fhewed how great a value the natives had fet upon our iron-work. The Refolution alone had two hundred and nine live hogs, thirty dogs, and about fifty fowls on board, when fhe failed, and the Adventure had not much lefs. We were fcarce got under way when Oree arrived along-fide in a fmall canoe, and came on board; he acquainted us that the robbers, and the things they had carried off, were taken, and defired both the captains, as well as Dr. Sparrman, to come on fhore, in order to fee the villains punifhed. But unfortunately his ftory was mifunderftood, and we loft an opportunity of feeing their method of inflicting punifhments. Captain Cook believing that Oree fpoke of fome of his countrymen who were embarked in the Adventure againft his will, immediately difpatched his boat to bring them back; but that veffel being a great way ahead, and we driving out to fea very faft, Oree became impatient, took a cordial leave of us all, and returned on fhore in his little

D d d 2　　　　canoe,

1774.
September.

canoe, with only one of his countrymen to assist him. A little while after our boat returned from the Adventure, and brought on board O-Mai, the only native who had embarked in that vessel with a view to go to England. He staid on board our ship till we reached Raïetea, whither we now directed our course. As soon as we were come to an anchor there, he returned on board the Adventure, and afterwards came to England in her, and has for some time engrossed the attention of the curious. He seemed to be one of the common people at that time, as he did not aspire to the captain's company, but preferred that of the armourer and the common seamen. But when he reached the Cape of Good Hope, where the captain dressed him in his own clothes, and introduced him in the best companies, he declared he was not a *teutou*, which is the denomination of the lowest class, and assumed the character of a *hòa*, or attendant upon the king. The world hath been amused at times with different fabulous accounts concerning this man, among which we need only mention the ridiculous story of his being a " Priest of the Sun;" a character which has never existed in the islands from whence he came. His stature was tall, but very slim, and his hands remarkably small. His features did not convey an idea of that beauty which characterizes the men at O-Taheitee; on the contrary, we do him no injustice to assert that, among all the inhabitants of Taheitee and the Society

Isles,

Isles, we have seen few individuals so ill-favoured as him- ~~1773.~~
self. His colour was likewise the darkest hue of the
common class of people, and corresponded by no means
with the rank he afterwards assumed. It was certainly
unfortunate that such a man should be selected as a specimen of a people who have been justly enrolled by all
navigators, as remarkably well featured and coloured,
considering the climate in which they live. The qualities
of his heart and head resembled those of his countrymen in
general; he was not an extraordinary genius like Tupaia,
but he was warm in his affections, grateful, and humane;
he was polite, intelligent, lively, and volatile. For a further account of O-Mai, I refer the reader to the preface,
where I have mentioned his stay in England, his progress
in knowledge, and his equipment at his return.

Having left Huahine we sailed to the westward, and Wedensday 1.
doubled the south end of an island, discovered by captain
Cook in 1769, which all the natives of Taheitee, and the
Society Isles call O-Raietea, but which (upon what foundation I know not) is named Ulietea in captain Cook's
charts *. The next morning we anchored in an opening
of the reef, and spent the whole day in warping into Hamaneno harbour. The country hereabouts afforded a
prospect much resembling Taheitee; for the island being
about three times the size of Huahine, had much broader

* See Hawkesworth, vol. II. p. 255, 260.

plains, and loftier hills. The natives surrounded us in a number of canoes, and brought a few hogs; but our people looked at them with a careless indifference, and offered very low prices, being difficult to please, since their success at Huahine. In one of the canoes a chief came on board, named Oruwherra, a native of the adjacent isle of Borabora (Bolabola.) He was very athletic, but his hands very small, and the punctuation, which the natives call tattow, confisted of the moft singular square blotches on his arms, and of large black stripes across the breaft, belly, and back. His loins and thighs were uniformly black. He brought some green branches, and a little pig which he presented to my father, being neglected by every body else. Having received a few iron-tools as a return, he descended immediately into his canoe, and was paddled to the shore. But in a little time, another canoe arrived from him with coco-nuts and bananas, which his servants offered to his new friend, refusing at the same time to accept of any retribution. The pleasure which we felt from this circumstance, can easily be conceived. Philanthropy is never better rewarded, than when its objects are endowed with good and amiable qualities.

In the afternoon another chief, a native of the same isle of Borabora, came on board, and exchanged names with my father. His name was Herea, and his person the most corpulent we ever saw in the South Sea islands; round his
waift

waift he meafured no lefs than fifty-four inches, and one of his thighs was thirty-one inches and ½ in girth. His hair was likewife remarkable; for it hung down in long black wavy treffes to the fmall of his back, and in fuch quantity that it encreafed the apparent bulk of his head confiderably. His corpulence, his colour, and his punctures, like thofe of Oruwherra, were very diftinguifhing marks of his rank, to which indolence and luxury are annexed here as well as at Taheitee. It may perhaps want fome explanation, how both thefe chiefs, who were natives of the adjacent ifle of Borabora, could have any authority and poffeffions on Raietea. Already, in captain Cook's former voyage, it was known that O-Poonee the king of Borabora, had conquered not only the ifle of Raietea, but likewife that of O-Taha, which is included in the fame reef, and that of Mowrua which lies about fifteen leagues to the weftward*. The warriors who had ferved under him in thefe expeditions had been rewarded with ample poffeffions, and a great number of his fubjects had received grants in the conquered iflands. The king of Raietea Oo-Ooroo, was however confirmed in his dignity, though his power was confined to the diftrict of Opoa; but at Taha, Poonee had placed a viceroy, named Boba, who was nearly related to him. Many of the natives of the conquered iflands had retreated to Huahine and Taheitee,

* See Hawkefworth, vol. II. p. 266, 267.

pre-

preferring a voluntary exile, to a submission to the conqueror, and hoping one day to refcue their country from oppreſſion. It ſeems, this was the motive which prompted Tupaïa and O-Maï, who were both natives of Raietea, to embark in British ſhips, as both of them always expreſſed a hope of obtaining a quantity of our fire-arms. Tupaïa might perhaps have carried his ſcheme into execution, if he had lived; but O-Maï's underſtanding was not ſufficiently penetrative, to acquire a competent idea of our wars, or to adapt it afterwards to the ſituation of his countrymen. He was, however, ſo fond of the thought of freeing his country from the Borabora men, that he has frequently ſaid, in England, if captain Cook did not aſſiſt him in the execution of his plan, he would take care that his countrymen ſhould not ſupply him with refreſhments. In this opinion he perſiſted till near the time of his departure, when he was perſuaded to adopt more peaceable principles. We were at a loſs to conceive the motives which could have induced a native of one of theſe iſlands to become a conqueror. If we believed the accounts of the Borabora men, their native iſland was as fertile and deſireable as theſe of which they had taken poſſeſſion; therefore nothing but a ſpirit of ambition could have ſtimulated them to contentions. Such a ſpirit ill agreed with the ſimplicity and generous character of the people, and it gave us pain to be convinced,

that

that great imperfections cannot be excluded from the beft
of human focieties.

On the day after our arrival, the captains went on fhore with us to a large houfe, clofe to the water's fide, which he knew to be the refidence of Orèa, the chief of the diftrict. We found him fitting in his houfe, with his wife, fon, daughter, and a great number of perfons of diftinction. Immediately after our arrival we fat down by them, and were fhut in on all fides by a thick croud of the natives, who made the place exceffively hot. Orèa was a middle-fized, lufty man, with a very lively intelligent countenance, and thin redifh-brown beard. He joked and laughed very heartily with us, and entirely banifhed all kinds of cere-mony and affectation. His wife was an elderly woman, but his fon and daughter, about twelve and fourteen years old. The latter was of a very white colour, and her fea-tures had not much of the general character of the nation, particularly her nofe, which was remarkably well-fhaped, and her eyes, which gave her fome refemblance to a Chi-nefe. Her flature was low, but her body elegantly pro-portioned, and her hands graceful beyond defcription ; only the legs and feet were too large for the reft of the figure, and the cuftom of cutting the hair fhort, appeared to be a great difadvantage. Her manners were very engaging, and fhe had a pleafing foft voice, like moft of her country-women, fo that fhe could not be refufed, when fhe afked

VOL. I.   E e e   for

for beads or other trinkets. As it did not agree with our
occupations, to stay in the house, we took a walk into the
groves, where we shot a few birds, and collected some
plants. We found here, to our great satisfaction, that confidence and familarity amongst the common people, which
we had not experienced at Huahine, and we were happy
at the same time not to be importuned by them, in the begging strain of the Taheitians. In the afternoon we made
another excursion, and shot several king-fishers. As soon
as we had shot the last, we met Orèa, and his family walking through the plain with captain Cook; the chief took
no notice of the bird which we had in our hands, but his
fair daughter lamented the death of her eatua, and ran
from us, when we attempted to touch her with it. Her
mother, and most of the women, seemed likewise to be
grieved at this accident, and at stepping into the boat, the
chief desired us with a very serious air, not to kill the king-
fishers and herons on his island, allowing at the same
time the liberty of shooting any other forts of birds. We
tried again to discover the nature of their veneration for
these two species, but all our enquiries were as fruitless
as they had been before.

We walked to the top of one of the neighbouring hills
the next day, and found several new plants in the vallies,
between them. The soil at the top was a kind of stone
marle; on the sides we found some scattered flints, and a
few

few fmall pieces of a cavernous or fpungy ftone-lava, of
a whitifh colour, which feemed to contain fome remains of
iron. This metal, which is of general and extenfive utility,
is difperfed through almoft all parts of the world, by the
benevolent hand of nature, and may perhaps even here be
contained in the mountains, In great quantity. The lava
indicated the exiftence of former volcanoes in this ifland,
which we had indeed fufpected, becaufe all the adjacent
ifles, we had hitherto feen, ftrongly, and fometimes evidently bore the marks of changes by fubterraneous fire. One
of the natives who had attended us, and carried fome refrefhments, pointed out the direction of feveral iflands in
the neighbourhood, but which lay out of fight. About
due weft, he faid, the ifle of Mopeehàh was fituated, and
about S. by W. another, named Whennua òwrah. Both
thefe, according to his accounts, were not inhabited, and
confifted only of circular ledges of coral, with palms on
them, but were occafionally vifited from this and the adjacent ifles. They feem to be Lord Howe's Ifland, and the
Scilly Ifles, difcovered by captain Wallis. We defcended
about noon, and found that captains Cook and Furneaux
had juft left the fhore, after feeing a great dramatic dance,
or heèva, performed by fome of the principal women in
the ifland. We haftened on board, as the day proved very
hot, and found both our veffels furrounded by a great number of canoes, in which were feveral perfons of diftinction

Eee2   of

of both fexes, who brought vaft quantities of cloth, made
of the mulberry-tree's bark, and offered them in exchange
for fmall nails. Our beads were much valued by the ladies
as ornaments, but by no means current like the nails, fo
that we could not even purchafe fruit with them. The Taheitians fet a much higher value on thefe trifles, which
have no intrinfic worth; may we not conclude therefore,
that a greater degree of general opulence is the caufe of
their particular affection for trinkets, efpecially as affluence
commonly tends to luxury?

The heat of the day prevented us from going on fhore
till near fun-fet. We landed at the watering-place, where
we found a little *tupapow*, or fhed, under which a dead
body was depofited on a ftage, and a thick grove of various
fhady trees furrounded it on all-fides. As I had never
feen the remains of the dead carelefsly expofed to all kinds
of accidents in thefe iflands, I was a little furprifed to
find the ground ftrewed with fculls and bones about this
fhed; nor could I meet with any native at this time, from
whom I could receive the leaft information on this fubject.
I rambled about here for fome time entirely alone, all
the inhabitants having repaired to the chief's houfe, where
the drums gave notice of another heeva, or public dance;
for they are fo fond of this amufement, that they croud
together from a confiderable diftance to have the pleafure
of feeing it performed. The ftillnefs of the evening, and
the

the beauty of the spot made this walk extremely pleasant, while the absence of the inhabitants encouraged some ideas of an enchanted country. Before we returned to our boat, we met, however, with a few of the natives, amongst whom one, a very intelligent man, gave us an account of nine islands in the neighbourhood, with most of which we were unacquainted. Their names were, 1. *Mopeehah*, 2. *Whennua-Ourah*, 3. *Aheeha*, 4. *Tewhheepa*, 5. *Wouwou*, 6. *Ooboroo*, 7. *Tubooai*, 8. *Aihaow*, and 9. *Rerotoa*. The two first we had already heard of in the morning, but of the rest he asserted that they all had their own* inhabitants, except *Aheeha*, which is occasionally visited. *Ooboorroo* he said was a *whennua* or high land, but all the rest he called *moroo*, that is low islands, or such as consist of ledges of coral.

Our curiosity was so much raised by these accounts, that we applied for farther information to the chief Orèa, who came on board the next morning with his son Tehaïura, and several other chiefs. They enumerated the first, second, seventh and ninth islands of the preceding account; but their relations differed in this respect, as they told us the second was regularly inhabited. Besides these they spoke of two more, one called Woredo or Wourèa, a large island, and Orèematàrra another, both which had settled inhabitants. The accounts of the situation and distances of these isles were so various and so vague, that we

could

could by no means depend upon them, for we never met with any man who had vifited them; however, they ferved to convince us, that the natives of the Society Ifles have fometimes extended their navigation farther than its prefent limits, by the knowledge they have of feveral adjacent countries. Tupaya, the famous man who embarked at Taheitee in the Endeavour, had enumerated a much more confiderable lift of names, and had actually drawn a map of their refpective fituations and magnitudes, of which lieutenant Pickerfgill obligingly communicated a copy to me. In this map we found all the names above-mentioned, except Ooborroo and Tubooai: but if his drawing had been exact, our fhips muft have failed over a number of the iflands which he had laid down. It is therefore very probable that the vanity of appearing more intelligent than he really was, had prompted him to produce this fancied chart of the South Sea, and perhaps to invent many of the names of iflands in it, which amounted to more than fifty.

The chief and his fon breakfafted with us, and went afhore with a number of prefents in return for fome of theirs. We followed foon after, and were invited by him to become fpectators of a dramatic dance or heeva; which was the more readily accepted by us, as we had never feen one before. The place where it was performed was an area, about twenty-five yards long and ten wide, enclofed between two houfes which ftood parallel to each other.

The

The one was a spacious building, capable of containing a great multitude of spectators; but the other was only a narrow hut, which was supported on a row of posts, and open towards the area, but perfectly closed up with reeds and mats on the opposite sides; one corner of it was matted on all sides, and this was the dressing-room of the performers. The whole area was spread with three large mats of the best workmanship, striped with black on the edges. In the open part of the smaller hut we saw three drums of different sizes, cut out of solid wood, and covered with shark's skin, which were continually struck with the fingers only by four or five men with amazing dexterity. The largest of these drums was about three feet high and one in diameter. We had already sat some time under the opposite roof, amidst the principal ladies of the island, when the actresses appeared. One of them was Poyadua, the fair daughter of the chief Orèa, and the other a tall well shaped lady, of very agreeable features, and likewise a very fair complexion *. Their dress was remarkably different from the usual fashion of these islands. It consisted of a piece of the brown cloth, of the country fabrick; or, instead of that, of a piece of blue European cloth, closely wrapped round the breast, so as to resemble the close dresses which our ladies wear; a kind of ruff of four rows of their cloth, alternately red and

* That is, considering her as a native of the Society Isles.

white,

white, refled on their hips, being tied on with a ftring; and
from thence a great quantity of white cloth defcended to
the feet, forming an ample petticoat, which we expected,
from its length, would be a confiderable impediment to
their agility, as it fairly trailed on the ground on all fides.
The neck, fhoulders, and arms were left uncovered, but
the head was ornamented with a kind of turban, about
eight inches high, made of feveral fkains of plaited human
hair, which they call tamòw.   Thefe being laid above each
other in circles, which enlarged towards the top, there was
a deep hollow left in the middle, which they had filled up
with a great quantity of the fweet-fcented flowers of the
(gardenia) Cape jafmine. But all the front of the turban was
ornamented with three or four rows of a fmall white flower,
which formed little ftars, and had as elegant an effect on
the jetty black hair as if it had been fet out with pearls.
They moved to the found of the drums, and to all appearance under the direction of an old man, who danced with
them, and pronounced feveral words, which, from the
tone of his voice, we took to be a fong.   Their attitudes
and geftures were much varied, and fometimes might admit of being conftrued into wantonnefs; but they were entirely free from that pofitive degree of grofs indecency
which the chafte eyes of Englifh ladies of fafhion are *forced*
to behold at the opera.   The movement of their arms is
certainly very graceful, and the continual gefticulation of
                                        their

their fingers has something extremely elegant. The only
action which gives offence to all our ideas of gracefulness
and harmony, is the frightful custom of writhing their
mouths into the strangest distortions, which it was impossible for any one of us to imitate. They screwed their
mouth into a slanting direction, and at last threw the lips
into a waving or undulated form, which seemed to us to
be performed by means of an habitual and sudden convul-
sion. After they had danced for about ten minutes, they
retired into the part of the house which I called their dressing room, and five men, dressed in mats, took their place,
performing a kind of drama. This consisted of dancing in
an indecent manner, and of a dialogue which had some
cadence, and in which they sometimes pronounced a few
words shouting all together. This dialogue seemed to be
closely connected with their actions. One of them kneeled
down, and another beat him and plucked him by the
beard, repeating the same ceremony with two others; but
the last seized and beat him in his turn with a stick. After
this they withdrew, and the drummers gave notice of the
second act of dancing, which the two ladies performed
with little variation from the first. The men took their
turn a second time; the ladies succeeded them again, and
concluded with a fourth act. Then they sat down to rest
themselves, appearing fatigued to a great degree, and in a
most profuse perspiration; one of them in particular, being

rather luftier and of a lively difpofition, had a fuffufion of
red in her cheeks, which was the ftrongeft proof of her
fair complexion.   The other, Orèa's daughter, had performed her part to admiration, notwithftanding the fatigue
of the preceding day, when fhe had acted both in the
morning and evening.   The officers of both fhips, who
were prefent, and ourfelves, loaded them with a great variety of beads and ornaments, which they had fo well de-
ferved.

In the afternoon Oo-òoroo, the king of the ifle of Raietea, came on board with Orèa and feveral ladies, to vifit
captain Cook.   He brought a hog as an introductory prefent, and was well repaid with a great quantity of European goods.   Among the ladies was one of the dancers,
named Teina or Teinamai, who had performed in the
morning, and whofe complexion we had much admired.
She now appeared to much greater advantage than in the
cumbrous drefs which fhe wore during the ceremony.
Her own hair, which fortunately was not cut, formed finer
ebon ringlets than ever the luxuriant fancy of a painter
produced, and a narrow fillet of white cloth was carelefsly
paffed between them.   Her eyes were full of fire and expreffion, and an agreeable fmile fat in her round face.
Mr. Hodges took this opportunity of drawing a fketch of
her portrait, which her vivacity and reftlefs difpofition
rendered almoft impoffible.   This was, perhaps, the reafon
that

that he was lefs fuccefsful than ufual, as the reprefentation which is inferted in captain Cook's own account of this voyage, is infinitely below the delicacy of the original, notwithftanding the excellence of Mr. Sherwin's engraving. But though it has loft the refemblance to Teinamal, it may ferve as a fpecimen of the generality of features in this and the neighbouring iflands, and gives a tolerable idea of a Taheitian boy about ten years old. Towards fun-fet, all our noble vifitors returned afhore, extremely well pleafed with the reception which they had met with; a number of women of the loweft rank, however, remained on our decks, with a complaifance equal to that of the Taheitian girls, (fee pag. 336.)

It was remarkable that they were not without fome degree of vanity, as they never gave themfelves any other name than that of *tedùa*, (lady,) which is the title of their female nobility, and which, by way of eminence, is particularly applied to the princeffes of thefe iflands. If the king's fifter happened to pafs by while we fat in a houfe at Taheitee, the natives who furrounded us were warned to uncover their fhoulders, by fome one who fpied her at a diftance, fimply faying *tedua barremai*, (the lady comes hither!) or elfe they only faid *aree!* which on fuch occafions always denoted one of the royal family. Our failors, who did not underftand the language, took it for granted that

F f f 2

their

their dulcineas were all of one name, which frequently occasion some pleasant mistakes.

We spent the two next days in various rambles along the shores, in which we found many deep creeks towards the northern part, with marshes at the bottom, where wild-ducks and snipes resided in great plenty. These birds were more shy than we expected, which we soon learnt was owing to their being much pursued by the natives, who looked upon them as dainty bits. On the first of these days we were likewise entertained with another heeva or dramatic dance, by the same persons who had performed it before. It was in every respect the same with that which we saw on the 11th, only its duration was much shorter.

On the 14th, at day-break, captain Cook sent his launch, and captain Furneaux another boat, to the isle of O-Tahá, which was two or three leagues distant, and inclosed in the same reef within which we lay at anchor. They were in hopes of purchasing some fruit there, which was very scarce at Raietea, and to that purpose provided lieutenant Pickersgill and Mr. Rowe the mate of the Adventure, with a quantity of beads and nails. Dr. Sparrman and my father, unwilling to miss this opportunity of examining another island, likewise embarked with them.

ORBA, the chief of this part of the island, having invited us to come and dine on shore, the captains, with several officers and passengers of both ships, and myself, went

on

on shore about noon, taking with us a little pepper and salt, some knives, and a few bottles of wine. A great part of the chief's spacious house was spread with quantities of leaves, which served as a table-cloth, round which we seated ourselves, with the principal inhabitants. We had not waited long, before one of the common people arrived with a hog smoking on his shoulders, roasted whole, and wrapped in a large bundle of plantane-leaves, which he threw upon the floor in the midst of us: a second tossed a smaller to us in the same manner; and these were followed by several others bringing baskets, full of bread-fruit, bananas, and the fermented paste of bread-fruit, called mahei. Our host now desired us to help ourselves, and in a short time we had cut the two hogs in pieces. All the women, and the common sort of people, applied to us with a begging tone for portions, and what we distributed was handed from our neighbours, to the remotest persons in the croud. The men consumed their share with every mark of a good appetite, but the women carefully wrapped theirs up, and preserved it till they should be alone. The eagerness with which they repeated their importunities, as well as the envious looks of the chiefs, whenever we granted the request, convinced us, that the commonalty were in this island deprived of all sorts of luxuries and dainties. We all agreed that the pork which was set before us, tasted infinitely better, than if it had been

dressed

1773.
September.

dressed after the European manner. It was much juicier
than our boiled, and beyond comparison more tender than
roasted meat. The equal degree of heat with which it
stews under-ground, had preserved and concentrated all
its juices. The fat was not luscious and surfeiting, and
the skin instead of being hard as a stone, which is always
the case with our roasted pork, was as tender as any other
part. After dinner our bottles and glasses were brought
in, and our friend Orèa drank his share without flinching,
which appeared to us rather extraordinary, since almost
all the natives of these islands expressed a great dislike to
our strong liquors. Sobriety is a virtue almost universal
with them, and particularly among people of inferior rank.
They are however acquainted with an intoxicating beverage, which is much admired by some of the old chiefs.
It is made in the most disgustful manner that can be
imagined, from the juices contained in the root of a species
of pepper-tree. This root is cut small, and the pieces
chewed by several people, who spit the macerated mass into
a bowl, where some water (milk) of coco-nuts is poured
upon it. They then strain it through a quantity of the fibres of coco-nuts, squeezing the chips, till all their juices
mix with the cocoa-nut-milk; and the whole liquor is de-
canted into another bowl. They swallow this nauseous
stuff as fast as possible; and some old topers value themselves
on being able to empty a great number of bowls. I was
                                                    present

prefent at the whole procefs one of the firft days after our arrival at this ifland. Our paffenger, Porea, who was not fo referved with the natives here as he had been at Huahine,
brought one of his new acquaintances into the captain's
cabin, and immediately fat down with him to perform the
operation. He drank about a pint, which in lefs than a
quarter of an hour made him fo dead drunk, that he lay
down on the floor without motion; his face was inflamed,
and his eyes fwelled out of his head. A found fleep of feveral hours was neceffary to reftore him to his fenfes; but as
foon as he had recovered them, he appeared thoroughly
afhamed of his debauch. The pepper-plant is in high
efteem with all the natives of thefe iflands as a fign of peace;
perhaps, becaufe getting drunk together, naturally implies
good fellowfhip. It feems, however, that drunkennefs here
is punifhed, like all other exceffes, by difeafe. The old
men who make a practice of it are lean, covered with a
fcaly or fcabby fkin, have red eyes, and red blotches on all
parts of the body. They acknowledge thefe evils to be the
confequence of drinking; and to all appearance, the pepper-
plant, which they call awa, tends to produce leprous complaints.

As foon as we had dined, our boat's crew and fervants
feafted on the remains; and the fame croud who had profited by our liberality before, now paid their court to them.
The failors were complaifant only to the fair fex; and giving

ing way to their natural difpofition for fenfuality, for every piece of pork required the performance of an indecent denudation. To complete our entertainment this day, the chief gave orders for performing another heeva, and we were admitted (behind the fcenes) to fee the ladies drefling for that purpofe. They obtained fome ftrings of beads on this occafion, with which we took it into our heads to improve upon their ornaments, much to their own fatisfaction. Among the fpectators we obferved feveral of the prettieft women of this country; and one of them was remarkable for the whiteft complexion we had ever feen in all thefe iflands. Her colour refembled that of white wax a little fullied, without having the leaft appearance of ficknefs, which that hue commonly conveys; and her fine black eyes and hair contrafted fo well with it, that fhe was admired by us all. She received at firft a number of little prefents, which were fo many marks of homage paid at the fhrine of beauty; but her fuccefs, inftead of gratifying, only fharpened her love of trinkets, and fhe inceffantly importuned every one of us as long as fhe fufpected we had a fingle bead left. One of the gentlemen fortunately happened to have a little padlock in his hand, which fhe begged for as foon as fhe had perceived it. After denying it for fome time, he confented to give it her, and locked it in her ear, affuring her that was its proper place. She was well pleafed for fome time; but finding it too heavy, defired

fired him to unlock it. He flung away the key, giving her
to underftand at the fame time, that he had made her the
prefent at her own defire, and that if fhe found it incumbered her, fhe fhould bear it as a punifhment for importun-
ing us with her petitions. She was difconfolate upon this
refufal, and weeping bitterly, applied to us all to open the
padlock; but if we had been willing, we were not able to
comply with her requeft for want of the key. She applied
to the chief; and he as well as his wife, fon and daughter,
joined in praying for the releafe of her ear; they offered
cloth, perfume-wood, and hogs, but all in vain. At laft a
fmall key was found to open the padlock, which put an end
to the poor girl's lamentation, and reftored peace and tran-
quility among all her friends. Her adventure had however
this good effect, that it cured her and fome of her forward
country-women of their idle habit of begging. In the
evening we returned on board, highly pleafed with the hofpitality and general good difpofition of the natives towards
us. We were therefore furprifed the next morning, that
not a fingle canoe would come off to us, and going to
Orea's houfe, in order to enquire the reafon of this fudden
change of behaviour, we to our farther aftonifhment found
it abandoned by him and his family. A few of the natives,
who came to us with a good deal of diffidence, told us that
he had retired towards the north point of the ifland, being
afraid that we meant to take him prifoner. It was imme-

diately refolved upon to follow, in order to undeceive him, and give him frefh affurances of friendſhip. We rowed along ſhore for feveral miles, till we came to the place to which he had retired. At our interview all were in tears, fo that we were obliged to have recourfe to a variety of careffes, to infpire them with new confidence towards us, and our beads, nails, and hatchets, were not the leaft efficacious arguments. They told us they believed captain Cook would confine them, in order to force their countrymen to bring back thofe people who were run away from us to O-Taha. We now faw through their miſtake, and affured them that our party had not run away, but was fent on purpofe, and would certainly return this night. Orèa not yet fatisfied, named each of the principal perfons in that party fingly, and enquired concerning every one, whether he would come back, and the pofitive anfwers which we returned, at laſt quieted his apprehenfions. While we were fitting in a circle with them, Porea our Taheitian, who intended to go to England, came running to the captain, returned the powder-horn, which he had hitherto carried for him, and faid he would come back to us prefently. We waited in vain a good while, and at laſt were obliged to return on board without him; nor did we fee him again during the little time we remained on the iſland. From the natives we could gather but little information, and the captain fearing leſt they ſhould take new alarm,

If

if he interested himself too strongly in his behalf, entirely
dropped the enquiry.   After dinner I accompanied him
to the shore again, on a visit to Orèa.   A very handsome
youth, about seventeen years of age, who went by the name
of O-Hedeedee, and who appeared to be of the better sort of
people by his complexion and good garments, addressed
himself to me, expressing a defire to embark for England.
I was not inclined to believe at first, that he would forsake
the easy way of life, which persons of his rank enjoyed in
these islands, and smiling at his proposal, told him the difagreeable circumstances to which he exposed himself by
leaving his country.   But, though I represented to him the
rigours of climate which we had to endure, and the bad
provisions to which he should be reduced in time, he was
not to be dissuaded from his resolution, and a number of
his friends joined with him to defire his admittance into
our ship.   Upon this I presented him to captain Cook, and
he having granted his request, we all returned on board
together.   Before sun-set our boats returned from O-Taha,
where they had collected a load of bananas and coco-nuts,
and a few hogs.   They landed there on the 14th in the
morning, after a few hours sail, in a fine bay on the east
side, called O-Hamene.   The country and its inhabitants
perfectly resembled those of the other islands in this archi-
pelago.   Their productions, vegetable and animal, were
in general the same, varying only in the abundance or

scarcity

scarcity of some articles. Thus, for instance, the tree, which our sailors called the apple-tree, (*spondias,*) was plentiful at Taheitee, extremely rare at Raietea and Huahine, and not very common at Tahà; fowls were hardly to be met with at Taheitee, but common in the Society Isles; and rats, which infested Taheitee in numberless myriads, were not quite so numerous at O-Tahà; still less frequent at Raietea, and seen in very inconsiderable numbers at Huahine.

After our party had dined in O-Hamene harbour, they removed to the next creek to the north, and walked to the house of a chief named O-Tàh, where the natives said there would be a heeva or public dance. The crowd increased prodigiously as they approached it, and in their way they saw a woman at a considerable distance, dressed in a singular habit*, and blacked all over. They were told she performed the burial rite, or mourned for a dead person. They found the aree, who was an elderly man, sitting on a wooden stool, of which he offered one half to my father. The dance was begun some time after by three young girls, the eldest not exceeding ten, and the youngest about five years of age. The usual music was performed on three drums, and in the intervals of the dance three men performed something of a pantomime drama, which represented travellers asleep, and thieves dextrously convey-

* This is to be described in the sequel.

ing

ing away their goods, round which they had, for greater security, placed themselves. During their performance the croud made way for several people who advanced towards the house in pairs, but stopped at the entrance. They were well dressed, with sashes of their red cloth round their loins, and skains of the tamow or plaited hair round their heads, and the whole upper part of their body was naked and anointed with coco-nut oil. Some among them were grown men and some boys. O-Tàh called them the O-DA-WIDDEE *, which, from the gestures he made to explain himself, our people understood to be mourners. When they appeared the area of the entrance was spread with cloth of bark, which was, however, taken up immediately and given to the drummers. One of the latter quarrelled with another native, and they fought, pulling each other by the hair, and giving some hearty blows. However, that the entertainment might not be interrupted, another drummer was substituted, and the boxers turned out of the house. Towards the end of the dance the croud made way, and the O-Da-widdee appeared once more, but stood still, as they had done at first, without performing any other particular rite.

A great number of canoes were hauled up along the shore before the chief's house, and in one of them, which

* Mahine and Omai called them by the name of Hea-biddhee and explained the word to signify relations.

had

had a roof or covering, there was a dead corfe, for which
the mourning rites were inftituted. Our gentlemen were
obliged, therefore, to lay up their boats a little farther on,
where they paffed the night under fhelter of a good houfe,
whilft it blew and rained exceffively hard.

The next morning the chief, O-Tah, went into the boat
with them, and they failed round the north point of the
ifle, feeing a number of long low iflands, covered with
palm and other trees, which lay in the reef. They bought
a quantity of good bananas about ten o'clock, and dined
a little farther to the fouthward, near the houfe of the
greateft chief in the ifland, whofe name was Boba, and
who governed it as a viceroy for O Poonee, the king of
Borabora, (Bolabola) but was not on the ifland at that
time. After dinner they miffed a bag, which contained a
number of nails, fome looking-glaffes, and feveral ftrings
of beads, being their whole ftock in trade. After a fhort
debate, the officers refolved to feize as much of the property of the inhabitants as poffible, in order to force them
to a reftitution. They immediately began at the place
where they traded, and took away a hog, fome mother of
pearl fhells, and a quantity of cloth, not without being
obliged to threaten with fire-arms. The party was then
divided; fome guarded the boats, fome the goods which
were feized, and fome, with the lieutenant at their head,
advanced into the country in queft of greater feizures. The

old

old chief, O-Tah, accompanied them, and was under the strongest influence of fear, which manifested itself like that of the dogs in the fable *. Wherever they came the inhabitants hurried away before them, and drove their hogs into the mountains. The officer ordered three muskets to be fired to frighten them, upon which a chief, who had one leg and foot swelled to an enormous size by the *elephantiasis*, returned and surrendered his hogs and several large bales of cloth. Our people next proceeded to Boba's house, which they stripped of two targets and a drum, and with these spoils they retired to the house which they had occupied before. O Tàh left them in the evening, but returned soon after with the stolen bag, containing about one half of the nails, beads, &c. which were taken away with it, and passed the night among our party. Early the next morning the proprietors of the goods which our people had seized, were told that every thing should be restored on condition that they procured the remaining beads and nails. In the mean time they advanced towards O Herurua Bay on the S. W. part of the island, and, on their way, the chief, O-Tàh, together with the other chief with the elephant's leg, who walked as well as any one of the rest, produced most of the missing iron and trinkets, which had been hid in bushes; upon which our people gave up the cloth, hogs, targets, &c. which had

* See Phædr. Fab.

hitherto

1771.
September.
hitherto remained in their hands, and rewarded the owner
of the hut, where they had paſſed the night, as well as
the old chief, for their fidelity and kindneſs. The beads
which they had recovered, enabled them to purchaſe a
quantity of bananas in the diſtrict of Herurua, and afterwards in a bay called A-Poto-Poto, or the Round Bay,
where they ſaw one of the largeſt houſes in all the Society
Iſles. It was full of inhabitants, many of whom lodged
with their families in different parts of it; the whole appearing to be rather a public building, erected for the caſual
ſhelter of travellers, like the carvanſaras of the Eaſt, than
a private dwelling-houſe. Here they dined, and after diſ-
poſing of every bead and nail which they had brought with
them, ſet out on their return to the ſhips, where they arrived about four o'clock in the afternoon, thoroughly wet
by the waves which beat into their boats.

The next morning, the chief Orèa with his family came
to take leave of us, and the ſhip was filled with the friends of
O-Hedeedee, who embarked with us, bringing him cloth of
the country fabric, and a ſea-proviſion of their balls of fermented bread-fruit (mahei) which they are very fond of,
and which is one of the moſt nutritive ſubſtances in the
world. The daughter of Orèa, who had never ventured
to viſit us before, came on board on this occaſion, to beg for
the green awning of the captain's boat, which had mightily
ſtruck her fancy. She received abundance of preſents, but
the

the captain could not possibly grant her request. The trade for their tools, cloth, &c. was very brisk all round the ship about this time, till the anchor was weighed. Our friends parted from us, with the sincerest expressions of grief, and shedding floods of tears, reproached some of us with a want of sensibility. Our civilized education in general tends to stifle the emotions of our heart; for as we are too often taught to be ashamed of them, we unhappily conquer them by custom. On the contrary, the simple child of nature, who inhabits these islands, gives free course to all his feelings, and glories in his affection towards the fellow-creature.

> Mollissima corda
> Humano generi dare se natura fatetur,
> Quæ lacrymas dedit; hæc nostri pars optima sensus.   JUVENAL.

A

V O Y A G E

ROUND THE

W O R L D.

B O O K II.

CHAP. I.

Run from the Society Isles to the Friendly Isles, with an Account of our Transactions there.

1773,
SEPTEMBER.

WE cleared the reefs of Hamaneno towards ten
o'clock, and steered to the W. S. W. having the
islands of Raietea, Tahâ, and Borabora in sight. Only one
month had elapsed since our arrival at Taheitee, and yet
we found ourselves recovered from the effects of a long
uncomfortable cruize in cold wet climates, and during the
worst of seasons; and all those who had the strongest symptoms of the scurvy at that time, were now as perfectly restored to their health as the rest. The vegetables of this
delightful group of islands had, in all likelihood, principally effected our cure, especially as we left our first place
of refreshment, Aitepèha, in a tolerable state of convalef-
cence,

cence, though we had not then tasted any fresh animal food. Our prospect for the next month to come promised a continuance of health, for we carried with us between two and three hundred hogs in each ship, besides a number of fowls and some dogs, together with a great quantity of bananas, which formed a kind of orchard on our poop. It is true the want of room occasioned the death of several hogs, and the obstinacy of the old dogs in refusing to take any sustenance, deprived us of the greatest number of those animals. But we soon took an effectual method of saving our provisions by killing all the hogs which were weakened by confinement, and strewing the meat with salt. By this means it was preserved, and remained palatable and juicy without being so unwholesome as the pickled meat we brought from England, which was now so penetrated with salt, that if we attempted to sweeten it in water, we extracted all the remaining juices. The only inconvenience which the stay among these isles had brought upon our seamen, was a complaint which arose from their own intemperance, in carrying on a free connection with common women. But this, though many of them were affected with it, was fortunately of so slight a nature, that it did not, in general take them from their duty, and yielded quickly to the gentlest remedies.

Our young friend Hedeèdee, whom we had taken with us instead of the Taheitian Porèa, felt himself much affect-

ed

ed with the fea-ficknefs, occafioned by the motion of the
fhip, to which he was not accuftomed. He told us, however, as we were looking at the high peak of Borabora,
that he was born in that ifland, and was nearly related to
O-Poonee, the great king who had conquered Tahà and
Raietea. He acquainted us, at the fame time, that his own
name was properly Mahine, he having exchanged it for
that of Hedeedee with a chief in Eimeo; a cuftom which,
as I have already obferved in another place, is common in
all thefe iflands. His relation, king O-Poonee, was at
prefent, according to his account, at Mowrùa, an ifland
which we paffed in the afternoon. It confifted of a fingle
mountain, of a conic form, rifing into a fharp point; and,
from the reports of the inhabitants of Raietea, fome of
whom had frequently vifited it, we had reafon to conclude
that its productions are perfectly fimilar to thofe of all the
other ifles in this group.

Our poor friend did not recover his appetite till the next
afternoon, when he feafted on part of a dolphin of twenty-
eight pounds weight, which had been caught by one of our
feamen. We offered to have it dreffed for him immediately, but he affured us it tafted much better raw; and accordingly we provided him with a bowl of fea-water, in
which he dipped the morfels as in a fauce, and eat them
with great relifh, alternately biting into a ball of mahei, or
four bread-fruit pafte, inftead of bread. Before he fat
down

down to his meal, however, he separated a little morsel of
the fish and a bit of the mahei, as an offering to the Eatua
or Divinity, pronouncing a few words at the same time,
which we understood to be a short prayer. He performed
the same ceremony two days after, when he dined on a raw
piece of shark. These instances served to convince us,
that his countrymen have certain fixed principles of religion, and that a kind of ceremonial worship takes place
among them, which they have perhaps preserved ever since
their first separation from their ancestors on the continent.

We continued our course without any event worthy of
of notice till the 23d, in the morning, when a low island
appeared on our larboard bow. We steered towards it,
and about noon found it was divided into two parts; the
latitude which we observed at that time was 19° 8' south.
We soon distinguished a quantity of shrubs and tufted trees
upon it, over which rose a prodigious number of coco-
palms. By the help of our glasses we observed that the
shore was sandy, but here and there over-run with verdure,
which probably was occasioned by the common bindweed
of these climates (convolvulus Brasiliensis). A reef as we apprehended, connected the two parts of the island together,
which notwithstanding its agreeable appearance, seemed to
be entirely uninhabited. Captain Cook gave it the name
of Hervey's Isle, in honour of the present earl of Bristol.
A bird which resembled a sand-piper in its flight, and

note,

note, had appeared about the ship, the day before we made this island, and might be said to have announced its proximity, but though we observed another of the same sort on the 26th, which actually settled in the rigging, yet we did not fall in with another island. We held a westerly course from Hervey's Isle, which lies in 19° 18' south latitude and 158° 54' west longitude from Greenwich, till
the first of October, when we saw land before us about two o'clock in the afternoon. In four hours time we came within two or three leagues of it, and found it of a moderate height; the hills were covered with trees, and offered a pleasing, though not magnificent prospect. At the south-west extremity we observed a small rocky islet, and to the northward a low land of greater extent. From thence we judged, that the isle before us was the same which Abel Janssen Tasman named Middleburg Isle, in 1643, and that the other to the north, was that of Amsterdam, discovered by the same navigator. We lay to all night, and with day-break passed round the S. W. point of Middleburg Isle, and ranged its western coast. There appeared to be some low land at the bottom of the hills, which contained plantations of fine young bananas, whose vivid green leaves contrasted admirably with the different tints of various shrubberies, and with the brown colour of the coco palms, which seemed to be the effect of winter.

The

1773.
OCTOBER.

The light was still so faint, that we distinguished several fires glimmering in the bushes, but by degrees we likewise discerned people running along the shore. The hills which were low, and not so high above the level of the sea as the Isle of Wight, were agreeably adorned with small clumps of trees scattered at some distance, and the intermediate ground appeared covered with herbage, like many parts of England. It was not long before we perceived some of the inhabitants busied in launching several canoes, and paddling towards us. We threw a rope into one of these canoes which ran up close to us, and one of the three people in her came on board, and presented a root of the intoxicating pepper-tree of the South Sea Islands, touched our noses with his like the New Zeelanders, in sign of friendship, and then sat down on the deck without speaking a word. The captain presented him with a nail, upon which he immediately held it over his own head, and pronounced *fagafetai*, which was probably an expression of thanksgiving. He was naked to the waist, but from thence to the knees he had a piece of cloth wrapped about him, which seemed to be manufactured much like that of Taheitee, but was covered with a brown colour, and a strong glue, which made it stiff, and fit to resist the wet. His stature was middle-sized, and his lineaments were mild and tolerably regular. His colour was much like that

of

of the common Taheitians [*], that is, of a clear mahogany
or chefnut brown; his beard was cut fhort or fhaven, and
his hair was black, in fhort frizzled curls, burnt as it were
at the tips. He had three circular fpots on each arm,
about the fize of a crown piece, confifting of feveral concentric circles of elevated points, which anfwered to the
punctures of the Taheitians, but were not blacked; befides
thefe, he had other black punctures on his body. A fmall
cylinder was fixed through two holes in the lap of his ear,
and his left hand wanted the little finger. He continued
his filence for a confiderable while, but fome others, who
ventured on board foon after him, were of a more com-
municative turn, and after having performed the ceremony
of touching nofes, fpoke a language which was unintelligible to us at that time. In the mean while we arrived
at the N. W. point of the ifland, where we ftruck foundings
on a good bottom, in an open road, and let go our anchors
about nine in the morning. We were prefently furrounded
by a number of canoes, each containing three or four

* As I fhall frequently mention the inhabitants of Taheitee, and of the Society Iflands, in comparifon with other iflanders, it will be proper to obferve,
th t fince the natives both of Taheitee and of the Society Iflands, are perfectly
alike in moft refpects, I fhall indifferently call a cuftom Taheitian, or ufual at
the Society iflands, which is common to them both. Therefore, unlefs I exprefsly put thefe terms in contradiftinction to each other, I wifh to have them
underftood in general as fynonymous.

people,

people, who offered great quantities of their cloth for sale. The canoes were small, about fifteen feet long, very sharp built, and decked or covered at each extremity. Most of them had out-riggers made of poles, like the small canoes at Taheitee, but the workmanship of these boats was infinitely preferable, as they were joined together with an exactness which surprised us, and the whole surface had received an excellent polish. Their paddles had short broad blades, something like those of Taheitee, but more neatly wrought, and of better wood. They made a great deal of noise about us, every one shewing what he had to sell, and calling to some one of us, who happened to look towards them. Their language was not unpleasing, and whatever they said, was in a singing kind of tone. Many were bold enough to come on board, without expressing the least hesitation, and one of these seemed to be a chief, or a man of some quality, and was accordingly treated with a number of presents, which he severally laid on his head, when he received them, saying *fagafetai* every time. Our English cloth and linen he admired most, and iron wares in the next degree. His behaviour was very free and unconcerned; for he went down into the cabin, and where-ever we thought fit to conduct him. He likewise told us, upon our enquiry, that the island near which we lay at anchor, (the same which Tasman called Middleburg) was called Ea-Oowhe among his country-men; and that the

VOL. I.   I i i   other

other to the north (or Tafman's Amflerdam ifland) bore the
name of Tonga-Tabboo. We confulted feveral of the
natives, in order to have greater certainty on this point,
and always received the fame names in anfwer.

After breakfaft, the captains went on fhore with us and
the chief, who had continued on board all that time. A
bed of coral rocks furrounded·the coaft, towards the landing-place ; but many canoes occupied the deep channels
between thefe rocks, and a great number of inhabitants in
them as well as on the fhore, fhouted for joy at our approach. The canoes immediately came along fide the boat,
and the natives threw great bales of cloth into it, without
afking for any thing in return ; while many of both fexes
fwam about perfectly naked, holding up fome trifles, fuch
as rings of tortoife-fhell, fifh-hooks of mother of pearl, and
the like, for fale. As foon as we could make way through
the throng of canoes, we approached as near as poffible to
the fhore, and were carried to it out of our boat, for which
the natives very readily offered their backs. The people
thronged about us with every expreffion of friendfhip, and
offered a few fruits, with a variety of arms and utenfils.
The cordial reception which we met with, was fuch as
might have been expected from a people well acquainted
with our good intentions, and accuftomed to the tranfitory
vifits of European fhips. But thefe kind iflanders had never
feen Europeans among them, and could only have heard
of

1773.
October.

of Tafman who vifited the adjacent Amfterdam ifland, by imperfect tradition. Nothing was therefore more confpicuous in their whole behaviour than an open, generous difpofition, free from any mean diftruft. This was confirmed by the appearance of a great number of women in the croud, covered from the waift downwards, whofe looks and fmiles welcomed us to the fhore. Mr. Hodges defigned this memorable interview in an elegant picture, which has been engraved for captain Cook's account of this voyage. The fame candour with which I have made it a rule to commend the performances of this ingenious artift, whenever they are characteriftic of the objects which he meant to reprefent, obliges me to mention, that this piece, in which the execution of Mr. Sherwin cannot be too much admired, does not convey any adequate idea of the natives of Ea-oowhe or of Tonga Tabbo. The plates which ornamented the hiftory of captain Cook's former voyage, have been juftly criticifed, becaufe they exhibited to our eyes the pleafing forms of antique figures and draperies, inftead of thofe Indians of which we wifhed to form fome idea. But it is alfo greatly to be feared, that Mr. Hodges has loft the fketches and drawings which he made from NATURE in the courfe of the voyage, and fupplied the deficiency in this cafe, from his own elegant ideas. The connoiffeur will find Greek contours and features in this picture, which have never exifted in the South Sea. He

l i i 2   will

will admire an elegant flowing robe which involves the whole head and body, in an island where the women very rarely cover the shoulders and breast; and he will be struck with awe and delight by the figure of a divine old man, with a long white beard, though all the people of Ea·oowhe shave themselves with muscle-shells.

We soon left the landing place, and followed the chief, who invited us up into the country. The ground from the water's side rose somewhat steep for a few yards, above which it flattened into a beautiful green lawn, surrounded by tall trees and tufted shrubberies, and open only to the sea. At the bottom of it, which might be about one hundred yards from the landing-place, we saw a very neat well-looking house, of which the roof sloped down within two feet of the ground. We advanced across the delightful green, which was so smooth, that it put us in mind of the finest spots in England, and were entreated to sit down in the house, which was most elegantly laid out with mats of the best workmanship. In one corner of it we saw a moveable partition of wicker-work standing upright, and, from the signs of the natives collected, that it separated their bed-place. The roof, sloping down on all sides, was formed of a great number of spars and round sticks very firmly connected, and covered with a sort of matting made of banana leaves.

We

We were so sooner seated in the house, surrounded by
a considerable number of natives, not less than a hundred,
than two or three of the women welcomed us with a song,
which, though exceedingly simple, had a very pleasing effect, and was highly musical when compared to the Taheitian songs. They beat time to it by snapping the second
finger and thumb, and holding the three remaining fingers
upright. Their voices were very sweet and mellow, and
they sung in parts. When they had done they were re-
lieved by others, who sung they same tune, and at last
they joined together in chorus. A very ingenious gentleman, who was on this voyage with us, has favoured me
with one of the tunes which he heard in this island, which
may serve as a specimen to the musical part of my readers.

In this little specimen the music is in the minor key, (a flat
third.) They varied the four notes without ever going
lower than A or higher than E; singing them rather slow,
and sometimes ending with the chord

The kindness of the people was expressed in every look
and gesture, and they freely offered us some coco-nuts, of
which we found the liquor very palatable. We were likewise regaled with a most delicious perfume in this place,
which the breeze wafted towards us. It was a considerable
time

time before we difcovered from whence it proceeded; but
at laft having looked at fome fhady trees at the back of the
houfe, we perceived they were of the lemon tribe, and
covered with beautiful branches of white flowers, which
fpread this fragrant fmell. The natives foon brought us
fome of the fruits, which we knew to be of the kind called fhaddocks in the Weft-Indies, and pomplemofes at Batavia and the adjacent Eaft-Indian ifles. Their fhape was
perfectly globular, their fize almoft as large as a child's
head, and their tafte extremely pleafant.

On both fides of the lawn we took notice of a fence or
enclofure made of reeds, diagonally plaited in an elegant
tafte. A door, which confifted of feveral boards, and was
hung on a rope inftead of hinges, gave admittance into a
plantation on each fide. We feparated, in order to examine
this beautiful country, and at every ftep had reafon to be
well pleafed with our difcoveries. The door was fo contrived as to fhut after us without any affiftance, and the
enclofures were over-run with climbers, and efpecially a
bind-weed, having flowers of a beautiful fky-blue. The
profpect now changed into an extenfive garden, where we
faw a number of tufted fhaddock-trees, tall coco-palms,
many bananas, and a few bread-fruit trees. In the midft of
this fpot the path led us to a dwelling-houfe, like that on
the lawn, furrounded by a great variety of fhrubs in blof-
fom, whofe fragrance filled the air. We roamed through
these

thefe bufhes, and collected a variety of plants which we had never met with in the Society Ifles. The inhabitants feemed to be of a more active and induftrious difpofition than thofe of Taheitee, and inftead of following us in great crouds wherever we went, left us entirely by ourfelves, un-lefs we entreated them to accompany us. In that cafe we could venture to go with our pockets open, unlefs we had nails in them, upon which they fet fo great a value that they could not always refift the temptation. We paffed through more than ten adjacent plantations or gardens, feparated by enclofures, communicating with each other by means of the doors before mentioned. In each of them we commonly met with a houfe, of which the inhabitants were abfent. Their attention to feparate their property feemed to argue a higher degree of civilization than we had expected. Their arts, manufactures, and mufic were all more cultivated, complicated, and elegant than at the So-ciety Iflands. But, in return, the opulence, or rather luxury, of the Taheitians feemed to be much greater. We faw but few hogs and fowls here, and that great fupport of life, the bread-tree, appeared to be very fcarce. Yams, therefore, and other roots, together with bananas, are their principal articles of diet. Their cloathing too, com-pared to that of Taheitee, was lefs plentiful, or at leaft not converted into fuch an article of luxury as at that ifland. Laftly, their houfes, though neatly conftructed, and always

placed

placed in a fragrant shrubbery, were less roomy and convenient. We made these reflections as we advanced towards
the landing place, where several hundred natives were af-
sembled; and their appearance immediately struck us with
the idea, that if they did not enjoy so great a profusion of
the gifts of nature as the Taheitians, those gifts were perhaps distributed to all with greater equality. We advanced among them, and were accosted with caresses by
old and young, by men and women. They hugged us
very heartily, and frequently kissed our hands, laying them
on their breast, with the most expressive looks of affection
that can be imagined. The general stature of the men was
equal to our middle size, from five feet three to five feet
ten inches. The proportions of the body were very fine,
and the contours of the limbs extremely elegant, though
something more muscular than at Taheitee, which may be
owing to a greater and more constant exertion of strength in
their agriculture and œconomy. Their features were extremely mild and pleasing, and differed from the Taheitian
faces, in being more oblong than round; the nose sharper,
and the lips rather thinner. Their hair was generally
black and strongly curled, and the beard shaven or rather
clipt by means of a couple of sharp muscle shells, (*mytili*.)
The women were, in general, a few inches shorter than
the men, but not so small as the lower class of women at
Taheitee and the Society Isles. Their body was exquisitely
pro-

proportioned down to the waift, and their hands and arms were to the full as delicate as thofe of the Taheitian women; but like them they had fuch large feet and legs as did not harmonize with the reft. Their features, though without regularity, were as agreeable as we had in general obferved them at the Society Ifles; but we recollected many individuals there, efpecially of the principal families, to which none of thefe could be compared. The complexion of both fexes here was the fame, a light chefnut-brown, which had commonly the appearance of perfect health. That difference of colour and corpulence, by which we immediately diftinguifhed the ranks at Taheitee, was not to be met with in this ifland. The chief, who had vifited us on board and accompanied us to the fhore, was in nothing different from the common people, not even in his drefs; it was only from the obedience which was paid to his orders that we concluded his quality. The cuftom of puncturing the fkin and blacking it, was in full force among the men, and their belly and loins were very ftrongly marked in configurations more compounded than thofe of the Taheitians. The tendereft parts of the body were not free from thefe punctures, the application of which, befides being very painful, muft be extremely dangerous on glandulous extremities, and juftly excited our aftonifhment.

——— et picta pandit fpectacula cauda! Hor.

The women, however, were exempted from this custom
of disfiguring themselves, and had only a few black dots
on their hands.   But besides these, both sexes had three
spots on the arms, consisting of concentric circles of punctures, without any blacking, which I have mentioned before.   The men in general went almost naked, having only a small bit of cloth round the loins.   Some, however,
wore a dress nearly resembling that of the women.   This
was a long piece of cloth made of bark, in the same manner as the Taheitee cloth, but afterwards painted chequer-
wise, or in patterns nearly resembling our painted floor-
cloths, and covered with a size, which turned the wet for a
long while.   This they wrapped round their waist, the
men nearly about their middle, the women more immediately under the breast, and in both it commonly descended
below the knees.   Instead of the cloth they likewise substituted mats, extremely well wrought, in form resembling
those of Taheitee, and sometimes, though rarely, covered
even their shoulders and breasts with them.   The men frequently wore a string round their necks, from which a
mother of pearl shell hung down on the breast.   The women
often had loose necklaces, consisting of several strings of
small shells, intermixed with seeds, teeth of fishes, and in
the middle of all the round *operculum*, or cover of a shell,
as large as a crown-piece.   Both their ears were perforated,
and sometimes with two holes, and a little cylinder cut out

of

of tortoise-shell or bone, was stuck through both the holes. Sometimes these cylinders were only of reed, filled with a red solid substance, painted and lacquered with different colours in regular compartments. The most singular circumstance which we observed among these people was, that many of them wanted the little finger on one and sometimes on both hands; the difference of sex or age did not exempt them from this amputation; for even amongst the few children, whom we saw running about naked, the greater part had already suffered this loss. Only a few grown people, who had preserved both their little fingers, were an exception to the general rule. We immediately conjectured that the death of a near relation or friend might require these strange mutilations, in the same manner as is customary among the Hottentots, in Africa*; the Guaranos, in Paraguay; and the Californians; and our enquiries, though unsuccessful at first, afterwards confirmed the conjecture. Another singularity, which we observed to be very general among these people, was a round spot on each cheek-bone, which appeared to have been burnt or blistered. Some had it quite recent, in others it was covered with a scurf, and many had a very slight mark of its former existence. We could never learn how and for what purpose it was made; but we supposed it could only be

* See Kolben's account of the Cape of Good Hope; also the Recherches Philosophiques sur les Americains, par M. Pauw, vol. II. p. 224, 229.

used

ufed like the Japanefe *moxa*, as a remedy againſt various complaints.

Notwithſtanding the engaging manners of the natives, we forefaw that we ſhould make but a very ſhort ſtay among them, becaufe our captains could not obtain refreſhments in any confiderable quantity; which might be owing not ſo much to their ſcarcity upon the iſland, as to the difficulty of making our goods current for ſuch valuable articles, when they could obtain them in exchange for arms and utenſils. They had brought indeed a few yams, bananas, coco-nuts, and ſhaddocks for fale, but they foon dropt that branch of trade. Our people purchaſed an incredible number of fiſh hooks made of mother of pearl, barbed with tortoife-ſhell, but in ſhape exactly refembling the Taheitee fiſh-hooks, called witte-witte *; fome of which were near feven inches long. They likewife bought their ſhells, which hung on the breaſt, their necklaces, bracelets of mother of pearl, and cylindrical ſticks for the ear. They had the neateſt ornamental combs that can be imagined, confifting of a number of little flat ſticks about five inches long, of a yellow wood like box, moſt firmly and elegantly connected together at the bottom by a tiſſue of the fibres of coco-nut, fome of which were of their natural colour, and others dyed black. Thefe fibres were likewife employed

* See Hawkefworth, vol. II. p. 218. Alfo Parkinfon's Journal, p. 77, and Tab. XIII. fig. 25.

in

In making a great variety of baskets, wrought with regular compartments of two colours, brown and black, or sometimes all brown, and ornamented with rows of round flat beads, which were made by cutting pieces of shells into that shape. The taste and the workmanship of these baskets were elegant in the highest degree, and varied into different forms and patterns. Those little stools, which serve as pillows for the head, were much more frequent here than at Taheitee; flattish bowls, in which they place their meat, and spatulas with which they mix up the bread-fruit paste, were likewise in great abundance, and made of the club-wood (*casuarina equisetifolia*), which had this name from supplying all the islanders in the South Sea with weapons. The clubs of the people of this isle, were of an infinite variety of shapes, and many of them so ponderous that we could scarce manage them with one hand; the most common form was quadrangular, so as to make a rhomboid at the broad end, and gradually tapering into a round handle at the other. But many were spatulated, flattish, and pointed; some had long handles and a blade which resembled the blade of a fleam; others were crooked, knobbed, &c. But by far the greatest part were carved all over in many chequered patterns, which seemed to have required a long space of time, and incredible patience, especially when we consider, that a sharp stone, or a piece of coral, are the only tools which the natives

can

can employ in this kind of work. All the different
compartments were wrought and divided with a regularity which quite surprised us, and the whole surface
of the plain clubs was as highly polished, as if our
best workmen had made them with the best instruments. Besides clubs, they had spears of the same wood,
which were sometimes plain, sharp pointed sticks, and
sometimes barbed with a sting-ray's tail. They had likewise bows and arrows, of a peculiar construction. The
bow which was six feet long, was about the thickness of a
little finger, and when slack, formed a flight curve. Its
convex part was channelled with a single deep groove, in
which the bow string was lodged, and which was likewise
big enough sometimes to contain the arrow made of reed,
near six feet long, and pointed with hard wood. When the
bow was to be bent, instead of drawing it so as to encrease
the natural curvature, they drew it the contrary way, made
it perfectly strait, and then formed the curve on the other
side. The bow-string by this means never needed to be
tense, as the arrow received sufficient moment by changing
the natural bent of the bow; the recoil of which was never
violent enough to hurt the arm. Our seamen, unacquainted with the nature of these weapons, broke several
of them by drawing them like other bows. The immense
quantity of arms belonging to the natives, corresponded
very ill with the pacific disposition, which had strongly
shone

shone through their whole behaviour towards us, and which still manifested itself in their readiness to dispose of them. It is probable that they have sometimes quarrels amongst themselves, or wage war with the neighbouring islands, but we could by no means discover any thing from their conversation or signs, which might have served to throw a light on this subject. The several articles above enumerated, together with all their sorts of cloth, their elegant mats, which for workmanship and variety excelled even those of Taheitee, and a great many other trifles too tedious to mention, they brought to sell, and with great eagerness exchanged for small nails, and sometimes for beads. But in respect of the latter their taste was different from that of the Taheitians; for the latter always chose those that were transparent, but the people of Ea-oowhe would take no other than black opaque beads, with red, blue, and white stripes. We traded with them till dinner-time, and then re-embarked in order to return on board the ships; but were obliged to sit down contented with the loss of a grapnel, which the natives had contrived to steal almost as soon as it was let down into the water. Their kind looks and acclamations followed us till we returned on board, where a number of them traded in their canoes with the same sorts of goods which we had purchased on shore. We saw several persons among them afflicted with leprous complaints, in some of which the disorder had risen to a

                                                   high

high degree of virulence; one man in particular had his whole back and shoulders covered with a large cancerous ulcer, which was perfectly livid within, and of a bright yellow all round the edges. A woman was likewise unfortunate enough to have all her face destroyed by it in the most shocking manner; there was only a hole left in the place of her nose; her cheeks were swelled up and continually oozing out a purulent matter; and her eyes seemed ready to fall out of her head, being bloody and sore. These were some of the most miserable objects I recollect ever to have seen; and yet they seemed to be quite unconcerned about their misfortunes, traded as briskly as any of the rest, and what was most nauseous, had provisions to sell.

After dinner Dr. Sparrman remained on board with me, in order to arrange our acquisitions of the morning, and my father again accompanied the captains to the shore, with a view to collect a fresh supply. They returned about sunset, and my father gave the following account of this excursion.

" At the landing-place the natives welcomed us with shouts as in the morning, and the croud being as numerous as ever, the trade was carried on very briskly, but provisions were scarce, and shaddocks in particular not at all to be had, as the season was not yet sufficiently advanced. Mr. Hodges, myself, and one servant, left the trading-place with

two

two of the natives, whom we engaged to become our guides in case of necessity, and walked up the hill to view the interior part of the country. Our walk lay through a number of rich plantations or gardens, enclosed as before mentioned with fences of reeds, or with quick-hedges of the beautiful coral flower, *(erythrina coralladendron.)* Beyond these we entered into a lane between two enclosures, and observed bananas and yams planted in rows on both sides, with as much order and regularity as we employ in our agriculture. This lane opened into a fine extensive plain, covered with rich grasses. Having crossed it, we met with a most delightful walk about a mile in length, formed of four rows of coco-nut trees, which ended in another lane between plantations of great regularity, surrounded by shaddocks and other trees. It led through a cultivated valley to a spot where several paths crossed each other or met in one. Here we saw a fine lawn covered with a delicate green turf, and surrounded by large shady trees on all sides. In one corner of it there was a house, which was empty at present, its inhabitants being probably by the water's side. Mr. Hodges sat down to draw this delightful spot. We breathed the most delicious air in the world, fraught with odours which might have revived a dying man; the sea breeze played with our hair and gently cooled us; a number of small birds twittered on all sides, and many amorous doves cooed harmoniously in the deepest shade of

the tree under which we were seated. The tree was remarkable for its roots, which came out of the stem near
eight feet above the ground, and for its pods of more than
a yard long, and two or three inches broad. This secluded
spot, so rich in the best productions of nature, where we
sat solitary with no other human being besides our two
natives, struck us with the idea of enchanted ground, which
being the creation of our own gay fancy, is commonly
adorned with all possible beauties at once. In fact, there
could not have been a more desirable spot for a little place
of retirement, according to the elegant imagination of
Horace, if it had only been supplied with a crystal foun-
tain or a little murmuring rill! But water is unfortunately
the only blessing denied this charming little island. To the
left of this spot we discovered a shady walk, that brought
us to another grassy lawn, at the bottom of which we perceived a little mount with two huts upon it. A number
of reeds stuck into the ground, at the distance of one foot
asunder, encompassed this rising, and several casuarinas,
with their slender branches and thread-like leaves, were
planted before it. The natives, whom we had engaged to
accompany us, would not approach this mount; but we
advanced and looked into the huts, though with great difficulty, because the bottom of the roof was not above a
span from the ground. We found a corse in one of these
huts, which had been lately deposited; but the other was
                                             empty.

empty. Thus the cafuarina or club-wood *(toa)*, here, as in the Society Iſlands, pointed out the repoſitories of the dead. Its dull browniſh-green colour, and its long ſpreading branches, where the leaves are thinly ſcattered and hang weeping down, certainly become theſe melancholy places to the full as well as the funereal cypreſs. It is therefore probable that the ſame train of ideas, which conſecrated the latter in one part of the world to ſhade the tombs, might fix upon the former in theſe regions for a ſimilar purpoſe. The mount on which the huts were placed was formed of ſmall pieces of coral rock, like gravel, accumulated without any particular order. From thence we proceeded a little farther, and ſtill found the ſame elegant plantations and the ſame kind of houſes in the middle as before. Our natives conducted us through one of them, where they entreated us to ſit down, and procured ſome coco nuts, which proved extremely refreſhing. At our return we found our boats juſt ready to put off, and embarked with them immediately. We had only ſeen a few of the natives on our walk, who paſſed unconcernedly by us towards the place where the captains traded; and I believe we ſhould have been entirely left to ourſelves if we had not engaged two of them to become our conductors. The diſcharge of our guns, and their effect, neither excited their admiration nor their fear; but they always appeared kind and courteous towards us. Their women were, in general,

L l l 2 reſerved,

referved, and turned with difguft from the immodeft behaviour of ungovernable feamen, fome of them however
appeared to be of eafy virtue, and beckoned to our people
with lafcivious geftures."

The next morning early the captain went on fhore with
us, and prefented the chief with a variety of garden feeds,
explaining by figns how ufeful they would prove to him.
This was as yet our only mode of converfation, though we
had picked up a number of words, which, by the help of
the principles of univerfal grammar, and the idea of dia-
lects, we eafily perceived had a great affinity with the language fpoken at Taheitee and the Society Ifles.   O-Mai and
Mahine (or O-Hedeèdee,) the two natives of Raietea and
Borabora who embarked with us, at firft declared that the
language was totally new and unintelligible to them;
however, when we explained to them the affinity of feveral
words, they prefently caught the peculiar modification of
this dialect, and converfed much better with the natives
than we could have done after a long intercourfe with
them.   They were extremely well pleafed with this country, but foon perceived its defects, and told us there was
but fcanty provifion of bread-fruit, few hogs and fowls, and
no dogs, which was really the cafe.   In return, however,
they liked the abundance of fugar-canes and of intoxicating pepper, of which the drink had been offered to captain Cook.

As

As foon as the captains had delivered their prefent, they returned to the fhips, and the chief came on board with us. Our anchor was weighed, our fails were fpread to the wind, and we forfook this happy ifland when we had fcarce difcovered its beauties. The chief, after felling a number of fifh-hooks for nails and beads, hailed one of the canoes which were pafling by, and left us with looks which fpoke his friendly, open difpofition.

We now failed along the weftern fhore of Tafman's Amfterdam ifland, which the natives called Tonga-Tabboo, and found it a very low flat land, compared with that which we had left. The middle of this ifland is nearly in 21° 11' S, latitude, and 175° W. longitude. Its higheft elevation above the level of the fea, appeared to the eye never to exceed fix or feven yards perpendicular. On the other hand, its extent was much more confiderable than that of Eaoowhe, and by the help of our fpying-glaffes, we difcovered the fame regular plantations which we had fo much admired there, and faw the fhores crouded with inhabitants, who gazed at us, probably with as much attention as we beftowed upon them. When we were about half way between both iflands, or nearly three leagues from each, we were met by feveral canoes full of men, who attempted to come along-fide, but as we happened to be too far to windward, they could only fetch the Adventure, where they came on board.

In.

1775.
October.

In the afternoon we approached the northernmost end of the island, and perceived some small isles connected by reefs to the eastward. Their situation and that of the shoal to the north-west, where the sea broke with great violence, convinced us that we were now arrived at the very place where Tasman anchored in 1643, and which he called Van Diemen's Road. Here we dropped an anchor upon a rocky bank, and were immediately surrounded with numbers of the natives, some in canoes, and some swimming, though we lay about a quarter of a mile from the shore. We found them to be of the same nation which inhabited Ea-oowhe, and their mercantile turn prompted them to bring an immense quantity of their cloth, mats, nets, utensils, arms, and ornaments, which they eagerly exchanged for beads and nails. The ships were no sooner moored, than a prohibition was made against purchasing curiosities, and the natives were told to bring coco-nuts, bread-fruit, yams, and bananas, as well as hogs and fowls, of which we had already learnt the names. We purchased a small quantity of provisions the same evening, to give an example to the rest of the inhabitants, who were obliged to take their merchandize on shore again. The good effects of this step appeared the next morning, when the natives returned from shore at day-break, and had loaded their canoes with vegetables and fowls. Many of them came on board as freely as if we had been old acquaintances, and did not

appear

appear to have the least idea of diftruft. One of them, a well made man, with a handfome open countenance, feemed to have fome authority among them, like the chief whom we had feen on Ea-oowhe. He defcended into the cabin, acquainted us that his name was Attahha, and received feveral prefents, among which he fat a high value on iron, and on red European broad-cloth. After breakfaft he went on fhore with us in the pinnace. A coral reef furrounded the coaft, at the diftance of a mufket-fhot, and a fingle narrow pafs admitted us within it, where we found the water fo full of rocks and fo fhallow, that we were obliged to be carried out of the boat. A party of the marines were pofted on the beach in cafe of danger, to protect the cap-tain's clerk, who traded for provifions. The natives did not exprefs either furprize or diflike at this proceeding, perhaps becaufe they were unacquainted with its meaning. They received us with acclamations of joy as at Ea-oowhe, and defired us to fit down with them on the rocks along fhore, which confifted of coral, and were covered with fhell fand. We purchafed feveral beautiful parroquets, pigeons, and doves, which they brought to us perfectly tame; and our young Borabora-man Mahine (or Hedeedee) traded with great eagernefs for ornaments made of bright red feathers, which he affured us had an extraordinary value at Taheitee and the Society Iflands. Here they were commonly pafled to aprons ufed in their dances, and made of the fibres of

coco-

coco-nut, or fixed upon banana leaves, forming rhomboidal frontlets or diadems, &c. With a degree of extasy which gave the greatest weight to his assertion, he shewed us that a little piece of feathered-work, as broad as two or three fingers, would purchase the largest hog in his island. Both this youth and O-Mai were much pleased with the inhabitants of these islands, and began to understand their language tolerably well.

We left the beach after the first acquaintance with the natives, and ascended a few feet into a wild forest consisting of tall trees, intermixed with shrubberies. This wood though narrow, being in many places not above one hundred yards wide, was continued along the shore of Van Diemen's road, being more or less open in various parts. Beyond it the whole island was perfectly level. We walked across a piece of uncultivated land, about five hundred yards wide, which adjoined to the wood. Part of it appeared to have been planted with yams, but the rest was full of grass, and had a little swamp in the middle, where the purple water-hen, or *poule sultane*, resided in great numbers. As soon as we left this, we entered into a lane about six feet wide, between two fences of reed, which enclosed extensive plantations on each side. Here we met many of the natives, who were travelling to the beach with loads of provisions, and courteously bowed their heads as they passed by us in sign of friendship, generally pronouncing some monosyllable or

other,

other, which feemed to correfpond to the Taheitian *tayo*. The enclofures, plantations, and houfes were exactly in the fame ftyle as at Ea-oowhe, and the people had never failed to plant odoriferous fhrubs round their dwellings. The mulberry, of which the bark is manufactured into cloth, and the bread-tree, were more fcarce than at the Society Ifles, and the apple of thofe iflands was entirely unknown, but the chaddock well fupplied its place. The feafon of fpring, which revived the face of all nature, adorning every plant with bloffoms, and infpiring with joyful fongs the feathered tribe, doubtlefs contributed in a great meafure to make every object pleafing in our eyes. But the induftry and elegance of the natives, which they difplayed in planting every piece of ground to the greateft advantage, as well as in the neatnefs and regularity of all their works, demanded our admiration, whilft it gave us room to fuppofe, that they enjoyed a confiderable degree of happinefs.

One of the lanes between the enclofures led us to a little grove, which we admired for its irregularity. An immenfe cafuarina tree far out-topped the reft, and its branches were loaded with a vaft number of blackifh creatures, which we took for crows at a diftance, but which proved to be bats when we came nearer. They clung to the twigs, by the hooked claws, which are at the extremity of their webbed fingers and toes; fometimes they hung with the head downwards, and fometimes the reverfe. We fhot

at them, and brought down fix or eight at once, befides
wounding feveral others which held faft on the tree. They
were of the kind which is commonly called the vampyre *,
and meafured from three to four feet between the expanded
wings. A great number of them were difturbed at our
firing, and flew from the tree very heavily, uttering a
fhrill piping note; fome likewife arrived from remote parts
at intervals to the tree, but the greateft number remained in
their pofition, and probably go out to feed only by night.
As they live chiefly upon fruit, it is likely that they commit great depredations in the orchards of the natives, fome
of whom being prefent when we fired, feemed very well
pleafed with the death of their enemies. We had feen
fome of them who had caught thefe bats alive, and placed
them in a cage of wickerwork very ingenioufly contrived,
with an entrance like that of a fifh-bafket, where the animal could eafily be put in, but could not come out again.
They likewife affured us the bats were very mordacious, for
which purpofe they feemed indeed to be well provided with
large fharp teeth.

We had already obferved at Taheitee, at the Society
Iflands, and even at Ea-oowhe, that wherever we met with
a cafuarina, a burying-place was at hand. Therefore, at
fight of this venerable tree, which was hung with ill-
omened creatures, we immediately conjectured that it would

* La Rougette, of M. de Buffon. Vampyrus of Linné, and Pennant.

lead

lead us to a cemetery or place of worſhip, and the event
ſhewed that we were not miſtaken. We found a beautiful
green lawn, encloſed on all ſides by ſhady buſhes and trees,
amongſt which caſuarinas, pandangs, and wild ſago-
palms appeared with their various tints of green. A row
of Barringtonias, as big as the loftieſt oaks, formed one ſide
of it, and ſtrewed it with their large bluſhing flowers. At
the upper end of it, there was a riſing two or three feet
high, ſet out with coral-ſtones cut ſquare. The area above
was covered with a green ſod, like the reſt of the lawn.
Two ſteps, likewiſe of coral rock, led up to this part, in
the midſt of which a houſe was ſituated, exactly like that
which we ſaw at Ea-oowhe. Its length was about twenty,
the breadth fifteen, and the height of the ridge ten feet.
The roof deſcended ſloping nearly to the ground, and was
made of banana leaves. We entered into this building
with only one of the natives, the reſt keeping at ſome
diſtance. We found the floor covered with broken pieces
of white coral rock, and in one corner a heap of blackiſh
pebbles, about eight feet long, which was elevated a foot
above the white ſtones. The native told us that a man lay
buried there, and pointing to the place where his little
finger had formerly been cut away, he plainly ſignified that
when his *madua* or parents[*] died, they mutilated their
hands. We found two pieces of wood a foot long, carved

[*] Perhaps any relations in the aſcending line.

into

into fome refemblance of the human figure, like thofe which are called *e-tee* at Tahekee, but they were treated in the fame manner, that is without the leaft degree of refpect or veneration, being frequently trod upon and kicked about. Thefe burying-places, which are called *o-Fsytoora* in the language of the country, are always delightfully fituated on green lawns, and furrounded with the fineft groves. That which I have here defcribed, was drawn by Mr. Hodges, and an exact reprefentation of it is inferted in captain Cook's own account of this voyage.

We continued our walk through the plantations, and met with very few inhabitants, they being almoft all gone towards the trading-place. Thofe we faw paffed by us, or continued their occupations without ftopping on our account. Neither curiofity, nor diftruft and jealoufy excited them to prohibit our farther progrefs; on the contrary, they always fpoke in a kind tone to us, which fufficiently characterized their difpofition. We looked into many of the houfes and found them empty, but always laid out with mats, and delightfully fituated among odoriferous fhrubs. Sometimes they were feparated from the plantations by a little fence, through which a door, like thofe of Ea-oowhe, gave admittance, which could be fhut on the infide. In that cafe only the area, which this fence enclofed around the hut, was planted with the odoriferous grove, which is fo much in requeft with the natives. A walk of three

miles

miles brought us to the eastern shore of the island, where
it forms a deep angle, which Tasman called Maria Bay.
Where we fell in with it, the ground sloped imperceptibly
into a sandy beach; but as we walked along towards the
north point, we found it rose perpendicularly, and in some
places it was excavated and overhanging. It consisted,
however, entirely of coral, which is a strong proof of some
great change on our globe, as this rock can only be formed under water. Whether it was left bare by a gradual
diminution of the sea, or perhaps by a more violent revo-
lution which our earth may formerly have suffered, I shall
not venture to determine. So much, however, may be affumed as a certainty, that if we suppose a gradual diminution of the sea, at the rate which they pretend to have observed in Sweden *, the emersion of this island must be of
so modern date, that it is matter of astonishment how it
came to be covered with soil, herbage, and forests; so well
stocked with inhabitants, and so regularly adorned as we
really found it. We picked up a quantity of shells at the
foot of the steep rock, where we sometimes waded in water
to the knees upon a reef, on account of the flood tide
which was advancing. We likewise met with several natives returning from the trading-place, who sold us a number of fish-hooks and ornaments, a fish-net made like our
casting-nets, knit of very firm though slender threads, some

* See the Memoirs of the Swedish Academy of Sciences at Stockholm.

man

mats and pieces of cloth. We likewife purchafed of them
an apron, confifting of many wheels or ftars of plaited
coco-nut fibres, about three or four inches in diameter, co-
hering together by the projecting points, and ornamented
with fmall red feathers and beads cut out of fhells. Finding that the water encreafed too faft upon us, we looked
out for an afcent to the top of the rock, and having with
fome difficulty found one, we re-entered the plantations,
where we obferved the weeds rooted out with great care
and laid in heaps to dry. After a long walk, during which
we miffed our way, and engaged one of the natives to become our guide, we entered a long narrow lane between
two fences, which led us directly to the *Fayetoue* or burying-place we had left before. Here we found captains
Cook and Furneaux, and Mr. Hodges, with a great number
of natives, feated on the fine lawn. They were in converfation with an old blear-eyed man, who had a good deal
of weight among the reft of the people, and was always
accompanied by a number of them wherever he went. We
were told that he had conducted our gentlemen to two *fye-
toear*, and had pronounced a folemn fpeech or prayer, with
his face directed to the building, but at times turning to
captain Cook, and addreffing the words to him, in a quef-
tioning tone. In thefe moments he always made a fhort
paufe, as if he expected an anfwer, and feeing a nod enfue,
proceeded with his fpeech. Sometimes, however, his memory

mory feemed to fail, upon which he was prompted by another man who fat near him. From this ceremony, and the
place where it was performed, we conjectured that he was
a prieſt. However, as far as we could fee into their religious notions, it did not appear that they practiſed any
kind of idolatry; neither did they feem to have any particular veneration for birds like the Taheitians, but to worſhip a ſupreme inviſible Being. What may have induced
them, as well as the people of Taheitee and the Society Iſles,
to unite their repoſitories of the dead and their places of
worſhip in one, remains in obſcurity. The religious tenets
of a people are the laſt things which ſtrangers become acquainted with, whoſe knowledge of the language is commonly too imperfect. Beſides this, the dialect of the church
frequently differs from the common dialect, and thus religion is veiled in myſteries, eſpecially where there are prieſts
to take advantage of the credulity of mankind.

From this place we returned to the fea ſhore, where a
briſk trade for vegetables, fowls, and hogs was carried on.
Here we bought a large flat ſhield or breaſt-plate, of a
roundiſh bone, white and poliſhed like ivory, about eighteen inches in diameter, which appeared to have belonged
to an animal of the cetaceous tribe. We likewiſe found a
new muſical inſtrument, conſiſting of eight, nine, or ten
ſlender reeds, about nine inches long, joined to each other
by ſome fibres of coco-nut core. The length of its reeds

ſeldom

seldom varied much, and the long and short ones were placed promiscuously; a notch was formed at the top of each, and the method of playing was only to slide the instrument backwards and forwards along the lips. It had commonly not above four or five different notes, and we never met with one which included a whole octave. Its resemblance to the syrinx, or Pan's flute of the civilized Greeks, dignified it much more than any music which it contained. From the method of playing it, the lovers of music will easily conceive that this divine art is entirely in its infancy among the inhabitants. The vocal part, which is the same as we had already observed it at Ea-oowhe, is very far from being unharmonious, and the women beat time to it by snapping their fingers very exactly; but its whole extent is only of four notes, and therefore cannot admit of any variety. They had likewise a flute of a bamboo-reed, nearly of the thickness of a German flute, which they played with the nostrils, like the Taheitians. They commonly had ornamented it with various little figures, burnt in, and pierced four or five holes in it, whereas the Taheitian flute had but three in all. The method of ornamenting wood by burning figures into it, was frequently observed in their bowls and various other utensils.

It was near sun-set when we returned on board with our collection, and found the vessels still surrounded by many canoes, and the natives swimming about extremely vocife-

vociferous. Among them were a confiderable number of women, who wantoned in the water like amphibious creatures, and were eafily perfuaded to come on board, perfectly naked, without profeffing greater chaftity than the common women at Taheitee, and the Society Ifles. Our feamen took advantage of their difpofition, and once more offered to our eyes a fcene worthy of the Cyprian temples. A fhirt, a fmall piece of cloth, nay a few beads, were fometimes fufficient temptations, for which fome of the women of Tonga-Tabboo, proftituted themfelves without any fenfe of fhame. This lubricity was, however, very far from being general, and we had reafon to believe that not a fingle married woman was guilty of infidelity. If we had been acquainted with the diftinction of ranks as at Taheitee, it is highly probable, that we fhould have obferved no other proftitutes than fuch as belonged to the loweft clafs of people. Still it remains an unaccountable fingularity in the character of the nations of this part of our globe, that they fuffer any of their unmarried women to admit the promifcuous embraces of a multitude of lovers. Can they imagine, that after giving fuch an unlimited courfe to the impulfes of nature, they will make better wives, than the innocent and the chafte? But it is in vain that we endeavour to find reafons for the arbitrary whims of mankind. Their opinions in refpect of the fex in particular, have been infinitely various in all ages and countries.

In some parts of India, no man of consequence will condescend to marry a virgin; in Europe she who has lost that character is universally rejected. Turks, Arabs, Tartars, and Russians are jealous even of an imaginary characteristic of virginity, which the native of Malabar bestows upon his Idol.

None of these women ventured to stay on board after sun set, but returned to the shore to pass the night, like the greater part of the inhabitants, under the shade of the wild wood which lined the coast. There they lighted numerous fires, and were heard conversing during the greatest part of the night. It seems their eagerness to continue the trade with us, would not permit them to return to their dwellings, which were probably situated in the remotest part of the island. Our goods were in great repute with them. Nails, which the natives commonly hung on a string round the neck, or stuck through the ear, were very current for fowls, and smaller ones for bunches of bananas, and coconuts. Their fowls were the largest we had ever seen, and extremely well-tasted. Their plumage was commonly very glossy, and beautifully coloured with red and gold. Our sailors bought numbers of them, in order to enjoy the barbarous amusement of seeing them fight. From the time of our leaving Huahine, they had daily followed the cruel occupation of tormenting these poor birds, by trimming their wings, and incensing them against each other. They had

had fo well fucceeded with thofe of Huahine, that fome of them fought with the moft defperate fury of true game-cocks; but they were well difappointed with thofe which they purchafed at Tonga-Tabboo, and as they could not make them fight, they were forced to eat them in revenge.

Early the next morning, the captain's friend Attahha or Attagha (fee p. 447.) came on board in one of the firft canoes, and breakfafted with us. He was dreft in mats, one of which, on account of the coolnefs of the morning, he had drawn over his fhoulders. He refembled all other uncivilized people in the circumftance that his attention could not be fixed to one object for any fpace of time, and it was difficult to prevail on him to fit ftill, whilft Mr. Hodges drew his portrait. An excellent print, executed by Mr. Sherwin, has been made from his drawing, which ex-preffes the countenance of this chief, and the mild character of the whole nation, better than any defcription. It is inferted in captain Cook's account of this voyage, and reprefents Attahha in the action of thankfgiving, laying a nail on his head, which he had received as a prefent. After breakfaft, the captains and my father prepared to return to the fhore with him; but juft as he was going out of the cabin, he happened to fee a Tahoitian dog running about the deck; at this fight he could not conceal his joy, but clapped his hands on his breaft, and turning to the captain, repeated the word *goorree* *

* *Oorri* fignifies a dog at Taheitee; and *ghurri* at New Zeeland.

near

near twenty times. We were much furprifed to hear that he knew the name of an animal which did not exift in his country, and made him a prefent of one of each fex, with which he went on fhore in an extafy of joy. That the name of dogs fhould be familiar to a people, who are not poffeffed of them, feems to prove either that this knowledge has been propagated by tradition from their anceftors, who migrated hither from other iflands, and from the continent; or that they have had dogs upon their ifland, of which the race, by fome accident, is become extinct; or laftly, that they ftill have an intercourfe with other iflands where thefe animals exift.

I remained on board all this day, to arrange the collection of plants and birds which we had made upon our firft excurfion, and which was far from defpicable, confidering the fmall fize of the ifland. The natives continued to croud about our veffels in a number of canoes, whilft many were fwimming to and from the fhore, who were probably not rich enough to poffefs a canoe. Thefe embarkations were of different conftruction. The common fmall trading-canoes were fharp-bottomed, and ended in a fharp edge at each extremity, which was covered with a board or deck, becaufe their narrow form frequently expofed thefe parts to an entire fubmerfion, which would have filled them with water without this precaution. They commonly had a flight out-rigger or balancer, made of a few poles, to pre-

vent

vent their overfetting. The body of the canoe confifted of feveral planks, of a hard brown wood, fewed together with ftrings made of the fibrous coco-nut core, and fo artfully joined that they appeared to be remarkably tight. The Taheitians fimply bore holes in each plank, through which they pafs their ftrings; but by this means their canoes are always leaky. At Tongo-Tabboo they dub the infide of the plank in fuch a manner as to leave a projecting lift or rim clofe to the edge, and through this they pafs their threads. Along the deck or narrow board at each extremity are placed feven or eight knobs, which feem to be an imitation of the little fins, (pinnulæ fpuriæ,) on the belly of bonitos, albecores, or mackarels; and I cannot but conjecture that the natives have taken thefe fwift fifhes for their models in the conftruction of their boats. Though thefe canoes are commonly fifteen or eighteen feet long, yet they are as neatly and fmoothly polifhed as our beft cabinet-work, which muft appear the more furprifing when we confider that the tools of the natives are only wretched bits of coral, and rafps made of the fkins of rays. Their paddles were equally well polifhed, of the fame wood as the canoe, and had fhort rhomboidal broad blades, like thofe of Taheitee. The other fort of canoes were conftructed for failing, and perfons fkilled in nautical matters acknowledge that they were admirably well adapted for this purpofe. We faw one of them in Maria Bay, confifting of two joined together,

together, of which the planks were fewed in the fame
manner as in the common canoe; but they were covered
all over, and had a kind of elevated ftage or platform, like
the Taheitian war-canoes *. Some of them may carry one
hundred and fifty men; and their fails, which are latine,
are made of ftrong mats, in which the rude figure of a tor-
toife or a cock, &c. is fometimes reprefented †. As a farther detail would be tedious to moft readers, and inftructive
only to mariners, I omit it in this place, and refer thofe
who wifh to be better acquainted with the fubject to the
accurate figures with which Mr. Hodges has ornamented
captain Cook's account of this voyage. I fhall only obferve, that it appears probable from the good conftruction
of the failing-boats, that the inhabitants of thefe iflands
are more experienced mariners than thofe of Taheitee and
the Society Ifles.

Among the great numbers of people who furrounded
our fhips, we obferved feveral whofe hair feemed to be burnt
at the ends, and were ftrewed with a white powder. Upon
examination we found that this powder was nothing elfe
than lime, made of fhells or coral, which had corroded or
burnt the hair. The tafte of powdering was at its height

* See Hawkefworth, vol. II. p. 221.

† The figure of a canoe in Schouten's voyage, gives a very good idea of one
of the failing-boats of Tonga-Tabboo. See Dalrymple's Collection, vol. II.
pag. 17, 18.

in

in this island. We observed a man who had employed a
blue powder, and many persons of both sexes who wore an
orange powder, made of turmerick. St. Jerom, who
preached against the vanities of the age, very seriously re-
prehends a similar custom in the Roman ladies: " *Ne irru-
fet crines, et anticipet sibi ignes Gehennæ!*' Thus, by an admirable similarity of follies, the modes of the former inhabitants of Europe are in full force among the modern antipodes; and our insipid beaux, whose only pride is the invention of a new fashion, are forced to share that slender
honour with the uncivilized natives of an isle in the South
Seas.

My father did not return from his excursion till the evening, having proceeded a considerable way towards the south
end of the island. At noon a smart shower had obliged
him to retire into a plantation and to take shelter in a house.
Fortunately for him the owner of this cottage was at home,
and immediately invited him to sit down on the clean mats
which covered the floor, whilst he went to provide some
refreshments. In a few moments he brought several coco-
nuts, and having opened his oven under ground, took out
some bananas and fishes, wrapped in leaves, which were
perfectly well done and delicious to the taste. The manner of cooking provisions is therefore exactly the same as at
Taheitee; nor are the natives less inclinable to acts of hospitality and benevolence, though these virtues were not so

frequently

frequently exercifed towards us, becaufe we commonly found the country quite deferted, the inhabitants being drawn together towards our trading-place. The hofpitable man was rewarded with nails and beads, with which he performed the *fagafetai*, by laying them on his head, and accompanied my father back to the beach, carefully carrying a number of fpears and clubs for him, which he had purchafed on the road.

The harmlefs difpofition of thefe good people could not fecure them againft thofe misfortunes, which are too often attendant upon all voyages of difcovery. Our goods tempted them at leaft as much as they had tempted the Taheitians, and they were confequently equally difpofed to pilfer. The captains had not been long on fhore the next day, when one of the natives took an opportunity of ftealing a jacket out of our boat. In a few moments no lefs than feven fhot were fired, without the captain's orders, though in his prefence, at the thief, who firft dived in the water, and at laft ran into the croud, by which means feveral innocent people were wounded. Notwithftanding this feverity, the good-nature of the people was fuch, that they did not forfake the trading-place, or take umbrage at our proceeding, but heard with unconcern the balls whiftling about their ears. A few hours afterwards, one of them was equally nimble on board our fhip, and luckily flipping into the mafter's cabin ftole from thence feveral mathematical books,
a fword,

a fword, a ruler, and a number of trifles of which he could never make the leaft ufe. He was feen making his efcape in a canoe, and a boat being difpatched after him, he threw all the ftolen effects overboard. Thefe were picked up by another of our boats, whilft the firft continued in the purfuit of the thief. Our men fired a mufket into the ftern of his canoe, upon which he and fome others with him jumped into the fea. The thief was ftill hunted with incredible eagernefs, but difplayed a moft wonderful agility, diving feveral times under the boat, and once unfhipping the rudder. At laft one of our people darted the boat-hook at him, and catching him under the ribs, dragged him into the boat ; but he watched his opportunity, and notwith-ftanding his lofs of blood, leaped into the fea again, and efcaped to fome canoes, which came from the fhore to his affiftance. It is remarkable that even fuch a difpofition for cruelty, as had been difplayed in the purfuit of this poor wretch, did not deprive us of the confidence and affection of his country-men. The captains brought Attagha and another chief on board with them to dinner, and the trade was carried on as quietly as if nothing had happened. The chief who came with Attagha appeared to be of a fuperior rank, becaufe the latter, who ufed to fit at table with us on former occafions, now retreated a few fteps, fat down on the floor, and could not be prevailed upon to eat in his fight. He was a blear-eyed, elderly man, and having a great influence on the people in the canoes, was called the admiral by our sea-men. His dress did not in the least indicate his superior dignity, probably because these islanders are little acquainted with the refinements of luxury, though on the other hand they seem to behave with great submission to their men of rank, directly contrary to what we had observed at the Society Isles. The respect which Attagha paid to the other chief, was however trifling in comparison of that which we heard of on shore after dinner. Here we found a well-looking middle-aged man, sitting on the ground at the trading-place, and all the croud forming a circle about him. Some of our sportsmen acquainted us, that they had met with him near Maria Bay, where the other natives passing by had prostrated themselves on the ground before him, kissed his feet, and put them on their necks. Upon enquiry, they had been repeatedly told, that he was the chief of the whole island, in the same manner as Cookee (captain Cook) was chief of our ships, and that they called him Ko-Haghee-too-Fallango *. Whether this was his name or his title I cannot determine, as we never heard it mentioned again by the natives ; but they all agreed in telling us, that he was their † Areegbee or king. They added that his name was Latoo-Nipooroo, of which we concluded

* Ko is the article in these Islands and at New Zeeland, which answers to the Taheitian O or E.

† The same word in the Taheitee dialect is pronounced Aree.

that

that the former part (Latoo) was a title, it being fame which Schouten and Le Maire, the Dutch navigators in the year 1616, found at the Cocos, Traytors, and Horne iſlands, which are fituated in this neighbourhood, only a few degrees to the northward [*]. We were confirmed in this opinion by the great correſpondence of the vocabularies, which theſe intelligent ſeamen have left us, with the language which was ſpoken at Tonga-Tabboo, and ſtill more ſo by the entire ſimilarity in the behaviour and cuſtoms of theſe iſlanders. The captains walked up to the Latoo, and made him a number of preſents, which he received with ſo much gravity and ſeeming indifference, as bordered upon ſtupidity. Amongſt other things they put a ſhirt on him, with a great deal of trouble, becauſe his behaviour was moſt aukwardly paſſive. He did not return any thanks for the preſents which he received, till an old woman ſitting behind him, had repeatedly excited him to expreſs his gratitude. Upon this he held each ſeparate article over his head, and pronounced the word *fagofetai*, like the meaneſt of his ſubjects. The prieſt, who had led our captains to the places of worſhip, on the firſt day after our arrival, was ſeated in the ſame circle, and drank vaſt quantities of the intoxicating pepper-water [†], which was

[*] See Dalrymple's Hiſtorical Collection of Voyages and Diſcoveries in the South Pacific Ocean, 2 vols. quarto, 1771. London. Vol. II. p. 27, 28, &c.

[†] Called *ava* at Taheitee, and *kava* at Tonga-Tabboo, and Horne Iſland.

ſerved

ferved in little fquare cups made of banana-leaves curioufly
folded.   At his defire, we were very politely prefented with
this dainty beverage, and in pure civility tafted of it.   It
had a naufeous infipid tafte, which was afterwards followed
by a ftrong pungency, and its colour was fomewhat milky.
The holy man took fuch large and frequent draughts of
this ftuff every evening, as to become perfectly intoxicated.
No wonder then that his memory failed him, when he was
at prayer (fee p. 454.) that his whole habit of body was
lean and fcabby, his face wrinkled, and his eyes red, and
" purging thick amber *." He had great authority among
all the people, and a number of fervants attended to fupply
him with replenifhed cups. The prefents which he received from us, he retained in his own cuftody, whereas
Attagha and feveral other chiefs, gave up to their fuperiors
whatever the captains had prefented to them.   The prieft
had a daughter, who received many prefents from our people.   She was extremely well featured, and fairer than moft
of the women of this country, who feemed to pay her fome
degree of deference.   A fairer complexion, and fofter features
than thofe of the common people, are the natural effects of
an eafy inactive life, unexpofed to the blaze of a tropical fun,
and pampered with a profufion of the beft productions of the
country. Muft we not conclude therefore that the beginnings
of luxury will be introduced even here under the cloak of

* Shakefpeare.

1C–

religion, and that another nation will be added to the many
dupes of voluptuous priest-craft? So small a spark as the
cunning of a single man may in time kindle a dreadful
and irresistible fire! The obedience and submission with
which these people revere their chiefs, are evident proofs
that their government, though perhaps not perfectly des-
potic, is yet far from being democratical; and this kind of
political constitution seems likely to facilitate the introduction of luxury. This seems to hold good likewise in regard
to many islands in the western part of the Pacific Ocean,
since the faithful descriptions of Schouten, Le Maire, and
Tasman, who visited them, correspond in every material
particular with our own observations. The general disposition for trading, and the kind and friendly reception
which strangers have almost constantly met with in every
island belonging to this group, prevailed upon us to give
these discoveries of Schouten and Tasman the name of the
FRIENDLY ISLANDS. Schouten's boats were indeed attacked at Cocos, Traitors, Hope, and Horne Islands; but these
attacks were inconsiderable, though severely punished on
the part of the Dutch navigator, who, after the first disturbance at Horne Island, lay there nine days in perfect good
understanding with the natives. Tasman, who twenty-
seven years afterwards saw several islands near six degrees
to the southward of those which Schouten had visited, was
received with every demonstration of peace and friendship,
though

though he was the first European that discovered them.
Whether this behaviour was only a consequence of the intelligence which the natives of Tonga-Tabboo and Ana-
mocka, (Amsterdam and Rotterdam Islands,) might have received from those of Cocos, Hope, and Horne Islands, concerning the superior strength of the strangers and the havock which they had made; or whether it was the natural
effect of their peaceable disposition, I cannot venture to determine, though I am inclined to adopt the former opinion.
Captain Wallis probably saw Cocos and Traitors Islands in
1767, which he called Boscawen's and Keppel's Isles; but
his people did the natives no hurt, except frightening them
with the discharge of a single musket. M. de Bougainville
saw some of the north-eastermost isles belonging to this
group, of which the inhabitants had the same general character. He called his discovery the *Archipel des Navigateurs*, justly enough, as many ships have fallen in with it. Since
Tasman's time, no other navigator has had any intercourse
with the isle of Amsterdam, which he discovered, previous
to our arrival. During a space, therefore, of one hundred
and thirty years, they have not materially changed their
manners, dresses, way of living, disposition, &c. &c. Our
ignorance of their language prevented our obtaining positive proof that they still preserved, by tradition, the memory
of former visitors; but they possessed some nails, which
must have been brought to the island in Tasman's time.

We

We purchased one of these nails, which was very small and almost consumed with rust, but had been carefully preserved by being fixed on a wooden handle, probably to serve the purposes of a gouge or borer, and is now deposited in the British Museum. We likewise bought some small earthen pots, perfectly black with soot on the outside, and suspected them to be memorials of Tasman's voyage; but afterwards we rather believed that they were manufactured by the natives themselves. The accounts of Schouten, Tasman, and M. de Bougainville agree with ours, in respect of the agility with which the natives committed petty thefts; Tasman and captain Wallis have likewise observed their custom of cutting off the little finger; and according to Schouten's and Le Maire's circumstantial narratives, the natives of Horne Island were as submissive to their king as those of Tonga-Tabboo. The experience of the superior power of the strangers, made them respectful even to servility towards the Dutch; their king prostrated himself before a Dutch purser, and their chiefs placed their necks under his foot *. These excessive marks of submission seem to border upon meanness and cowardice; but we never had reason to suppose them tinctured with these vices. Their behaviour towards us was commonly accompanied with that freedom and boldness which the rectitude of intentions

* See Mr. Dalrymple's Historical Collection of Voyages in the Pacific Ocean, vol. II. p. 41.

inspires;

infpires; and though really polite, was never unbecoming. Here, however, as in all other focieties of men, we found exceptions to the general character, and had reafon to lament the behaviour of vicious individuals. Dr. Sparrman and myfelf having left the beach where the Latoo attracted the attention of all our people, entered the wood in purfuit of farther difcoveries in our branch of fcience. The firft difcharge of my fowling-piece at a bird brought three natives towards us, with whom we entered into converfation, as far as our fuperficial knowledge of their tongue would permit. Soon after, Dr. Sparrman ftepped afide into a thicket in fearch of a bayonet, which he had loft from the end of his mufket. One of the natives, finding the temptation of the moment irrefiftible, grafped my fowling-piece, and ftruggled to wreft it from me. I called to my companion, and the two other natives ran away, unwilling to become accomplices in this attack. In the ftruggle our feet were entangled in a bufh, and we both fell together; but the native, feeing he could not gain his point, and perhaps dreading the arrival of Dr. Sparrman, got up before me, and took that opportunity of running off. My friend joined me immediately; and we concluded, that if there was fomething treacherous or vicious in the behaviour of this fellow, our feparation was alfo imprudent, becaufe it had furnifhed him with an opportunity to exercife his talents. We continued ftrolling about for fome time, without

any

any finister accident, and returned to the trading-place on the beach, where we found almost all the people whom we had left. Many of them were now feated in different little groups, which appeared to be fo many feparate families, and confifted of perfons of various ages and fexes. They were all in converfation, of which no doubt the arrival of our ships furnished the topics; and many of their women amufed themfelves either with finging or playing at ball. There was a young girl in particular, whofe features were more regular than common, her eyes fparkling with vivacity, her whole frame admirably proportioned, and, what was moft remarkable here, her long jetty hair hanging down in graceful curls on her neck. This girl, lively and eafy in all her actions, played with five gourds, of the fize of fmall apples, perfectly globular; fhe threw them up into the air one after another continually, and never failed to catch them all with great dexterity, at leaft for a quarter of an hour. The mufical ladies again performed the fame tune which we had already heard at Ea-oowhe, the different voices falling in with each other very harmonioufly, and fometimes joining all together as in chorus. Though I never faw the natives of thefe iflands dance, yet we may add this amufement to the lift of thofe which they are acquainted with, from their own accounts and geftures whenever they fold us their aprons made of flars of coco-nut core, and ornamented with fhell-work and red feathers, or fuch

VOL. I.   P p p   as

as were curioufly wrought of mats in refemblance of fretwork. From thefe geftures I have great reafon to fuppofe
that their dances are of a dramatic kind, and public, like
thofe which I have fpoken of in the Society Ifles, (fee
pag. 398.) Schouten and Le Maire likewife ftrongly confirm this fuppofition by their account of the dances at Horne
Ifland *. It appeared, upon the whole, that the cuftoms
and language of thefe iflanders have a great affinity with
thofe of the Taheitians, and that it would not therefore
be very fingular to find a coincidence even in their amufements. The greateft differences between thefe two tribes,
who muft have originated from the fame ftock, feem to be
owing to the different nature of their iflands. The Society
Ifles are well furnifhed with wood, and the tops of their
mountains are ftill covered with inexhauftible forefts. At
the Friendly Ifles this article is much fcarcer, the furface
(at leaft of thofe which we have feen) being almoft entirely
laid out in plantations. The natural confequence is, that
the houfes are lofty and of immenfe extent in the firft
group of iflands; but much fmaller and lefs convenient in
the laft. In one the canoes are numerous, I may almoft
fay innumerable, and many of a vaft fize; and, in the
other, very few in number, and much fmaller. The
mountains of the Society Ifles continually attract the vapours from the atmofphere, and many rivulets defcend

* See Mr. Dalrymple's Collection of Voyages, vol. II. p. 47.

from

from the broken rocks into the plain, where they wind
their serpentine course and glide smoothly to the sea. The
inhabitants of those islands take advantage of this gift
of bountiful nature, and not only drink of the salutary
element, but likewise bathe so frequently in it that no im-
purity can long adhere to their skin. It is very different
with a people who are absolutely denied this blessing, and
who must either content themselves with putrid stagnant
rain-water in a few dirty pools, or go entirely without it.
They are obliged to have recourse to expedients in order to
preserve a certain degree of cleanliness, which may preclude
various distempers. They therefore cut off their hair, and
shave or clip their beards, which doubtless makes them
look more unlike the Tahcitians than they would otherwise
do. Still these precautions are not sufficient, especially as
they have no fluid for drinking in any quantity. The body
is therefore very subject to leprous complaints, which are
perhaps irritated by the use of the pepper-root water or
ava. Hence also that burning or blistering on the cheek-
bones which we observed to be so general among this tribe,
that hardly an individual was free from it, and which can
only be used as a remedy against some disorders. The soil
of the Society Isles in the plains and vallies is rich, and the
rivulets which interfect it, supply abundance of moisture.
All sorts of vegetables therefore thrive with great luxuriance
upon it, and require little attendance or cultivation. This

P p p 2   profusion

profusion is become the source of that great luxury among the chiefs which we do not meet with at Tonga-Tabboo. There the coral rock is covered only with a thin bed of mould, which sparingly affords nourishment to all sorts of trees; and the most useful of all, the bread-fruit tree, thrives imperfectly on the island, as it is destitute of water, except when a genial shower happens to impregnate and fertilize the ground. The labour of the natives is therefore greater than that of the Taheitians, and accounts for the regularity of the plantations, and the accurate division of property. It is likewise to this source we must ascribe it, that they have always set a higher value on their provisions than on their tools, dresses, ornaments, and weapons, though many of these must have cost them infinite time and application. They very justly conceive the articles of food to be their principal riches, of which the loss is absolutely not to be remedied. If we observed their bodies more slender and their muscles harder than those of the Taheitians, this seems to be the consequence of a greater and more constant exertion of strength. Thus, perhaps, they become industrious by force of habit, and when agriculture does not occupy them, they are actuated to employ their vacant hours in the fabrick of that variety of tools and instruments on which they bestow so much time, patience, labour, and ingenuity. This industrious turn has also led them, in the cultivation of all their arts, to so much greater perfection than the
Taheitians.

Taheitians. By degrees they have hit upon new inventions, and introduced an active spirit and enlivening chearfulnefs even into their amufements. Their happinefs of temper they preferve under a political conftitution, which does not appear to be very favourable to liberty; but we need not go fo far from home to wonder at fuch a phænomenon, when one of the moft enflaved people in all Europe, are characterifed as the merrieft and moft facetious of mankind. Still there may be more fincerity in the chearfulnefs of the natives of Tonga-Tabboo; for, exclufive of great and almoft fervile fubmiffion, their king does not feem to exact any thing from them, which, by depriving them of the means to fatisfy the moft indifpenfible wants of nature, could make them miferable. Be this as it may, fo much feems to be certain, that their fyftems of politics and religion, from their fimilarity with the Taheitian, as far as we could judge, muft have had one common origin, perhaps in the mother country, from whence both thefe colonies iffued. Single diffonant cuftoms, and opinions may have acceded to the primitive ideas, in proportion as various accidents, or human caprices have given rife to them. The affinity of their languages is ftill more decifive. The greateft part of the neceffaries of life, common to both groups of iflands, the parts of the body, in fhort the moft obvious and univerfal ideas, were expreffed at the Society and Friendly Ifles nearly by the fame words.

We

1773.
O. rosen.

We did not find that fonoroufnefs in the Tonga-Tabboo
dialect, which is prevalent in that of Taheitee, becaufe the
inhabitants of the former have adopted the F, K, and S, fo
that their language is more replete with confonants. This
harfhnefs is compenfated however by the frequent ufe of
the liquid letters, L, M, N; and of the fofter vowels E and I,
to which we muft add that kind of finging tone, which
they generally retain even in common converfation.——
But it is time to return from this digreffion.

We did not part from our friends till fun-fet, promifing
to return to them once more the next morning. Our fhips
were well provided with bananas, yams, and coco-nuts;
and, confidering the fmall fize of the ifland, as well as our
fhort ftay, fixty or eighty hogs, befides a vaft number of
large fowls, were a furprifing acquifition. During our ftay
we had fearched the country in vain for water, and the
mafter had been fent to the eaftward to furvey Maria Bay,
and the low ifles which fhelter that harbour. The fituation
of thefe iflands he found very exactly reprefented in the
charts of the ever accurate Tafman, and on one of them
where he landed, he faw an aftonifhing number of fpeckled
water-fnakes, with flat tails, which are harmlefs, and diftinguifhed in the fyftem of Linnæus, by the name of *colubri
laticaudati.* In our branch we had not been unfuccefsful,
this little ifland having afforded us feveral new plants,
among which was a new fpecies of jefuit's bark, or *cinchona,*
of

of which the bitter bark may perhaps be equally efficacious
with that of Peru. We also collected several birds unknown
before, and purchased some live species, particularly of the
parrot and pigeon tribe, of the natives, who seem to be
very expert fowlers. But it did not appear to us, that the
pigeons, which many carried perched on crooked sticks,
were marks of distinction, though Schouten at Horne Island
where the same custom prevails, is of that opinion *. In
the last boat which had brought our people on board in the
evening, the Latoo or king had sent a great quantity of
vegetables, together with a whole hog roasted, or dressed
under-ground, as a present to the captain. In the morning
therefore, we embarked early in the pinnace, and rowed to
the shore to make a present in return. We found the Latoo
sitting at a little distance from the beach ; and captain Cook
gave him a shirt, a saw, a hatchet, a brass kettle, and several
articles of less moment, all which he received with sullen
gravity ; this deportment he never varied, except once, when
he was seen to smile as he conversed with Attagha. Among
the croud, we observed a single man, who differed from all
the rest, by having suffered his hair to grow, and having
twisted it into several round bunches, which hung wildly
about his ears. This man, and the young girl mentioned
page 468. were the only persons we met with, who had

* See Mr. Dalrymple's Historical Collection, vol. II. p. 46.

not

not conformed to the general custom of cutting off the
hair.

After a short conversation with the natives, of whom we
bought a variety of their tools, on account of their elegant
carving, we returned on board to breakfast, and immediately after weighed the anchors and set sail. The provisions lying in confused heaps on the decks, prevented
our going into the open sea immediately. We therefore
kept standing off and on, under shelter of this island, and
did not take our departure till towards evening, when we
shaped our course southerly.

Friday 2. The next morning, the weather being nearly calm, we
caught a shark, eight feet long, consequently bigger than
any we had seen before. In the afternoon we saw the
little isle which Tasman calls Pylstaerts Island. This name
refers to the birds, which the Dutch navigators observed
there, and which in all probability were tropic birds. Pyl-
staert literally signifying arrow-tail, alludes to the two long
feathers in the tail of this bird, from whence its French
name of *paille-en-queue* is likewise derived *. Its latitude is
22° 26′ S. and its longitude 170° 59′ W. A contrary S.
W. wind which sprung up towards evening, obliged us to
Sunday 10. cruize about till the 10th in the morning, when we came

* See Mr. Dalrymple's Collection, vol. II. p. 75. where they are called *wild
ducks.*

in

in fight of this little iflet again. It is of a moderate height, and has two hummocks, of which the fouthernmoft is the higheft. We recovered the trade-wind by degrees, fo that we were out of fight of this ifland about two o'clock In the afternoon, and having bid adieu to the tropical iflands of this ocean, directed our courfe a fecond time towards New Zeeland. We had now made fuch good ufe of the four months, after our departure from thence, as to have croffed the South Sea in the middle latitudes, in the depth of winter, examined a fpace of more than forty degrees of longitude between the tropics, and refrefhed our people at Taheitee, the Society Iflands, and the Friendly Iflands during one and thirty days. The feafon for profecuting our dif-coveries in high fouthern latitudes advanced, and the favage rocks of New Zeeland were only to give us fhelter, whilft we changed our fair-weather rigging, for fuch as might refift the ftorms and rigours of more inhofpitable climates.

CHAP. II.

Course from the Friendly Isles to New Zeeland.—Separation from the
Adventure.—Second stay in Queen Charlotte's Sound.

WE had no sooner left the torrid zone, than flocks of
sea-fowls attended us on our course, and hovered
lightly on the waves, which a favourable gale had raised.
On the 12th an albatrofs appeared, among the reft of the
inhabitants of the temperate zone, which never dare to
crofs the tropic, but roam from thence even to the polar
circle; fo carefully has nature allotted to each animal its
proper place of abode.'

The weather continued fair till the 16th in the morning,
when we had a fall of rain. Some of the people who examined the pump-well, found there a dog, which they
brought upon deck. This creature, which had been purchafed at the ifland of Huahine, like many others of the
fame fpecies, had obftinately refufed to take any nourifhment, and in all probability had lived ever fince in that
hole without the leaft fupport of food, for a fpace of
thirty-nine or forty days. The whole body was reduced
to a mere fkeleton, the legs were contracted, and he voided
blood

blood at the anus. The torments in which this poor animal muft have lived, were a leffon to our people, to purchafe only young puppies of this race for the future, as the grown dogs conftantly refufed to eat on board.

The next night feveral blubbers paffed by the fhip, which were vifible on account of their phofphoric light. Their luminous quality was fo great, that the bofom of the fea, feemed to contain brighter ftars than the æther.

Sea-weed, fheer-waters, and albatroffes daily appeared, as we advanced towards New Zeeland. On the 19th, the fea was luminous, and on the 20th, the diving petrels arrived in flocks about us, and indicated the proximity of the land, which we faw the next morning at five o'clock. We ftood in fhore all the day, till four in the afternoon, when we were abreaft of the Table Cape *, and Portland Ifland which adjoins to it by a ledge of rocks. The fhores were white and fteep towards the fea, and we could perceive the huts and ftrong bolds of the natives, like eagles airies on the top of the cliffs. A great number of natives ran along the rocks, in order to gaze at us, as we paffed by them, and many feated themfelves at the point which extends to the fouthward, but did not care to come off to us in their canoes. We failed between the funken rock and the land, and continued our courfe acrofs Hawke's Bay, and then along fhore, as it was growing dark.

* See the chart of New Zealand, in vol. II. of Hawkefworth's Compilation.

In

In the morning we were to the fouth of Cape Kidnappers, and advanced to the Black Cape. After breakfaft three canoes put off from this part of the fhore, where fome level land appeared at the foot of the mountains. They foon came on board as we were not very far from the land, and in one of them was a chief, who came on deck without hefitation. He was a tall middle-aged man, clothed in two new and elegant dreffes, made of the New Zeeland flag or flax-plant. His hair was dreffed in the higheft fafhion of the country, tied on the crown, oiled, and ftuck with white feathers. In each ear he wore a piece of albatrofs-fkin covered with its white down, and his face was punctured in fpirals and curve lines. Mr. Hodges drew his portrait, and a print of it is inferted in captain Cook's account of this voyage. His companions fold us fome fifh, while he was entertained in the cabin. The captain prefented him with a piece of red baize, fome garden-feeds, two young pigs of each fex, and likewife three pairs of fowls. Our young Borabora man, Mahine; who did not underftand the language of the New Zeelanders at the firft interview like Tupaya, hearing from us that thefe people were not poffeffed of coco-nuts and yams, produced fome of thefe nuts and roots with a view to offer them to the chief; but upon our affuring him the climate was unfavourable to the growth of palm-trees, he only prefented the yams, whilft we made an effort to convince the chief of the value of the

prefents

prefents which he had received, and that it was his intereſt
to keep the hogs and fowls for breeding, and to plant the
roots. He ſeemed at laſt to comprehend our meaning, and
in return for ſuch valuable preſents, parted with his *maere-
peb* or battle-axe, which was perfectly new, its head well
carved, and ornamented with red parrot's feathers and
white dog's hair. After a ſhort ſtay he returned on deck,
where captain Cook preſented him with ſeveral large nails.
He received thoſe with ſo much eagerneſs that he ſeemed to
value them above any other preſent; and having obſerved
that the captain took them out of one of the holes in the
capſtan, where his clerk had put them, he turned the capſtan all round, and examined every hole to ſee if there were
not ſome more concealed. This circumſtance plainly ſhews
how much the value of iron tools is advanced in the eſti-
mation of the New Zeelanders ſince the Endeavour's voyage,
when they would hardly receive them in many places. Before their departure they gave us a heeva or warlike dance,
which conſiſted of ſtamping with the feet, brandiſhing ſhort
clubs, ſpears, &c. making frightful contorſions of the face,
lolling out the tongue, and bellowing wildly, but in tune
with each motion. From their manner of treating the
fowls which we had given them, we had no great reaſon
to expect ſucceſs in our plan of ſtocking this country with
domeſtic animals, and we much feared whether the birds
would reach the ſhore alive. We comforted ourſelves, however,

1773.
OCTOBER. ever, with the thoughts of having at least attempted what
we could not hope to see accomplished.

The wind, which had shifted during our interview with
these savages, blew right off shore, and was very unfavourable. It encreased towards evening into a hard gale, during
which we hauled our wind, and stood on different tacks for
fear of being blown too far from the coast. Heavy rains
attended this gale, and penetrated every cabin in the ship.
Squalls were likewise frequent, and split some old sails,
which were not fit to resist the violence of the tempest.
We had not expected such a rough reception in the latitude
of 40° south, and felt the air from the bleak mountains of
New Zeeland very cold and uncomfortable, the thermome-
Saturday 23. ter being at 50 degrees in the morning. A few hours of
moderate and almost calm weather succeeded these boisterous
beginnings, after which the gale freshened to the same
height as the night before. By day it abated again, and
permitted us to run in shore, but every night it encreased
and blew in furious gusts, which demanded all our attention. On the 24th, in the evening, we had reached the
entrance of Cook's Strait, and saw Cape Palliser before us;
Monday 25. but the next morning a gale sprung up, which was already
so violent, at nine o'clock, that we were forced to hand our
sails and lay to, under a single one. Though we were
situated under the lee of a high and mountainous coast, yet
the waves rose to a vast height, ran prodigiously long, and
were

were difperfed into vapour as they broke by the violence of
the ftorm. The whole furface of the fea was by this means
rendered hazy, and as the fun fhone out in a cloudlefs
fky, the white foam was perfectly dazzling. The fury of
the wind ftill encreafed fo as to tear to pieces the only fail
which we had hitherto dared to fhew, and we rolled about
at the mercy of the waves, frequently fhipping great quantities of water, which fell with prodigious force on the
decks, and broke all that ftood in the way. The continual ftrain flackened all the rigging and ropes in the fhip,
and loofened every thing, in fo much that it gradually gave
way and prefented to our eyes a general fcene of confufion.
In one of the deepeft rolls the arm-cheft on the quarter-
deck was torn out of its place and overfet, leaning againft
the rails to leeward. A young gentleman, Mr. Hood, who
happened to be juft then to leeward of it, providentially
efcaped by bending down when he faw the cheft falling, fo
as to remain unhurt in the angle which it formed with the
rail. The confufion of the elements did not fcare every
bird away from us: from time to time a black fhear-
water hovered over the ruffled furface of the fea, and arti-
fully withftood the force of the tempeft, by keeping under
the lee of the high tops of the waves. The afpect of the
ocean was at once magnificent and terrific; now on the
fummit of a broad and heavy billow, we overlooked an un-
meafurable expanfe of fea, furrowed into numberlefs deep
channels;

1773.
October.

channels ; now on a fudden the wave broke under us, and
we plunged into a deep and dreary valley, whilft a frefh
mountain rofe to windward with a foaming creft, and
threatned to overwhelm us. The night coming on was not
without new horrors, efpecially for thofe who had not been
bred up to a feafaring life. In the captain's cabin the
windows were taken out and replaced by the dead-lights,
to guard againft the intrufion of the waves in wearing the
fhip. This operation difturbed from its retreat a fcorpion,
which had lain concealed in a chink, and was probably
brought on board with fruit from the iflands. Our friend
Mahine affured us that it was harmlefs, but its appearance
alone was horrid enough to fill the mind with apprehenfion [*]. In the other cabins the beds were perfectly foaked
in water, whilft the tremendous rear of the waves, the
creaking of the timbers, and the rolling motion deprived
us of all hopes of repofe. To complete this catalogue of
horrors, we heard the voices of failors from time to time
louder than the bluftering winds or the raging ocean
itfelf, uttering horrible vollies of curfes and oaths.
Without any provocation to ferve as an excufe, they
execrated every limb in varied terms, piercing and complicated beyond the power of defcription. Inured to danger
from their infancy, they were infenfible to its threats, and
not a fingle reflection bridled their blafphemous tongues. I

[*] See Hawkfworth's Compilation, vol. II,

know

know of nothing comparable to the dreadful energy of their curfes, than that difgrace to chriftianity the Anathema of Ernulphus *. In this comfortlefs fituation we continued till two o'clock the next morning, when the wind died away fuddenly, and was fucceeded in an hour's time by another from a favourable quarter. In the calm interval between thefe two winds, the fhip rolled more violently than ever, fo that the main-chains were repeatedly dipped under water, with part of the quarter-deck.

We failed all this day towards the land, having been driven off many leagues during the ftorm. Pintadas, black fhear-waters, and other peirels now furrounded us in great flocks, and we paffed an albatrofs fitting faft afleep in the water, perhaps fatigued by the violence of the preceding gale.

The next day we were difappointed once more at the mouth of the ftrait, and got a contrary wind, which blew a ftorm before night. The fame weather continued for two days following, almoft without Intermiffion. On the 29th, early in the morning, feveral water-fpouts were feen by the officer at watch; and foon after we had a flight fhower and a favourable change of wind. In the evening we loft fight of the Adventure our confort, whom we never rejoined again during this voyage. The foul wind which in the morning on the 30th certainly contributed to fepa-

* See Triftram Shandy.

VOL. I.   R r r   rate

1771.
October.
rate her from us entirely, she being so far astern that this wind must have had infinitely more effect upon her than upon our ship.

It would be useless and tedious to repeat the many changes from adverse tempests to favourable gales which succeeded those already mentioned, and which made us despair of ever coming to an anchor in New Zeeland again. We were buffetted about for nine nights together, during November,
Monday 1. which sleep scarce ever visited our eyes. On the 1st of November we got into Cook's Strait, but the weather proved so inconstant, that it became contrary to us as soon as we had approached Cape Tera-wittee upon the Northern Island. Our situation permitted us, however, the next day Tuesday 2. to come to an anchor in a new bay, which we discovered immediately under this promontory to the westward. The environs of this bay were dreary, blackish, barren mountains, of a great height, almost wholly destitute of woods and shrubs, and running out into long spits of sharp columnar rocks into the sea. The bay itself seemed to extend a considerable way up between the mountains, and by its direction left us in doubt, whether the land on which Cape Tera-wittee is situated, is not a separate island from Eaheino-mauwe. This miserable country was, however, inhabited, and we had not been half an hour at anchor, before several canoes full of natives came on board. They were very despicably habited in old shaggy cloaks,
which

which they called *bógbee-bógbee*. The fmoke to which they are perpetually expofed in their wretched habitations, and a load of impurities which they had probably never wafhed off fince their birth, perfectly concealed their real colour, and made them look of a vile brownifh yellow. The feafon of winter, which was juft at an end, had in all likelihood forced them at times to make their meals on putrid fifhes, which, together with the ufe of rancid oil for the hair, had fo penetrated them with an infufferable ftench, that we could fmell them at a diftance. They brought a few of their fifh-hooks and fome dried tails of craw-fifh to fell, for which they eagerly received our iron-ware and Taheitee cloth. Captain Cook likewife prefented them with two pair of fowls, with ftrong injunctions to keep them for breeding; but it is hardly to be expected that thefe wretched favages will attend to the domeftication of animals. In their unthinking fituation, the firft moment they have nothing ready at hand to fatisfy the cravings of appetite, our fowls muft fall the victims to their voracity. If there are any hopes of fucceeding in the introduction of domeftic animals in this country, it muft be in the populous bays to the northward, where the inhabitants feem to be more civilized, and are already accuftomed to cultivate feveral roots for their fubfiftence.

About three o'clock in the afternoon the weather fell perfectly calm; but in a little time a foutherly wind came

up

up the strait, at sight of which curling the water at a distance, we weighed anchor and got out of the bay. And
very fortunate it was that we did so, for the gale encreased
after a few minutes to such a furious pitch, that we were
hurried along with astonishing speed, and after passing close
to the dangerous rocks of the Brothers, on which a most
dreadful surf was breaking, we came to an anchor at night,
under shelter of Cape Koa-maroo in Queen Charlotte's
Sound.

The next day, about noon, we came safely into the Ship-
Cove, from whence we sailed on the 7th of June, near five
months before. We were in great hopes of being rejoined
here by the Adventure, because captain Cook intended to
make some stay at this place, though the early season of
the year did not promise such abundance of refreshments
as we had enjoyed at our first visit.

We had hardly dropped our anchor, before several of the
inhabitants, who had been out fishing, came to see us in
their canoes, and disposed of the fish which they had
caught. We recollected them as some of our old friends,
and called them by their names, at which they expressed
great satisfaction, doubtless because it served to persuade
them that we were particularly concerned for their welfare
by retaining them in memory. The weather was fair and
warm, considering the season, but our New Zeelanders were
all covered with shaggy cloaks, which are their winter
dresses.

dreſſes. We queſtioned them concerning the health of their absent countrymen, and received various anſwers; but among the reſt they acquainted us, that GooBAIA, one of their old chiefs, had chaced the two goats which we had left in the woods of Grafs-Cove, and had killed and eaten them. This news was moſt unwelcome to us, as it deſtroyed all our hopes of ſtocking the foreſts of this country with quadrupeds.

In the afternoon we viſited all the plantations which we had left on the beach in Ship-Cove, on the Hippah-Rock, and on moru-Aro. We found almoſt all the radiſhes and turneps ſhot into ſeed, the cabbages and carrots very fine, and abundance of onions and parſley in good order; the peas and beans were almoſt entirely loſt, and ſeemed to have been deſtroyed by rats. The potatoes were likewiſe all extirpated; but, from appearances, we gueſſed this to have been the work of the natives. The thriving ſtate of our European pot-herbs, gave us a ſtrong and convincing proof of the mildneſs of the winter in this part of New Zeeland, where it ſeems it had never frozen hard enough to kill theſe plants, which periſh in our winters. The indigenous plants of this country were not yet ſo forward; the deciduous trees and ſhrubs, in particular, were but juſt beginning to look green, and the vivid colour of their freſh leaves well contraſted with the dark wintery hue of the evergreens. The flag, of which the natives prepare their

hemp,

hemp, was however in flower, together with some other early species. We collected all we could find, gathered a quantity of celery and scurvy-grass, and shot some water-fowl, with all which we returned on board in the evening. We immediately made drawings and descriptions of all that was new to us, and particularly of the flag, *(phormium tenax,)* which, on account of the excellent flax that may be prepar-ed from it, deserves to be more universally known. De-sirous to promote every improvement which may turn out a real benefit to mankind, we did not hesitate a moment to permit an engraving to be made from our drawing, at the request of the Earl of Sandwich, which is intended to orna-ment captain Cook's account of this voyage.

The natives returned the next morning in more canoes than the preceding day, and among them was Teiratu, the chief, who had made acquaintance with us on the fourth of June, and had pronounced a long harrangue that day. He was now in his old clothes, or what the polite world would call *desbabillé;* quite destitute of the finery of che-quered matts edged with dog-skin, and his hair carelessly tied in a bunch, instead of being combed smooth, and delectably greased with stinking oil. In short, from being the orator and leader of a troop of warriors, he seemed to be degraded to a simple fishmonger. It was with some dif-ficulty that we recognized his features under this disguise, upon which he was taken into the cabin, and presented
with

with some nails. Our iron ware, and our provision of Taheitee cloth, were articles of such importance to Teiratu and his people, that they resolved to establish themselves near us, in order to be the first to profit by our commerce, and perhaps to lose no opportunity of laying their hands on any thing which belonged to us. Our ship lay very near the beach where we intended to fill our empty casks with fresh water. Here we had already set up a tent for the people who were employed in this branch of our preparations; another for our wood-cutters, and the astronomical observatory. We went on shore at this place, both before and after-noon, and made our way through a labyrinth of climbers which crossed from one tree to another. Mahine (or Hedeedee) likewise came on shore with us, and roamed through its intricate forests, surprised at the number of different birds, their sweet melody, and their beautiful plumage. One of our gardens where the radishes and turneps were in flower, was remarkably full of small birds, which sucked the nectareous juices of the blossoms, and not seldom plucked them from the stalk. We shot several of them, and Mahine, who had never made use of fire-arms in his life before, killed his bird at the first discharge. The senses of all nations, not more polished than his countrymen, are infinitely more acute than ours, which a thousand accidents tend to impair. We never were more clearly convinced of this, than at Taheitee; it was very usual for the natives there, to point out small birds to us in the thickest trees,

of

Novʏᴍʙᴇʀ. or ducks and other water-fowl between buſhes of reeds, where not one of us could ever perceive them.

The weather, which was warm and pleaſant, facilitated our zoological reſearches, ſo that we brought home a number of birds in the evening.

Friday ʃ. The firſt intelligence which we received from the ſhore the next day, was a complaint againſt the natives, who had ſtolen during the night, a watch-coat from the waterers tent, and a bag filled with linen. The captain immediately went into the cove, where the ſavages had taken up their quarters, which was only ſeparated by a ſingle hill from our watering-place, and to which he had given the name of Indian Cove. Here he addreſſed himſelf to their chief Teiratu, who ſent for the ſtolen goods, and returned them without heſitation, pretending that the theft was committed without his knowledge. Our people were politic enough to believe him on his word, becauſe the addreſs of his countrymen had hitherto ſupplied us with abundance of fiſh, for a very moderate compenſation of Taheitee cloth, whilſt we caught them but very ſparingly. In this place they found one of the ſows, which captain Furneaux had left in Canibal Cove; and Teiratu being queſtioned concerning its two companions, pointed to different quarters of the bay, whither he ſaid they had been carried. Thus by ſeparating the animals, and dividing them as a ſpoil, theſe barbarians effectually deſtroy the poſſibility of propagating

the

the species. Too much occupied with the wants of the present moment, they overlook the only means of securing a certain livelihood to themselves, and reject every attempt to civilize them.

They were joined by a strong party on the 6th in the afternoon, who came from various parts of the bay, with a great quantity of fish, and abundance of their clothes, arms, &c. which they exchanged for Taheitee cloth. In the evening they retired to a beach opposite the ship, where they hauled their canoes ashore, made some temporary huts, lighted fires, and broiled some fish for their suppers. Early the next morning looking about us, we found they were all gone off, not excepting those who had lived at the Indian Cove. We were at a loss to guess the reason of their sudden departure, till we perceived that they had taken away six small casks from our watering-place, probably for the sake of the iron-hoops. It is certain, that by supplying us with fish for another day, they would have received three or four times the value of this iron, manufactured for their use; but we have already observed that they are not much troubled with reflections, and probably value a bird in hand more than two in a bush. We were the greatest sufferers on this occasion, being now reduced to catch fish for ourselves, though we could not spare a sufficient number of hands, and were not acquainted with the haunts of the fishes as well as the natives. Our people were occupied

in

in cleaning, caulking, and breaming the ship, setting up and repairing the rigging, and, in short, in fitting her for the next southern cruize. A great party were on shore to fill our empty casks with fresh-water, to make provision of fuel, and to revise the ship's biscuit, which was in a very decayed condition. It had unfortunately been packed into new, or what are called green casks, the staves of which being damp, had communicated the moisture to the bread, a considerable part of which was perfectly rotten, and all the rest, more or less covered with mould. To prevent the fatal effects of this corruption, all the bread was carried ashore, the bad carefully selected from that which was still eatable, and this last put into an oven and baked over again, till it was thoroughly dried.

The weather during this time was as boisterous and inconstant, as that which had so long kept us out of this harbour. Scarce a day passed without heavy squalls of wind, which hurried down with redoubled velocity from the mountains, and strong showers of rain, which retarded all our occupations. The air was commonly cold and raw, vegetation made slow advances, and the birds were only found in vallies sheltered from the chilling southern blast. This kind of weather in all likelihood prevails throughout the winter, and likewise far into the midst of summer, without a much greater degree of cold in the former, or of warmth in the latter season. Islands far remote from any

continent,

continent, or at least not situated near a cold one, seem in
general to have an uniform temperature of air, owing perhaps to the nature of the ocean which every where sur-
rounds them. It appears from the meteorological journals
kept at Port Egmont on the Falkland Islands *, that the extremes of the greatest cold, and the greatest heat observed
there throughout the year, do not exceed thirty degrees on
Fahrenheit's scale. The latitude of that port is 51° 25′
south; and that of Ship Cove in Queen Charlotte's Sound,
only 41° 5′. This considerable difference of site, will
naturally make the climate of New Zeeland infinitely
milder than that of Falkland's Islands, but cannot affect
the general hypothesis concerning the temperature of all
islands; and the immense height of the mountains in New
Zeeland, some of which are covered with snow throughout
the year, doubtless contributes to refrigerate the air, so as to
assimilate it to that of the Falkland's Isles, which are not so
high.

The inclemency of the season did not prevent the natives
from rambling about in this spacious sound. Having been
entirely forsaken by them for three days together, a party
arrived near us on the 9th, in three canoes, one of which
was elegantly carved in fretwork on the stern. They sold

* See the Journal of the Winds and Weather, and Degrees of Heat and Cold
by the thermometer at Falkland's Island, from February 1766, to January 1767.
Inserted in Mr. Dalrymple's Collection of Voyages in the Southern Atlantic
Ocean.

us some curiosities, and then went on shore abreast of the
ship; but we did not remember having ever seen them
before. The next day two wretched canoes joined these, in
which was our friend Towahanga with his family*. He
came immediately on board, with his little boy Khoâa and
his daughter Ko-parree, and disposed of a great number of
green nephritic stones wrought into chissels and blades of
hatchets. He was introduced into the cabin, where captain
Cook gave him many little presents, and dressed his little
boy in one of his own white shirts. The boy was so overjoyed at his finery, that we found it absolutely impossible
to keep him in the cabin by fair words. He was bent upon
parading it before his countrymen on the deck, and persisted to importune us till we let him out. His little vanity,
however, had the most disastrous consequences. An old he-
goat, which went about our decks, to the great terror of all
the New Zeelanders, took offence at the ludicrous figure of
poor Khoâa, who was lost in the ample turns and folds of
his shirt, and awkwardly trotted along with self-complacen-
cy. The sturdy mountaineer stepped in his way, and raising himself on his hind-legs, butted with his head full
against him, and laid him sprawling on the deck in an instant. The unsuccessful efforts which the boy made to
rise, together with his loud lamentations, so provoked the
goat, that he prepared to repeat the compliment, and would

* See page 209.

probably

probably have filenced this knight of the rueful countenance, if fome of our people had not interpofed. His
fhirt was now fullied, and his face and hands covered with
dirt; and in this pitiful plight he returned into the cabin.
His air was quite dejected, his eyes full of tears, and he
feemed to be perfectly cured of his vanity. He told his
misfortune, crying, to his father; but far from exciting pity,
he provoked the favage's indignation, and received feveral
blows as a punifhment of his folly, before we could make
his peace. We cleaned his fhirt and wafhed him all over,
which had perhaps never happened to him before during
his life, and thus fucceeded to reftore him to his former
tranquillity. However, his father, dreading a future misfortune, carefully rolled up the fhirt, and taking off his
own drefs, made a bundle of it, in which he placed all the
prefents which he and his fon had received.

The natives continued to fell their artificial curiofities
and fome fifh to our people this day and the following,
both which proved very rainy. On the 12th, in the morning, the weather being clear again, Dr. Sparrman, my father,
and myfelf, went to the Indian Cove, which we found uninhabited. A path, made by the natives, led through the foreft
a confiderable way up the fteep mountain, which feparates
this cove from Shag Cove *. The only motive which could
induce the New Zeelanders to make this path, appeared to

* See the chart of Cook's Strait in Hawkefworth's Compilation, vol. II.

be

be the abundance of ferns towards the summit of the mountain, the roots of that plant being an article of their diet. The steepest part of the path was cut in steps paved with shingle or slate, but beyond that the climbers impeded our progress considerably. About half way up, the forest ended, and the rest was covered with various shrubs and ferns, though it appeared to be naked and barren from the ship. At the summit we met with many plants which grow in the vallies and by the sea-side at Dusky Bay, owing to the difference of climate, which is so much more rigorous in that southern extremity of New Zeeland. The whole to the very top consists of the same talcous clay which is universal all over the island, and of a talcous stone, which when exposed to the sun and air, crumbles in pieces and dissolves into lamellæ. Its colour is whitish, greyish, and sometimes tinged with a dirty yellowish-red, perhaps owing to irony particles. The south side of the mountain is clad in forests almost to the summit. The view from hence was very extensive and pleasing; we looked into East Bay as into a fish-pond, and saw Cape Terà-wittee beyond the strait. The mountains in the south arose to a vast height, and were capt with snow; and the whole prospect on that side was wild and chaotic. We made a fire as a memorial of our expedition, and then came down the same path by which we had ascended. The next morning we made an excursion to Long Island, where we found a number of

plants

plants and some birds which were new to us. In the woods
on the east side we heard some petrels in holes under ground
croaking like frogs and cackling like hens; and we supposed them to be of the little diving species, which I have
noticed before. It seems to be a general custom of the petrel
tribe to make their nest in subterraneous holes, as we found
the blue or silvery sort lodged in the same manner at
Dusky Bay.

Ever since the 12th the weather was mild and very fair;
the natives resided abreast of the ship, and supplied us with
plenty of fish, whilst our sailors carried on their former
amours with the women, amongst whom there was but one
who had tolerable features, and something soft and feminine
in her looks. She was regularly given in marriage by her
parents to one of our shipmates, who was particularly beloved by this nation, for devoting much of his time to them,
and treating them with those marks of affection which, even
among a savage race, endear mankind to each other. To-
gheeree, for so the girl was called, proved as faithful to her
husband as if he had been a New Zealander, and constantly
rejected the addresses of other seamen, professing herself a
married woman, (tirra-tàne.) Whatever attachment the
Englishman had to his New Zeeland wife, he never attempted to take her on board, foreseeing that it would be highly
inconvenient to lodge the numerous retinue which crawled
in her garments and weighed down the hair of her head.

Ile

He therefore visited her on shore, and only by day, treating
her with plenty of the rotten part of our biscuit, which we
rejected, but which she and all her countrymen eagerly devoured. Mahine, the native of Borabora, whom we had on
board, had been so much accustomed in his own country to
obey every call of nature, that he did not hesitate to gratify his appetites in New Zeeland, though he was too clear-
sighted at the same time not to perceive the vast falling off
from his own country-women. The force of instinct tri-
umphed over his delicacy,—and can we wonder at it, when
our civilized Europeans set him the example? His conduct
towards the New Zeelanders in general deserves to be com-
mended. There needed not much penetration to discover
that their present existence was very wretched in comparison of that of the tropical islanders; but he also frequently
expressed his pity, whilst he enumerated to us a variety of
articles of which they were ignorant. He distributed the
roots of yams to those who visited the ship at the Black
Cape, and always accompanied the captain whenever he
went to plant or sow a piece of ground in this harbour. He
was not, like Tupaya, so much a master of their language
as to converse freely with them, but he soon understood
them much better than any one of us, from the great ana-
logy of their language to his own. Our visit to the tropical islands had, however, contributed to make the New Zeeland dialect more intelligible to us than before, and we
                                                        plainly

plainly perceived that it had a great affinity to that of the
Friendly Isles, which we had just left. From such little
data we can only guess at the probable route by which a
country, so far to the south as New Zeeland, has been
peopled.

The weather continuing fair on the 14th at night, the
captain and my father went on shore to the observatory
with telescopes, to observe the emersion of one of Jupiter's
satellites. The result of a great number of observations,
made at different times by our accurate and indefatigable
astronomer, Mr. William Wales, F. R. S. has ascertained the
longitude of Queen Charlotte's Sound to be 174° 25′ East
from Greenwich.

The next morning we accompanied the captain to East
Bay, where we visited several small parties of the natives, in
three different places. They received us very amicably, presented us with fish, which was always the most valuable
article they had to give, and sold us several large hoop-
nets * for our iron and Taheitee cloth. Towards the bottom of the bay we mounted on the same hill which captain
Cook had ascended in his first voyage †, intending to look
out on the sea if we could perceive the Adventure. But
when we reached the summit, we found so thick a haze on
the water, that we could see no farther than two or three

---

* Of the kind mentioned in Hawkesworth's Compilation, vol. II. p. 392.
† See Hawkesworth, vol. II. p. 397.

leagues. The monument which captain Cook had erected
here formerly, confifting of a pile of loofe ftones, under
which fome coins, bullets, &c. had been buried, was entirely demolifhed at prefent; the natives having probably
fufpected that a treafure of European goods was depofited
there. At the foot of this hill fome friendly people, like
thofe of which captain Cook took notice at this place in his
firft voyage, came to us, and difpofed of many of their arms,
utenfils, and dreffes. In the afternoon we tried the hoop-
nets which we had bought of the natives, and had tolerable fuccefs. Thefe nets are made of the fplit leaves of
the flag, fo often mentioned, after they have been dried and
beaten. No plant promifes to become fo ufeful to Europe
by tranfplantation as this flag. The hemp or flax which
the New Zeelanders make of it, with their coarfe materials,
is exceffively ftrong, foft, gloffy, and white; and that which
has been prepared again in England, has almoft equalled
filk in luftre. It grows on all kinds of foil, and, being
perennial, may be cut down to the root every year, and
requires fcarce any attendance or care in the cultivation.

On the 17th, we fpent the forenoon in cutting down a
number of very tall trees, of which we wifhed to gather
the flowers, but all our efforts were in vain. We had no
fooner cut a tree, than it hung in a thoufand bindweeds
and climbers from top to bottom, from which it was not
in our power to difengage it. The three following days
we

we had much rain, which confined us on board; nor did
we receive any visits from the natives during that time.

On the 21st in the morning, none but women came
from the shore in two canoes, and seemed to be under
great apprehensions for their men, signifying to us that
they were gone to fight with another party. From the direction in which they pointed, we concluded that their
enemies dwelt somewhere in Admiralty Bay.

On the 22d, the weather being mild and fair, the captain, accompanied by Dr. Sparrman, my father, and myself,
went into West Bay, and in its deepest recess carried ashore
two sows and a boar, with three cocks and two hens, which
we set at liberty a good way up in the woods. We flattered
ourselves that having chosen a marshy spot, which is not
likely to be frequented by the inhabitants, the animals
would be left to multiply their species without any mo-
lestation. A few natives only in a single canoe had seen
us in the entrance of the bay, and probably would not sus-
pect that we were come on so particular an errand. If
therefore the southern isle of New Zeeland should in course
of time be stocked with hogs and fowls, we have great
reason to hope that the care with which we concealed them
in the woods, has been the only means of preserving the
race.

At our return seven or eight canoes arrived from the
northward, some of which, without paying any attention

to

to us, went directly into Indian Cove, whilst the rest came on board with a great variety of dresses and arms, which they sold to our people. They were more dressed than we had commonly seen any, during this second stay at Queen Charlotte's Sound, their hair was tied up, and their cheeks painted red. All these circumstances conspired to confirm the account which the women had given us the day before, that their husbands were gone to fight, as it is usual for them to put on their best apparel on those occasions. I am much afraid that their unhappy differences with other tribes, were revived on our account. Our people not satisfied with purchasing all the hatchets of stone, patoo-patoos, battle-axes, clothes, green jaddes, fish-hooks, &c. of which the natives of our acquaintance were possessed, continually enquired for more, and shewed them such large and valuable pieces of Taheitee cloth, as would not fail to excite their desires. It is not improbable that as soon as this appetite prevailed among the New Zeelanders, they would reflect that the shortest way to gratify it, would be to rob their neighbours of such goods, as the Europeans coveted. The great store of arms, ornaments, and clothes which they produced at this time, seemed to prove that such a daring and villainous design had really been put in execution; nor was it to be supposed that this could have been accomplished without bloodshed.

In

In the morning, which was very foggy, the natives at
our watering-place were seen to eat a root boiled or baked by means of hot stones; and Mr. Whitehouse the first mate brought some of it on board, which tasted rather better than a turnep. My father returned on shore with him; for a few trifles obtained some large pieces of this root, and with some difficulty prevailed on two of the natives to accompany Mr. Whitehouse and him into the woods, in order to point out to them the species of plant to which the root belonged. They walked up a considerable way without any arms whatsoever, trusting to the honesty of their guides. These men pointed out a species of fern-tree, which they called *mamaghoo*, as having the eatable root; and at the same time shewed the difference between this, and another kind of fern-tree, which they named *ponga*. The first is full of a tender pulp or pith, which when cut exsudes a reddish juice of a gelatinous nature, nearly related to sago. This is so much the less singular, as the real sago-tree is a species of fern. The good nutritive root of the mamaghoo must not, however, be confounded with that wretched article of New Zeeland diet, the common fern-root, or *acrostichum furcatum* Linn. The latter consists of nothing but insipid sticks, which after being broiled over the fire for some time, are beaten or bruised on a stone with a piece of wood much resembling the Taheitian cloth-beater, but round instead of square, and without

any

any grooves. The bruised mafs is chewed, what little juice there may be in it fucked out, and the reft thrown afide. The marnaghoo on the contrary is tolerably good eating, and the only fault feems to be, that it is not plentiful enough for a conftant fupply. At their return they were witneffes of an inftance of the ferocity of manners of this favage nation. A boy about fix or feven years old demanded a piece of broiled pinguin, which his mother held in her hands. As fhe did not immediately comply with his demand, he took up a large ftone and threw it at her. The woman incenfed at this action ran to punifh him, but fhe had fcarcely given him a fingle blow, when her hufband came forward, beat her unmercifully, and dafhed her againft the ground, for attempting to correct her unnatural child. Our people who were employed in filling water, told my father they had frequently feen fimilar inftances of cruelty among them, and particularly, that the boys had actually ftruck their unhappy mother, whilft the father looked on left fhe fhould attempt to retaliate. Among all favage nations the weaker fex is ill-treated, and the law of the ftrongeft is put in force. Their women are mere drudges, who prepare raiment and provide dwellings, who cook and frequently collect their food, and are requited by blows and all kinds of feverity. At New Zeeland it feems they carry this tyranny to excefs, and the males are taught from their earlieft age, to hold their mothers in contempt,

contempt, contrary to all our principles of morality. I leave
this barbarity without a comment, in order to relate the
remaining occurrences of this day, which was pregnant in
discoveries relative to the New Zeelanders. The captain,
with Mr. Wales, and my father, went to Motu-Aro in the
afternoon, where they looked after the plantations, collected
greens for the ships, &c. In the mean while some of the
lieutenants went to the Indian Cove, with a view to trade
with the natives. The first objects which struck them were
the entrails of a human corse lying on a heap a few steps
from the water. They were hardly recovered from their
first surprize, when the natives shewed them several limbs
of the body, and expressed by words and gestures that they
had eaten the rest. The head without the lower jaw-bone,
was one of the parts which remained, and from which it
plainly appeared, that the deceased was a youth about fifteen
or sixteen years old. The skull was fractured near one of
the temples, as it seemed by the stroke of a pattoo-pattoo.
This gave our officers an opportunity of enquiring how they
came in possession of the body. The natives answered, that
they had fought with their enemies, and had killed several
of them, without being able to bring away any of the dead
besides this youth. At the same time they acknowledged
that they had lost some of their friends, and pointed to several women who were seated apart, weeping and cutting their
foreheads with sharp stones, in commemoration of the dead.

Our

Our former conjectures were now amply verified, our apprehensions that we were the innocent causes of this disaster encreased, and the existence of anthropophagi confirmed by another strong proof. Mr. Pickersgill proposed to purchase the head, in order to preserve it till his return to England, where it might serve as a memorial of this voyage. He offered a nail, and immediately obtained the head for this price †, after which he returned on board with his company, and placed it on the taffarel *. We were all occupied in examining it, when some New Zeelanders came on board from the watering-place. At sight of the head they expressed an ardent desire of possessing it, signifying by the most intelligible gestures that it was delicious to the taste. Mr. Pickersgill refused to part with it, but agreed to cut off a small piece from the cheek, with which they seemed to be well satisfied. He cut off the part he had promised, and offered it to them, but they would not eat it raw, and made signs to have it dressed. Therefore, in presence of all the ship's company, it was broiled over the fire; after which they devoured it before our eyes with the greatest avidity. The captain arriving the moment after with his company, the New Zeelanders repeated the experiment once more in his presence. It operated very

† The head is now deposited in the collection of Mr. John Hunter, F. R. S.

* The upper part of the stern.

strangely

strangely and differently on the beholders. Some there were who, in spite of the abhorrence which our education inspires against the eating of human flesh, did not seem greatly disinclined to feast with them, and valued themselves on the brilliancy of their wit, while they compared their battle to a hunting-match. On the contrary, others were so unreasonably incensed against the perpetrators of this action, that they declared they could be well pleased to shoot them all; they were ready to become the most detestable butchers, in order to punish the imaginary crime of a people whom they had no right to condemn. A few others suffered the same effects as from a dose of ipecacuanha. The rest lamented this action as a brutal depravation of human nature, agreeably to the principles which they had imbibed. But the sensibility of Mahine, the young native of the Society Islands, shone out with superior lustre among us. Born and bred in a country where the inhabitants have already emerged from the darkness of barbarism, and are united by the bonds of society, this scene filled his mind with horror. He turned his eyes from the unnatural object, and retired into the cabin, to give vent to the emotions of his heart. There we found him bathed in tears; his looks were a mixture of compassion and grief, and as soon as he saw us, he expressed his concern for the unhappy parents of the victim. This turn which his reflections had taken, gave us infinite pleasure; it spoke a humane heart, filled with the warmest sentiments of social affection, and habituated to sympathize with its fellow-creatures. He was so deeply affected, that it was several hours before he could compose himself, and ever after, when he spoke on this subject, it was not without emotion. Philosophers, who have only contemplated mankind in their closets, have strenuously maintained, that all the assertions of authors, ancient and modern, of the existence of men-eaters are not to be credited; and there have not been wanting persons amongst ourselves who were sceptical enough to refuse belief to the concurrent testimonies in the history of almost all nations in this particular. But captain Cook had already, in his former voyage, received strong proof that the practice of eating human flesh existed in New Zeeland; and as now we have with our own eyes seen the inhabitants devouring human flesh, all controversy on that point must be at an end. The opinions of authors on the origin of this custom are infinitely various, and have lately been collected by the very learned canon Pauw, at Xanten, in his *Recherches Philosophiques sur les Americains*, vol. I. p. 207. He seems to think that men were first tempted to devour each other from real want of food and cruel necessity *. Many weighty objections, however, may be made against this hypothesis; amongst which the following is one of the greatest. There

---

* His sentiments are copied by Dr. Hawkesworth, who has disingenuously concealed their author. See his Compilation, vol. III. p. 447.

are

are very few countries in the world fo miferably barren as not to afford their inhabitants fufficient nourifhment, and thofe, in particular, where anthropophagi ftill exift, do not come under that defcription. The northern ifle of New Zeeland, on a coaft of near four hundred leagues, contains fcarcely one hundred thoufand inhabitants, according to the moft probable guefs which can be made; a number inconfiderable for that vaft fpace of country, even allowing the fettlements to be confined only to the fea-fhore. The great abundance of fifh, and the beginnings of agriculture in the Bay of Plenty and other parts of the Northern Ifle, are more than fufficient to maintain this number, becaufe they have always had enough to fupply ftrangers with what was deemed fuperfluous. It is true, before the dawn of the arts among them, before the invention of nets, and before the cultivation of potatoes, the means of fubfiftence may have been more difficult; but then the number of inhabitants muft likewife have been infinitely fmaller. Single inftances are not conclufive in this cafe, though they prove how far the wants of the body may ftimulate mankind to extraordinary actions. In 1772, during a famine which happened throughout all Germany, a herdfman was taken on the manor of Baron Boineburg, in Heffia, who had been urged by hunger to kill and devour a boy, and afterwards to make a practice of it for feveral months. From his confeffion it appeared, that he looked upon the flefh of young

U u u 2   children

children as a very delicious food; and the gestures of the
New Zeelanders indicated exactly the same thing. An old
woman in the province of Matogroffo, in Brasil, declared to
the Portuguese governor [*], that she had eaten human flesh
several times, liked it very much, and should be very glad
to feast upon it again, especially if it was part of a little
boy. But it would be abfurd to suppose from such circumstances, that killing men for the sake of feasting upon them,
has ever been the spirit of a whole nation; because it is
utterly incompatible with the existence of society. Slight
causes have ever produced the most remarkable events
among mankind, and the most trifling quarrels have fired
their minds with incredible inveteracy against each other.
Revenge has always been a strong passion among barbarians,
who are less subject to the sway of reason than civilized people, and has stimulated them to a degree of madness which
is capable of all kinds of excesses. The people who first
consumed the body of their enemies, seem to have been
bent upon exterminating their very inanimate remains, from
an excess of passion; but, by degrees, finding the meat
wholesome and palatable, it is not to be wondered that
they should make a practice of eating their enemies as often
as they killed any, since the action of eating human flesh,
whatever our education may teach us to the contrary, is

---

[*] M. de Pinto, now ambassador from Portugal at the British court; a nobleman equally eminent for his extensive knowledge and his excellent heart.

certainly

certainly neither unnatural nor criminal in itself. It can only become dangerous as far as it steels the mind against that compassionate fellow-feeling which is the great basis of civil society; and for this reason we find it naturally banished from every people as soon as civilization has made any progress among them. But though we are too much polished to be canibals, we do not find it unnaturally and savagely cruel to take the field, and to cut one another's throats by thousands, without a single motive, besides the ambition of a prince, or the caprice of his mistress! Is it not from prejudice that we are disgusted with the idea of eating a dead man, when we feel no remorse in depriving him of life? If the practice of eating human flesh makes men unfeeling and brutal, we have Instances that civilized people, who would perhaps, like some of our sailors, have turned sick at the thought of eating human flesh, have committed barbarities without example amongst canibals. A New Zeelander, who kills and eats his enemy, is a very different being from an European, who, for his amusement, tears an infant from the mother's breast, in cool blood, and throws it on the earth to feed his hounds *

> Neque hic lupis mos nec fuit leonibus.
> Nunquam nisi in dispar feris. Hor.

The New Zeelanders never eat their adversaries, unless they are killed in battle; they never kill their relations for

* Bishop Las Casas says, he has seen this atrocious crime committed in America by Spanish soldiers.

The

the purpofe of eating them; they do not even eat them if they die of a natural death, and they take no prifoners with a view to fatten them for their repaft*; though thefe circumftances have been related, with more or lefs truth of the American Indians. It is therefore not improbable, that in procefs of time they will entirely lay afide this cuftom; and the introduction of new domeftic animals into their country might haften that period, fince greater affluence would tend to make them more fociable. Their religion does not feem likely to be an obftacle, becaufe from what we could judge, they are not remarkably fuperftitious, and it is only among very bigoted nations, that the cuftom of offering human flefh to the gods, has prevailed after civilization. Tupaya †, the only man who could freely converfe with the New Zeelanders, foon learnt that they acknowledged a fupreme Being; and this fpark of divine revelation probably remains amongft all nations on the globe. To this they add the belief of fome inferior divinities, fo correfpondent to thofe of the Taheitians, that their fyftem of polytheifm muft be of very ancient date, and feems to derive its origin from their common anceftors. We never obferved a fingle ceremony in New Zeeland, which could be fuppofed to have a religious tendency; and I know of only two circumftances which may be diftantly conftrued to

* See Hawkefworth, vol. II. p. 389, 390.
† See Hawkefworth, vol. III. p. 471.

favour

favour of fuperftition. The firft is the name of *atua*, " the bird of the divinity," which they fometimes give to a fpecies of creeper * *(certhia cincinnata.)* This name feems to indicate a veneration like that which is paid to herons, and king-fifhers at Taheitee, and the Society Ifles; but I cannot fay that they ever expreffed the leaft wifh to preferve the life of this bird in preference to the reft. The fecond, is the cuftom of wearing an amulet of green jadde on the breaft, from a ftring round the neck. This piece of ftone is of the fize of two crown-pieces, and carved fo as to bear a rude refemblance to a human being. Thefe they call e-teeghee, a name which is doubtlefs equivalent to the Taheitian e-tee †. In that ifland, and the adjacent group, e-tee fignifies a wooden image of the human figure, erected on a pole at their cemeteries, in memory of the dead, but to which no worfhip nor particular refpect is paid. The New Zeeland teeghee feems to be worn with a fimilar view, but not to be better refpected; for though they did not part with it for a trifle, yet with half a yard of broad cloth or red kerfey, which were our beft goods in Queen Charlotte's Sound, we never failed to purchafe it. Befides this, they often wear feveral rows of human teeth round the neck, but we underftood that they were only the memorials of

* Our failors called this the poe-bird. Its common New Zeeland name is kogo.

† Better pronounced E-Tea-ee.

their

their prowefs, fince they had belonged to the enemies whom they had killed. It always appeared to us, that they have no priefts or jugglers of any kind among them, which accounts for their having fo little fuperftition. When the comforts of life are multiplied, it is poffible that fome individuals may be artful enough to improve upon their prefent ideas of religion, in order to enjoy exclufive advantages; for it has often been the fate of mankind, that the moft facred, and moft ineftimable gift of heaven, has ferved as a cloak under cover of which they have been deluded.

Having fitted the fhip to encounter the rigorous climate of the fouth, and received on board her provifion of frefh water and wood, as well as the bifcuit which had been baked over again, we re-imbarked all the tents from the fhore, and on the 24th, early in the morning, unmoored and rode by a fingle anchor. The natives immediately repaired to the beach which we had left, and finding there a heap of bread-duft which had been rejected as unfit for ufe at the revifal of our bifcuit, they fell to, and confumed it all, though our hogs had before refufed to touch it. We could not attribute this proceding to neceffity, becaufe they had plenty of frefh fifh, of which they daily fold us enough for our confumption. It was rather owing to the diverfity of their tafte from ours, or to the natural inclination for variety, which made them eat the worft of vegetable food,

because

because it was a rarity, in preference to fish, which is their conſtant diet. They had another motive for viſiting the place of our late eſtabliſhment; this was, to pick up any little trifles, ſuch as nails, rags, &c. which we might have left behind. Whilſt they were ſo employed, ſome others came from the interior parts of the bay, and offered a great quantity of their tools and weapons to ſell.

In the afternoon, a boat was ſent on ſhore to bury a bottle at the foot of a tree, with a letter for captain Furneaux, in caſe he ſhould come into the harbour after our departure. Another boat, with ſeveral officers, and my father, went to Indian Cove, where the entrails of the body ſtill lay on the ground. The war-canoe, in which the expedition had been made, had a carved head ornamented with bunches of brown feathers, and a double-forked prong projected from it, on which the heart of their ſlain enemy was transfixed. Our gentlemen purchaſed a quantity of their prepared hemp or flax, and many fiſh-hooks, armed with bone, which, according to the account of the natives, was taken from the human arm.

At four o'clock the next morning, a boat was ſent to the Motu-Aro, in order to take a few cabbages out of our plantations. My father took that opportunity of ſearching the ſhore for the laſt time, and was fortunate enough to find ſome plants which we had not ſeen before. In the mean while we hove the anchor, ſet ſail, and took up the boat on our way; but finding the current and wind against us, we were forced to come to again about seven o'clock, between Motu-Aro and Long Island. Here we lay an hour or two, and then set sail with a more favourable breeze, which carried us into Cook's Strait.

We stood close in shore under cape Tera-Wittee, and fired several guns to give the Adventure notice of our approach, in case she had lain in one of the adjacent harbours. Between the Capes Tera-Wittee and Palliser, we discovered a very deep bay, of which the shores had every where a gentle slope, and especially towards the bottom, where the hills were removed to such a distance, that we could but just discern them. If there is a sufficient depth of water for ships in this bay, and of that we had no room to doubt, it appears to be a most convenient spot for an European settlement. There is a great stretch of land fit for cultivation, and easily defensible; there is likewise plenty of wood, and almost certain indications of a considerable river; and lastly, the country does not seem to be very populous, so that there would be little danger of quarrels with the natives; advantages which are not frequently to be met with jointly in many spots of New Zeeland. The flag (*phormium tenax*) of which the natives make all their clothes, mats, ropes, and nets, affords such an excellent kind of flax, which is at once glossy, elastic, and strong, that it might become an article of commerce in India, where cordage and canvas is wanted.

wanted. Perhaps in future ages, when the maritime powers of Europe lose their American colonies, they may think of making new establishments in more distant regions; and if it were ever possible for Europeans to have humanity enough to acknowledge the indigenous tribes of the South Sea as their brethren, we might have settlements which would not be defiled with the blood of innocent nations.

We continued firing guns as we stood past this bay, and the next morning having doubled Cape Palliser, we ran along the coast to the northward till the evening, likewise firing guns from time to time. Our attempts to rejoin our consort were to no purpose; we heard no answer to all our signals, though we hearkened with an attention, and an eagerness which plainly shewed how unwillingly we ventured on a second cruize among numberless dangers without a companion. We were forced at last to give up the thought of seeing her again, and about six o'clock took our departure from Cape Palliser, steering to the S. S. E.

The scurvy, which had afflicted some of our people after the first tedious cruize to the south, between the Cape of Good Hope and Dusky Bay, had been entirely subdued by the wholesome diet on fish, and the drinking of spruce-beer in that harbour; and afterwards by the excellent greens in Queen Charlotte's Sound. Our disagreeable passage in winter from New Zeeland to Taheitee, had revived

X x x 2

the

the symptoms of the disease in many persons, and in some, to a considerable degree; but the continual supply of fresh vegetables, which we received at that island, together with the provision of excellent pork at the Society and Friendly Isles, had entirely re-established them. Our second stay at Queen's Charlotte's Sound had likewise furnished us, as before, with abundance of celery and scurvy-grass, which counteracted the noxious effects of salted meat; so that we were, to appearance, in a good state of health at our second departure from thence. It may, however, justly be questioned, whether the continual hardships and labours which we had undergone, had not in reality made the shew of health deceitful, and impaired the body so much that it was not able to resist so long as it had formerly done. The officers and passengers entered upon this second cruize under several difficulties which did not exist before. They had now no live-stock to be compared to that which they took from the Cape of Good Hope; and the little store of provisions which had supplied their table with variety in preference to that of the common sailor, was now so far consumed, that they were nearly upon a level, especially as the seamen were inured to that way of life by constant habit almost from their infancy; and the others had never experienced it before. The hope of meeting with new lands was vanished, the topics of common conversation were exhausted, the cruize to the south could not present any thing

new,

new, but appeared in all its chilling horrors before us, and the absence of our consort doubled every danger. We had enjoyed a few agreeable days between the tropics, we had feasted as well as the produce of various islands would permit, and we had been entertained with the novelty of many objects among different nations; but, according to the common vicissitudes of fortune, this agreeable moment was to be replaced by a long period of fogs and frosty weather, of fasting, and of tedious uniformity. The late Abbé Chappe, in his voyage to California, (or his compiler, M. Cassini, in his name,) observes *, " that variety alone has charms for " the traveller, who goes in quest of her from one country " to another." His philosophy is at the same time of such an exalted nature, that he pronounces † " the life which " is led at sea to be tedious and uniform only to those who " are not accustomed to look round them, and who be- " hold all nature with the eye of indifference." Had the good Abbé been unfortunate enough to make a visit to the antarctic circle, without the company of several hundred fattened fowls, which kept him in good humour on his short trip from Cadiz to Vera Cruz, his philosophy would not have taken so high a flight. But though he found variety at sea, he was not so fortunate in Mexico ‡. Here he crossed great tracts of uncultivated country and extensive forests, he saw nature in a savage state, allowed that she was rich and

* Pag. 11.   † Pag. 13.   ‡ Pag. 11.

beautiful;

beautiful; but, in the space of a few days, her multiplicity of charms became insipid and uniform in his eyes. And yet this traveller assures us, that he was astronomer, botanist, zoologist, mineralogist, chymist, and philosopher!

We quitted the shores of New Zeeland with ideas very different from those of Abbé Chappe; and if any thing alleviated the dreariness of the prospect with a great part of our ship-mates, it was the hope of completing the circle round the South-Pole in a high latitude during the next inhospitable summer, and of returning to England within the space of eight months. This hope contributed to animate the spirits of our people during the greatest part of our continuance in bad weather; but in the end it vanished like a dream, and the only thought which could make them amends, was the certainty of passing another season among the happy islands in the torrid zone.

CHAP.

C H A P. III.

The second course towards the high southern latitudes from New Zee-
land to Easter Island.

THE morning after we had taken our departure, we   Saturday 17.
had a N. N. W. wind, which raised the thermometer
to 64 deg. The two next days it stood at 54 deg. then at
48; and when we were in about 49° of south latitude, at
44½ deg. On the 28th of November, we observed a number of seals, or perhaps sea-lions, passing by us at a diftance towards the land which we had left. From that time
to the 6th of December we daily saw great flocks of blue   December.
                                                             Monday 6.
and other petrels, together with the different species of albatrosses, the skuas or grey gulls, many pinguins, and
abundance of sea-weed. About seven in the evening, on
that day, we were in the latitude of 51° 33' south, and
long. 180°; consequently just at the point of the antipodes of London. The remembrance of domestic felicity,
and of the sweets of society, called forth a sigh from every
heart which felt the tender ties of filial or parental affection.
We are the first Europeans, and I believe I may add, the
first human beings, who have reached this point, where it
is probable none will come after us. A common report
prevails indeed in England concerning Sir Francis Drake,.
                                                        who

1778.
December.
who is faid to have vifited the antipodes, which the legend
expreffes by " his having paffed under the middle arch of
" London-bridge:" but this is a miftake, as his track lay
along the coaft of America, and probably originates from
his having paffed the *periani*, or the point in 180° long. on
the fame circle of north latitude, on the coaft of California.

Friday 10.
In proportion as we advanced to the fouthward the thermometer fell; and on the 10th, in the morning, the wind
coming more ahead, it defcended to 37°. At noon we had
reached the latitude of 59° fouth, without having met
with any ice, though we fell in with it the preceding year
on the 10th of December, between the 50th and 51ft deg.
of fouth latitude. It is difficult to account for this difference; perhaps a fevere winter preceding our firft courfe from
the Cape of Good Hope, might accumulate more ice that
year than the next, which is the more probable, as we
learnt at the Cape that the winter had been fharper there
than ufual; perhaps a violent ftorm might break the polar
ice, and drive it fo far to the northward as we found it; and
perhaps both thefe caufes might concur, with others, to produce this effect.

Sunday 12.
On the 11th, at night, the cold encreafed, the thermometer ftanding at 34 deg. and at four o'clock the next
morning a large ifland of floating ice was feen ahead, which
we paffed an hour afterwards. At eight o'clock the thermometer was already at 31½ deg. the air being probably re-
frigerated

frigerated by the ice, though we did not see more than
this one piece. At noon we found the latitude to be 61°
46' south. The next morning the thermometer stood at
31 deg. and we ran to the eastward with a fresh breeze,
though we had a surprising fall of snow, which filled the
air to such a degree that we could not see ten yards before
us. Our friend Mahine had already expressed his surprize
at several little snow and hail showers on the preceding
days, this phænomenon being utterly unknown in his country. The appearance of "white stones," which melted in
his hand, was altogether miraculous in his eyes, and
though we endeavoured to explain to him that cold was
the cause of their formation, yet I believe his ideas on that
subject were never very clear. The heavy fall of snow this
day surprised him more than what he had seen before, and
after a long consideration of its singular qualities, he told
us he would call it the *white rain* when he came back to his
country. He did not see the first ice on account of the early
hour of the morning; but two days after, in about 65 deg.
of south latitude, he was struck with astonishment upon
seeing one of the largest pieces, and the day following presented him with an extensive field of ice, which blocked up
our farther progress to the south, and gave him great pleasure, supposing it to be land. We told him that so far from
being land, it was nothing but fresh water, which we
found some difficulty to convince him of at first, till we

VOL. I.　　　　Y y y　　　　shewed

shewed him the ice which was formed in the scuttled cask
on the deck. He assured us, however, that he would at all
events call this the *white land*, by way of distinguishing it
from all the rest. Already, at New Zeeland, he had collected a number of little slender twigs, which he carefully tied
in a bundle, and made use of instead of journals. For
every island which he had seen and visited, after his departure from the Society Isles, he had selected a little twig; so
that his collection amounted at present to nine or ten, of
which he remembered the names perfectly well in the
same order as we had seen them, and the white land, or
whennua teatea, was the last. He enquired frequently how
many other countries we should meet with in our way to
England, and formed a separate bundle of them, which he
studied every day with equal care as the first. The tedi-
ousness of this part of our voyage probably made him so
eager to know how it would end; and the salt provisions,
together with the cold climate, contributed to disgust him.
His usual amusement was to separate the red feathers from
the aprons, used in dancing, which he had purchased at
Tonga-Tabboo, and to join eight or ten of them together
into a little tuft, by means of coco-nut core. The rest of
his time he passed in walking on deck, visiting the officers
and petty officers, and warming himself by the fire in the
captain's cabin. We took this opportunity to improve in
the knowledge of his language, and, by degrees, revised
the

the whole vocabulary which we had collected at the Society Isles. By this method we became possessed of a fund of useful intelligence concerning his country and the adjacent isles, which led us to make many enquiries at our subsequent return to those islands.

The ice-fields appeared, in different parts of the horizon, about us on the 15th in the morning, so that we were in a manner embayed; and, as we saw no possibility of advancing to the south, we ran to the N. N. E. to get clear of them. The weather, which was already foggy, became thicker towards noon, and made our situation, amidst a great number of floating rocks of ice, extremely dangerous. About one o'clock, whilst the people were at dinner, we were alarmed by the sudden appearance of a large island of ice just a head of us. It was absolutely impossible either to wear or tack the ship*, on account of its proximity, and our only resource was to keep as near the wind as possible, and to try to weather the danger. We were in the most dreadful suspense for a few minutes, and though we fortunately succeeded, yet the ship passed within her own length to windward of it. Notwithstanding the constant perils to which our course exposed us in this unexplored ocean, our ship's company were far from being so uneasy as might have been expected; and, as in battle the sight of death becomes familiar and often unaffecting, so here, by daily experiencing

* i. e. To go round either with or against the wind.

Y y y 3   such

such hair-breadth efcapes, we paffed unconcernedly on, as
if the waves, the winds, and rocks of ice had not the power
to hurt us. The pieces of ice had a variety of fhapes, in
the fame manner as thofe which we had obferved to the
fouthward of the Indian Ocean; and many pyramids, obe-
lifks, and church-fpires appeared from time to time. Their
height was not much inferior to that which we had obferved among the firft iflands of ice in 1772; and many likewife refembled them in being of a great extent and perfectly
level at top.

The number of birds which we had hitherto met with
on our paffage, would have perfuaded any other voyagers
but ourfelves of the approach of land. We were, however,
fo much ufed to their appearance on the fea at prefent, as
never once to form any expectation of difcovering land
from that circumftance. Flocks of blue petrels and pintadas, many albatroffes, with now and then a folitary fkua
had attended us every day; and to thefe, fince our approach
to the ice, we could join the fnowy and antarctic petrels and
the fulmars. However, pinguins, fea-weed, or feals, had
not been obferved fince the 10th.

The weather, which was extremely moift and difagreeably cold, proved unfavourable to the doves and pigeons
which many people had purchafed at the Society and Friendly Iflands, and to the finging-birds which they had been at
great pains to catch alive at New Zeeland. We had five doves

21

at our departure from this country, all which died one after another before the 16th of December, being much more
expofed to the cold in our cabins, than in the failors births.
The thermometer in our cabins was never more than 5 deg.
higher than in the open air on deck, and their fituation
abreaft of the main-maft, where the ftrain of the fhip is
greateft, expofed them to currents of air, and made them
admit water like fieves.

On the 16th, in the afternoon, and on the 17th, we
hoifted out our boats and collected fome loofe pieces of ice
to fill our empty cafks with frefh water. The ice which
we picked up was old and fpungy, and impregnated with
faline particles, from having long been in a ftate of decay;
therefore did not afford us very good water, but it was
drinkable, particularly if we let the pieces of ice lie on deck
for fome time, by which means the falt-water was almoft
entirely drained off. From this time till the 20th we faw
no birds about us, which difappeared without any vifible
caufe; but on that day fome albatroffes appeared again.

Having left the ice behind which obftructed our paffage,
we had gradually advanced to the fouthward again, that
being our principal object, and on the 20th in the afternoon, we croffed the antarctic circle the fecond time during
our voyage. The weather was wet and foggy, ice iflands
were numerous around us, and the gale was very brifk.
Many antarctic petrels, and a whale which fpouted up the
water,

water near us, feemed to indicate our entrance into the frigid zone. At night two feals appeared, which we had not feen for fourteen days paft, and gave fome faint hopes of feeing land to feveral of our fhipmates; but our courfe difappointed their expectations, by continuing within the circle as far as 67° 12' S. lat. for feveral days following.

On the 23d in the afternoon, we were furrounded with iflands of ice, and the fea was in a manner covered with fmall fragments. The fhip was therefore brought to, the boats hoifted out, and a great quantity of good ice taken on board. The birds were at prefent very numerous about us again, and fome antarctic and other petrels were fhot and taken up, which we had an opportunity of drawing and defcribing. About this time many perfons were afflicted with violent rheumatic pains, head-aches, fwelled glands, and catarrhal fevers, which fome attributed to the ufe of ice-water. My father, who had complained of a cold for feveral days paft, was obliged to keep his bed to-day, having a fevere rheumatifm with a fever. His complaint feemed rather to arife from the wretched accommodations which he had on board, every thing in his cabin rotting in the wet which it admitted, and being mouldy. The cold was fo fenfible there this day in particular, that he found only a difference of two degrees and a half between the thermometer there, and that upon the deck.

After

After hoifting in our boats we made fail to the northward, as much as a contrary wind permitted, during all the night and the next day. On the 25th, the weather was clear and fair, but the wind died away to a perfect calm, upwards of ninety large ice iflands being in fight at noon. This being Chriftmas-day, the captain according to cuftom, invited the officers and mates to dinner, and one of the lieutenant's entertained the petty-officers. The failors feafted on a double portion of pudding, regaling themfelves with the brandy of their allowance, which they had faved for this occafion fome months before-hand, being follicitous to get very drunk, though they are commonly follicitous about nothing elfe. The fight of an immenfe number of icy maffes, amongft which we drifted at the mercy of the current, every moment in danger of being dafhed to pieces againft them, could not deter the failors from indulging in their favourite amufement. As long as they had brandy left, they would perfift to keep Chriftmas "like Chriftians," though the elements had confpired together for their deftruction. Their long acquaintance with a fea-faring life had inured them to all kinds of perils, and their heavy labour, with the inclemencies of weather, and other hardfhips, making their mufcles rigid and their nerves obtufe, had communicated infenfibility to the mind. It will eafily be conceived, that as they do not feel for themfelves fufficiently to provide for their own fafety, they

muft

muſt be incapable of feeling for others. Subjected to a very
ſtrict command, they alſo exerciſe a tyrannical ſway over
thoſe whom fortune places in their power. Accuſtomed to
face an enemy, they breathe nothing but war. By force
of habit even killing is become ſo much their paſſion, that
we have ſeen many inſtances during our voyage, where
they have expreſſed a horrid eagerneſs to fire upon the natives on the ſlighteſt pretences. Their way of life in
general prevents their enjoying domeſtic comforts; and
groſs animal appetites fill the place of purer affections.

> At laſt, extinct each ſocial feeling, fell
> And joyleſs inhumanity pervades
> And petrifies the heart.——— THOMSON.

Though they are members of a civilized ſociety, they
may in ſome meaſure be looked upon as a body of uncivilized men, rough, paſſionate, revengeful, but likewiſe
brave, ſincere, and true to each other.

At noon the obſervation of the ſun's altitude determined
our latitude to be 66° 22' ſouth, ſo that we were juſt returned out of the antarctic circle. We had ſcarcely any
night during our ſtay in the frigid zone, ſo that I find
ſeveral articles in my father's journal, written by the light
of the ſun, within a few minutes before the hour of midnight. The ſun's ſtay below the horizon was ſo very
ſhort this night likewiſe, that we had a very ſtrong twilight
all the time. Mahine was ſtruck with the greateſt aſtoniſh-
ment

ment at this phænomenon, and would fcarcely believe his fenfes. All our endeavours to explain it to him mifcarried, and he affured us he defpaired of finding belief among his countrymen, when he fhould come back to recount the wonders of petrified rain, and of perpetual day. The firft Venetians who explored the northern extremes of the European continent, were equally furprifed at the continual appearance of the fun above the horizon, and relate that they could only diftinguifh day from night, by the inftinct of the fea-fowl, which went to rooft on fhore, for the fpace of four hours [*]. As we were in all likelihood far diftant from any land, this indication failed us, and we have often obferved numerous birds on the wing about us all the night, and particularly great flocks of different fpecies, fo late as eleven o'clock.

At fix in the evening, we counted one hundred and five large maffes of ice around us from the deck, the weather continuing very clear, fair, and perfectly calm. Towards noon the next day we were ftill in the fame fituation, with a very drunken crew, and from the maft-head obferved o ne hundred and fixty-eight ice-iflands, fome of which were half a mile long, and none lefs than the hull of the fhip.

---

[*] Pietro Quirino failed in April 143?, and was miferably fhipwrecked at the ifle of Roeft or Ruften, on the coaft of Norway, under the polar circle, in January 143?.—See Navigationi et Viaggi raccolti di G. B. Ramufio. Venet. 1574. vol. II. p. 204, 210.

Z z z The

1773.
December.
The whole scene looked like the wrecks of a shattered world, or as the poets describe some regions of hell; an idea which struck us the more forcibly, as execrations, oaths, and curses re-echoed about us on all sides.

Monday 27.
A faint breeze sprung up in the afternoon, with which we made slow advances to the northward, the number of ice islands decreasing in proportion as we receded from the antarctic circle. About four the next morning, we hoisted out our boats, and took in a fresh provision of ice. The weather changed soon after, the wind coming about to the north-eastward, which brought on much snow and sleet. My father, and twelve other persons were again much afflicted with rheumatic pains, and confined to their beds. The scurvy did not yet appear under any dangerous form in the ship, and all those who had any slight symptoms of it, amongst whom I was one, drank plentifully of the fresh wort, quite warm, twice a day, and abstained as much as possible from salt-diet. A general languor and sickly look however, manifested itself in almost every person's face, which threatened us with more dangerous consequences. Captain Cook himself was likewise pale and lean, entirely lost his appetite, and laboured under a perpetual costiveness.

1774.
January.
Saturday 1.
We advanced to the northward as much as the winds would permit us, and lost sight of the ice on the first of Tuesday 4. January 1774, in 59° 7' S. latitude. On the 4th, the
wind

wind blowing from the weſtward was very boiſterous, and
obliged us to keep all our ſails double-reefed; the ſea ran
high, and the ſhip worked very heavily, rolling violently
from ſide to ſide. This continued till the 6th at noon,
when, having reached 51° of S. latitude, we bore away
from the wind, to the N. N. E. We were now within a
few degrees of the track which we had made in June and
July laſt, in going from New Zeeland to Taheitee, and had
directed our courſe towards it, in order to leave no conſiderable part of this great ocean unexplored. As far as
we had hitherto advanced, we had found no land, not even
indications of land; our firſt track had croſſed the South
Sea in the middle latitudes, or between 40 and 50 degrees.
In our courſe till Chriſtmas, we had explored the greateſt
part of it between 60 degrees and the antarctic circle; and
the preſent courſe to the northward had croſſed the ſpace
between the two former runs. If any land has eſcaped us,
it muſt be an iſland, whoſe diſtance from Europe, and
ſituation in an uncouth climate cannot make it valuable
to this country. It is obvious that to ſearch a ſea of ſuch
extent as the South Sea, in order to be certain of the exiſtence, or non-exiſtence of a ſmall iſland, would require many
voyages in numberleſs different tracks, and cannot be effected in a ſingle expedition. But it is ſufficient for us,
to have proved that no large land or continent exiſts in the

South

South Sea within the temperate zone, and that if it exists at all, we have at least confined it within the antarctic circle.

The long continuance in these cold climates began now to hang heavily on our crew, especially as it banished all hope of returning home this year, which had hitherto supported their spirits. At first a painful despondence, owing to the dreary prospect of another year's cruize to the South, seemed painted in every countenance; till by degrees they resigned themselves to their fate, with a kind of sullen indifference. It must be owned however, that nothing could be more dejecting than the entire ignorance of our future destination, which, without any apparent reason, was constantly kept a secret to every person in the ship.

We now stood to the north-eastward for a few days, till we came so far as $47^{\circ} 52'$ south latitude, where the thermometer rose to 52 degrees. On that day, which was the
11th, at noon, the course was directed to the S. E. again, though this frequent and sudden change of climate could not fail of proving very hurtful to our health in general.
On the 15th the wind encreased very much, and in a short time blew a tempestuous gale, which took

> ———— the ruffian billows by the top
> Curling their monstrous heads and hanging them
> With deaf'ning clamours in the flippery shrouds.   SHAKESPEARE.

At nine o'clock a huge mountainous wave struck the ship on the beam, and filled the decks with a deluge of water.

It

It poured through the sky-light over our heads, and extinguished the candle, leaving us for a moment in doubt, whether we were not entirely overwhelmed and sinking into the abyss. Every thing was afloat in my father's cabin, and his bed was thoroughly soaked. His rheumatism, which had now afflicted him above a fortnight, was still so violent as to have almost deprived him of the use of his legs, and his pains redoubled in the morning. Our situation at present was indeed very dismal, even to those who preserved the blessing of health; to the sick, whose crippled limbs were tortured with excessive pain, it was insupportable. The ocean about us had a furious aspect, and seemed incensed at the presumption of a few intruding mortals. A gloomy melancholy air loured on the brows of our shipmates, and a dreadful silence reigned amongst us. Salt meat, our constant diet, was become loathsome to all, and even to those who had been bred to a nautical life from their tender years: the hour of dinner was hateful to us, for the well known smell of the victuals had no sooner reached our nose, than we found it impossible to partake of them with a hearty appetite.

It will appear from hence that this voyage was not to be compared to any preceding one, for the multitude of hardships and distresses which attended it. Our predecessors in the South Sea had always navigated within the tropic, or at least in the best parts of the temperate zone; they had almost

almoſt conſtantly enjoyed mild eaſy weather, and ſailed in ſight of lands, which were never ſo wretchedly deſtitute as not to afford them refreſhments from time to time. Such a voyage would have been merely a party of pleaſure to us; continually entertained with new and often agreeable objects, our minds would have been at eaſe, our converſation cheerful, our bodies healthy, and our whole ſituation deſirable and happy. Ours was juſt the reverſe of this; our ſouthern cruizes were uniform and tedious in the higheſt degree; the ice, the fogs, the ſtorms and ruffled ſurface of the ſea formed a diſagreeable ſcene, which was ſeldom cheered by the reviving beams of the ſun; the climate was rigorous and our food deteſtable. In ſhort, we rather vegetated than lived; we withered, and became indifferent to all that animates the ſoul at other times. We ſacrificed our health, our feelings, our enjoyments, to the honour of purſuing a track unattempted before. This was indeed as the poet ſays,

———— propter vitam vivendi perdere cauſas.   JUVENAL.

The crew were as much diſtreſſed as the officers, from another cauſe. Their biſcuit, which had been ſorted at New Zeeland, baked over again, and then packed up, was now in the ſame decayed ſtate as before. This was owing partly to the reviſal, which had been ſo rigorous, that many a bad biſcuit was preſerved among thoſe that were eatable, and partly to the neglect of the caſks, which had not

not been sufficiently fumigated and dried. Of this rotten
bread the people only received two thirds of their usual
allowance, from œconomical principles; but, as that portion is hardly sufficient, supposing it to be all eatable, it
was far from being so when nearly one half of it was rotten. However, they continued in that distressful situation
till this day, when the first mate came to the captain and
complained bitterly that he and the people had not where-
with to satisfy the cravings of the stomach, producing, at
the same time, the rotten and stinking remains of his biscuit. Upon this the crew were put to full allowance.
The captain seemed to recover again as we advanced to the
southward, but all those who were afflicted with rheuma-
tisms continued as much indisposed as ever.

The first ice islands which we met with on this run were
in 62° 30' south, on the 20th, but they did not accumulate in number in proportion to our progress, so that we
crossed the antarctic circle again on the 26th, without seeing more than a few solitary pieces. On that day we were
amused with the appearance of land; for after standing on
towards it for some hours, it vanished in clouds. The next
day, at noon, we were in 67° 52' south; consequently to the
southward of any of our former tracks, and met with no
ice to stop us. The blue petrels, the little storm petrels,
and the pintadas still accompanied us, but albatrosses had
left us some time ago. We were now once more in the
regions

Thursday 19.

Wednesd. 25.

Thursday 27.

regions of perpetual day *, and had sunshine at the hour of midnight.

On the 28th, in the afternoon, we passed a large bed of broken ice, hoisted out the boats, and took up a great quantity, which afforded a seasonable supply of fresh water. At midnight the thermometer was not lower than 34°, and the next morning we enjoyed the mildest sunshine we had ever experienced in the frigid zone. My father therefore ventured upon deck for the first time after a month's confinement.

We now entertained hopes of penetrating to the south as far as other navigators have done towards the north pole; but on the 30th, about seven o'clock in the morning, we discovered a solid ice-field of immense extent before us, which bore from E. to W. A bed of fragments floated all round this field, which seemed to be raised several feet high above the level of the water. A vast number of icy masses, some of a very great height, were irregularly piled up upon it, as far as the eye could reach. Our latitude was at this time 71° 10' south, consequently less than 19 deg. from the pole; but as it was impossible to proceed farther, we put the ship about, well satisfied with our perilous expedition, and almost persuaded that no navigator will care to come after, and much less attempt to pass beyond us.

* In the frozen zone, where the sun remains six months above and six months below the horizon, dividing the year into one long day and night.

Our

Our longitude at this time was nearly 106° W. The thermometer here was at 32°, and a great many pinguins were heard croaking round us, but could not be seen on account of the foggy weather which immediately succeeded.

As often as we had hitherto penetrated to the southward, we had met with no land, but been stopped sooner or later by a solid ice-field, which extended before us as far as we could see. At the same time we had always found the winds moderate and frequently easterly in these high latitudes, in the same manner as they are said to be in the northern frozen zone. From these circumstances my father has been led to suppose, that all the south pole, to the distance of 20 degrees, more or less, is covered with solid ice, of which only the extremities are annually broken by storms, consumed by the action of the sun, and regenerated in winter.

——— flat glacies iners
Menses per omnes.———   HORAT.

This opinion is the less exceptionable, since there seems to be no absolute necessity for the existence of land towards the formation of ice *, and because we have little reason to suppose that there actually is any land of considerable extent in the frigid zone.

We ran to the northward with moderate winds till the 5th of February, when we got a fine fresh breeze after a

* See vol. I. page 95.

short calm. The day after it shifted to S. E. and freshened
so as to blow very hard at night, and split several sails. As
it was favourable for the purpose of advancing to the
northward, the only circumstance that afforded us comfort,
we were far from being concerned at its violence, and in
the next twenty-four hours made upwards of three degrees
of latitude. The same gale assisted us till the 12th, when
we observed the latitude to be 50° 15′ south, our thermometer being once more returned to the milder temperature
of 48 degrees. We were now told that we should spend
the winter season, which was coming on apace, among the
tropical islands of the Pacific Ocean, in the same manner as
we had passed that immediately preceding. The prospect
of making new discoveries, and of enjoying the excellent
refreshments which those islands afford, entirely revived
our hopes, and made us look on our continuance on the
western side of Cape Horne with some degree of satisfaction.

A great number of our people were however afflicted
with very severe rheumatic pains, which deprived them of
the use of their limbs; but their spirits were so low, that
they had no fever. Though the use of that excellent pro-
phylactic the four krout, prevented the appearance of the
scurvy during all the cold weather, yet being made of
cabbage, it is not so nutritive that we could live upon it
without the assistance of biscuit and salt-beef. But the
former

former of these being rotten, and the other almost confumed by the salt, it is obvious that no wholesome juices
could be secreted from thence, which might have kept the
body strong and vigorous. Under these difficulties all our
patients recovered very slowly, having nothing to restore
their strength; and my father, who had been in exquisite
torments during the greatest part of our southern cruize,
was afflicted with tooth-aches, swelled cheeks, fore-throat,
and universal pain till the middle of February, when he
ventured on deck perfectly emaciated. The warm weather
which was beneficial to him, proved fatal to captain Cook's
constitution. The disappearance of his bilious complaint
during our last push to the south, had not been so sincere,
as to make him recover his appetite. The return to the
north therefore brought on a dangerous obstruction, which
the captain very unfortunately flighted, and concealed from
every person in the ship, at the same time endeavouring to
get the better of it by taking hardly any sustenance. This
proceeding, instead of removing, encreased the evil, his
stomach being already weak enough before. He was afflicted with violent pains, which in the space of a few days
confined him to his bed, and forced him to have recourse
to medicines. He took a purge, but instead of producing
the desired effect, it caused a violent vomiting, which was
assisted immediately by proper emetics. All attempts however to procure a passage through his bowels were inef-

4 A 2

fectual;

fectual; his food and medicines were thrown up, and in a few days a moft dreadful hiccough appeared, which lafted for upwards of twenty-four hours, with fuch aftonifhing violence that his life was entirely defpaired of. Opiates and glyfters had no effect, till repeated hot baths, and plafters of theriaca applied on his ftomach, had relaxed his body and inteftines. This however, was not effected till he had lain above a week in the moft imminent danger. Our fervant fell ill about the fame time with the captain, of the fame diforder, and narrowly efcaped, but continued weak and unferviceable the greateft part of our cruize between the tropics.

During this time we advanced to the northward very faft, fo that on the 22d we reached 36° 10 S. latitude, where the albatroffes left us. Our longitude being about 94½ degrees weft from Greenwich, we fteered to the fouth-weftward, in queft of a fuppofed difcovery of Juan Fernandez, which, according to Juan Luis Arias, a Spanifh author, is faid to lie in 40° fouth latitude, and by Mr. Dalrymple's chart in 90° weft from London [*]. We ftood on to the weftward till the 25th at noon, where being in 37° 50′ S. and about 101° W. and feeing no figns of land, we altered our courfe fomething to the northward. The dangerous fituation of captain Cook, was perhaps the reafon, why our track was not continued farther to the

[*] See Mr. Dalrymple's Hiftorical Collection, vol. I. p. 53, and the Chart.

fouth,

south, so as to put this matter entirely out of doubt for the future. It was indeed of the utmost importance at present, to hasten to a place of refreshment, that being the only chance to preserve his life.

On the 26th, captain Cook felt some relief from the medicines which had been administered to him, and during the three following days, recovered so far as to be able to sit up sometimes, and take a little soup. Next to Providence it was chiefly owing to the skill of our surgeon, Mr. Patton, that he recovered to prosecute the remaining part of our voyage, with the same spirit with which it had hitherto been carried on. The care and assiduity with which this worthy man, watched him during his whole illness, cannot be sufficiently extolled, as all our hopes of future discoveries, as well as union in the ship, depended solely on the preservation of the captain. The surgeon's extreme attention however, had nearly cost him his own life. Having taken no rest for many nights together, and seldom venturing to sleep an hour by day, he was so much exhausted, that we trembled for his life, upon which that of almost every man in the ship in great measure depended. He was taken ill with a bilious disorder, which was dangerous on account of the extreme weakness of his stomach, and it is more than probable, that if we had not speedily fallen in with land, from whence we collected some slight refreshments, he must have fallen a sacrifice to that rigorous perseverance and

extreme

extreme punctuality with which he difcharged the feveral duties of his profeffion.

We had eafterly winds ever fince the 22d of February, which was probably owing to the fituation of the fun, ftill continuing in the fouthern hemifphere. The weather was warm and comfortable again, the thermometer being at 70 degrees; and fome grey terns were feen from time to time, which according to our friend Mahine's account,

never went to a great diftance from land. On the firft of March, fome bonitos appeared fwiftly fwimming paft the fhip, and the next day, being in 30° degrees of latitude, we faw tropic birds again.

The fcurvy now appeared with very ftrong fymptoms in the fhip, and I was particularly afflicted with it. Excruciating pains, livid blotches, rotten gums, and fwelled legs, brought me extremely low in a few days, almoft before I was aware of the diforder; and my ftomach being very weak, through abftinence from an unwholefome and loathed diet, I could not take the wort in fufficient quantity to remove my complaint. The fame cafe exifted with regard to a number of other people, who crawled about the decks with the greateft difficulty.

We had almoft calm weather from the 3d to the 6th, the fky was clear, and the warmth and ferenity of the weather remarkably pleafing; but we were impatient to proceed to

a place

a place of refreshment, and this delay ill suited with our wishes.

On the 5th, at night, we saw some towering clouds and a haze on the horizon to the southward, from whence we hoped for a fair wind. Already, during night, we had some smart showers, and at eight o'clock the next morning we saw the surface of the sea curled to the south-eastward, upon which we trimmed our sails, and advanced again with a fair wind. The next morning four large albecores were caught, the least of which weighed twenty-three pounds. They afforded us a most delicious repast, it being now an hundred days since we had tasted any fresh fish. Shearwaters, terns, noddies, gannets, and men of war birds appeared numerous about us, hunting the shoals of flying-fish which our ship, the bonitos, albecores, and dolphins had frightened out of the water.

We reached the 27th degree of S. latitude on the 8th at noon, and then shaped our course due west in search of EASTER ISLAND, discovered by Jacob Roggewein in 1722, and since visited by the Spaniards in 1770 *, who gave it the name of St. Charles's Island. On the 10th, in the morning, the birds of the grey tern-kind were innumerable about us, whilst we advanced at the rate of seven miles an hour. We lay to during night, being apprehen-

* See Mr. Dalrymple's Historical Collection of Voyages, vol. II. pag. 851. also his letter to Dr. Hawkesworth, 1773.

five

1774.
March. five of falling in with the land, which we actually discovered at five o'clock the next morning. The joy which this
fortunate event spread on every countenance is scarcely to
be described. We had been an hundred and three days
out of sight of land; and the rigorous weather to the south,
the fatigues of continual attendance during storms, or
amidst dangerous masses of ice, the sudden changes of
climate, and the long continuance of a noxious diet, all
together had emaciated and worn out our crew. The expectation of a speedy end to their sufferings, and the hope
of finding the land stocked with abundance of fowls and
planted with fruits, according to the accounts of the Dutch
navigator, now filled them with uncommon alacrity and
cheerfulness.

> E l'uno e 'l altro il mostra, e in tanto oblia
> La noia, e 'l mal de la passata via.   TASSO.

We advanced but slowly towards the land by day, to the
great disappointment of all on board, who became more
eager in proportion as new difficulties arose to prolong
their distresses. The land appeared of a moderate height,
and divided into several hills, which gently sloped from
their summits; its extent did not seem to be considerable,
and we were at too great a distance to be able to form any
Saturday 12. conjecture as to its productions. The next morning we
were becalmed within five leagues of the island, which had
then a black and somewhat disagreeable appearance. We
amused

amufed ourfelves with catching fharks, feveral of which fwam about the fhip, and eagerly fwallowed the hook, which was baited with falt pork or beef. In the afternoon a breeze fprung up, with which we flood towards the fhore, in great hopes of reaching an anchoring-place before night. The land did not look very promifing as we advanced, there being little verdure, and fcarcely any bufhes upon it; but to us who had lingered fo long under all the diftreffes of a tedious cruize at fea, the moft barren rock would have been a welcome fight. In our way we perceived a great number of black pillars ftanding upright, near two hummocks, and in different groups. They feemed to be the fame which Roggewein's people took for idols*; but we gueffed already, at that time, that they were fuch monuments, in memory of the dead, as the Taheitians and other people in the South Seas erect near their burying-places, and call E-TEE.

The wind, which was contrary and very faint, the approach of night, and the want of an anchoring-place on the caft fide of the ifland, difappointed us once more, and forced us to pafs another night under fail, during which we faw feveral fires in the neighbourhood of the pillars above-mentioned. The Dutch, who likewife obferved them, called them facrifices to the idols; but it feems to be more probable that they were only lighted to drefs the food of the natives.

---

* See Mr. Dalrymple's Hiftorical Collection of Voyages, &c. vol. II. p. 91.

We passed the night in making several trips, in order to keep to windward of the island and as near it as possible, resolving to pursue our search of anchorage the next day. In the mean time we reflected on the excellent means of ascertaining the longitude, with which our ship had been furnished, and which had carried us exactly to this island, though several former navigators, such as Byron, Carteret, and Bougainville had missed it, after taking their departure from islands at so short a distance from it as those of Juan Fernandez [*]. Captain Carteret it seems was only missed by an erroneous latitude in the geographical tables which he confulted; but this could not be the case with the rest. We had the greatest reason to admire the ingenious construction of the two watches which we had on board, one executed by Mr. Kendal, exactly after the model of that made by Mr. Harrison, and the other by Mr. Arnold on his own plan, both which went with great regularity. The last was unfortunately stopped immediately after our departure from New Zeeland in June 1773, but the other went till our return to England, and gave general satisfaction. It appears, however, that in a long run the observations of distances of the moon from the sun or stars, are more to be depended upon, if they be made with good instruments, than the watches or time-keepers, which frequently change their rates of going. The method of deducing the longitude

[*] Juan Fernandez, properly so called or la de Tierra, and la Mas a fuera.

from

from the diſtances of the ſun and moon, or moon and ſtars, one of the moſt valuable acquiſitions to the art of navigation, muſt immortalize its firſt inventors. TOBIAS MAYER, a German, and profeſſor at Gottingen, was the firſt who undertook the laborious taſk of calculating tables for this purpoſe, for which his heirs received a parliamentary reward. Since his death the method was ſo much facilitated by additional calculations, that the longitude will perhaps never be determined with greater preciſion at ſea by any other means.

The latitude of Eaſter Iſland correſponds within a minute or two with that which is marked in admiral Roggewein's own MS. journal *, and his longitude is only one degree erroneous, our obſervations having aſcertained it in 109° 46′ weſt from Greenwich. The Spaniſh accounts of the latitude are likewiſe exact, but they err in longitude about thirty leagues.

* See the Lives of the Governors of Batavia.—It is there expreſſed 27° 04′ S. latitude, and 265° 42′ E. from Teneriff, or 110° 45′ W. from London.

CHAP.

C H A P.   IV.

An Account of Easter Island, and our Stay there.

ON the 13th, early in the morning, we ran close to the south point of the island, where the shore rose perpendicularly, and consisted of broken rocks, whose cavernous appearance, and black or ferruginous colour, seemed to have been produced by subterraneous fire. Two detached rocks lay about a quarter of a miles off this point; one of them was singular on account of its shape, resembling a huge column or obelisk, and both were the habitations of numerous sea-fowls, which stunned our ears with their discordant screams. Soon after we opened another point about ten miles distant from this, and as we advanced we perceived the ground gently sloping to the sea. On the slope we discovered several plantations by the help of our glasses; but the surface of the isle in general appeared to be extremely dreary and parched, and these plantations were so thinly scattered upon it, that they did not flatter our hopes of meeting with considerable refreshments. However, our eyes, long unused to the enchanting prospect of verdure, were constantly directed towards the shore, where we distinguished a number of people nearly naked, hastily running down from the hills towards the sea-side.

We

We could not perceive that they had any arms, which we immediately interpreted into a sign of a peaceable difposition. In a few minutes we faw them launch a canoe, in which two men came off towards us. They were along fide in a fhort time, having paddled very brifkly, and immediately called out for a rope, naming it by the fame word as the Taheitians. We had no fooner thrown them the rope, than they tied a great clufter of ripe bananas to it, making figns for us to haul it up. The fudden emotions of joy in every countenance, at the fight of this fruit, are fcarcely to be defcribed; they can only be felt in their full extent by people in the fame wretched fituation with ourfelves at that time. At leaft fifty perfons endeavoured to begin a converfation with the people in the canoe, who being addreffed by fo many at once, could not anfwer one of them. Captain Cook fent for fome ribbands, to which he tied fome medals and beads, and lowered them down. in return for their prefent. They feemed to admire them much, but haftened afhore with them immediately. In dropping aftern, they faftened a fmall piece of cloth to a fifhing line which we towed after us; it was immediately hauled up, and appeared to be made of the fame bark as the Taheitian cloth, and coloured yellow. From a few words which they pronounced, we concluded their language to be a dialect of the Taheitian, which we had now found. in both extremities of the South Sea. Their whole appearance

ance confirmed us in this opinion, and proved them issued
from the same stock.   They were of a middle stature, but
rather thin; their features resembled those of the Taheitians,
but were less agreeable: one of them had a beard, which
was cut to the length of about half an inch; the other was
a youth of about seventeen.   They had punctures of the
same nature with those used by the natives of the Society
and Friendly Islands and of New Zeeland; but their whole
body, which was perfectly naked, was marked with them.
The greatest singularity which we observed about them was
the size of their ears, of which the lap or extremity was
stretched out so as almost to rest on the shoulder, and pierced by a very large hole, through which four or five fingers
might be thrust with ease.   This circumstance entirely agreed
with the description which the serjeant-major of Roggewein's ship gives of these people[*].   Their canoe was another curiosity, being patched up of many pieces, each of
which was not more than four or five inches wide, and two
or three feet long.   Its length might be about ten or twelve
feet, its head and stern were raised considerably, but its
middle was very low.   It had an outrigger or balancer
made of three slender poles, and each of the men had a
paddle, of which the blade was likewise composed of several
pieces.   This description also exactly corresponds with the

[*] See Mr. Dalrymple's Historical Collection, vol. II. p. 90, 94, or Histoire
de l'Expedition de Trois Vaisseaux, tome I. p. 133, a la Haye 1739.

Dutch

Dutch account of Roggeweln's voyage, printed at Dort in 1728 *; and sufficiently proved that the island is very destitute of wood, though the contrary is ascertained in the serjeant-major's relation of that voyage †.

Though we struck soundings opposite the place from whence this canoe put off, yet in hopes of finding a better place of anchorage, we ran along the coast of the island, till we came in sight of its northern extremity, which we had already seen the day before from the other side. But being disappointed in our expectation, we put about with a view to return to the place which we had left. A great number of black pillars stood along the shore, many of which were elevated on platforms consisting of several ranges of stone. We could now distinguish something resembling a human head and shoulders towards their upper end; but the lower part appeared to be a rude stone, without being carved into a resemblance of the human shape. Sometimes we perceived two, sometimes four, and even five together in a row; but some were likewise placed by themselves. We saw but few plantations towards the north end, the land being much more bluff or steep there, than about the middle of the island, and we could easily perceive that there was not a tree upon the whole island, which exceeded the height of ten feet.

* See Mr. Dalrymple's Collection, vol. II. pag. 111.
† Ibid. vol. II. p. 951 or Histoire, &c. vol. I. p. 138.

In

In the afternoon we hoifted out a boat, and the mafter went towards the fhore to take foundings in the road, from whence the canoe had come off to us. As foon as the natives perceived our boat on the water, they affembled along fhore, near the place to which our people feemed to direct their courfe. Among a croud of naked men, we faw fome who feemed to be dreffed in a bright cloth of a yellow, or rather orange colour, from whence we fufpected that they were their principal people. We now likewife began to difcern their houfes, which feemed to be extremely low and long, higheft in the middle, and floping down towards both extremities. They much refembled a canoe turned with the keel or bottom upwards. In the middle there feemed to be a fmall entrance or door, which was fo low, that a man of a common fize muft ftoop to get in. Towards evening we let 'go our anchor in about forty fathom, gravelly bottom off the S. W. part of the ifland. The mafter returned prefently after, and brought one of the natives in the boat with him. This bold fellow had jumped into the boat without any ceremony or invitation, while it was clofe to the fhore, and expresfly defired to be brought on board. He was of the middle fize, about five feet eight inches high, and remarkably hairy on the breaft and all over the body. His colour was a chefnut brown, his beard ftrong, but clipped fhort, and of a black colour, as was alfo the hair of his head, which was likewife cut
fhort.

short. His ears were very long, almost hanging on his shoulders, and his legs punctured in compartments after a taste which we had observed no where else. He had only a belt round his middle, from whence a kind of net-work descended before, too thin to conceal any thing from the sight. A string was tied about his neck, and a flat bone, something shaped like a tongue, and about five inches long, was fastened to it, and hung down on the breast. This, he told us, was a porpoise's bone (eevee toharra), expressing it exactly by the same words which a Taheitian would have made use of. To explain himself better, he also called it eevee-eeka, which we well understood to signify the bone of a fish [*]. He was no sooner seated in the boat, than he complained of being cold by shivering, and making various gestures of a very intelligible nature. Mr. Gilbert, the master, therefore gave him a jacket, and put a hat on his head, and in that dress he appeared upon deck. The captain and passengers presented him with nails, medals, and strings of beads, the last of which, he desired to have tied round his head. At the beginning he shewed some marks of fear or diffidence, asking whether we should kill him as an enemy (matte-tao?) but upon being assured of good treatment and friendship on our part, he seemed perfectly secure and unconcerned, and talked of nothing but dancing

[*] Eeys at Taheitee, and eeka at New Zealand and the Friendly Isles mean a fish.

4 C (heeva).

(*Eheva*). It was with some difficulty that we understood him at first; but having enquired for the names by which he distinguished the parts of the body, we soon found them to be nearly the same with those which are used in the Society Isles. If we mentioned a word which he did not comprehend, he repeated it several times with a look which strongly expressed his ignorance of it. As night approached; he said he wanted to go to sleep, and complained of cold. My father gave him a large Taheitee cloth of the thickest sort, in which he wrapped himself, saying he found it comfortably warm. He was afterwards conducted into the master's cabin, where he lay down on a table, and slept very quietly the whole night. Mahine, who had already expressed his impatience to go on shore, was much pleased to find that the inhabitants spoke a language so similar to his own, and attempted to converse with our new visitor several times, but was interrupted by the questions which many other persons in the ship put to him.

We dragged our anchor during night, and drove off the bank, so that we were obliged to set sail again, in order to recover our situation. Immediately after breakfast, captain Cook went ashore with the native, whose name was Maroowahai, together with Mahine, my father, Dr. Sparrman, and myself, though my feet and legs were still swelled excessively, and I was hardly able to walk. We found a snug cove for boats, among a number of rocks which sheltered the

in upon the fhore. About a hundred, or a hundred and
fifty natives were affembled on the fpot where we landed,
almoft all of them naked, fome having only a belt round
the middle, from whence a fmall bit of cloth, fix or eight
inches long, or a little net, hung down before. A very
few of them had a cloak which reached to the knees, made
of cloth, refembling that of Taheitee in the texture, and
ftitched or quilted with thread to make it the more lafting.
Moft of thefe cloaks were painted yellow with the turmeric-
root. The people did not make the leaft unfriendly motion
at our landing, but expreffed a prodigious dread of our
fire-arms, of which they feemed to know the deadly effects.
We faw but few arms among them; fome however had
lances or fpears, made of thin ill-fhapen flicks, and pointed
with a fharp triangular piece of a black glaffy lava (*pumex
vitreus*, Linn.) commonly called Iceland agate. One of them
had a fighting club, made of a thick piece of wood about
three feet long, carved at one extremity; and a few others
had fhort wooden clubs, exactly refembling fome of the
New Zeeland patoo-patoos, which are made of bone. We
obferved fome who had European hats and caps, chequered
cotton handkerchiefs, and ragged jackets of blue woollen-
cloth, which were fo many indubitable teftimonies of the
vifit which the Spaniards had made to this ifland in 1770.
The general appearance of the natives feemed to argue a

4 C 2

great

great sterility of the country. They were inferior in stature to the natives of the Society and Friendly Isles, and to those of New Zeeland, there being not a single person amongst them, who might be reckoned tall. Their body was likewise lean, and their face thinner than that of any people we had hitherto seen in the South Sea. Their want of cloathing, and a great eagerness to obtain our goods without offering any thing in return, seemed altogether to be sufficient marks of poverty. They were all prodigiously punctured on every part of the body, the face in particular; and their women, who were very small and slender limbed, had likewise punctures on the face, which resembled the patches sometimes worn by our ladies. The number of women in the croud did not exceed ten or twelve; they were seldom satisfied with their natural clear brown colour, but painted the whole face with a reddish brown ruddle, over which they laid on the bright orange of the turmeric-root; or ornamented themselves with elegant streaks of white shell-lime. The art of painting is therefore not confined to those ladies who have the happiness to imitate French fashions. The women were all dressed in pieces of cloth, which appeared scanty when compared to the Taheitian-dresses. Both sexes had thin, but not savage features, though the little shelter which their barren country offers against the sun-beams, had contracted their brows sometimes, and drawn the muscles of the face up towards the eye.

eye. Their nofes were not very broad, but rather flat
between the eyes; their lips ftrong, though not fo thick as
thofe of negroes; and their hair black and curling, but
always cut fhort, fo as not to exceed three inches. Their
eyes were dark brown, and rather fmall, the white being
lefs clear than in other nations of the South Seas. Their
ears were remarkable for the great length of the lap, which
frequently hung on the fhoulder, and was pierced with fo
large a hole, that the extremity could be tucked up through
it. In order to bring it to this fize, they wore a leaf of a
fugar cane, which is very elaftic, rolled up in it like a fcroll;
by which means it was always on the ftretch. The violent
action of the fun upon their heads has forced them to contrive various coverings for that part. Many of the men
wore a ring about two inches thick, ftrongly and curioufly
plaited of grafs, and fitting clofe round the head. This
was covered with great quantities of the long black feathers
which decorate the neck of the man of war bird. Others
had huge bufhy caps of brown gulls feathers, which were
almoft as large as the full bottomed wigs of European law-
yers; and ftill others wore a fimple hoop of wood, round
which a number of the long white feathers of a gannet
hung nodding, and waved in the wind. The women wore
a great wide cap, made of very neat mat work; it was
pointed forwards, formed a ridge along the top, and two
large lobes behind on each fide, which we found extremely

1774.
March.

cooling for the head. Mr. Hodges drew the figure of a woman with this cap on, and of a man with one of the other head dresses; both are extremely characteristic of the nation, and have been engraved for captain Cook's account of this voyage. The only ornaments which we saw among them, were the flat pieces of bone in the shape of a tongue, or like a laurel leaf, which both sexes wore hanging on their breast, together with some necklaces and ear-jewels made of shells.

After staying among the natives for some time on the beach, we began to walk into the country. The whole ground was covered with rocks and stones of all sizes, which seemed to have been exposed to a great fire, where they had acquired a black colour and porous appearance. Two or three shrivelled species of grasses grew up among these stones, and in a slight degree softened the desolate appearance of the country. About fifteen yards from the landing-place we saw a perpendicular wall of square hewn stones, about a foot and a half or two feet long, and one foot broad. Its greatest height was about seven or eight feet, but it gradually sloped on both sides, and its length might be about twenty yards. A remarkable circumstance was the junction of these stones, which were laid after the most excellent rules of art, fitting in such a manner as to make a durable piece of architecture. The stone itself of which they are cut is not of great hardness, being a black-

ish

ish brown cavernous and brittle stony lava. The ground
rose from the water's side upwards; so that another wall,
parallel to the first, about twelve yards from it and facing
the country, was not above two or three feet high. The
whole area between the two walls was filled up with soil and
covered with grass. About fifty yards farther to the south
there was another elevated area, of which the surface was
paved with square stones exactly similar to those which
formed the walls. In the midst of this area, there was a
pillar consisting of a single stone, which represented a
human figure to the waist, about twenty feet high, and
upwards of five feet wide. The workmanship of this figure
was rude, and spoke the arts in their infancy. The eyes, nose,
and mouth were scarcely marked on a lumpish ill-shaped
head; and the ears, which were excessively long, quite in the
fashion of the country, were better executed than any other
part, though a European artist would have been ashamed of
them. The neck was clumsy and short, and the shoulders
and arms very slightly represented. On the top of the
head a huge round cylinder of stone was placed upright,
being above five feet in diameter and in height. This
cap, which resembled the head-dress of some Egyptian divinity, consisted of a different stone from the rest of the
pillar, being of a more reddish colour; and had a hole on
each side, as if it had been made round by turning. The
cap together with the head, made one half of the whole:

pillar

pillar which appeared above ground. We did not obferve
that the natives paid any worfhip to thefe pillars, yet they
feemed to hold them in fome kind of veneration, as they
fometimes expreffed a diflike when we walked over the
paved area or pedeftals, or examined the ftones of which it
confifted.

A few of the natives accompanied us farther on into the
country, where we had feen fome bufhes at a diftance,
which we hoped would afford us fomething new. Our road
was intolerably rugged, over heaps of volcanic ftones, which
rolled away under our feet, and againft which we continually hurt ourfelves. The natives, who were accuftomed to
this defolate ground, fkipped nimbly from ftone to ftone
without the leaft difficulty. In our way we faw feveral
black rats running about, which it feems are common to
every ifland in the South Sea. Being arrived at the fhrubbery which we had in view, we found it was nothing but
a fmall plantation of the paper mulberry, of which here, as
well as at Taheitee, they make their cloth. Its ftems were
from two to four feet high, and planted in rows, among
very large rocks, where the rains had wafhed a little foil
together. In the neighbourhood of thefe we faw fome
bufhes of the *bibifcus populneus*, Linn. which is common
alfo in the Society Ifles, where it is one of the numerous
plants made ufe of to dye yellow; and likewife a *mimofa*,
which is the only fhrub that affords the natives fticks for

their

their clubs and pattoo-pattoos, and wood sufficient to patch up a canoe.

We found the face of the country more barren and ruinous the farther we advanced. The small number of inhabitants, who met us at the landing-place, seemed to have been the bulk of the nation, since we met no other people on our walk; and yet for these few we did not see above ten or twelve huts, though the view commanded a great part of the island. One of the sightliest of these was situated on a little hillock, about half a mile from the sea, which we ascended. Its construction was such as evinced the poverty and wretched condition of its owners. The foundation consisted of stones about a foot long, laid level with the surface in two curve lines, converging at the extremities. These lines were about six feet asunder in the middle, but not above one foot at the ends. In every stone of this foundation we observed one or two holes, in each of which a stake was inserted. The middlemost stakes were six feet high, but the others gradually diminished to two feet. On the top the stakes all converged, and were tied by strings to transverse sticks, by which they were kept together. A kind of thatch, made of small sticks, and covered with a neat mat-work of sugar-cane leaves, leaned on each row of stakes, forming a very sharp ridge or angle at the top, and resting firmly on the ground at the bottom. A hole was left on one side, about eighteen inches or two

feet

feet high, over which the people had built a round projecting funnel to keep off the wet.   We crept on all fours
into this opening, and found the inside of the hut perfectly
naked and empty, there being not so much as a wisp of
straw to lie down upon.   We could not stand upright in
any part except just in the middle, and the whole place appeared dark and dismal.   The natives told us they passed
the night in these huts, and we easily conceived their situation to be uncomfortable, especially as we saw so very few
of them, that they must be crammed full, unless the generality of the people lie in the open air, and leave these
wretched dwellings to their chiefs, or make use of them
only in bad weather.

Besides these huts, we observed some heaps of stones piled
up into little hillocks, which had one steep perpendicular
side, where a hole went under ground.   The space within
could be but very small, and yet it is probable that these
cavities likewise served to give shelter to the people during
night.   They may, however, communicate with natural
caverns, which are very common in the lava currents of
volcanic countries.   Such caverns are very frequent in Iceland, famous for having been the dwelling-places of the
ancient inhabitants.   Mr. Ferber, the first mineralogical
historian of Vesuvius, has noticed such a subterraneous hole
in one of the modern lavas of that mountain.   We should
have

have been glad to have afcertained this circumftance, but the natives always denied us admittance into thefe places.

A plantation of fugar-canes and one of bananas adjoined to the houfe we had vifited, and both were in excellent order, confidering the ftony quality of the ground. The bananas were all growing in holes one foot deep, which we fuppofed to be contrived for collecting the rain, and preferving it for a longer time about the plant. The fugar-canes were about nine or ten feet high, even in this parched country, and contained a very fweet juice, which the inhabitants prefented to us very frequently, and particularly whenever we afked for fomething to drink. We concluded from thence that they had no water on the ifland; but coming back to the landing-place we met captain Cook, whom the natives had conducted to a well very clofe to the fea, which was cut deep into the rock, but full of impurities. When our people had cleared it, they found the water in it rather brackifh, but the natives drank of it with much feeming fatisfaction.

Captain Cook had not been very fortunate in trading with the people. They feemed indeed to be fo deftitute as to have no provifions to fpare. A few matted bafkets full of fweet potatoes, fome fugar-canes, bunches of bananas, and two or three fmall fowls ready dreffed, were the whole purchafe which he had made for a few iron tools, and fome Taheitee cloth. He had prefented the people with

4 D 2

beads,

beads, but they always threw them away with contempt, as far as ever they could. Whatever elfe they faw about us, they were defirous of poffeffing, though they had nothing to give in return. Their number was now decreafed nearly to one half, many of them having probably gone home to their dinners; however, the number of women was always remarkably fmall in proportion to the men, there being not above twelve or fifteen at our firft landing, and about fix or feven when we embarked again. They were neither referved nor chafte, and for the trifling confideration of a fmall piece of cloth, fome of our failors obtained the gratification of their defires. Their features were mild enough, and the large pointed cap gave them the air of profeffed wantons.

We returned on board the fhip before noon, and found it at anchor, though we had left it under fail. The frefh fruits and roots which we brought on board, were immediately diftributed as far as they would go, and proved a moft feafonable refrefhment to our fick. We tafted the fowls, which feemed to have been dreffed under-ground, by means of hot ftones being wrapped up in green leaves, in the manner practifed amongft all the nations of the South Sea, whom we had hitherto vifited. The potatoes were of a gold-yellow colour, and as fweet as carrots, therefore not equally palatable to us all; however they were extremely nourifhing, and very antifcorbutic. The juices of
this,

this, and all the other vegetables on this island, seemed to have been concentrated by the dryness of the soil. Their bananas were reckoned very delicious in their kind, by those who were fond of this fruit, and their sugar-canes were sweeter than any we had tasted at Taheitee.

In the afternoon we returned on shore again, and an officer went with another boat to fill water at the well. We found but few natives near the landing-place, and among them was one, who appeared to have some little authority, and readily accompanied the captain wherever he went. He was not so timorous as the rest of his countrymen, but walked boldly along with us, whilst the others were alarmed at the least motion which appeared unusual to them. This disposition, however, did not prevent them from picking our pockets, or stealing any thing which suited them. We had not been half an hour on shore, when one of them came behind Mahine, and very nimbly snatching a black cap from his head, ran off with the greatest velocity over the heaps of rugged stones, where it was impossible to follow him. Mahine was so surprised, that it was some time before he could find words to complain to the captain; and when he did it, the thief was already at a great distance. About the same time, as Mr. Hodges was sitting on a little eminence, and sketching a view of the country, one of the natives ran off with his hat in the same manner. Mr. Wales was standing by him

with

1774.
March. with a mufket in his hand, but very juftly reflected, that
fo flight a crime did not deferve the punifhment of a leaden
bullet.

In our walk along the fea-fhore, we difcovered a few
ftalks of the fame fpecies of celery which is plentiful on the
beaches of New Zeeland, and we alfo found two other little
plants common to that country. Whether thefe plants
originally exifted on the ifland, or fprung up from feeds,
which the current of the fea, or birds by their plumage
might tranfport from the oppofite fide of the ocean, I cannot
venture to determine. We likewife met with a plantation
of yams *(diofcorea alata,* Linn.*)* which in fo poor a *flora* as
that of Eafter Ifland was a great addition. The great cor-
refpondence in the features, cuftoms, and languages of
thefe people, to thofe of other natives of the South Sea
iflands, gave us fome room to hope for fuch domeftic animals among them, as we had obferved at Taheitee or New
Zeeland. But notwithftanding the moft diligent fearch,
we never met with any other than common fowls, which
were of a very fmall breed, and had a dull plumage. It
is true we obferved alfo two or three noddies, which were
fo tame as to fettle on the fhoulders of the natives, but
from thefe individuals we could not conclude, that they
kept a regular breed of them.

About fun-fet we left the watering-place, and walked to
the cove where our boat lay at a grapnel. In our way we
                                                                    paffed

paffed over the area on which the fingle pillar before-men-
tioned was placed. A few natives who ftill accompanied
us, made figns that we fhould defcend, and walk in the
grafs at the foot of the pedeftal; but feeing that we did
not care to underftand their geftures, they made no other
attempt to oppofe our progrefs. We put fome queftions to
the moft intelligent perfons among them, concerning the
nature of thefe ftones, and from what we could underftand,
we concluded that they were monuments erected to the
memory of fome of their areekees, or kings. This led us
to believe that the pedeftal was perhaps to be confidered as
a burying-place, and on looking carefully round it, we
found a number of human bones, which confirmed our
conjecture. The length of thefe bones was exactly fuch as
might be expected in perfons of a middle ftature, and a
thigh-bone which we meafured, exactly correfponded with
that of a perfon about five feet nine inches high. To the
weftward of the cove, there was a range of three pillars,
ftanding on a very large elevated area or pedeftal. This
range the natives diftinguifhed by the name of *hanga-roa*, and
the fingle pillar they called *obeena*. About ten or twelve
people were feated at a little diftance from the laft, round
a fmall fire, over which they had roafted a few potatoes.
Thefe ferved for their fupper, and they offered us fome of
them as we paffed by. We were much furprifed with this
inftance of hofpitality in fo poor a country, efpecially when

we

1774.
March.
we compared it to the cuſtoms of civilized nations, who
have almoſt entirely laid aſide all tender feelings for the
wants of their fellow-creatures.   At the ſame time we were
very glad to be convinced, that the conjectures of the Dutch
concerning the fires which they ſaw on this iſland, were
ill-founded, as we did not ſee the leaſt reaſon to ſuppoſe,
that they were lighted for religious purpoſes.   We now
embarked with a ſmall quantity of potatoes, and with about
ſix or ſeven common plants which we had gathered, and
returned on board.   Thoſe only who were ill of the ſcurvy,
reaped ſome benefit from their viſit to the ſhore.   I who
went out in the morning with my legs exceſſively ſwelled,
and ſo tender that I could hardly ſtand upon them, returned
on board much better ; the ſwelling was ſomething reduced,
and my pains at leaſt were gone.   I could not attribute this
ſudden change to any thing elſe, than the exerciſe I had
taken on ſhore, and perhaps to thoſe ſalutary antiſcorbutic
effluvia of the land, which it is ſaid, are alone ſufficient
to recover thoſe, who have contracted the ſcurvy on a long
cruize at ſea.

Tueſday 15.
Early the next morning, captain Cook appointed a party
of marines and ſailors, under the command of lieutenants
Pickerſgill and Edgecumbe, to reconnoitre the interior parts
of the country, in order to be convinced if poſſible, whether
any other part was better cultivated, or more cloſely inhabited than that which we had hitherto ſeen.   Mr. Wales,
                                                                           Mr.

Mr. Hodges, Dr. Sparrman, and my father affociated with them, fo that the whole party confifted of twenty-feven men.

After breakfaft I accompanied captain Cook and feveral officers afhore, where we found about two hundred inhabitants affembled, amongft whom were fourteen or fifteen women, and very few children. It was impoffible for us to guefs at the caufe of this difproportion in the number of the different fexes; but as all the women we faw were very liberal of their favours, I conjectured at that time, that the married and the modeft, who might be fuppofed to form the greater part, did not care to come near us, or were forced by the men to ftay at their dwellings in the remote parts of the ifland. Thofe few who appeared were the moft lafcivious of their fex, that perhaps have ever been noticed in any country, and fhame feemed to be entirely unknown to them; our failors likewife difclaimed all acquaintance with modefty, for nothing but the fhadow of the gigantic monument fcreened them from the fun.

Mr. Patton, lieutenant Clerke, and myfelf left the feafide, where the concourfe was greateft, and took a walk into the country. The heat of the fun was very violent, the beams being reverberated from the broken ground, and there was not a fingle tree to give us fhelter. My companions had taken their fowling-pieces in hopes of meeting with fome birds; but they were greatly difappointed, there

VOL. I.   4 E   being

being probably no other land-birds on the island than the
common fowl, which were tame and extremely scarce. We
followed one of the paths which the natives had made, till
we came to a cultivated spot, consisting of several fields
planted with sweet potatoes, yams, and eddoes, together
with a species of night-shade, which is made use of at Taheitee and the neighbouring islands as a vulnerary remedy,
(*solanum nigrum?*) and may, for ought I know, be cultivated here for the same purpose. The grass, which commonly springs up among the stones on the uncultivated
soil, was here carefully plucked up, and spread over the
whole plantation as a manure, or perhaps to preserve it in
some measure from the parching beams of the sun. It
should seem from these circumstances that the natives are
not altogether ignorant of rural œconomy, and till the
ground at a great expence of time and labour. At a little
distance from these fields we met with two huts, constructed exactly like that which I have mentioned page 569, but
much smaller. The entrance was stopped up with a great
quantity of small brushwood, and we at first imagined that
we heard the voices of women within, but after listening
for some time we heard nothing farther to confirm us in
this belief. We rambled from thence to the top of a hillock covered with shrubberies, which we found to consist
of nothing but a species of *mimosa*, that scarcely attained the
height of eight feet, and afforded us very little shelter from
the

the fun. Here we refled a while, and then defcended by a different route into another fet of fields, which were treated in the fame manner as the reft. None of them had any fort of enclofures, though the hiftorians of Rogge-wein's voyage, who feem to have confulted fancy more than truth, make mention of them. The encreafing heat of the day had entirely exhaufted us, when we had ftill a confiderable way to make down to the fea-fide. Fortunate-ly we paffed by a native who was at work, gathering pota-toes in one of the fields. We complained of great thirft to him, upon which, though he was an old man, he imme-diately ran to a large plantation of fugar-canes, and brought us a great load of the beft and juicieft on his back. We made him fome prefents in return for them, cut them into walking-fticks, and, as we went along, gradually peeled and fucked them, finding their juice extremely refrefhing.

At our return to the landing-place we found captain Cook ftill occupied in trading with the inhabitants, who brought him fome fowls ready dreffed, and fome matted bafkets full of fweet potatoes, but fometimes deceived him by filling the bafket with ftones, and only laying a few potatoes at the top. The moft valuable article of trade on our part were empty coco-nut fhells, which we had re-ceived at the Society and Friendly Iflands; but they were not current, unlefs the hole in them was very fmall, or un-lefs they had a cover. The Taheitian and European cloths

4 E 2

were

were valued in the next degree according to the size of the pieces; and iron-ware bore an inferior price. The greatest part of the natives who traded with us instantly ran off with the cloth, nut-shell, or the nail which had been given in exchange for their potatoes, as if they were apprehensive that we might repent of our bargain, even though they dealt honestly with us. Some among them were bold enough to run off with what they had received, as the price of their provisions, before they had delivered up the goods for which we had bargained. From such circumstances the deplorable condition of the natives became more and more conspicuous. The scarcity of cloth among them was extremely great, most of the people being forced to go naked; but this did not prevent their selling what little cloth they had in exchange for that of Taheitee. The desire of possessing this cloth prompted them to expose to sale several articles which perhaps they would not have parted with so easily under other circumstances. Among these were their different caps or head-dresses, their necklaces, ornaments for the ear, and several human figures, made of narrow pieces of wood about eighteen inches or two feet long, and wrought in a much neater and more proportionate manner than we could have expected, after seeing the rude sculpture of the statues. They were made to represent persons of both sexes; the features were not very pleasing, and the whole figure was much too long to be natural; however, there was something cha-

racteristic

1774.
March.

racteristic in them, which shewed a taste for the arts. The wood of which they were made was finely polished, close-grained, and of a dark-brown, like that of the casuarina. But as we had not yet seen this tree growing here, we eagerly expected the return of our party, hoping they would make some discoveries to explain this circumstance. Mahine was most pleased with these carved human figures, the workman of which much excelled those of the *e Tees* in his country, and he purchased several of them, assuring us they would be greatly valued at Taheitee. As he took great pains to collect these curiosities, he once met with a figure of a woman's hand, carved of a yellowish wood, nearly of the natural size. Upon examination, its fingers were all bent upwards, as they are in the action of dancing at Taheitee, and its nails were represented very long, extending at least three fourths of an inch beyond the fingers' end. The wood of which it was made was the rare perfume-wood of Taheitee, with the chips of which they communicate fragrance to their oils. We had neither seen this wood growing, nor observed the custom of wearing long nails at this island, and therefore were at a loss to conceive how this piece of well-executed carving could be met with there; we hoped, however, to unravel this circumstance also at the return of our party. Mahine afterwards presented this piece to my father, who has in his turn made a present of it to the British Museum. Mahine was likewise very eager

to

to collect as many feathered caps as he could meet with, especially those which had the feathers of a man of war bird, that bird being very scarce about Taheitee, and much valued on account of its glossy black colour.

Whilst captain Cook continued in the cove, another trade for potatoes was carried on at the watering-place. Here the desire of possessing our goods, made some of the natives guilty of a crime against their own countryman. A field of sweet potatoes was situated close to the well, and a considerable number of people of different ages and sizes, busied themselves in digging them up, and bringing them for sale to our people. They had carried on this occupation for some hours, when another native arrived, who was in a vehement passion with them, and drove them all away, remaining alone to dig the roots up himself. He was the owner of the field, whom the rest had robbed of the fruits of his labour, finding an easy method to dispose of their stolen goods. It is not to be doubted that these offences against the laws of civil society, are sometimes committed even at the Society Isles, because the inhabitants have often told us, that they inflicted a capital punishment upon such offenders; but we never saw any instances of it there. On this occasion at Easter Island, we did not observe that they annexed any penalty to the crime, though we saw it committed. Perhaps this is owing to the different degree of civilization of those two cogeneric tribes.

We

We went on board at noon, where we dined on some fowls and potatoes, which we found delicious after the fatigues of the morning. We obferved a few natives on board, who had ventured to fwim off, though the fhip lay about three quarters of a mile from the fhore. They exprefled the moft unbounded admiration at every thing they faw, and every one of them meafured the whole length of the veflel from head to ftern, with his extended arms; fuch a great quantity of timber of fo ftupendous a fize, being altogether incomprehenfible to people whofe canoes were patched of many fmall bits of wood. Among them was one woman, who had arrived on board in the fame manner, and carried on a particular traffic of her own. She vifited feveral of the inferior officers, and then addreffed herfelf to the failors, emulating the famous exploits of Meffalina *. A few Englifh rags, and fome pieces of Taheitee cloth, were the fpoils which fhe carried away with her, being fetched off by a man in the patched canoe, which was perhaps the only one in the ifland. Another of her country-women had vifited our fhip the day before, and been equally unbounded in her revels. It remained a doubt with us, whether we fhould moft admire their fuccefs among a fickly crew, exhaufted by the long continuance of a noxious diet, or their own fpirit and infatiate temper.

* See Plin. Hift. Nat. lib. x. c. 63. Tacit. Annal. lib. xi. Juvenal. Sat. vi. 129.
——laffata viris, nec fatiata receffit.

In

In the afternoon we returned to the shore again, and
I walked on the hills to the southward, which rose with a
very easy slope. Here I met with a large plantation of
bananas, beyond which I found some remains of a stone
wall, which was perhaps once the base of a statue. From
thence I crossed some fields, where I saw a family of the
natives at work, taking potatoes out of the ground. I
walked up to their hut, which was one of the smallest I
had yet seen, and as they came about me, I sat down among
them. Their whole number amounted to six or seven
persons, one of whom was a woman, and two were young
boys. They presented me with some sugar-canes, and in
return, I made them a present of a small piece of Taheitee
cloth, which they immediately wrapped about the head.
They did not express that great curiosity which we had
observed among the people of the Society Isles, but soon
returned to their former occupation, in which all were employed without exception. Some of them had head-dresses
made of feathers, which they readily offered to exchange
for pieces of cloth no bigger than a handkerchief. About
the hut I perceived a few fowls, the only ones which I
had seen alive on the island. Their behaviour towards me
was wholly inoffensive, agreeably to the general character
of the nations in the South Sea. From the expressions of
the historians of Roggewein's voyage, it should seem, that
the Dutch very wantonly fired upon the natives, who gave

no

no provocation, and killed a confiderable number of them, intimidating the reft to a great degree. It is probable, that the terror with which they looked upon the deftructive arms of Europeans at that time, and during the late vifit of the Spaniards, was revived among them at our appearance, and had an influence on their general timid behaviour towards us; but it is not to be doubted, at the fame time, that there is a mildnefs, fellow-feeling, and good-nature in their difpofition, which naturally prompts them to treat their vifitors kindly, and even hofpitably, as far as their wretched country will permit.

I returned the fame way by which I came, and foon after went on board the fhip with captain Cook. About nine o'clock a mufket was fired on fhore, as a fignal for a boat, and the pinnace being fent off, returned foon after with our party, who had been to examine the ifland. My father being more fatigued than any body elfe, on account of his long rheumatic complaint, was obliged to go to bed immediately; but the other gentlemen fupped with us, on a few fowls which we had purchafed on fhore, and gave us fome account of their travels. As it will be moft agreeable to fee it in connection, I fhall here infert that which I have extracted from my father's journal.

" Immediately after landing, we walked directly inland or acrofs the country, under the higheft hill which lies towards the fouth, till we came to the other fide of the ifland.

About an hundred natives, and among them four or five women, accompanied us on our march, and fold us a quantity of potatoes and a few fowls, which we added to our stock of provisions. We found the whole country strewed with stones of various sizes, of a cavernous or spongy texture, and of a black, brown, or reddish colour, which had indubitable marks of having been in a volcanic fire. The paths through this rugged ground are in some measure cleared of the stones, but so very narrow, that we were obliged to turn our toes inwards, at which the natives are perfectly expert, and to set one foot exactly before the other. This mode of walking was excessively fatiguing to us who were not used to it, so that we continually hurt our feet or stumbled. On both sides the ground was covered with a thin perennial Jamaica-grass, (paspalum,) which grew in bunches or tufts, and was so slippery that we could not walk on it. We reached the east side of the island, near a range of seven pillars or statues, of which only four remained standing, and one of them had lost its cap.. They stood on a common pedestal, like those which we had seen on the other side, and its stones were square and fitted exactly in the same manner. Though the stone of which the statue itself is formed seems to be soft enough, being nothing but the red tufa which covers the whole island, yet it was incomprehensible to me how such great masses could be formed by a set of people among whom

we

we saw no tools; or raised and erected by them without machinery. The general appellation of this range was *Hanga Tebòw*; hanga being the word which they prefix to every range. The names of the statues were *Ko*-Tomaï, Ko-Tomiderte, Ko-Hòo to, Morchèena, Oomardèraa, Weenàbm, Weenapè.*

" From hence we continued our march to the northward along the sea, having a precipice on our right. The ground was the same ferrugineous *tufa* for a considerable way, covered with small fragments; but after some time we came to a spot which was a single coherent rock or lump of black melted lava, which appeared to contain some iron. There was no soil, grass, or plant whatsoever upon it. Beyond it we passed through a number of plantations of bananas, potatoes, and yams, and one of eddoes. The grass between the stones was plucked up and spread on the land, to screen it from the sun, to keep the moisture of the rain in it, and at last to manure it.

" The natives continued to offer some potatoes for sale ready dressed, and, at a hut where we halted, they sold us some fish. Some of them carried arms, which were no other than the thin sticks we had seen before, and which were headed with a black vitreous lava, carefully wrapped in a small piece of cloth. Only one of them had a battle-axe, resembling that of the New Zeelanders, though much shorter. It had a head carved on each side, and a small

---

* Ko is the article, as at New Zeeland and in the Friendly Isles.

round

round portion of the black glafs above-mentioned inftead of eyes. They had likewife fome fmall crooked human figures made of wood, of which we could not learn the ufe or fignification ; we did not, however, think that our ignorance on this fubject intitled us to call them idols, which is too commonly the judgment paffed upon the works of art of unknown nations.

" After leaving this hut we ftill advanced to the northward, without feeing any new objects. A man and a woman met us from fome neighbouring houfes, each with a large matted bag, of very neat workmanfhip, filled with hot potatoes, and placed themfelves by the fide of the path where we were to pafs. As we came on, the man prefented each of us with fome of the roots, and having diftributed a portion to the whole party, he ran with amazing fwiftnefs to the head of our file to fhare out the reft, till he had given away the whole. He received a large piece of cloth from me, which was the only requital for an inftance of hofpitality, of which I never faw the like even at Taheitee. Soon after the natives told us their aree, or bareekee, or king was coming towards us. Several men came on before him, and diftributed fugar-canes to us all in fign of friendfhip, at the fame time pronouncing the word tee*, which fignifies friend. We now faw the king ftanding on a hill, and walked up to him, Mr. Pickerfgill and myfelf making him

----

* Tee at the Society Ifles ; Whee at the Friendly Ifles.

some

some presents. We asked for his name, which he told us was Ko Toheetai, adding that he was *aree* or king. We were desirous of knowing whether he was only the chief of a district, or of the whole island; upon which he spread out his arms, as it were to include the whole island, and said *Waihu*. To shew that we understood him, we laid our hands on his breast, and, calling him by name, added his title, king of Waihu, at which he expressed very great satisfaction, and conversed a great deal with his people on that subject. He was a middle-aged man, rather tall; his face and whole body strongly punctured. He wore a piece of cloth made of the mulberry bark, quilted with threads of grass, and stained yellow with turmerick; and on his head he had a cap of long shining black feathers, which might be called a diadem. We did not perceive any great degree of homage or attention paid to him by the people; and indeed in so poor a country there seems to be nothing which he could have reserved for himself, without a manifest incroach-ment on the natural rights of mankind, which might have produced dangerous effects. When we wanted to continue our march he seemed to dislike it, and desired us to return, offering to accompany us; but seeing our officer determined to proceed at all events he desisted, and went with us.

" We marched to an elevated spot, and stopped a little while to take some refreshments, and to give Mr. Hodges time to draw some of the monuments, near one of which

we

we found an entire skeleton of a man. A good view of some of these monuments is inserted in captain Cook's account of this voyage. Our people sat down on the ground, and laid their bundles of provision before them, whilst the officers, and other gentlemen with myself, conversed with the natives. One of our sailors, who carried my plant-bag, in which were a few nails, &c. being less careful of his bundle than the rest, a native snatched it up and ran off with it. None of us saw it, except lieutenant Edgecumb, who immediately fired his musket, loaded with small shot, at the thief, and thus gave the alarm to us all. The native being wounded threw down the bag, which our people recovered, but he fell soon after; his countrymen took him up, and fled to a little distance, till we beckoned to them to return, which almost all of them did. Though this was the only instance of firing at a native during our stay at Easter Island, yet it is to be lamented that Europeans too often assume the power of inflicting punishments on people who are utterly unacquainted with their laws.

" From this spot we continued our march a good way inland, and were conducted to a deep well, which appeared to have been formed by art, and contained good fresh water, though somewhat troubled. We all drank heartily of it, and then went on, passing by several large statues, which had been overturned, till we came in sight of the two hummocks, near which we had perceived the greatest number of

pillars

pillars or statues, from the ship, on the 12th. We mounted on an eminence in the neighbourhood, from whence we
beheld the sea on both sides of the island, across a plain
which we had likewise discovered from the ship at that
time. We viewed the whole eastern coast, and its numerous pillars, and were convinced that there was no bay or
harbour on that side of the island. With this information
we returned back to a large statue, which the natives called
Mogooo, and in the shade of which we dined. In its neighbourhood we met with another huge statue, which lay overturned; it was twenty-seven feet long, and nine feet in diameter, exceeding in magnitude every other pillar which we
had seen on the island.

"In returning, we stopped once more at the well, and
quenched our thirst, which the raging heat of the sun,
reverberated from barren rocks, had excited. From thence
we directed our march something nearer the ridge of hills
which run along the middle of the island, but found the
path more rugged and fatiguing than ever, the country
being strewed with volcanic cinders, and desolate all round
us, though we found many remaining proofs of its having
been formerly cultivated. I now felt how much I had
been weakened by the long continuance of the rheumatism,
which had crippled all my limbs, and was hardly able to
keep up with the rest, though I had formerly, upon similar
occasions, been indefatigable. The natives seeing us strike
into

into a difficult path had all left us, except one man and a little boy. Finding that our officers with their party, went too much out of their way, by mistaking the direction of our ship, I left them; and with Dr. Sparrman, a sailor, and the two natives, pursued the nearest path, which the latter had plainly pointed out. The man seeing me very faint, offered me his hand, and walking on the loose stones by the side of the path, with amazing dexterity supported me for a considerable way; the little boy going before, and picking up the stones which obstructed the path. By resting several times, we were at last enabled to reach the summit of the hill, from whence we saw the sea to the west, and the ship at anchor. The hill was covered with a shrubbery of the *mimosa*, which grew here to the height of eight or nine feet, and some of whose stems near the root, were about the thickness of a man's thigh. We found another well hereabouts, of which the water was infected with a putrid taste, and the smell of *hepar sulphuris*, but of which we drank, notwithstanding its nauseousness. The sun set very soon after we had left this well; so that we continued our walk downwards, for more than two hours entirely in the dark, during which my Indian's assistance was particularly valuable to me. I waited for Mr. Pickersgill and the rest of the party, having gained near three miles upon them, and arrived safely at the sea-side with them, after walking at the lowest computation, at least five and twenty miles on the most detestable

detestable roads, where not a single tree appeared to give us shelter from the scorching sun. I rewarded my friendly conductors with all the Taheitee cloth, and iron ware, which I had about me, and arrived safely on board with the party."

From this narrative it is evident, that the most diligent enquiries on our part, have not been sufficient to throw a clear light on the surprising objects which struck our eyes in this island. We may however, attempt to account for those gigantic monuments, of which great numbers exist in every part; for as they are so disproportionate to the present strength of the nation, it is most reasonable to look upon them as the remains of better times. The nicest calculations which we could make, never brought the number of inhabitants in this island beyond seven hundred [*], who, destitute of tools, of shelter, and clothing, are obliged to spend all their time in providing food to support their precarious existence. It is obvious that they are too much occupied with their wants, to think of forming statues, which would cost them ages to finish, and require their united strength to erect. Accordingly, we did not see a single instrument among them on all our excursions, which

---

[*] The Spaniards in the S. Lorenzo, and frigate Rosalia, make the population of Easter Island amount to between two and three thousand; but it may be doubted whether they examined the interior country, as well as our people. See Mr. Dalrymple's Letter to Dr. Hawkesworth.

could

1774.
MARCH. could have been of the leaſt uſe in maſonry or ſculpture.
We neither met with any quarries, where they had recently
dug the materials, nor with unfiniſhed ſtatues which we
might have conſidered as the work of the preſent race.
It is therefore probable, that theſe people were formerly
more numerous, more opulent and happy, when they could
ſpare ſufficient time to flatter the vanity of their princes,
by perpetuating their name by laſting monuments. The
remains of plantations found on the ſummits of the
hills, give ſtrength and ſupport to this conjecture. It is
not in our power to determine by what various accidents
a nation ſo flouriſhing, could be reduced in number, and
degraded to its preſent indigence. But we are well convinced that many cauſes may produce this effect, and that
the devaſtation which a volcano might make, is alone ſufficient to heap a load of miſeries on a people confined to
ſo ſmall a ſpace. In fact, this iſland, which may perhaps,
in remote ages, have been produced by a volcano, ſince all
its minerals are merely volcanic, has at leaſt in all likelihood been deſtroyed by its fire. All kinds of trees and
plants, all domeſtic animals, nay a great part of the nation
itſelf may have periſhed in the dreadful convulſion of nature : hunger and miſery muſt have been but too powerful
enemies to thoſe who eſcaped the fire. We cannot well
account for thoſe little carved images which we ſaw among
the natives, and the repreſentation of a dancing woman's
hand,

hand, which, as I have mentioned above, are made of wood, at present not to be met with upon the island. The only idea which offers itself, is that they were made long ago, and have been saved by accident or predilection, at the general cataftrophe which feems to have happened. All the women whom we faw in different parts of the island, did not amount to thirty, though our people croffed it almoft from one end to the other, without feeing the leaft probability that the women had retired to any fecluded part. If there are really no more than thirty or forty women, among fix or feven hundred men, the whole nation is in a fair way of becoming entirely extinct in a fhort fpace of time, unlefs all our phyfical principles on the plurality of hufbands are erroneous. The greater part of the women whom we faw gave us no reafon to fuppofe that they were accuftomed to a fingle partner; on the contrary, they feemed habitually to have arrived at the fpirit of Meffalina, or of Cleopatra. But this difproportion is fuch a fingular phænomenon in human nature, that we cannot without difficulty give credit to it, and would willingly lay hold of any argument which, though incumbered with difficulties, might reftore the proportion between the fexes. It is true our party did not fee any valley or fecluded glen, to which the women might have confined themfelves during our ftay; but I muft remind the

4 G 2   reader

reader of thofe caverns mentioned before, to which the natives always refufed to admit us.　The caverns of Iceland
are fpacious enough to contain feveral thoufand inhabitants;
and nothing is more probable than that, in a fimilar volcanic country, fuch caverns may afford room for a few
hundreds.　What reafons the Eafter Iflanders may have to
be more jealous of their women than the Taheitians, we
know not; but we are acquainted with the outrageous and
wanton behaviour of the failor, wherever he has fo great a
fuperiority over the Indian, as the Dutch and Spaniards muft
have had over the people of Eafter Ifland.　The principal
objection againft this fuppofition is, however, the fmall number of children which we faw, there being no reafon to fe-
clude them from our eyes, whatever might be thought neceffary with regard to the women.　In fhort, this matter
muft remain unafcertained, and if, in fact, the number of
women is inconfiderable, it muft have been diminifhed by
fome extraordinary accident, which none but the natives
could have explained; but, in all our doubts, our ignorance
of their language prevented us from acquiring any information.

The next morning we fent a boat afhore to take in fome
water, and the weather continuing calm, another went off
to trade with the natives in order to encreafe our little ftock
of potatoes.　One of the natives likewife plied between the
 fhip

ship and the shore, bringing off potatoes and bananas in
the patched canoe. In the mean while a smart shower
falling on board the ship, enabled our people to collect a
quantity of fresh water in the awnings and sails of the ship,
which were spread to catch it. Another boat went off to
the shore in the afternoon, but towards evening a faint
breeze springing up, the ship fired a gun, in consequence
of which the boat came on board, and we sailed N. W. by
W. from Easter Island.

We had been greatly disappointed in the expectation
which we had formed of this island, as a place of refreshment. The only article of any importance was their sweet
potatoes; but after we had regularly shared out all we had
purchased, the common people had only a few scanty meals
of them. As to the bananas, yams, and sugar-canes which
we had bought, they were in such inconsiderable quantities,
that they scarce deserve to be mentioned. All the fowls
which we had obtained, and which, in general, were of a
very small breed, did not amount to fifty; and even the
quantity of water which we had filled was inconsiderable
and ill tasted. However, this small supply was so seasonable, that it preserved us from the too violent attacks of
the scurvy and bilious disorders, till we could reach a better
place of refreshment. Indeed, when I consider the wretched situation of the inhabitants, I am surprised that they

parted

parted with a quantity of provisions to us, of which the
cultivation muſt have coſt them great pains and labour.
The barren refractory ſoil of their iſland, the ſcarcity of domeſtic animals, and the want of boats and proper materials
for fiſhing, all concur to render their means of ſubſiſtence
extremely difficult and precarious. Yet the deſire of poſſeſſ-
ing the new toys and curioſities which ſtrangers bring
among them, hurried them away, and prevented their reflecting on the urgency of their own moſt natural and unavoidable wants.   In this, as in numberleſs other circumſtances, they agree with the tribes who inhabit New Zeeland, the Friendly and the Society Iſlands, and who ſeem
to have had one common origin with them.   Their features are very ſimilar, ſo that the general character may
eaſily be diſtinguiſhed.   Their colour, a yellowiſh brown,
moſt like the hue of the New Zeelanders; their art of
puncturing, the uſe of the mulberry-bark for clothing, the
predilection for red paint and red dreſſes, the ſhape and
workmanſhip of their clubs, the mode of dreſſing their victuals, all form a ſtrong reſemblance to the natives of the
iſlands above mentioned.   We may add to theſe, the ſimplicity of their languages, that of Eaſter Iſland being a dialect which, in many reſpects, reſembles that of New Zeeland, eſpecially in the harſhneſs of pronunciation and the
uſe of gutterals, and yet, in other inſtances, partakes of that
of

of Taheitee. The monarchical government likewise strengthens the affinity between the Easter Islanders and the tropical tribes, its prerogatives being only varied according to the different degrees of fertility of the islands, and the opulence or luxury of the people. Easter Island, or, as the natives call it, WAIHU, is so very barren, that the whole number of plants growing upon it does not exceed twenty species, of which far the greater part is cultivated[*]; though the space which the plantations occupy is inconsiderable, compared with that which lies waste. The soil is altogether stoney, and parched by the sun, and water is so scarce, that the inhabitants drink it out of wells which have a strong admixture of brine; nay, some of our people really saw them drink of the sea-water when they were thirsty. Their habit of body must, in some measure, be influenced by these circumstances; they are meagre, and their muscles hard and rigid; they live very frugally, and, in general, go almost wholly naked, only covering the head, which is the most sensible of heat, with feathered caps, and puncturing or daubing the rest with colours. Their ideas of decency are, of course, very different from those of nations who are accustomed to clothing. They cut short their hair and beards

---

[*] The Spaniards mention white calabashes, (pumpions,) among the vegetable productions of this island; but we did not see any.—See Mr. Dalrymple's judicious letter to Dr. Hawkesworth.

from

from motives of cleanliness, like the people of Tonga-Tabboo, but fortunately seemed to be less subject to leprous
complaints. It is easy to conclude that the king of
such a people cannot have great and conspicuous advantages over the commonalty, nor did our party observe any
thing of that kind. The religion of the Easter Islanders is
still wholly unknown to us, because abstract ideas are not
to be acquired in so short a time as our stay. The statues,
which are erected in honour of their kings, have a great affinity to the wooden figures, called TEE, on the chief's ma-
rais or burying-places at Taheitee; but we could not possibly consider them as idols, though Roggewein's people
would pass them for such upon us. The fires which the
Dutch interpret as sacrifices, were only made use of by the
natives to dress their meals; and though the Spaniards suspected them to be a kind of superstition, they were, perhaps,
equally mistaken, because the scarcity of fuel obliged the
inhabitants to be careful of it, and to prevent their provisions being uncovered after they had once been put under
ground with heated stones.

We are unacquainted with the amusements of the people
of Easter Island, having never seen them engaged in any
kind of diversion, nor taken notice of a single musical instrument among them. They cannot, however, be entire
strangers to amusements, since Maroo-wahai, who slept on
board,

board, talked a great deal of dancing, as foon as we had
quieted his fears with refpect to the fafety of his perfon.
The difpofition of thefe people is far from being warlike;
their numbers are too inconfiderable, and their poverty too
general, to create civil difturbances amongft them. It is
equally improbable that they have foreign wars, fince hitherto we know of no ifland near enough to admit of an
intercourfe between the inhabitants; neither could we obtain
any intelligence from thofe of Eafter Ifland upon the fubject. This being premifed, it is extraordinary that they
fhould have different kinds of offenfive weapons, and efpecially fuch as refemble thofe of the New Zeelanders; and
we muft add this circumftance to feveral others, which are
inexplicable to us in their kind.

Upon the whole, fuppofing Eafter Ifland to have undergone a late misfortune from volcanic fires, its inhabitants
are more to be pitied than any lefs civilized fociety, being
acquainted with a number of conveniencies, comforts, and
luxuries of life, which they formerly poffeffed, and of which
the remembrance muft embitter the lofs. Mahine frequently lamented their unhappy fituation, and feemed to feel for
them more than he had done for the New Zeelanders, becaufe he found them much more deftitute. He added another ftick to the bundle which compofed his journal, and
remembered Eafter Ifland with this obfervation, *idia maitai,*
wheanua eeno, that the people were good, but the ifland very

bad; whereas at New Zeeland he had found more fault with the natives than the country. His feelings were always warm from the heart, which education had filled with real philanthropy; they were likewife juft, in general, becaufe his fenfes were found and acute, and his underftanding, though uncultivated, was free from many prejudices.

END OF THE FIRST VOLUME.

ERRATA in VOL. I.

	for		read	
P. 13. l. 19,	for	Ribiera,	read	Ribeira.
32. l. 1. (margin)		1773,		1774.
48. l. 4.		drying,		dying.
51. l. 16.		vacuorum,		supervacaneum.
59. l. 10.		at the same,		at the same time.
92. l. antepenult,		as was,		as it was.
139. l. 9.		Ferro,		Ferrà.
172. l. 11.		family,		family.
174. l. 9. and 10.		musquets,		muskets.
196. l. last,		multiplicamini,		multiplicamini.
172. l. 7.		quaken,		quakin.
207. l. 20.		gurus,		gurus.
219. l. 2.		scamp-net,		bump-net.
253. l. 10.		O-Taheim,		O-Taheitee.
308. l. 11.		Juan de Langara		Domingo Boenechea.
		y Huarte,		

CPSIA information can be obtained
at www.ICGtesting.com
Printed in the USA
BVHW030520211221
624508BV00007B/297